Our World
GOD'S VISIBLE LANGUAGE

Visible Creation as Testimony to an Invisible Creator

JERRY SALLOUM

Copyright © 2022, 2024 by Jerry Salloum
Second Edition — 2022

All rights reserved. No part of this book may be reproduced, stored, or transmitted by any means—whether auditory, graphic, mechanical, or electronic—without written permission of both publisher and author, except in the case of brief excerpts used in critical articles and reviews. Unauthorized reproduction of any part of this work is illegal and is punishable by law.

Unless stated otherwise, all biblical quotations are taken from THE HOLY BIBLE, NEW INTERNATIONAL VERSION®, NIV® Copyright © 1973, 1978, 1984, 2011 by Biblica, Inc.® Used by permission. All rights reserved worldwide.

All biblical quotations taken from the King James Version are identified with the letters, KJV.

Biblical references labelled JBP are taken from The New Testament in Modern English, by J.B. Phillips. London: Geoffrey Bles, 1960.

All references from the Anglican Book of Common Prayer are identified with the letters, BCP. © The General Synod of the Anglican Church of Canada 1962.

All photos taken and all introductory commentaries by the author are identified with the initials JES.

All diagrams and sketch maps are the creation of the author. All rights reserved.

ISBN: 979-8-89031-896-1 (sc)
ISBN: 979-8-89031-897-8 (hc)
ISBN: 979-8-89031-898-5 (e)

Because of the dynamic nature of the Internet, any web addresses or links contained in this book may have changed since publication and may no longer be valid. The views expressed in this work are solely those of the author and do not necessarily reflect the views of the publisher, and the publisher hereby disclaims any responsibility for them.

One Galleria Blvd., Suite 1900, Metairie, LA 70001
(504) 702-6708

CONTENTS

Preface vii
Introduction xi

1   Cosmos 1
2   Earth 45
3   Moon 71
4   Shadow 91
5   Rock 107
6   Wilderness 143
7   Earth's Water and Atmosphere 159
8   Flood 203
9   Ice and Snow 227
10 Imago Dei 263

Postscript 301
Endnotes 305
Selected Bibliography 341
Acknowledgements 345
About the Author 349

Cover Photos

Earth: The Blue Marble

The Blue Marble: was photographed on December 7, 1972 by the crew onboard Apollo 17's mission to the Moon.

The image,
a pearl-like sphere,
displays an almost fully-
illuminated Earth hemisphere,
from Antarctica northward,
through the entire South American continent,
to most of the North American continent,
as far as Canada's high Arctic.

The prominence of water is obvious in all its forms (solid, liquid and vapour), with most resident as liquid in giant ocean containers.

No stars are visible
since the fully-illuminated Earth,
with the Sun behind the camera,
extinguishes all stellar light,
leaving a full Earth hemisphere
to shine in reflected brilliance,
seemingly alone in a Cosmos where
stars abound in countless numbers.

Photos courtesy NASA

Saturn and its Rings

This magnificent photo was taken by the Cassini-Huygens unmanned space probe in 1997, after a 7-year, 7.9 billion kilometre gravity-assisted journey. Following final capture by Saturn, the probe completed 294 orbits around it, greatly expanding human knowledge of this, the farthest planet visible with the naked eye.

The photo's elliptically-shaped rings indicate that Cassini was slightly above the plane of these rings when photographed. Saturn's black surface surrounded by its thin illuminated edge testifies to the location of the Sun in the photo, namely behind the planet. This means that Cassini was passing through Saturn's shadowy umbra, a condition producing a total eclipse of the Sun yet with light reflecting into that shadow from countless ring particles.

Cassini's demise occurred
on September 15, 2017 during a controlled plunge through Saturn's thick atmosphere, vaporizing after a 13-year, highly productive sojourn about this celestial jewel.

JES

To my one and only,
in whom I have a pearl of great price
and
to the five guys in my life
who are constant reminders of the importance of
leisure, laughter, play, and wonder.

PREFACE

For since the creation of the world God's invisible qualities—
his eternal power and divine nature—have been clearly seen,
being understood from what has been made,
so that people are without excuse.

Romans 1:20

Ours is a fascinating world of materials spread over incredible distances. Beholding its form and structure arrests us, provokes our wonder, generates questions, and beckons us to discover more of what's out there, where it came from, how it works, and what our place is within it.

Without doubt, the investigations and enjoyment of various components of our material world are, in themselves, all worthwhile human pursuits. This explains their place of primacy within this book. However, the reason for nature's attractiveness may not lie solely in, or be restricted to its physical appeal. How so?

The foundational statements for *Our World: God's Visible Language* are contained in scriptural verses from the books of Romans and Psalms. First, from Romans 1:20, we are presented with a provocative thought, namely that the natural world, with all its orderliness, beauty, and variety, with its harmony, seemingly limitless expanse, and with its countless patterns and processes, is much more than matter and energy. In some profound manner, as visible, and from what has been made, our world has the assigned task of reflecting specific attributes of an invisible Creator.

> *The heavens declare the glory of God;*
> *the skies proclaim the work of his hands.*
> *Day after day they pour forth speech;*
> *night after night they reveal knowledge.*
> *They have no speech, they use no words;*
>
> *Psalm 19:1–3a*

Secondly, from Psalm 19:1–3a, we discover that the natural world is a form of testimony that speaks without words or language. The persuasive power of this speech is demonstrated in the frequency with which the Bible, using words, makes reference to familiar elements of our physical world that speak, not with words, but through their forms and functions, through their patterns and processes, conveying a message that metaphorically links what is visible and familiar to a deeper reality largely hidden from sight. It declares that our world reflects the element of the sacred, thus inclining our minds toward what is beyond itself.

> *O come hither, and behold the works of the Lord,*
> *what wonders he hath wrought upon the earth.*
>
> *Psalm 46:9 (BCP)*

Thirdly, the words of Psalm 46:9 represent a clear invitation for humanity to investigate all of Creation's natural wonders at different scales: spatially, from the cosmic to the subatomic; and temporally, from its distant past to its present and even into its future. It is an invitation to delve into systems of orderliness and sheer beauty, but with an important qualifier. The word *behold* suggests the need for more than an observer's cursory glance. Rather, it implies a prolonged gaze, sustained over time, capturing the speech emanating from a variety of sources, from a multitude of places, and often at the most unexpected times. The fact that the act of beholding involves prolonged viewing suggests that we may not ultimately fully comprehend what we are seeing, and that after viewing repeatedly, we may have to become satisfied, not only with new knowledge, but with even more mystery.

Nevertheless, we are to mull, to contemplate, to wonder, to differentiate figurative expressions from those that are literal, and to dig beyond the works to the Creator of these works. And if the hands that made all things and gave them speech without words belong to the One from whom also came His written words, then it is reasonable to expect that the special revelation from each source will, in some remarkable fashion, both complement and supplement the other.

> *Nature never taught me that there exists a God of glory and of infinite majesty. I had to learn that in other ways. But nature gave the word 'glory' a meaning for me.*
>
> *C. S. Lewis*[1]

> *Teach me, my God and King, in all things Thee to see, and what I do in anything, to do it as for Thee.*
>
> *George Herbert*[2]

INTRODUCTION

And [Moses] said,
"I beseech thee, shew me thy glory."

Exodus 33:18 (KJV)

Grounded Iceberg off Northern Ellesmere Island, Nunavut[3]
(JES)

Only Supernaturalists really see Nature.
You must go a little away from her,
and then turn round, and look back.
Then at last the true landscape will become visible.
You must have tasted,
however briefly,
the pure water from beyond the world
before you can be distinctly conscious of the hot, salty tang
of Nature's current.

To treat her as God, or as Everything,
is to lose the whole pith and pleasure of her.
Come out, look back,
and then you will see:
this astonishing cataract of bears, babies, and bananas:
this immoderate deluge of atoms, orchids, oranges, cancers,
fleas, gases, tornadoes, and toads.

How could you ever have thought
[our world] was the ultimate reality?
How could you ever have thought
that it was merely a stage
set for the moral drama of men and women?

C. S. Lewis[4]

Introduction

With atmospheric clarity close to its maximum, the Arctic sky was a brilliant blue. The late afternoon sun cast long shadows over the mountainous tundra landscape as the Twin Otter aircraft flew low along the rugged coastline of Ellesmere, Canada's northern-most island and, at present, its most glaciated. Except for isolated pockets within land depressions where snow accumulations were greater through drifting, snow cover on this high Arctic land surface had largely disappeared. So too had most ice cover that had formed through the winter within the narrow but relatively deep waterways.

That August afternoon of light and warmth represented a brief respite from the seemingly endless season of cold. Already the sun, which at these latitudes moves more horizontally than vertically, was spiralling each day closer to the horizon, rapidly diminishing light and heat intensity as it descended. Soon it would begin its slow passage through the horizon, then disappear from this treeless wilderness to begin a four-month period of decreasing twilight, followed by uninterrupted night and countless stars.[5]

Seated near the pilot, I had become engrossed in the details of a largescale chart spread before me and was attempting to identify our plane's location by matching visible shoreline features with corresponding shapes on the chart. Suddenly, with finger jabbing forward, he motioned for me to look through my window and well ahead of the plane. His interest was an assemblage of icebergs. They sat motionless some distance offshore from a giant ice shelf from whose terminus these floating ice cubes had recently calved. As our plane approached them, their massiveness and beauty grew proportionately. Myriads of miniature ice mirrors on each glistening surface played with shafts of sunlight, scattering them in all directions in a dazzling display of reflected brilliance.

The pilot put our aircraft into a sharp turn, decreased altitude, and then levelled off on a track parallel to the glacier's terminus. I reached for my camera and readied myself to begin snapping photos. But something was wrong. My lens was out of focus. Rather than beholding the beauty of floating glacial fragments, my field of vision was cluttered with the blurry spots and random scratches on the aircraft's window. Unrecognizable forms appeared within a distant but equally blurry background. Responding quickly, I rotated the focus ring. With each twist, my visual field was altered. The mess of window spots and scratches faded and the background majesty beyond the mess, observed though distorted *through* that mess, came into sharp focus. The photo shoot was over quickly. But my silent reverence and wonder that had begun when these frozen giants first made their appearance persisted until well after they were out of sight. I had learned an important lesson on a pervasive impediment to properly observing reality, namely intervening clutter.

> *A man that looks on glass, on it may stay his eye.*
> *Or if he pleaseth through it pass,*
> *and then the heavens espy.*
>
> George Herbert[6]

We are long accustomed to the prominence of random clutter in our field of vision, which, while remaining unfiltered, frequently masks what is out there. Fortunately, since "spots and scratches" cannot entirely obscure all of nature's wonders, life treats us to moments of enrichment of things within or beyond that clutter that cause us to *"stay our eye"* and ponder. Such was the scene permanently etched on my mind that day over that remote fiord.

Within such experiences, our pondering leads to questions. What is the mysterious allure of the beautiful, whether expressed in colour, symmetry, pattern, or process, that is able to turn the head, capture our gaze, quicken the human spirit, and refresh us? From the Greek language, the scriptural word *kalos* helps to unwrap some of the mystery associated with what we speak of as *beautiful* or *good*.

As an adjective, *kalos* expresses something endowed with *matchless intrinsic excellence*. But also, as a verb, it is a form of invitation that calls or summons. Therefore, instead of being passive while one beholds matchless intrinsic excellence, what is beautiful and good actively initiates, then stirs within us all that the beautiful and good promote (namely wonder, joy, and delight). Employing descriptive words to capture these times, however, normally proves altogether inadequate. Yet *kalos* experiences, through direct exposure to elements of the natural world, seem strangely congruent with both holy scripture where the Word of God, with words, feasts liberally with seeming delight on familiar images from nature.

It was the awareness of *intrinsic excellence* that prompted those first lunar astronauts, when beholding the bleak lunar landscape through virtually no intervening clutter to describe what they saw as "magnificent desolation." It must have been *intrinsic excellence* within a thin strip of metal that riveted Albert Einstein's attention and imagination when, as a young boy, he first pondered the mysterious invisible influence that repeatedly forced his compass needle in the direction of geographic north. It was the *intrinsic excellence* within a newborn baby that captured my wife's adoring gaze the first time ever she saw our grandson's face.

My experience over Ellesmere Island on that August afternoon illustrates three mental responses when confronting the natural world. Each represents a central focus when engaging that world. For our purposes, let us call these responses *Wow! How So?* and *So What?*

The *Wow* response is principally an emotional response of surprise or delight to an encounter with a natural element through those mental ports of entry called our senses: the first *sighting* of an iceberg or a dazzling sunset; the first *hearing* of a Bach fugue or the song of a cardinal; the first *taste* of the chef's new recipe for spring lamb; or the captivating *smell* of a lover's fragrance. *Wow* responses involve the romantic, namely strange attractions toward adventure and mystery. Such responses are spontaneous and highly sensual. More to be enjoyed than analyzed, some things are best appreciated in their entirety. The whole appears somehow greater than the sum of its parts. With them, our responses are expressed more with spontaneous joy than with words.

The *How So* response is initiated the moment one moves from an appreciation of something in its entirety to a desire to comprehend its parts. This response is essentially academic, objective, and filled with questions. What a beautiful iceberg! But why is its ice blue? And why does it float with some of its mass above the waterline since, chemically, ice is the same substance as the stuff on which it floats? Or, why does the sun or full moon appear so much larger near the horizon than above us? Or, why can't we, from anywhere on Earth, ever see the far side of the moon even though the moon rotates on its axis once every month? And how do emperor penguins manage to incubate their eggs while exposed to the harshest climate on Earth? And why do Canada geese fly in a V-formation?

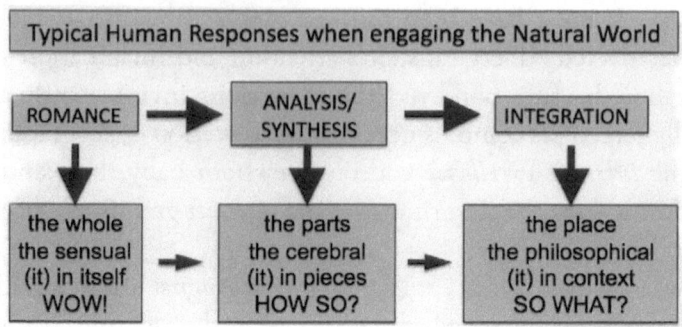

The *So What* response also asks many questions. But it attempts to pursue various phenomena within a larger context. For example, how does the reduction of ice cover over the Arctic Ocean influence world climate? Do the laws of nature common to our world operate in a similar fashion throughout the universe? Does the beauty of glistening icebergs testify to a greater glory beyond themselves? From apparent *design* in nature, can one assume a *Designer*? What place do we have in the grand scheme of things?

Thus, while the principal objective of the *How So* response is directed toward analysis and understanding, the *So What* response and questions are toward integration of phenomena within a wider sphere of influence, and into a big picture. If the *How So* response is dominant in the scientific mind, the *So What* response belongs in the realm of the philosophical. In the latter, the interest is on meaning, purpose, and significance, and less on comprehension.

Judging from lessons I have learned from my children and grandchildren, *Wow* responses (to colourful balloons, candles flickering on birthday cakes, and ribbons and paper hiding mysterious contents) make their debut early in life. Aging does not extinguish them, though aging may alter the various stimuli that trigger them. Part of being human involves enjoying each of the three responses to the natural world at different times. Most people would, however, identify one particular response that dominates, and with which they feel most comfortable.

INTRODUCTION

The contents of the pages that follow are an invitation to exult in aspects of the physical world—its bounteous beauty that can be seen and enjoyed *(Wow)*, and its intricate patterns and processes that can be studied, and in part understood *(How So?)*. But that's not all. The pages that follow are also an invitation to wonder about the physical world's apparent transparency that allows observers to peer through it as a window and beyond it to a context and a glory far greater than itself *(So What?)*. Certainly, especially in parables and metaphors, the scriptures testify in words to reality not seen (1 Cor 2:9), and to a natural world that has the capacity to speak without the use of words.

What we are capable of seeing in the here and now represents a minute, but attractive taste of what at present lies largely hidden. This idea is suggested in biblical writings where familiar images from the Creation: wind and water, storms and seas, planets and stars, and mountains and wilderness are among the many visual aids that scripture writers employ, not only to be enjoyed in themselves but, equally importantly, as illustrative windows through which and beyond which we are enabled to grasp much more. It appears that satisfaction in life is maximized when we enjoy both the windows themselves *and* the glimpses of the contents beyond them. For this reason, the following pages will seem, in many places, more like a science textbook. In fact, it links God's world with His written Word.

Yet, a story not authored by us is being told, not only about many things, but also about some *One* infinitely greater than ourselves. To tap into all this involves a mental journey: *up* into apparently endless space where invisible forces have organized and maintain an orderly and silent celestial dance of objects at incredible distances; but *down* and *through* the world's land and water surfaces, its massive ice sheets and deep oceanic sediments where stratified accumulations of materials over many millenniums have laid down, hidden, and preserved recoverable, long chronologies of atmospheric and geologic history. And all around us, amid the march of days and seasons, where nature's *intrinsic excellence* regularly engages our hearts and minds, there is speech without words about what has been made.

With all this, and more, we open ourselves up to repeated glimpses of both God's eternal power and divine nature. And with these discoveries, we become more prepared to receive and comprehend God's heart and mind when, in holy scripture, He chooses to speak *in words* that repeatedly reference aspects of His Creation, and in Someone named Emmanuel through whom He chose to disclose Himself by paying Earth a personal visit.

> *Beauty and grace are performed whether or not we will sense them. The least we can do is try to be there . . . so that creation need not play to an empty house.*
>
> *Annie Dillard*[7]

1
COSMOS

*O ALL ye Works of the Lord, bless ye the Lord:
praise him, and magnify him forever.*

Benedicite (BCP)[8]

**Distant Spiral Galaxy (Messier 31)
observed through stars in the Constellation Andromeda**[9]
(NASA)

What's out there?
Was it always out there?
Countless sources of light,
some as isolated points, most in giant assemblages.

What processes created them?
In whose brilliant mind were they first conceived
to perform an endless celestial dance for all to see?
And for what purpose?

JES

Who has measured the waters in the hollow of his hand,
or with the breadth of his hand
marked off the heavens?

Who has held the dust of the earth in a basket,
or weighed the mountains on the scales
and the hills in a balance?

Isaiah 40:12

THE ATTRACTIVENESS OF THE UNKNOWN

It was early in the day. A cold morning mist hung undisturbed over the lake's mirror-like surface. As promised, this was to be the place and the time of my four-year-old's introduction to the sport of fishing. With excitement and great anticipation, he approached his new adventure alongside a father who was still attempting to shake off the last remnants of sleep and who knew virtually nothing about the sport of fishing. But there we sat, oblivious to time, with feet dangling over the end of the dock, assembling crude fishing rods and lines from sticks and string, hooks, floats, and sinkers.

The worms were the challenge. After a few awkward attempts to bait the hooks without stabbing myself, all was ready. Rick watched intently as his worm, hook, and weight slowly descended and disappeared into a dark watery world. In silence, we waited, jerking the line now and then to awaken any life form below that fresh protein was being delivered for breakfast.

Suddenly, our wait was over; the anticipated event happened. A faint tremor passed through the line and into Rick's hands. "What was that?" We speculated as he assembled clues of a micro-world we could not see. Imagination offered a number of possibilities, each one more exaggerated than the one before. What had caused that tremor? How big was the thing that caused it? What did it look like? And how many similar beasts were down there? Rick pulled on the line. Whatever it was offered little resistance as up from the depths came his prize: a four-inch minnow. Persistence was rewarded; some questions had been answered. Though a little disappointed that this had not been the anticipated struggle between boy and beast, Rick's joy was obvious.

PURSUITS IN UNDERSTANDING

The watery world at the end of that dock represents a microcosm of the much larger natural world, a source of delight within much mystery. It is like a closed box that beckons its occupants to open and discover. Like young children, we peer into the unknown to enjoy and attempt to make sense of what is almost entirely beyond our vision. We might imagine a giant jigsaw puzzle that is set before us. Pieces are many, with almost all disassembled. We assume the puzzle can be completed, that all pieces will eventually fit properly, and that when assembled, its picture will make sense. On occasion, progress is rapid. But because of the puzzle's complexity and size, progression is normally slow as trials leading to success are interspersed with errors, necessitating backtracking and corrections.

During discouraging moments when progress grinds to a complete halt, we begin to question our assumptions. What explains our lack of progress? Is there something wrong with the puzzle? Has any part been assembled incorrectly? Maybe the manufacturer tricked us by including extraneous pieces that don't belong and will never fit. On the other hand, maybe the manufacturer *can* be trusted. Maybe all pieces before us belong; but perhaps not all pieces have been provided.

Similar questions surfaced in the minds of astronomers soon after the discovery of the methane-rich blue planet Uranus in 1781.[10] A century prior to its discovery, Sir Isaac Newton had formulated laws approximating the motion of objects in the heavens. However, observations of the orbit of planet Uranus soon indicated that its compliance with these laws appeared problematic.

The question then arose as to the validity of Newtonian laws at such distances. Suspicion focused on the possible existence of an unknown object that was of sufficient mass to significantly influence the path of this celestial giant. The answer to the dilemma soon proved to be an unknown object. The absence of a piece of the puzzle contributing to the planet's orbital perturbations had rendered the puzzle confusing and incomprehensible. That puzzle piece proved to be the yet undiscovered planet and more distant giant Neptune, whose periodically close proximity to and large gravitational influence on it at the time was the explanation that resolved the mystery. In fact, because of its distance from the sun, resulting in relatively slow orbital speed, it had been considered a star and not a planet.

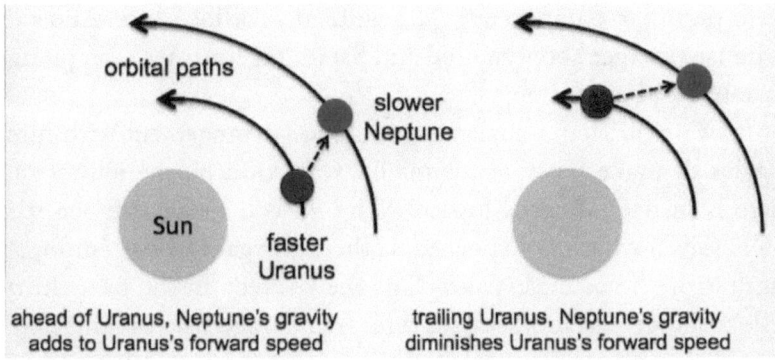

Locations of Uranus Relative to Neptune in the Early 1800s[11]

Ironically, in the end, doubt concerning the validity of Newton's Law actually enhanced public confidence in it. Moreover, the event demonstrated how well established scientific laws survive periodic apparent contradictions. In the case of the perturbations associated with planet Uranus, no established facts were erroneous. Existing laws were valid. While nothing but the truth had been provided, this truth did not constitute the *whole* truth.

The presence of confusion in the minds of people attempting to make sense of things frequently appears in the Bible. A classic example surfaces in the story of Job, a man who could not understand why so much misfortune had come his way. The story confronts us, not with a planet whose behaviour didn't seem to make sense, but with an individual whose personal misfortunes didn't seem to make sense, and, even more importantly, with a God whose long silence and apparent indifference to human misery was a mystery.

The earliest verses of the Book of Job establish the reason for all that follows. In a strange confrontation between Satan and God, Satan questions the purity of Job's love for God, implying this love is equivalent to a farmer loving cows for their milk or hens for their eggs, and that if blessings were withdrawn from Job, he would surely curse and discard the One who supposedly provides them. Satan's meaning is clear: all love (Job's love, and even God's) contains a utilitarian element. That is, one's value is based upon one's usefulness. Love is conditional, involving a type of quid pro quo based upon an exchange of favours. God counters with a limited permit to Satan to test the genuineness of Job's love. And so, with this unusual wager between God and Satan, misfortunes soon plunge Job into doubt and confusion.

Unaware of Satan's challenge and God's arrangement with him, Job struggles to make sense of his plight. Can God be the author of evil? Where is justice? *What* is justice? Why do bad things happen to good people? Given what has happened, is there any gain in *not* sinning? Does God destroy the blameless as well as the wicked? In the next thirty-five chapters of the story, Job, with his three friends, agonizes over his miserable state. Throughout the lengthy deliberations, God remains agonizingly silent. Then suddenly, as a voice out of a storm, God speaks. But instead of addressing Job's questions directly, God's response is a lengthy set of questions of His own. No question relates to Job's plight. Rather, each relates surprisingly to the natural world. God's questions initiate an adventure in wonder through an imaginative tour of the cosmos with God as Job's Tour Guide:

- *Where were you when I laid the earth's foundation? (Job 38:4)*
- *Have you ever given orders to the morning? (38:12a)*
- *Who cuts a channel for the torrents of rain? (38:25a)*
- *From whose womb comes the ice? (38:29a)*
- *Can you bring forth the constellations in their seasons? (38:32a)*
- *Do you know the laws of the heavens? (38:33a)*

One might wonder about the tour's duration. Given the profundity of each question, might it have stretched over Job's entire life? What was the Tour Guide's tone of voice? Was it thunderous? Was it disdainful? What captures our attention most is not the duration of the tour or God's tone of voice, but rather the *content* of God's questions. While they appeared to be all about the cosmos, they were, in fact, all about its Creator. God had used elements of the cosmos to introduce *Himself*. Written within the cosmos is a grand story about infinite variety in design and function, about vastness, unimaginable power, meticulous care, about everything controlled by Someone superior and separate from it, all hidden in deep mystery.

> *To the natural philosopher*
> *there is no natural object unimportant or trifling . . .*
> *a soap bubble . . . an apple . . . a pebble. . . .*
> *He walks in the midst of wonders.*
>
> *John Herschel*[12]

Each teaching aid bore God's fingerprints. Each question constituted an invitation to wonder: wonder about constellations, about storms, about life and the nature of nature. And Job's response to God? From his first words, "My ears had heard of you but now my eyes have seen you" (Job 42:5), it is clear that he saw more than the physical Creation. His response testifies both to the reason for the tour and to the reason for God's gift of wonder, a gift allowing Job to dabble in and to discover that great context in which all life exists. This was the missing puzzle piece. Its absence had rendered the grand story incomprehensible. Its inclusion strangely satisfied.

With each question, God invited Job to discover that life does not consist merely of self, of boils, of property or personal convenience. Each element of the cosmos is an icon, a window through which Job was permitted to see something beyond and greater than self. Each was a light that diminished Job's darkness. Job learned he was made for more than mere preservation of body and possessions. Like the astronomer Copernicus, Job awakened to the realization that neither he nor his world occupies the centre of the cosmos and that God is infinitely more than a convenient waiter or cosmic bellhop to be employed and activated for human convenience, and then to be set aside. More importantly, Job's experience with God enhanced his confidence in God's trustworthiness, despite experiences that seemed to diminish it.

> *I know now, Lord, why you utter no answer. You are yourself the answer. Before your face, questions die away. What other answer would suffice?*
>
> *C. S. Lewis*[13]

Our own tours of the natural world make us anything but bored. Its vastness and apparent endlessness speak to us of the infinite in language without words. Its apparent age, though not believed to be eternal, speaks to us of eternity. Buried and scattered within its contents are stories of its past. It is both a picture of beauty and extravagance, as well as a great mystery. It possesses pattern and design and immense variety. It is a work of art. All of it, from its smallest particles to its largest components, falls subject to the authority of natural laws established and governed by a Super-Power—a Sovereign, a personal God. Always in constant change, His world nevertheless possesses elements of constancy and integrity within change.

> *Who can be bored with such a world? Who can tire of its many patterns? Who can grow weary of discerning the fingerprints of a greater Glory?*
>
> *Bruce Prewer*[14]

THE BIG PICTURE OF UNMATCHED SPLENDOUR

"Universe" is the word we assign to the sum total of all physical matter and the space it occupies. Since the volume of space overwhelms the mass of matter within it, one can say that the universe is largely empty. In fact, space is an almost perfect vacuum, a characteristic nature supposedly abhors. Each increase in telescopic power has revealed more matter and even greater emptiness.

Given this vastness, we cannot help but wonder about the outer edges of our cosmos. Does it have an edge with a measurable breadth and volume? What shape does the sum of all matter assume? Is it spherical like a tennis ball or flat like a sheet of paper? Or is it randomly scattered with no recognizable shape? And did it have a temporal beginning? Possibly the biggest thing of all, the universe, is spatially indefinable, goes on forever with no temporal beginning. If so, one cannot speak of it having an edge, or a geographic centre, or even a creator.

What matter there is, however, is bound together by an invisible force, a type of natural glue called gravity. Somehow, gravitational attraction, like light, but unlike sound, can spread its influence over vast distances and through a vacuum. Gravitational strength is a function of mass. Because of this, surface gravity on the Earth exceeds surface gravity on the moon. Moreover, the gravitational force *between* objects varies with distance. Thus, an object exerting the greatest "pull" on another object in space is the most massive and the closest.

A study of the heavens reveals that matter appears not to be spread homogeneously through space. Instead, it is found in countless concentrated assemblages. The largest assemblages are called galaxies and galactic clusters. Each galaxy consists of countless point sources of light whose numbers stagger the imagination. Most point sources are stars, varying in mass from giants to dwarfs and varying in surface temperature from the hotter blue stars to the relatively cooler red stars. Being so massive, stars serve as giant gravitational vacuums capable of capturing, with their enormous gravitational fields, space debris over vast distances.

Our own galaxy (the Milky Way) contains some 200 billion stars. Structurally, it resembles a flattened circular disc, similar in shape to our own solar system, but packaged along spiral arms that radiate pinwheelstyle about its galactic centre.

Our sun, a star of average mass, along with its orderly cluster of planets, moons, asteroids and scattered debris, is located closer to the end of its galactic arm than to its galactic centre. Knowledge of galactic motion allows astronomers to determine that a single circuit about its centre (known as a galactic year) takes some 200 million years, a number that is consistent with the enormity of time needed for structures of galactic proportions to assume orderly patterns from earlier conditions of chaos. In considering the stars in the heavens and the great distances between them, one stands in awe before a realm of incredible sizes and distances, fascinating history and great mystery, a reality within which our own planet is minute by comparison and before which the human spirit is humbled.[15]

> *Surely I spoke of things I did not understand,*
> *things too wonderful for me to know.*
>
> **Job 42:3b**

Stars are nature's furnaces. This is true because they possess the proper ingredients, sufficient mass and gravity to generate nuclear reactions that release incredible amounts of energy. In addition, they serve as nature's factories where the chemical elements of the cosmos are born. Deep within a star's interior, where extremely high temperatures and pressures prevail, solar mass is converted into solar energy through the fusion of lighter atoms like hydrogen into heavier atoms like helium.[16] Converted solar mass in the form of radiation streams out of each star at great speeds and in all directions. Stars become, therefore, the mechanism by which nature not only alters mass, but also redistributes mass and energy through space. We are able to appreciate some of this violent activity from afar since a small amount of the total energy package emanating from individual stars scatters as visible light and since a very small fraction of the total (1 unit per 2 billion units) is directed toward Earth.[17]

EMBRYONIC IMPRESSIONS ABOUT THE BIG PICTURE

The earliest astronomers date back to the centuries before Christ, inhabiting what are presently the lands of Greece, Egypt, China, and India, and the ancient lands of Babylonia and Arabia (now Iraq and Saudi Arabia). With a great capacity to imagine and the inquisitiveness that prompts exploration and wonder, ancient people studied their physical world and formulated ideas about its contents and patterns. They knew nothing of stars as violent furnaces or chemical factories. They began with little appreciation of the size of celestial objects or the enormity of stellar distances, believing that objects were both small and close. Moreover, they were unaware that the Earth rotates about an imaginary axis. Instead, because they trusted that appearance accurately reflects reality, they saw themselves at the geographic centre of a black canopy that slowly pivoted about them once each day from east to west. Within this overhead canopy, countless point sources of light resembling white holes appeared in the night sky, drifting west, maintaining fixed positions relative to each other before their disappearance in the morning. Through each hole streamed light from beyond the canopy.

Early students of the heavens saw identifiable shapes within specific groupings of holes. They imagined these to be the residences of various deities and assigned each grouping, or *constellation*, a name.

Further study of the heavens revealed strange behaviour associated with a few brighter sources of light. Mysteriously, they did not maintain fixed positions on the canopy. Instead, they displayed certain movements, unlike other visible objects. With unaided vision, curious observers identified seven of these anomalies: Mercury; Venus; Mars; Jupiter; and Saturn; as well as the extended sources of light, the moon and sun. They were the *planeetais* (planets), nature's celestial renegade *wanderers*.

Though wanderers, their movements were restricted to a narrow band in the celestial canopy (the *zodiac*). From these wanderers, the names of our seven days of the week were derived, names more easily recognizable in French than in English (see Chapter 2, Endnote 42). Normally progressing eastward at different rates relative to the white holes, they appeared to periodically reverse direction and describe elongated loops against the celestial canopy. To the ancient mind, nature was at play, throwing objects into our limited field of vision, beckoning us to speculate about a distant realm. Thus, nature was provoking human imagination with light that squirted through the billions of pin pricks in the firmament's canopy and adding additional entertainment with this batch of anomalous wanderers.

Though the contents of space remained largely a mystery to the earliest astronomers, two characteristics within the cosmos were recognizably accurate, namely *movement* and *regularity*, each cyclical and therefore recurring and predictable. These characteristics rendered certain celestial objects useful as time-measuring devices. It is believed that the Chinese developed one of the earliest calendars linked to the 365-day annual cycle of the sun. Later, the Babylonians developed a lunar calendar based upon the repeated monthly cycles of lunar phases. Babylonians, as well as Egyptians, employed the regular passage of the sun across the sky to perfect the sundial as a convenient hourly measuring device.

It is believed that much of the attention paid to monitoring precise locations and movements of celestial bodies was motivated by beliefs associated with the pseudo-science of astrology. The stuff of the heavens was believed to be, and among some people still is strongly influential in human destiny. Of great significance to them was the *horoscope*, a detailed circular chart that displays the configuration of celestial objects at the time of one's birth. The charts were considered windows into the future because of their perceived predictive properties. With the precise configurations produced by nature's celestial rhythms over time, it is clear that astrology had a vital role in the development and expansion of the then embryonic science of astronomy.

CONTRIBUTIONS OF EARLY GREEKS TO THE BIG PICTURE

History records occasional periods during which knowledge and wisdom moved human progress ahead in quantum leaps. This was true, especially within early Greek culture, in the centuries that preceded the birth of Christ. Within the philosophical framework assembled by brilliant minds, seminal ideas and inspiration stimulated probes into the nature of nature. A sample of early Greek astronomers and philosophers includes Aristotle, Aristarchus, Eratosthenes, Hipparchus, Ptolemy, Socrates, and Plato. Among all these mental giants, Aristotle's writings are most prolific.

- **Aristotle** correctly explained the phenomena of lunar phases and eclipses. He offered solid arguments supporting the spherical shape of the Earth. However, his conclusions were mainly founded on hunches, reason. and some observations, rather than on experimentation. He rejected the heliocentric view that the Earth revolves about the sun and erroneously argued that it is the celestial sphere that pivots about the Earth each day. With his work, we are reminded again that knowledge grows incrementally and that both erroneous conclusions along with accurate knowledge can proceed from the brightest of minds.
- **Aristarchus** employed geometry, direct observations, and reasoning to determine the relative distances to the sun and moon, as well as their sizes relative to the size of Earth. Though he properly perceived the sun larger, and the moon smaller than the Earth, his estimated diameters were inaccurate. Aristarchus grossly underestimated both the sun's diameter and its distance

from Earth. Nevertheless, he correctly surmised that stars are extremely distant objects and that the earth orbits the sun.

- **Eratosthenes**, like Aristarchus, focused on observations and geometry. His calculation of the circumference of the earth, given the rudimentary equipment at his disposal, is surprisingly accurate. In fact, his calculations were later found to be within 1% of the actual value of its circumference of 40 075 kilometres.

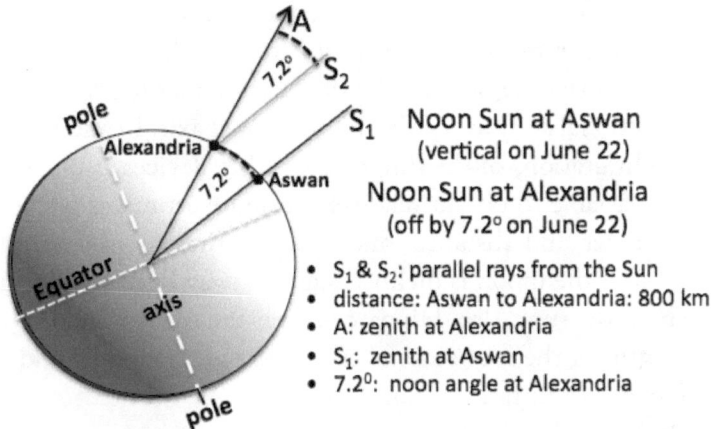

Simple Geometry to determine the Earth's Circumference[18]

To determine his results, Eratosthenes employed a simple method. It consisted of determining the difference in the noon angles of the sun (i.e. its elevation) at two places in Egypt conveniently located roughly on the same meridian: Alexandria on the Mediterranean coast, and Aswan some 800 kilometres to the south on the Nile River. At Aswan on the first day of summer, and at precisely the instant of solar noon, the sun was found to shine to the bottom of a vertical well. In other words, at that time and place, the rays of the sun were vertical (noon angle = 90°). On the same date, at the same time at Alexandria, the sun's rays were off the vertical toward the south by some 7.2 degrees (noon angle = 82.8°). Using a simple geometric construction, applying the rules of geometry concerning parallel lines, and assuming a spherical Earth, Eratosthenes calculated that the Aswan-Alexandria distance, represented by an arc of a circle, was 360/7.2 or one-fiftieth the entire circumference of the Earth.

Knowing the actual distance on land represented by this arc, namely 800 kilometres, he was able to perform his final calculation:

Earth Circumference = 50 x 800 km = **40 000 km**

- **Hipparchus** is known as the greatest among the early group of astronomers. He compiled an exhaustive catalogue of stars, assigning each a set of coordinates as well as a number expressing the magnitude of stellar brightness. So precise were his measurements and so thorough were his observations of the heavens that he became the first astronomer to identify the slow directional shift in the Earth's rotational axis. In addition, despite the limitations of the simple measuring devices available to him, he was able to obtain relatively accurate estimates of the moon's diameter and distance, and was the first to discover that the orbit of the moon is inclined slightly away from the Earth's orbit about the sun. Also, Hipparchus was the first to discover that the lengths of the four seasons of the year are not equal and that the Earth-Sun distance is not constant.
- **Ptolemy**, an early astronomer and mathematician, completed an exhaustive 13-volume compilation of writings on astronomy. By means of observations and simple geometry, he determined a measure of the moon's distance that he expressed as a multiple of Earth diameters. Compared to calculations made centuries later, Ptolemy's estimate turned out to be very close to the correct value. However, the model he developed to explain the apparent and periodic backward movement of planets in their orbits (known today as *retrograde motion*) proved incorrect since it was founded on an error, namely that planets orbit Earth and not the sun.

LATER IMPRESSIONS OF THE BIG PICTURE

Concerning the heavens, it gradually became clear that many early perceptions did not completely correspond to reality. As with most foundational changes in human thinking, there was a persistent reluctance to jettison the old and embrace the new. In many circles, loyalty to tradition outweighed loyalty to truth. Nevertheless, inventions like the telescope brought radical alterations to our understanding of the contents of the sky.

New discoveries were surprising, and sometimes disturbing, since new knowledge could not always be reconciled with cherished belief systems, especially those embedded within religion. Objects previously thought to be close proved to be distant. What was perceived to be small turned out to be remarkably large. Surfaces of objects like the moon, thought to possess perfect surface "complexions," were marred with *blemishes*. And shapes long considered to resemble perfect spheres were not so. Moreover, ancient observers had reversed the structure of the heavens just as with light in a photographic negative. What was for centuries believed to be matter (canopy) was found, in fact, to be empty space. What was once considered space (hole) was found to be concentrated matter (star).

Perhaps the most profound of all discoveries related to our own planet's place in the scheme of things. To the surprise of many, our place proved not to be central to our solar system. Neither did our sun occupy a central place in our galaxy. If we are special in the mind of a Creator, special status is not expressed in being assigned a geographically central place in His Creation.

> *Much of the practice of science . . . consists of the gradual correction of the mistakes of previous generations. You could say that science progresses by bringing mistakes to light, not by trying to hide them.*
>
> *Philip Ball*[19]

As mentioned above, the separation of fact from fiction is difficult, especially when loyalty to tradition is favoured over commitment to truth. The tendency is to resist the innovator and maintain the status quo. It was in the world of late Medieval Europe, dominated by the conservatism of the Roman Church, that the brilliant minds of Nicolaus Copernicus, Johannes Kepler, Galileo Galilei, and Isaac Newton made their appearance.

1. Nicolaus Copernicus (1473–1543)

Nicolaus Copernicus was a Polish mathematician and astronomer whose principal contributions to the corpus of human knowledge related to the fundamental structure of our solar system. In the early 1500s, through reason and observation, he set forth an unorthodox, and to many, heretical argument for a heliocentric solar system that displaced the Earth from its central place. He established the correct sequence of the orbits of the six known planets, from Mercury through to Saturn (no planet was then known to exist beyond Saturn), and calculated their relative distances from the sun with what later proved to be a high degree of accuracy. In addition, he correctly surmised that planetary orbital speeds depend upon their proximity to the sun (with slower speeds linked to greater distances). Then, having arrived at the correct structure for the solar system, Copernicus tackled the puzzling issue of the perceived relative motion of planets, namely *retrograde motion.*

The difficulty of appreciating the true orbital behaviour of various planets within our system is related to the fact that earliest observations were made from platform Earth, a part of that system. Relative motion of a planet (that is, its observed, and not necessarily its actual motion) can best be understood with reference to a series of concentric racetracks (representing individual planetary orbits), with each track occupied by a single horse (an individual planet), and with all horses running in the same direction about a central clubhouse (representing the sun). Away from the clubhouse, tracks get progressively longer. In addition, away from the clubhouse, horses get progressively slower. Thus, the horse that occupies the inside track not only travels the shortest circuit; it does so at the fastest speed. If we suppose that the race begins with all horses alongside each other, we can readily understand why the initial alignment of horses is immediately destroyed.

Eventually, differential speeds and distances cause a horse on a more inside track to circle more quickly, and eventually lap all horses on more outside superior tracks. If one imagines observing the race from the vantage point of a single inside horse, there would be times when adjacent horses on all superior tracks would be seen to be travelling *backwards,* a common observance on highways when our faster car overtakes and passes a slower car travelling in the same direction. This is, in fact, what we observe from Earth as we approach and pass slower planets like Mars and Jupiter. Each appears to move backwards in orbit relative to distant fixed stars.

This appearance of periodic backward motion, so puzzling to earlier astronomers, and observable around the time we lap a superior planet, is called *retrograde motion*. But from the vantage point of a plane flying over all these tracks and the movement of planets within them, no object would ever exhibit retrograde motion. All would appear to be travelling in the same direction. Copernicus had solved a confusing observation of *apparent* planetary behaviour with simple logic.

2. Johannes Kepler (1571–1630)

Like Copernicus, Johannes Kepler was both a mathematician and an astronomer. Early in his career, he came to accept his predecessor's heliocentric view of the solar system.

Kepler believed that mathematics was the language of God and that the precision of mathematical expressions could be used to express the precision of the heavens God created. For many years, aided by the research of a contemporary, he studied the orbit of Mars, Earth's close neighbour. Hypothesizing that the orbit of Mars is circular, Kepler attempted to fit the extensive observational data collected from that planet into a simple mathematical model approximating a circular shape. However, all his attempts met with failure. In fact, the orbit of Mars later proved not to be circular, but oval, matching the mathematical shape known as the ellipse.

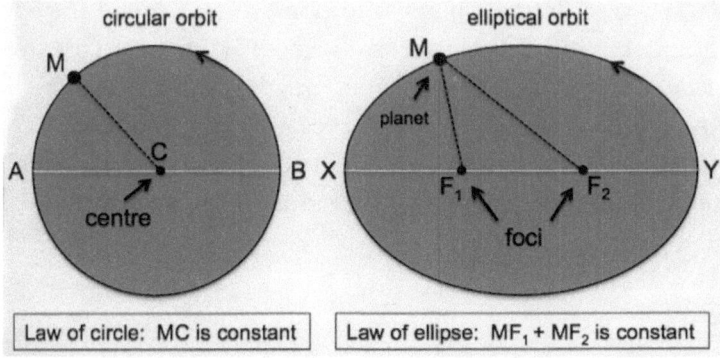

Comparisons of two geometric shapes: the circle and the ellipse[20]

While a circular pathway represents a set of points that are all the same distance from a single point (the focus), an elliptical pathway represents a set of points that move such that the sum of the distances from each point to *two* fixed points (the foci) is constant. The longest line that can be drawn through any ellipse passes through both foci. It is the *major axis* of the ellipse (xY).

Any line joining two points on a circle's circumference that passes through its centre is called a *diameter*. One special characteristic of any circle is that its circumference length, divided by its diameter, always produces the same number, referred to in mathematics as the constant quantity, pi (π). This constant shows all circumferences of circles, regardless of length, possess lengths slightly greater than three times their diameters and explains the well-known numerical value of pi (π) to be slightly greater than 3.14. Calculated as a ratio, 3.14 has no units.

If one imagines the elliptical shape squeezed in such a way as to reduce the length of xY to make the oval into a circle, both foci would migrate toward each other to eventually become a single focus. The ellipse would then become a circle with a single focus at its centre. Thus, a circle is a special form of an ellipse.

The degree to which an elliptical shape deviates from that of a perfect circle is called its *eccentricity*. A perfect circle has zero eccentricity. Earth's orbital eccentricity is close to zero and much smaller than the highly elongated orbit of Halley's Comet that, when closest to the sun (perihelion), falls within the orbit of Venus, but when at its farthest point (aphelion), drifts beyond the orbit of Neptune. Highly eccentric orbits, with their frequent crossovers of orbits of other bodies, mean that eventual collisions are more likely. With an orbital period of some 76 years, Halley is next expected to pass perihelion in the year 2061. One can imagine how the size of the sun would vary if it were observed on this comet through a full orbital period.

Kepler's investigations of the Martian orbit led to his formulation of three laws of planetary motion he believed had equal application to all other planets. His *first law* (**Law of Orbits**) is a simple statement defining the orbital shape about the sun as an ellipse, with the sun at one focus and with the second focus empty.

His *second law* (**Law of Areas**) describes the manner in which the variable planet-sun distances in an elliptical orbit are linked to the variable speeds of that planet in orbit (the fastest speed linked to the shortest distance).

Kepler's *third law* (**Law of Periods**) is an example of just how simple a mathematical relationship can be in describing a process in nature. This law came to be known as his *Harmonic Law*. It was as much an expression of his interest in amorphous mysticism as it was of his love for the precision of mathematics. To the imaginative mind of Kepler, the heavens in their harmonious movements "sing" music that Kepler represented in notes on musical scales. In his third law, (P), the period of time a planet takes to complete a single orbit of the sun, increases with (D), its average distance to the sun. Expressed in simplified form, this direct proportion reads:

$$\mathbf{P}^2 \propto \mathbf{D}^3$$

In other words, knowing a planet's distance means knowing also its orbital period, or year. Unfortunately, what Kepler correctly described, namely planetary motion, he couldn't explain. For explanations, the world would have to wait for the formulation of Isaac Newton's laws of motion and his *Universal Law of Gravitation*.

3. Galileo Galilei (1564–1642)

Galileo Galilei was another outstanding mathematician and astronomer who was a principal architect of experimental modern science. Among his many interests was the subject of *classical mechanics*, a scientific field dealing with the motion of physical objects from simple machines to planets and stars. He investigated phenomena such as the behaviour of falling bodies, balls rolling down an inclined plane, and the swing of a pendulum. He discovered the principle of *inertia*—that things at rest remain at rest, and things in motion remain in motion unless an external force is applied to them. Unfortunately, without the benefit of Newton's laws, he was unable to explain why planets move along curved pathways rather than in straight lines.

To Italy's Roman Catholic Church, Galileo represented a major disturbance. Over the years, the Church had fallen into line with the thinking of Aristotle and Ptolemy. Obscurantist in its receptivity to many new ways of thinking, it stubbornly held to the Ptolemaic view of planetary behaviour. Galileo's beliefs, however, were solidly Copernican. But to the church hierarchy, his beliefs lacked scriptural support. More importantly, they lacked congruency with church tradition. Given these diametrically opposed views, a clash was inevitable. To Galileo, beliefs concerning the behaviour of matter were not necessarily true just because they were always considered true. A clear demonstration of this fact involves a simple experiment.

Imagine a heavy steel ball and a light feather are dropped from the same height, released at the same instant to fall the same distance. In response to the pull of gravity, we might ask which of these objects will hit the ground first. The answer appears obvious: the steel ball, of course! Experiments with heavy steel balls and light feathers repeatedly demonstrate this.

But such an experiment is flawed. The reason is that gravity is not the sole variable affecting the behaviour of the two objects. Steel balls and feathers fall at different rates, not because they differ in mass, but rather because different shapes and sizes of objects offer differing resistance to the air that surrounds them during their fall. It is clear that feathers offer the greatest resistance to the air. To prove this, one merely removes the factor of air resistance. How? Let both feather and steel ball fall in a complete vacuum. In such circumstances, it is clear that both objects hit the ground at the same instant. In fact, *all* objects, regardless of mass, behave in like manner, even if one were to drop a feather and an automobile.

Such tests clearly demonstrate the difference between the concepts of experimental *reliability* and experimental *validity*. Experimental reliability prevails whenever test results show consistency. Experimental validity prevails whenever a test measures what it is supposed to measure. A bathroom scale, with its number system set incorrectly at 2 kilograms and not zero, will give consistent results of 2 kilograms *above* one's correct weight (consistent, therefore reliable, but definitely not valid). Thus, in the experiment with the steel ball and the feather falling through air, test results, though somewhat reliable on average, are definitely *not* valid.

Discomfort with Galileo's unconventional thinking reached a climax when someone discovered that combining pieces of specially machined glass produce an optical instrument that enlarges the apparent size of distant objects and enhances visual clarity. Thus, the telescope, through magnification, made clearer and visually proximal distant planets that had only been observed as fuzzy smudges.

To the ecclesiastical mind—which thought of planetary shapes as perfect spheres, planetary orbits as perfectly circular, and planetary surfaces as unblemished—Galileo's flattened planets, elliptical orbits, sunspots, and newly discovered moons orbiting not the Earth but the distant planet Jupiter, were impossible and could not be accepted. One may ask why planetary flattening, blotches on the lunar surface, or orbits not perfectly circular but elliptically shaped qualify as nature's imperfections.

Galileo was called before the Roman Inquisition and charged with subscribing to beliefs the Church claimed were in opposition to the teachings of holy scripture. Forbidden to hold to the Copernican view, he was placed under house arrest and surveillance for the last ten years of his life.

Truly, this was not the Church's finest hour. Many in it had failed to enter into a fuller appreciation of the glory of a real universe because of its reluctance to jettison a partially unreal one. Absent was a humble posture before truth and an equally serious and stubborn refusal to consider the possibility of error. Regrettably, not until 1992, a full 350 years after the death of this brilliant scientist, did the Roman Church admit its errors with regard to Galileo's condemnation and formally acknowledge that his views on the solar system were correct.[21] Among his many profound assertions to his adversaries were the following:

> *Take note, theologians, that in your desire to make matters of faith out of propositions relating to the fixity of Sun and Earth you run the risk of eventually having to condemn as heretics those who would declare the Earth to stand still and the Sun to change position —eventually, I say, at such a time*

as it might be physically or logically proved that the Earth moves and the Sun stands still.[22]

It is very pious to say and prudent to affirm that the Holy Bible can never speak untruth—whenever its true meaning is understood. But I believe nobody will deny that it is often very abstruse, and may say things which are quite different from what its bare words signify.[23]

To command the professors of astronomy to confute their own observations is to enjoin an impossibility, for it is to command them not to see what they do see, and not to understand what they do understand, and to find what they do not discover. The Bible does not tell how the heavens go, but how to go to heaven.[24]

4. Isaac Newton (1643–1727)

Within the beauty and rich traditions of London's Westminster Abbey can be found the burial sites of famous people: poets Geoffrey Chaucer and Alfred, Lord Tennyson; composers Vaughn Williams and George Frideric Handel; and politicians William Pitt and Oliver Cromwell. First among the scientific community to be honoured with such a distinctive site of last repose was Sir Isaac Newton, recognized as a genius of extraordinary calibre and, along with his predecessor, Francis Bacon, an outstanding contributor to the expanding field of natural science.

Nature and Nature's laws lay hid in Night.
Then God said: "Let Newton be," and all was Light.

Alexander Pope[25]

A contemporary of the poet, Alexander Pope, Newton was born the year after Galileo's death. Those were the years when the resurgence of the Black Death brought back the horrors and misery that prevailed during the Great Plague of the 14th century. Newton's parents wanted him to take up farming. However, a relative proposed an alternate direction for his life: to enter Cambridge University, studying physics and mathematics, and prepare for the Anglican ministry.

Using theoretical analyses and detailed experimentation, Newton began to write prolifically on many subjects. He probed the field of optics. He studied the spectrum of colours produced by the passage of light through a prism. He invented the first reflector telescope with a concave mirror (instead of a glass lens) to concentrate light. He is considered by many to be the inventor of the branch of mathematics known as calculus.

Newton wrote on lunar and planetary behaviour. He theorized that natural elements consist of atoms and that each atom contains particles that determine an element's distinct properties. He formulated three laws of motion, using principles of inertia, force, acceleration, action, and reaction. He also assembled his *Universal Law of Gravitation*, mathematically linking the magnitude of gravitational force to quantities of mass and distance. This law was regarded as *universal* in that it was non-restrictive. It applied not only to apples falling from trees, but equally to moons orbiting planets and to planets orbiting distant suns. His calculations resulted in the first accurately predicted return of Halley's Comet in 1758.[26]

Newton regarded mathematics, with its precision of expression, as reflecting something of the nature of God. He held firm to God as the Universal Ruler and Sovereign over all, a God who is eternal and perfect. His belief about a God whose authority encompasses all things fit very well with the universal application of the laws he formulated. Among his famous quotes:

> *If I have seen further than others, it is by standing upon the shoulders of giants.*[27]
>
> *I do not know what I may appear to the world, but to myself, I seem to have been only like a boy playing on the sea-shore, and diverting myself in now and then finding a smoother pebble or a prettier shell than ordinary, whilst the great ocean of truth lay all undiscovered before me.*[28]

Newton is reported to have been an avid reader of holy scripture. Gravity was his hypothetical construct, the invisible glue that governs planetary motion, establishing and maintaining order within the cosmos. By this, Newton was not explaining phenomena. Rather, he was providing elaborate descriptions of them. Newton believed that the order, beauty, design, and regularity within the natural world could proceed only from the mind of a superior Being and Designer, and never by blind chance. Moreover, his was not a pantheistic belief in multiple gods infused *within*, and *part of* nature. On the contrary, his was a monotheistic belief in a single Governor God who is Lord *over* nature. The science espoused by Newton served to encourage, rather than threaten, those who hold to belief in a God who not only exists but is Lord over all Creation.

> *This most beautiful system [The Universe] could only proceed from the dominion of an intelligent and powerful Being.*[29]

Newton was identified as the father of modern science. It was in his time that the refinement and use of the *scientific method* moved ahead in giant leaps. Recognized as universally applicable to all branches of science, the method, with its hypotheses and structured experimentation, became the recognized means of discovering the regularities within the natural world and the relationships between events in space and time. Acquisition of knowledge was recognized as incremental, involving both trial and error. Methodology involved observation, description, measurement, quantification, replication, and peer review, with the scientist formulating the experiment, but with nature free to *speak* its results.

> *I keep the subject of my inquiry constantly before me, and wait till the first dawning opens gradually, by little and little, into a full and clear light.*[30]

> *If I have ever made any valuable discoveries, it has been owing more to patient attention, than to any other talent.*[31]

In commentaries written about scientists of Newton's stature, superlatives abound. In addition, it is telling to examine the personal comments Newton made about himself. The above quotations point to a person of the patience one hopes would characterize anyone standing daily before the overwhelming vastness and complexities of nature with the humility required to receive and evaluate the input of fellow colleagues within the scientific community.

Firmly established as a means of understanding the natural world, the scientific method now awaited yet another quantum leap forward with the advent of new questions and theories, new technology, new exploratory toys, and minds as brilliant as Einstein, Hubble, and Hawking, introducing us to a radically new world of relativity, Quantum Theory, an expanding universe, black holes, artificial intelligence, dark matter, and something called *the Big Bang*. Given the rates at which scientific discoveries are coming forward, one wonders what other parts of the cosmic puzzle will eventually be uncovered that presently lie beyond our mental horizons.

THE COSMOS AS SEEN BY THE CASUAL OBSERVER

As inhabitants of a single celestial orb, humans occupy a moving observational platform that is completely surrounded by an overhead canopy. This canopy presents as a celestial screen where countless images appear spatially and disappear temporally in response to the Earth's movements of rotation and revolution and in response to the modifying and distorting influences of our thick atmosphere. Considering this, what can casual observers on our planet see and appreciate by viewing what is above us?

1. Light and movement

The origin of celestial light is found in immense stellar concentrations of gas. Human imagination envisions a Master Blacksmith, wielding a giant hammer, slamming it down on his giant anvil. The impact creates a shower of sparks that fly in all directions. In this way, one could imagine how the countless stars were formed. Putting aside this fanciful nature of an image of a Master Blacksmith, it is clear that elements of this metaphor such as temporal beginnings, high temperatures, and rapid dispersal of matter away from a common point of origin come close to approximating certain aspects of what we believe actually occurred. Indeed, if anything is eternal, it is not matter, but rather the Blacksmith. And, like the flying sparks, no matter in the universe is static. Everything moves at great speeds in all directions from a common point of origin, yet bound invisibly by the ever-present force of gravity. It is only because of the enormity of stellar distances that individual sparks appear both tiny and motionless.

2. Vastness and emptiness

On each clear night, as rotation swings us toward the darkness of outer space and away from the sun's brilliance, we are permitted to behold the grandeur of the heavens. What we see are assemblages of matter suspended in and separated by vast stretches of empty space, space that is completely silent and black. It is silent because sound cannot propagate through a vacuum. It is black because light is neither generated nor reflected by emptiness and because insufficient light arrives from the most distant stars to be rendered visible. Despite the emptiness and blackness of space, what stellar matter *is* visible easily testifies to the order and extravagance of nature. Moreover, no part behaves in isolation. No part acts independently. All parts move and are bound together by the invisible universal glue called gravity.

3. Celestial patterns and celestial dance

The geometric configurations of sun, moon, and Earth, arising from their regular and predictable movements relative to each other, generate various monthly lunar phases and the spectacular phenomenon of the eclipse. Solar wind particles in collision with the top of our atmosphere create colourful light displays known as aurora borealis and aurora australis.[32] In his book, *Fatal Passage*, Ken McGoogan vividly describes an Arctic aurora:

> *On the horizon, as if celebration, the aurora borealis emerged out of nothingness to form a great, shimmering rainbow across the northern sky . . . Its arch slowly grew larger, filling more than half the heavens before resolving itself into a series of vertical, grass-green rays cascading toward the horizon. Then began a shimmering dance*

of violet light, folding and unfolding across the sky in a thousand shades of purple, advancing, retreating, and finally shattering in a liquid explosion that ended with a sparkling, multi-coloured shower.

from Fatal Passage, p.135

4. Glimpses of the past, NOT the present

We behold events from afar because the One who made all things gave light the property of propagation. If gravity is nature's *glue*, light is nature's *messenger*. It has the ability to transfer information very rapidly over vast distances from its place of origin. Yet, despite enormous speed, no information is received at the exact instant it is sent. Light transmission over distance, like slower sound transmission over distance, takes time. The sound of the bat hitting the baseball reaches our ears a noticeable time after we see the bat impact the ball. The sound of distant lightning is heard some time after the flash is seen. But neither the sound of the bat hitting the ball nor the lightning flash is experienced at the exact instant it occurs. Lags of time with light, like those with sound, increase with distance. Because of this, we are never able to see objects in the heavens as they *are*, but as they *were*.

No speeding tickets here![33]

When objects are close, time lags are negligible. But on scales associated with galactic distances, delays are highly significant. Time delays associated with our nearby moon exceed one second. Those associated with our more distant sun are over eight minutes. Light from Neptune takes approximately four hours to reach us, while light from the nearest star beyond our sun involves a lag of over four years. Thus, in surveying the present *geography* of the heavens, we cannot avoid also peering into its *history,* simultaneously into different moments in history, at some incredibly ancient where the farthest distances create lags of time in excess of ten billion years. Thus the vastness of the spatial world testifies to the enormity of its temporal lifespan, estimated to be about thirteen billion years: a mere sampling of eternity.

5. Glimpsing objects that aren't *"there"*

Imagine yourself stopped at an intersection waiting for the light to turn green. It is nighttime and in the still air large snowflakes are lazily falling vertically through the beams projected by your headlights. It is obvious to you that the flakes are coming from somewhere directly above you. As your car moves forward, the snowflakes no longer appear to fall vertically but seem to come toward you on an angle from somewhere in front of you. As car speed increases, snowflakes appear to approach you more horizontally than vertically.

This simple but common experience helps to explain a phenomenon called *stellar aberration,* a complex visual event relating to the apparent location of stars in the heavens. In the analogy, the car represents our planet orbiting our sun and the snowflakes represent particles of light streaming toward us from above. As a result of our movement, a star is *not* where it appears to be, but rather is displaced in the direction of Earth's motion.

However, our illustration is not perfect. In reality, both incoming light from a star and progression of planet in orbit travel at much faster speeds, with starlight speed far exceeding planetary movement, and doing so about ten thousand times faster than our orbital progression. The net effect is to cause the location of a star to still be displaced ahead of its actual location, but by a mere fraction of a degree of arc. Although of little worth to most of us, such knowledge is critical to any astronomer who, with highly accurate tracking devices, is attempting to locate and study feeble light sources many light years away.

6. Glimpsing with nearby orbiting optical aids

Our principal means of interpreting incoming light packages from afar is the telescope. If microscopes enlarge small objects that are nearby, telescopes enlarge giant objects that only appear small because of their vast distances.

Since the telescope's invention, we have lived with a major problem: light that has traversed great distances to reach Earth must then negotiate a thick planetary atmosphere, which is able to reflect, absorb, scatter, and distort what is seen. In order to minimize these effects, observational sites are carefully selected. Preferred sites include: high altitudes (since atmospheric density decreases with altitude); low latitudes (since more of the celestial sphere can be observed over a period of a year nearer the equator than near either pole); dry climate locations (where water vapour and annual cloud cover are minimal); and sites far from urban areas (where starlight is not extinguished by urban glare). A quantum leap forward in high-quality telescopic imaging came in 1990 with the introduction of the powerful Hubble Space Telescope.[34] Lifted to an altitude of some 560 kilometres by the Space Shuttle *Discovery*, Hubble became an Earth satellite, circling Earth every 97 minutes. At this altitude, virtually all atmospheric distortion is eliminated.

While distance from the Earth's surface has advantages in terms of visual acuity, remoteness makes upgrading and periodic repair of space telescopes difficult and costly. At Hubble's inception, upgrades to its primary mirror became necessary to eliminate blurry images being relayed back to Earth. Later on, the main data processing instrument onboard Hubble failed. In addition, because its orbit is subject to a gradual speed reduction caused by atmospheric drag, the telescope requires periodic lifting and re-insertion into its original orbit to offset drag-induced orbital decay.

When operating as an efficient "light bucket," Hubble's light-gathering capability and powers of resolution permit observations of deep space, and hence of very ancient light sources. Recently, a new full-colour deep space image from Hubble captured light that had left distant galaxies some 13.2 billion years ago. This is remarkable, given that the most recent estimates of the age of our universe are in the order of 13 billion years. When Hubble became operational as a sophisticated optical aid, the distances at which we were able to observe the vastness around us virtually doubled.

The data relayed to us from Hubble show clear evidence that the universe is expanding. Pieces of galactic matter are moving away from a common centre. The motion is attributed to a cosmic explosion of unimaginable proportions—the so-called *Big Bang*. This may have been the instant that time and matter began. However, there is no explanation of conditions immediately prior to the Big Bang event, if such an instant occurred. Today, billions of years after this supposed gargantuan blast, we are still able to observe countless fragments of matter scattering at incredible speeds, even though their great distances from us make them appear stationary.

Given that matter appears to be moving *away from us* in all directions, it is natural to conclude that by some unbelievable stroke of luck, we on Earth just happen to reside on that one special fragment at the centre of the explosion. By applying laws of probability, this is almost certainly *not* the case. A common and simple explanation makes reference to the analogy of raisins in a transparent batch of dough. Imagine that our planet is a raisin suspended randomly in a slowly rising lump of dough. Imagine that other raisins suspended nearby represent matter in distant galaxies. As the dough rises, the whole lump expands. As it does, *all raisins move away from all other raisins*. Thus, if we were to switch our observation platform to any other raisin, we would still be drawn toward the same erroneous conclusion, namely that our new lump of matter appears to occupy the central place in the expansion process.

> *When I consider thy heavens, the work of thy fingers,*
> *the moon and the stars, which thou hast ordained;*
> *What is man, that thou art mindful of him?*
>
> *Psalm 8:3–4 (KJV)*

7. Glimpsing with more distant optical aids

From the perspective of the cosmos, the Earth has less significance than a single molecule of water within all the world's oceans. It exists as a member of a small community of eight planets that race about a single central star, itself a member of a single galaxy—the Milky Way. Included within our solar system is a collection of moons, an assortment of rock fragments called asteroids, a few tiny comets with eccentric orbits and very little mass, and scattered debris that has yet to be captured by larger objects during the galaxy's gravity-induced tidying up process.

The distribution of mass within our solar system is non-uniform, with over 99% of it resident in the sun and well over half of what remains belonging to the single giant planet—Jupiter. Thus, our solar system is essentially a single massive bright object surrounded by a tidy and relatively sparse debris field. What is visible to the naked eye is paltry compared to what is out there: the sun, five of our planets, a myriad of the brightest stars within our galaxy, and nothing but faint, tantalizing smudges beyond the Milky Way.

In the late 1960s, with the aid of energy-rich propellants and a powerful and massive Saturn-V rocket, humans managed to overcome local gravitational restraints to traverse some 384 000 kilometres of nearby space to accomplish a successful landing on our only moon. This "giant leap for mankind", though true, was erroneously labelled our *conquest of space*.

In the late 1970s, the United States launched two unmanned Voyager spacecraft to explore well beyond our nearest neighbour. One of these, *Voyager 1*, launched in 1977, made close approaches to Jupiter in 1979 and the more distant Saturn in 1980. Using the massive gravity of these planetary giants as accelerants, *Voyager 1* was propelled forward toward our two most distant planets: Uranus and Neptune.

By 2005, it had flown so far that radio transmission from it to Earth exceeded 14 hours. In September 2013, NASA announced it had become the first man-made object to leave our solar system. In 2021, 44 years after its initial launch, it had moved past the orbits of Neptune and Pluto and was about 22 billion kilometres from the sun. Barring unforeseen collisions, both Voyager spacecraft are expected to continue journeying many billions of kilometres and wander the galaxy, possibly forever.

Astronomical distances of these magnitudes involve lags in radio transmissions in the order of 10 hours for each one-billion-kilometre increase in distance. To date, our various forays into space, though minuscule when we consider the enormity of the cosmos, have nevertheless been remarkable. Each "small step for Man," like the recent ones directed to the planet Mars, bears testimony to the imagination and ingenuity of the human mind to develop technology to meet the many challenges and hazards of space travel. Each also testifies to both the universality and the reliability of natural laws formulated by a divine Mind and discoverable by finite and mortal beings.

THE MIRACULOUS WITHIN THE WORLD OF THE NATURAL

Whether the scenes we observe arrive by unaided vision or with the aid of giant light-gathering buckets such as Hubble, they all depict something truly remarkable about our natural world. But what makes something *natural*? Is something deemed natural because it is usual, ordinary or predictable? Planets spinning, waters flowing, mountains forming, landscapes degrading, vapours rising, climates changing, and continents drifting: all these exemplify both the natural, and the usual. Each involves processes that occur over time that are known as comprehensible, orderly, reasonable, and normal.

However, some events considered natural fall into an additional category, namely the *un*-usual or abnormal. For example, while it is both natural and usual that wheat seeds planted in the spring mature into a golden field of wheat in the fall, Canadian wheat can also be destroyed by a swarm of insects. Though natural, such an event is fortunately unusual. Here, outcomes are less certain, and surprises are more common.

Against these examples is the situation in which the sowing of wheat results in a harvest of barley. Of course, this is absurd since it is altogether *un*-natural and totally surprising since it is inconsistent with nature's behavioural reputation. According to human experience, such an event is deemed impossible since the probability of it happening is virtually zero. It is when something considered impossible occurs that the subject of *miracle* arises.

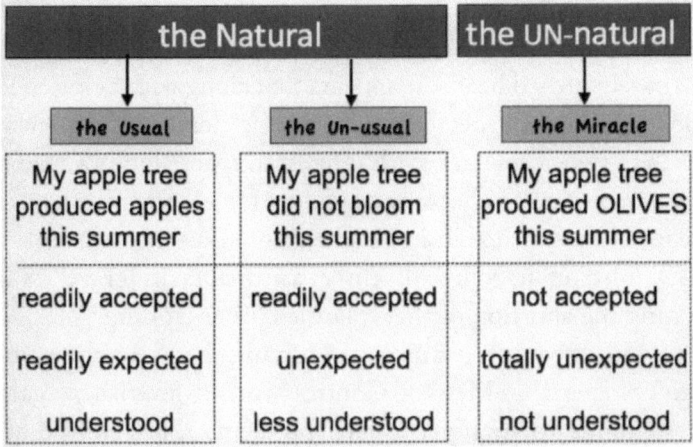

In our world, miracles are considered the stuff of the impossible—those events that are unique, have no known explanation, and cannot by any human effort be replicated, since replication would prove they are *not* unique. Yet, regardless of their perceived impossibility, most of us have prayed for miracles, especially in times of dire circumstances. Childlike, in desperation, having no other option, we call out to an invisible Supreme Being to do the impossible, to arrest or even reverse the progress of horrible happenings. And when we hear stories of spectacular rescues against impossible odds, or amazing survivals from accidents, or recoveries from illnesses when all hope was lost (since certain illnesses have no known cure), the word *miraculous* is frequently the descriptive term used. Consider the following:

1. "Miracles" in our present world?

The *Apollo 8* voyage to the moon in the late 1960s drew the attention of many millions of people worldwide whose minds were captured by the magnitude of what was unfolding. Three astronauts, accelerating to almost 11 kilometres per second in a small space capsule, managed with extreme precision to rendezvous with the moon. Using state-of-the-art communication and computer technology, they achieved insertion into a lunar orbit and completed ten circuits about the moon in twenty hours before safely returning to Earth. It was a near-flawless mission. The event was described by many observers as miraculous. Yet, subsequent Apollo missions barely turned heads. It appears that along with being spectacular, miraculous events are expected to possess the element of uniqueness.

Less than two years later, with interest in space flights already waning and television networks choosing to feature far less spectacular events, the world learned that an explosion had ruptured an oxygen tank onboard *Apollo 13*, placing its crew of three astronauts in grave danger and necessitating the abortion of their planned lunar landing.

Faced with great uncertainty, and forcing themselves to think rather than panic, experts at Mission Control worked feverishly against time to find solutions to highly complex problems. How would they deal with diminishing oxygen levels and increasing concentrations of CO_2 gas? How best to conserve limited energy supplies? Approaching Earth, how would they navigate with the precision required for a safe angle of reentry? Failure was deemed not an option. As minutes passed into hours, with millions watching, and with brilliant minds tackling a situation never confronted before, disaster was somehow averted. In the moments after the astronauts' safe splashdown in the Pacific, NASA labelled their mission *a successful failure*, and the astronauts' return miraculous.

During the cataclysmic events that followed the massive earthquake off the Japanese coast in 2011, giant tsunami waves invaded coastal villages, destroying human habitation and life, burying people in a chaotic mess, and carrying wreckage through backwash off the land and into the sea. Three days later, it was reported that search and rescue crews had discovered a survivor, a four-month-old baby girl lying unharmed amid broken glass, home contents, wood fragments and mud. In the vicinity, over 2000 people had disappeared.

What was miraculous about the *Apollo 8* journey to the moon? What was miraculous about *Apollo 13*'s incredible escape from tragedy? What was miraculous about a baby surviving an earthquake and tsunami, alone in a vast chaotic mess of debris? Most people would insert each of these events into the category of the extraordinary, even the miraculous, but not because of anything that was unnatural. Indeed, everything that happened, though improbable, occurred within the wide range of what is termed *natural variability*, and in response to natural law and the known properties and tolerances of naturally occurring materials. Each event bore testimony to the fact that the miraculous is not necessarily restricted to the unnatural.

We do not consider miraculous events restricted to the unnatural. Our sense is that the miraculous doesn't require something to be either extraordinary or unique. On the contrary, it is within the usual, the ordinary, the expected or even the unexpected that events described as miraculous reside: in the birth of a baby, or the survival of one for many hours amid widespread carnage and destruction; in the orderly progression of seasons; in the harmony and integrity of the cosmos; in the precision of a space flight; in the multi-million human heartbeats in a single lifetime; or, in the unexpected safe return of some astronauts.

2. "Miracles" in biblical times:

Now, if miracles are not restricted to the unnatural, do they actually happen within it? When reading about the familiar workings of our world in scripture, one is often confronted with the altogether impossible, with events not contained within the range of natural variability but which reach beyond what is both normal and natural. We sense we are seeing into another world that is operating by different rules.

We read stories of a Creator making something out of nothing (Gen 1); of the sun suddenly arrested in its motion across the sky (Josh 10:13); of Jesus being born to a virgin (Luke 1); of Jesus walking on water (Matt 14); of a person blind from birth suddenly being able to see (John 9); and, of Jesus rising from the dead (John 20). Each alludes to a *super-natural* realm where wolves live peaceably with lambs (Isa 11:6) and where defenseless infants play in perfect safety near the hole of venomous snakes (Isa 11:8). We would all agree that all these events are not only unusual but clearly *not* natural.

The existence of such a realm is not merely hinted at in scripture. We are told of *signs and wonders*, seemingly outrageous events that stretch our imaginations to think audacious thoughts. Such thoughts require us to step out of what is considered conventional thinking. Can we dismiss these events as merely fiction? Has non-biblical human history any examples of moments when natural laws did not apply or when they appeared temporarily suspended? Do similar apparent suspensions of natural law occur today?

In ruminating over specific examples, care must be taken to distinguish what is *truly* unnatural from what is unusual. For example, how are we to think about the star of Bethlehem? Did God construct a unique star just for a most special occasion? Postulating an omnipotent God, we have to assume He could have done so in an instant. To believe otherwise is disturbing since it suggests a tampering with the reliability of scripture. Or is it possible that a supremely imaginative God chose not to add an additional star, but to use what was already created? Maybe the Star of Bethlehem was not a star at all, but an alignment of planets *in conjunction*; that is, visually so close to one another that they appeared to ancient observers as a single bright object.

Though relatively infrequent, such an alignment of planets observed from Earth does occur. And coincidentally, it did, in 7 BC, involving Jupiter and Saturn, our two largest planets, each about ten times the size of Earth. This was followed a year later by a second conjunction of Jupiter, Saturn, and Mars (one of our smallest planets). Both events have been verified through retrievable historical data from the orbital periods of these planets. If so, it seems a correction to the numbering of AD years is necessary!

Whichever explanation regarding Bethlehem's star is true, both capture our wonder and allude to something miraculous. It might have been a unique object created for a unique purpose. Or it might have been an entirely natural orchestration and alignment of celestial objects whose occasional appearance as a single brighter *"star"* was precisely timed to correspond to the event of Christ's Incarnation. In either case, we witness God's sovereignty over all.

Does a natural explanation diminish the wonder associated with that star, moving *it* outside the category of the miraculous, possibly moving *us* away from beholding the far greater glory of the Incarnation? Or is wonder actually enhanced when we consider the precision and timing associated with the normal behaviour of all planets and stars?

Regardless of our conclusion, it is important that anyone seeking to submit to biblical truths must be satisfied that congruency between what scripture *"says"* in specific statements and what it *"teaches"* on the same subject is evident. For us to do otherwise is to drift from the God who made us and toward a god that we created.

3. "Miracles" as foretastes of what is to come

Having argued the above, the idea that *all* phenomena can eventually find their explanation within the natural order seems inadequate. In our most desperate times, when elements of severe mental and physical pain attack us with disharmony, uncertainty, disappointment, pain, and ultimately death, the human heart finds itself longing for and being comforted by yearnings for conditions that reside beyond the natural order. Our minds turn to audacious thoughts. Audacious thoughts defy conventional thinking and frequently enter the category of what experiences have shown to be impossible.

Why are audacious thoughts so frequently resident in the human mind? And why must such thoughts always be regarded as merely human fancy? Such thoughts are not restricted to the desperate among us, but rather may be universally present. What generates lasting hope in individuals is the discovery that an ultimate reversal of human misfortune is central to the plan of God. This plan is called redemption, an act involving restoration of all things, from the largest entities of reality to the smallest. And so we ask, "Does God, who in the beginning established the rules by which nature plays, sometimes suspend the normal and reliable operation of these rules? And if He does, for what reasons would He do something so radical?"

In attempting an answer these questions, care must be taken to determine just what constitutes the *natural*. Let us assume for the moment that the gold standard for determining what is truly natural is defined by God, and not by what is perceived as the normal reputation of natural law. Recall what happened at the tomb of Lazarus (John 11). At death, life ceases and decay slowly commences to obliterate all evidence that an individual ever existed. But in the presence of witnesses and at the command of Jesus, a dead man, described as rotting in his tomb for four days, stood up and walked.

Few among us would argue against this startling event constituting a suspension of the laws of nature, a disturbing act when we imagine how chaotic our world would be if a fickle deity arbitrarily chose to render natural laws undependable.

But consider this. Maybe causing a dead man to rise and walk is exactly what Jesus did! Rather than suspending the laws of nature, maybe Jesus was opening up, just for an instant, a window displaying what the truly natural looks like, an idyllic world in which reside pure delight and fulfillment, sheer beauty, harmony, and goodness. The window opens into a reality in which the created order functions in perfect congruency with the original purposes of God, a situation that prevailed so long ago in Eden, that idyllic Garden in an existence that time has failed to fully erase from our memory.[35]

Perhaps the form of miracle that to us represents a suspension of natural law is, in fact, a foretaste or glimpse of how all will be after future restoration destroys forever the truly *un*-natural, dysfunctional part of our world—namely sorrow and pain, crying and tears, death and decay (Rev 21:3–4). If so, then miracles take on a significance that goes beyond providing temporary comfort for the individual but extends rather to every part of the cosmic order, providing an encapsulated preview of what is truly permanent and real. Audacious thinking outside the box of conventional thinking? Without question, an altogether radical thought![36]

IMAGES OF THE COSMOS WITHIN SCRIPTURE

The prophet Isaiah, alluding to the glory of God and His immense power over, knowledge of, and interest in the Creation, beckons us with these words:

> *Lift up your eyes and look to the heavens: Who created all these?*
> *He who brings out the starry host one by one,*
> *and calls forth each by name.*
> *Because of his great power and mighty strength,*
> *not one of them is missing.*
>
> **Isaiah 40:26**

Similarly, the psalmist announces that the glory of God, namely, the essence of His character, is declared in the heavens and that day after day, heavens pour forth speech without words (Ps 19:1–2). Psalm 8:3 captures the image of God as Artist, fashioning the moon and the stars with His fingers, then meticulously inserting each of them into a special place. A vivid expression of both God's care of and sovereignty over all Creation is contained in the psalmist's lofty words, *"He determines the number of the stars and calls them each by name"* (Ps 147:4). The abundance of stars in the sky is a useful tool to capture how numerous Abraham's descendants would eventually be (Heb 11:12). The enormity of stellar distances is referenced to illustrate the everlasting nature of God's mercy (Ps 103:12), while the span of natural history expresses the eternal nature of God (Ps 90:2). The image of the heavens being *"higher"* than the Earth is a powerful visual aid expressing the loftiness of God's ways and thoughts over ours (Isa 55:9).

At the time of Creation, God *was*; but the cosmos wasn't. The fact that God never *wasn't* and that He pre-existed His Creation is inferred in the very first verse of the Bible (Gen 1:1). Elsewhere, parts of this Creation are depicted in beautiful figurative language as choristers entering into joyful acts of praise by singing together (Job 38:7). Without words, hills and valleys sing songs of praise (Ps 65:12) and floods clap their hands (Ps 98:8).

The contrast between how we view our place in the cosmos and how God views it is striking. Confronting the immensity of the cosmos, we find it incredible that God could ever be mindful of us (Ps 8:4). However, the scriptures paint a very positive picture of our significance within His created order. In the Old Testament, we are described as His "delight" (Isa 62:4), His "sought after" (Isa 62:12), and His "planting for the display of his splendour" (Isa 61:3). In the New Testament, we are described as His "beloved", His "children," shining like stars in the universe as we "hold out the word of life" (Phil 2:15–16). And as if these expressions of God's affection for His children are not enough, Ephesians 2:10 describes us as God's "workmanship": translated from the Greek word, *poema*. The English equivalent of poema is the word poem!

PONDERING COSMIC ORIGINS FROM SCRIPTURE

All things were made by him,
and without him
was not anything made that was made.

John 1:3 (KJV)

According to Genesis 1, things came into being, not by chance or accident, but by direct commands from God who only is eternal: "And God said, 'let there be light', and there was light." Genesis does not debate the point. Rather, it declares it. Elsewhere in scripture, the same point is made in the same manner:

By the word of the LORD the heavens were made,
their starry host by the breath of his mouth. . . .
For he spoke, and it came to be;
he commanded, and it stood firm.

Psalm 33:6, 9

For in him all things were created:
things in heaven and on earth, visible and invisible,
whether thrones or powers or rulers or authorities;
all things have been created through him and for him.

Colossians 1:16

The whole of scripture affirms the truth of Genesis 1. Thus, it is thoroughly appropriate for the Apostles' Creed to begin with the words, "I believe in God the Father Almighty, maker of heaven and earth."

It is absurd for the Evolutionist to complain that it is unthinkable for an admittedly unthinkable God to make everything out of nothing, and then pretend that it is more thinkable that nothing should turn itself into everything.

G. K. Chesterton[37]

While the focus of the story is on the creative acts of God, it is not a clear scientific statement on the methods by which these creative acts were accomplished. With conspicuous gaps, the story is shrouded in mystery. How could it be otherwise? We are told *what* is done and *who* does it, but are told little about *how* it was done or *when* it was done. As a result, the story leaves us with a sense of wonder and also with a multitude of legitimate questions that we, born with inquisitiveness and the capacity to think and imagine, ought to be asking. Moreover, it leaves us with the responsibility to investigate for ourselves the vast array of evidence strewn about in God's creation that contains delicious clues to those provocative *hows* and *whens*.

The Creation story begins with God making something out of nothing. This boggles our minds because anything *we* make requires ingredients. In the beginning, no ingredients existed for the fashioning of the universe— no wood, no plastics, no metals, no earth, no anything. God alone, with the Son and the Holy Spirit, was there in the beginning. Equally boggling is the statement from Hebrews 11:3: "What is seen was not made out of what was visible." Thus, while God is eternal, matter isn't. Matter had a beginning; God didn't. If matter was always, it would not have required a creator. Furthermore, scripture makes it abundantly clear that, contrary to pantheistic beliefs, the Creation is distinct from its Creator. We are cautioned neither to blur this distinction nor to worship creation rather than Creator.

The story also makes clear that while God fashioned first things out of nothing, first things became the stuff from which God fashioned subsequent things. Thus, Adam was not created out of nothing, but rather out of stuff from the ground. Eve was created from the stuff of Adam. In like manner, beasts of the field and fowls of the air came from already created materials.

This is a thrilling story. Curiosity abounds about a God who creates stuff out of nothing, who creates stuff out of stuff, about a God who is not satisfied creating a single shape or a single size or a single colour but prefers creating stuff of infinite variety. We find fascination in a God who is like a child in a sandbox, delighting in fashioning various things for sheer pleasure by mere command, by His *breath* and by His *fingers*, then exulting in it all, and calling it all *good*. And we continually wonder about a God who hides most of His stuff, making it necessary for us to assemble a somewhat confusing puzzle and sometimes to patiently await inventions like the microscope (to discover the smallest stuff), the telescope (to find distant stuff) or the slow-motion camera (to better appreciate fast-moving stuff).

But is this story believable? If it doesn't contain *the whole* truth, does it contain *nothing but* the truth? Does one take the Genesis account of creation literally? Does God *want* us to take the Genesis account of creation literally? If not literally, why did He choose to write it figuratively? These questions are legitimate since God delights in conversations with His children, whether our questions arise out of sheer inquisitiveness or out of skepticism.

Surely, serious doubts can find residency in honest believers. They are certainly resident in various scriptural characters. But those who ask such questions must do so with humility and not with arrogance. Humility characterized Mary's question to the angel before she conceived: "How will this be?" (Luke 1:34). Last-minute doubts characterized John the Baptist's question to Jesus just before his death: "Are you the one who is to come, or shall we look for another?" (Matt 11:3). Questioning God for purposes of clarification does not dishonour him. What dishonours God is neglecting to wonder about His mighty acts. Wonder is that which naturally resides in a healthy, God-given mind.

Among the questions that continue to generate controversy are these: How long ago did God create the heavens and the Earth? Also, how long did God take to complete His acts of creation? Herein lies controversy involving scriptural interpretation that has frequently taken many minds away from fully appreciating the Genesis story of Creation. From scripture, we read that God did it in six days, then rested on the seventh! Could He have done it that fast? Without doubt! In fact, faster! As Christians, we have no argument that an omnipotent God is capable of doing anything He wants to do, like constructing an entire universe in an instant.

That being the case, one might ask, "Why did a God, who is able in an instant to call into existence anything He wishes, take *so long*? Why did He take almost a week to do something He could have completed in a flash? Does the Genesis reference to the *day* mean something different from a 24-hour period?" A literal interpretation of the time factor in

Genesis 1 makes any agreement with what the physical sciences put forth as Creation's timeline virtually impossible. And the Bible is clear in its assertion that the natural world adds its powerful voice to the acts of God in the Creation Story.

If one acknowledges the validity of both natural and special revelation in speaking to the issue of Creation (as scripture clearly affirms), then both sources of revelation must be taken seriously. If "the heavens declare the glory of God and the Earth shows forth his handiwork" (Ps 19:1), there is little justification in jettisoning legitimate and well-documented scientific studies on the subject since to do so would mean jettisoning part of God's revelation in Creation. One does not jettison a large piece of legitimate testimony just to eliminate apparent contradictions. Rather, one doggedly investigates the evidence to determine why the contradictions exist.

But just as no part of God's counsel can be discarded, no part can be contradictory. The package must possess integrity. And yet, those who struggle with it must be ready to accommodate mystery and to live in dynamic tension. If contradictions arise, then one or both sources of His counsel have been misinterpreted. And there are many reasons for misinterpretation. Thus, for us who now "know only in part" (1 Cor 13:12), a humble posture before truth is critical. In time, we may know fully. But by then, it may matter little.

Regardless of whether the time language of Genesis 1 is to be interpreted as figurative or literal, or both, one must not be distracted from appreciating the enormity, mystery and incredible grandeur of the Creation story. How can such a story be adequately described with mere words? Whatever God chooses to do must be regarded with awe and wonder. Could it be that by calling all things into being, sometimes instantaneously, and sometimes through detailed and complex processes over periods of time far longer than a day, God was demonstrating not only supreme sovereignty over our natural world, but also immense pleasure and imagination in all His acts of creation?

With each creative act, we perceive an unmistakable air of exultation and rejoicing. We who live in the dimension of time know that anything involving celebration, by its very nature, must never be rushed. What is true within human realms, I suspect, is probably also true within the divine. To many, it is thoroughly consistent with the Bible's image of

God to think this way. For it appears that the delight and joy of God is as much in the *processes* of Creation as in its finished products. On Creation, scripture speaks in eloquent pictures:

> *He who made the Pleiades and Orion,*
> *who turns midnight into dawn and darkens day into night,*
> *who calls for the waters of the sea and pours them out*
> *over the face of the land—the LORD is his name.*
>
> *Amos 5:8*

> *Like the appearance of a rainbow in the clouds on a rainy day,*
> *so was the radiance around him.*
> *This was the appearance of the likeness of the glory of the Lord.*
> *When I saw it, I fell facedown,*
> *and I heard the voice of one speaking.*
>
> *Ezekiel 1: 28*

How wondrous is the ineffable splashed all over Creation. Without words, it exemplifies universal language whose 'speech' is not restricted to any human language employing nouns, adjectives or verbs. Its value is clearly expressed by the reliance in scripture on elements of Creation in the construction of parables and metaphors. It is here that the Bible employs nouns, adjectives and verbs to allude to the ineffable.

JES

2

EARTH

Sing to the LORD a new song;
sing to the LORD, all the earth . . .
Let the heavens rejoice, let the earth be glad;
let the sea resound, and all that is in it;
let the fields be jubilant, and everything in them.
Then all the trees of the forest will sing for joy.

Psalm 96:1, 11-13

Earthrise out of the Lunar Horizon[38] **(NASA)**

*The Earth,
sub-microscopic on a galactic scale;
a rather secondary mass within its solar system;
with a single Sun and a single Moon,
a colourful ball hanging out there in emptiness
with no visible support,
spinning about itself and revolving,
thereby creating variations in light and temperature,
and rendering visible to all observers
the entire celestial sphere surrounding them.
Is this magnificent orb unique
as a human dwelling within the universe?
Many doubt it.
Given the laws of probability,
such a combination of environmental conditions
could be duplicated elsewhere,
and frequently.*

JES

Suddenly, from behind the rim of the Moon, in long, slowmotion movements of immense majesty, there emerges a sparkling blue and white jewel, a light, delicate sky-blue sphere laced with slowly swirling veils of white, rising gradually like a small pearl in a thick sea of black mystery. It takes more than a moment to realize this is Earth . . . home.

Edgar Mitchell, Apollo Astronaut [39]

The thought of flying like birds may be as old as human imagination. However, the conversion of dream into reality occurred only relatively recently. The first humans to fly were lifted upwards in baskets attached by ropes to large balloons. Lift was provided either by air made buoyant through thermal heating and expansion or through the use of naturally buoyant gases such as hydrogen or helium, both lighter than air.

Following aviation's primitive beginnings, the field of aeronautics grew rapidly. Major innovations in the early design and function of flying machines included the introduction of the internal combustion engine and propeller for forward thrust, and the application of aerodynamically designed wings for lift. Combining thrust and lift, flight now possessed both horizontal and vertical capabilities. At present, with metals that can tolerate the stresses of rapid motion and very high temperatures; with computers capable of rapid processing and storing large volumes of information and maintaining precise flight paths; and with fuels that deliver enormous power safely and on demand, speeds have become supersonic, flight altitudes have reached the near vacuum of the Earth's upper atmosphere, and destinations, beginning with Earthorbiting missions, have come to include the extra-terrestrial and faraway places at the margins of our solar system.

It was the 1950s, and the world had entered the so-called space race involving two principal competitors—the United States and the then Soviet Union. Human desire to oppose the restrictive influences of planetary gravity had spawned the development of new designs, new propellants, new flying machines, and a host of adventurous pilots to fly them.

Given its close proximity to the Earth, the moon, though inhospitable to life, was the obvious choice as our first extra-terrestrial destination. On a cosmic scale, an Earth-moon distance is hardly noteworthy. However, in terms of human achievement, traversing such a distance with a human cargo represented a monumental accomplishment. For the first time in history, humans penetrated their thin protective atmospheric envelope and entered that hostile place called space. In doing so, we never escaped the force of gravity. According to Newton, we never can. But for the first time in history, we were able to travel to a point in space beyond which the gravity of another object pulling astronauts forward came to exceed the Earth's force of gravity pulling them backward. And as Earth became more distant and its apparent size slowly diminished, astronauts were eventually able, in a single photograph, to capture through their space capsule window almost 50% of Earth's entire surface. It was our first-ever opportunity to glimpse our planet in its context within the glorious cosmos.

For astronauts fortunate enough to be selected for such an incredible ride, views of the Earth are spectacular. Nothing impedes or obscures their vision. Our planet presents itself as a coloured spherical ball resembling a blue and white marble. Photos from space display it as a delicate Christmas tree ornament suspended without string in black space. Both ocean and land surfaces are clearly visible. The giant ice sheet over the Antarctic continent, the world's oceans and swirling cyclonic cloud patterns give evidence of the ubiquitous presence of water in solid, liquid, and condensed vapour form. To astronauts, this beautiful jewel-like orb appeared motionless against a virtually empty black background. From a distance, it displayed almost no visible marks of human occupancy.

Space shuttle astronaut Charles Walker, like Edgar Mitchell, used superlatives in his description of Earth's appearance from afar. Interestingly, despite the arresting beauty before him, he sensed that a critical element, a last brush stroke of a created masterpiece was missing. Leaving his readers with the thought that this last stroke is ours to contribute, Walker wrote:

> *Here was a tremendous visual spectacle, but viewed in silence. There was no grand musical accompaniment; no triumphant, inspired sonata or symphony. Each one of us must write the music of this sphere for ourselves.*[40]

THE SIZE OF THE EARTH

The Earth, ranking fifth among our eight planets in mass, orbits a central sun whose own mass is 333 000 times greater and whose radius is 110 times greater. Among the planets, most mass belongs to a single giant—Jupiter, possessing more than twice the matter of the seven other planets combined. Among our planets, Mercury is the least massive. If we judge the significance of the system's various members solely on the basis of mass, then clearly our own planet's presence in that system is of little significance.

Appreciating the size of the Earth relative to the size of the sun is difficult, given the large scales involved. But if we reduce sizes and distances proportionately, some appreciation emerges. One popular reduction in sizes and distances involves a basketball, a BB pellet, and a basketball court. If the basketball represents the sun, *half* the diameter of a single BB pellet would represent the Earth, with ball and BB pellet separated by the full length of the court.[41] Also, if one were to imagine standing on the pellet and looking at the basketball, that sphere, resting one full court away, would have an angular diameter of half a degree of arc (approximating the appearance of a pencil's eraser at arm's length).

THE SHAPE OF THE EARTH

A sky-blue sphere; a small pearl: like other planets, ours is a celestial ball. Judging from the shapes of stars and planets, natural laws favour spheres over cones, cubes, and cylinders. But why favour *any* shape? The simple answer is the existence of gravity, the mysterious attractive force that is able to influence all matter. As nature's glue operating between objects, gravity pulls and holds our flock of planets within fixed orbital paths about the sun. And as it does, it collects up extraneous space debris, depositing it onto larger masses. Also, as nature's force operating within each object, gravity causes the collapse of materials in the direction of the object's centre, an action that eventually produces a spherical shape at a rate proportional to the force of gravity operating within the object. However, due to other active forces in nature, our planet isn't a perfect sphere. Among these forces, two predominate. Both result in sizable redistributions in planetary mass.

Firstly, we know that our crustal surface is subject to continuous change from forces acting both from below and above. Mountains thrust up by sub-crustal tectonic forces lift and buckle solid rock and extrude hot liquid material to form topographic features consisting of lofty heights and deep valleys (see Chapter 5). Meanwhile, from above, relentless gradational forces of wind and water erode and transport weathered rock, diminishing heights and elevating valleys. The dynamic equilibrium thus created is sufficient to render the Earth a slightly imperfect sphere, but so slightly, in fact, that from space, one cannot distinguish loftiest heights from deepest valleys.

Secondly, mass redistribution is also generated by planetary rotation, or spin. Rotation contributes a strong centrifugal force that opposes gravitational collapse. The result of our planet twisting its entire mass once every twenty-four hours about its axis of spin is a slow transfer of mass outward in the region of its equator and a corresponding flattening at either pole. With an equatorial bulge and two flattened polar regions, our equatorial diameter exceeds its polar diameter by slightly over forty-two kilometres. This difference is about double the elevation difference between the world's tallest mountaintop and its deepest ocean trench.

For any rotating object, degrees of planetary distortion vary with rates of spin and the densities of materials being spun. For the Earth, spherical distortion due to rotation is slight. Visually, it is barely noticeable. Yet, it is sufficient to cause our body weight to be less at the equator than at either pole. Moreover, comparing poles, our weight at 90°N (standing at sea level) would exceed our weight at 90°S (standing on a thick ice sheet) because at the North Pole, our distance to the Earth's centre is less. Rates of spin, and hence distortion from centrifugal forcing, are greatest among the planetary giants, namely Jupiter and Saturn. They are minimal among the least massive planets, namely Mercury and Venus.

THE SPIN OF THE EARTH: FURTHER EFFECTS

Polar flattening and equatorial bulging are by no means the only effects of planetary spin. There are many more:

1. Rotation, Axis of Spin, Geographic Poles, and Equator:

Rotation is defined as the movement of an object about an imaginary line called an *axis of spin*. The two points where an axis of spin intersects the surface of a rotating object are called *geographic poles*. All points on a rotating object that lie equidistant from either pole form an imaginary line called the object's *equator*. Since our sun, moon, and all solar system planets spin, each possesses an axis of spin, two geographic poles, and an equator.

2. The Phenomenon of the "Day":

The planetary motion called rotation resembles the movement of a child's spinning top in that it spins with a slow wobble. This wobble, called *precession*, causes the axis of rotation to change its orientation, slowly describing a full circle through a field of stars once every 26 000 years. And while it does this, the axis itself twists one full turn every 24 hours, dragging our planet through one full rotation to complete an Earth *day*. Fortunately, spin is much below the rate needed for centrifugal forces to break our planet apart. Nevertheless, this is a relatively rapid rate when compared to the most lethargic of spinners like Mercury, Venus, and the moon, but markedly slower than the spin rates of the solar system's giants—Jupiter, Saturn, Uranus, and Neptune. Over time, our spin rate is slowing, making rotation periods progressively longer by microseconds per year. Nevertheless, its relative constancy makes spin rate a convenient and reliable method to measure time.[42]

3. Spiral Patterns in Our Atmosphere:

Atmospheric winds travel over our planet from areas of high pressure to lower pressure. But since the surface over which they travel is rotating, they are subject to an influence—the *Coriolis Effect*. This effect causes a deflection in wind pathways. North of the equator, wind deflection is to the right of its pathway; south of the equator, deflection is left. In Canada, the results of Coriolis deflection are clearly seen on weather maps, where winds spiral clockwise (right) out of centres of higher pressure and counter-clockwise (right again) into centres of lower pressure. Similar patterns are readily apparent in the cloud and debris associated with the more violent structures of tornado funnels and hurricane spirals.

Coriolis's influences are maximized at the highest latitudes, with the most rapidly moving particles, and over the most rapidly rotating planets. The phenomenon was noticed during the First World War when shells fired from powerful long-range "Big Bertha" artillery and lobbed long distances over a mid-latitude war zone fell consistently to the right of their intended pathways. South of the equator, all deflections would be to the left.

4. The Westward Drift of our Celestial Canopy:

The rotation of Earth eastward about its axis creates a continual slow westward migration of sun, moon, and stars across our sky. Thus, once each rotational period, for all latitudes between the Antarctic and Arctic circles, moon, sun, and stars rise somewhere in the east and set somewhere in the west (with rise and set positions, and timing determined by season).

More careful observations of the heavens at each pole reveal that stars do not rise and set but, rather, pivot in giant circles about a single stationary point in the sky, disappearing during the brightness of the day, but never setting. Such stars are called *circumpolar*, with the number of such stars increasing as one nears each pole. At each pole, all stars are circumpolar; at the equator, none is.

In the northern hemisphere, the point of pivot, almost over the North Pole, is occupied by the bright star, Polaris. This special positioning renders it almost stationary despite rotational spin, a fact that makes it a most useful star for celestial navigation, remaining over $90°N$ as the Earth rotates. One's latitude in degrees is simply the elevation of the star Polaris above the northern horizon. All that is needed is a device such as a sextant to determine its elevation angle (E). At the North Pole, E equals $90°$. For Toronto observers, E is about $43°$, and remains $43°$ on any night, and at any time of night an observation is taken. Of course, Polaris cannot be a navigational aid south of the equator since it cannot be seen.

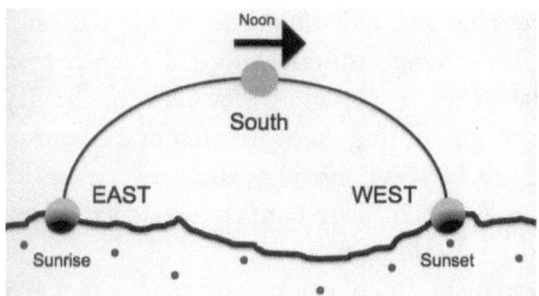

Daily Path of the Sun across the Sky[43]

5. Diurnal Variations in Solar Light Intensity:

The brightness of our sun depends upon its elevation above the horizon. A sun at our zenith is the brightest. As it approaches the horizon, its light intensity diminishes since pathways through an energy-absorbing atmosphere are longer. The influence of the atmosphere on lesser lights such as stars is most apparent throughout the celestial canopy. Toward the horizon in any direction, many disappear entirely, depending on atmospheric clarity and urban glare.

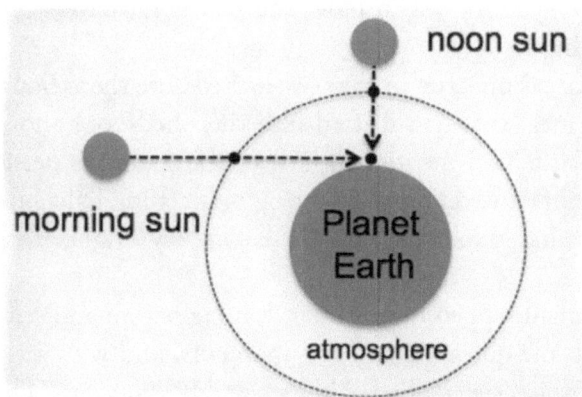

Longer and Shorter Pathways through the Atmosphere[44]

Throughout the night hours, solar radiation is next to zero. With daylight emerging out of darkness at dawn, and with increasing elevations of the sun, increasing solar radiation concentrations cause a corresponding rise in atmospheric temperatures. Daily radiation is maximum at solar noon when the sun is at its highest elevation for the day. Beyond solar noon, it drops to zero during dusk. Maximum 24-hour temperatures lag behind maximum radiation, arriving about two hours after solar noon. A similar lag in lowest 24-hour temperatures delays them to just before dawn, rather than at midnight.

Given our planet's 24-hour rate of spin, daily temperature ranges are not extreme since, on average, places face into the sun for a mere twelve hours. By contrast, places on the much slower-rotating moon, which takes a month to complete a single rotation, experience a far greater temperature range since a daytime warming up period of 14 days is followed by an equally lengthy cooling-off period at nighttime. Lunar temperature swings are also enhanced by the absence of both surface water and an atmosphere.

6. The Phenomenon of Twilight:

As parents of small children, after-supper activities involved the oftrepeated ritual of bath, horseplay, story, and prayers. Often, this ritual would generate a comment or question that would trigger wonder and discussion. The venue was usually the bedroom, covers pulled up and kids tucked in.

On one occasion, after prayers, we locked onto the various smells from the evening meal that had drifted into their bedroom and still lingered in the air. Casually, I mentioned how cooking odours persist long after they are manufactured. Then, pointing to a ceiling light bulb, I asked if light behaves like odours. "Does the room stay bright after the bulb is turned off?"

I knew I had tapped into Richard's imagination and curiosity, for he suddenly became quiet. After a few moments, and with an authoritative tone in his voice, he replied, "Nope, daddy. No way. The light goes away really REALLY fast." Knowing his pleasure in playing with such provocative thoughts and his normal reluctance to end days with something as mundane as sleep, I persisted. "How fast? If you raced into bed as soon as you turned off the light, would you get there before the room gets dark? Are you faster than a speeding bullet? . . . Ya wanna try?" Of course, he wanted to try. I had offered him a challenge he could not refuse. Equally important was the fact that the game delayed the final lights out. Now action was resuming!

He tore off his covers, jumped out of bed, positioned himself beside the light switch a short distance away, and readied himself for the dash across the room. The switch went *flick*, and Rick put his body into overdrive. Robert watched with great interest, awaiting his turn to try. Both were fast but not fast enough. Repeated tries, primarily to further delay final lights out, produced the same result. Of course, Richard's initial comment had proven correct: when lights are turned off, light disappears from the room really REALLY fast, far faster than odors.

Why do things such as cooking odours and light from sources disappear? The answer relates to processes of diffusion and absorption. Cooking smells are deemed to have disappeared when particle absorption causes their concentrations to reach levels that are insufficient to trigger recognizable olfactory responses. Similarly, light disappears when, through absorption of light energy by surrounding surfaces, residual light is insufficient to render visual images recognizable. Comparing the rates of light absorption relative to the rates of odour diffusion, the former is far more rapid than the latter. In other words, though both light and odours eventually disappear, light disappears faster than smells.

Now concerning the speed at which sunlight disappears, one might ask, "Why doesn't light disappear from the sky immediately after sunset and return with the same suddenness at the instant of sunrise? Why do we experience a gradual transition between light and darkness?" In other words, "How do we explain the phenomenon of twilight?"

We have just noted that sunlight begins to dim, not at sunset when the disc of the sun disappears, but rather immediately after the instant of high noon when the elevation of the sun begins to drop. Initially, light reduction after high noon is slow and seldom recognized as such, but gradually becomes more rapid and observed as the sun approaches and traverses the horizon line to totally disappear at the end of dusk. A corresponding pattern of increasing light intensity occurs as the sunlight reappears at dawn through sunrise to reach maximum intensity at noon.

So, why is there light from the sun when it is in the twilight zone? Presence of additional sunlight, after sunset (dusk) and before sunrise (dawn), relates to the existence of our planet's atmosphere and its ability to scatter light. This scattering is capable of adding brightness to the sky when the sun resides in a region not far below the horizon, a region it enters before sunrise and again just after sunset. That region is called the *twilight zone.*

From the accompanying diagram, it is apparent that the length of time it takes for the sun to traverse the twilight zone depends not only on its width, but also upon how the path of the sun is oriented relative to it. Pathway orientations depend upon a location's latitude. At the equator, passage through the zone of twilight is perpendicular to the equator's horizon. This corresponds to the shortest route, and therefore the quickest route through it. Canadians vacationing in the Caribbean are surprised at the brevity of southern twilights compared to twilights back home.

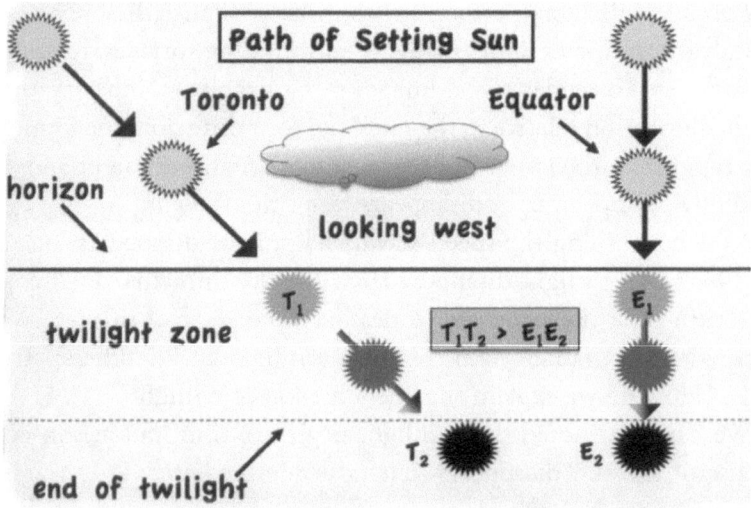

Two Tracks of the Setting Sun[45]

By contrast, on an icebreaker at the top of Canada and approximately ten degrees from the North Pole, I watched a brief portion of a sunset progressing slowly downward along a path similar to a plane approaching an airport runway. Its behaviour was similar to a person crossing a road, not perpendicular to the curb, but almost parallel to it. Imagine the distance the solar disc would have to move laterally in order for its total diameter to traverse the horizon line to begin an even longer period of dusk. One can now imagine why Arctic sunsets and dusks are such long events. At the North Pole, where the rising and setting paths of the sun are roughly *parallel* to the horizon, these events are even longer. Here the single sunset for the year occurs in September while the only dusk period continues into October.

EARTH'S ORBITAL MOTION CALLED REVOLUTION

*What though in solemn silence
all move round the dark terrestrial ball,
What though no real voice, nor sound, amidst their radiant
orbs be found; In reason's ear they all rejoice,
and utter forth a glorious voice,
Forever singing, as they shine,
"The hand that made us is divine."*

Joseph Addison, 1712[46]

Just as planetary rotation creates the concept of the day, planetary revolution creates the concept of the *year*, the period of time required for a single planetary circuit about the sun. Thus, both days and years are temporal concepts related to planetary movements.

Since orbital periods of planets depend upon distance to the sun, years are shortest on Mercury (closest planet) and get progressively longer toward Neptune (farthest planet). For Earth, a year is much longer than a day, slightly more than 365 times longer, in fact. But surprisingly, the condition of years being longer than days is not applicable to all planets. For planet Venus, the time for a single rotation about its axis (a day) is slightly *longer* than the time for a single revolution about the sun (a year). Thus, because of the manner in which terms are defined, a day on Venus is longer than its year!

REVOLUTION AND THE LINKS TO TIME AND THE MODERN CALENDAR

Like many foundational concepts, such as gravity and light, the concept of time is difficult to define. In practical terms, however, one may simply say that time is the interval between specific recurring events and is a form of temporal *distance*. Time progresses as distance from an initial event increases and distance toward some similar final event diminishes. Thus, farmers speak of the growing season as that time interval from seedtime to harvest; and airline pilots refer to flight times as intervals between takeoffs and landings.

Human perception of the length of any time interval depends greatly upon the degree to which one finds the intervening time pleasurable, or the amount we are distracted from thinking about time. Children's waits for Christmas morning or for the ending to a long car ride seem an eternity of time while, by contrast, times of celebration with delicious foods in the presence of loved ones seem to pass quickly. My recollection during childhood of the interval between falling asleep and morning awakening seemed but a fraction of a second, a far different experience from personal nocturnal endurances that have become all too common in recent years.

But regardless of how time is perceived, all time is measured against natural events with which most of us are familiar and by which reliability and regular repetition in constant intervals render them standards for measuring time. Our earliest time measurements relied on the behaviour of celestial objects visible to us all. Planetary rotation about an axis generates the day. Planetary revolution about the sun generates the year and the progression of the seasons. And it is upon the regular orbiting about us of our moon with its accompanying cycle of lunar phases that we base the concept of the month. Unfortunately, the length of a day, a month, and a year are *not* exact multiples of each other.

Our need to develop more precise measuring devices took a giant leap forward when, to our practical methods based upon astronomical events, were added methods at the atomic level with the extremely precise atomic clock. The clock achieves extreme regularity by defining a *second of time* in terms of a precise number of vibrations of a certain atom: 9 192 631 770 times!

Yet despite the inclusion of atomic clocks to the world, it is the behaviour of the sun in response to the Earth's revolution that remains our most prominent and useful timepiece, daily drifting westward over us, migrating north and south with the seasons, and crossing the equator twice each year. The instant of its passage into the northern hemisphere is called the *vernal equinox*, the official commencement of spring season in that hemisphere.

The time interval between successive such passes is called a *tropical year*. However, a minor math problem arises because we have chosen to link our annual calendar to the tropical year. Simply put, the 365-day calendar year is *shorter* than a tropical year by about six hours. Thus, it takes about six hours more than 365 full rotations (days) for the Earth to complete a tropical year.[47]

Why should we care if our calendar is shorter than a tropical year by a mere quarter of a day per year? It doesn't matter, so long as we don't mind seasons of the year, and specific events in those seasons relating to day length and temperatures slowly drifting into different months of the year. Our preference to coordinate seasons with specific months explains two important calendar reforms:

1. In 45 BC, the calendar year was increased in length by a single day (a leap day) every fourth year, thus creating the concept of the *leap year* (366 days). It was agreed upon that for convenience and uniformity, leap years would occur in all years divisible by four. The product of this reform was the *Julian calendar*. It largely corrected the problem between tropical and calendar years. But alas, it then made the new calendar longer than the tropical year by a paltry 11 minutes, 14 seconds per year; thus, accumulating a full day discrepancy every 128 years. Good enough? For most, yes! But not for all.

2. By 1582, with the accumulated drift of the vernal equinox forward some eleven days toward early March, a second calendar correction, known as the *Gregorian Calendar Reform*, was instituted. It slightly shortened the Julian year by a slight modification relating to leap years. The revision was that all years divisible by four would remain leap years, except for some century

years. For a century year to be a leap year, it would have to be **divisible by 400.** This change eliminated three leap years in each 400-year period, thus reducing the length of the average calendar year by three days in 400 years, thereby increasing the time to accumulate a full day discrepancy to 3300 years. The correction created our present calendar, still slightly too long, but only by a few minutes per year—an insignificant amount in one's lifetime.

Our world: blessed with a host of years!

> The *tropical year* begins sometime around March 21. But there are many other *years* to which we refer. And each has its own beginning and importance. For example, the present ***calendar year*** begins in January. By contrast, the ***Church year*** begins sometime in November, with the period of time known as Advent. To these are added a host of other cycles of time: the ***fiscal year*** within the business world; the ***school year*** within the world of academia; in the realm of astronomy, the ***anomalistic year***, the ***lunar year***, based upon the cyclical phasing and movements of the moon; and, the giant of all years, the ***galactic year***, the roughly 220 million Earth years needed for our sun and its planets to complete a single trip about our galactic centre.

EARTH'S ORBITAL SHAPE

Planetary orbits are neither parabolic nor perfectly circular in shape.[48] Rather, they are elliptical. If parabolic, they would not be orbits performing repeated movements about the same sun. Since elliptical in shape, orbits do occur, but no single orbit maintains a constant planet-sun distance or a fixed place in space.

As Earth nears the sun, total radiation received rises toward its maximum for the year. Decreasing distances correlate with increasing gravitational pull and therefore increasing planetary speed. Since this orbital speed is most rapid in early January, the trip through our winter's portion of the orbit takes the shortest time, making the winter season slightly shorter than all others.

For the six months from early January, the Earth-sun distance increases to a maximum in early July. Throughout this period, Earth's orbital speed declines with the sun's reducing gravitational pull. In addition, the sun's apparent size as well as Earth's total radiation received drops to their minimum values. Since orbital speed is minimal in early July, the length of our summer season is the longest season of the year (about four days longer than winter). But since the elliptical shape of Earth is not extreme, neither are the changes that result from our planet following an elliptical orbit.

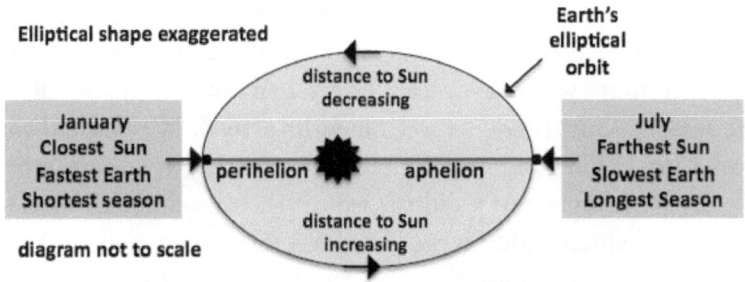

A Year in the Life of an Earth Orbit[49]

Having stated that the shape of the Earth's orbit causes variations in incoming radiation from the sun, we might conclude that shape of orbit explains the phenomenon of seasons. But such is not the case. While shape of orbit is a factor affecting monthly radiation received by the entire planet, seasons do not owe their existence primarily to orbital shape, but rather to the orientation of Earth's axis of rotation relative to the sun.

THE PERIODS OF TIME CALLED SEASONS

My birthplace of Kirkland Lake sits on the hard igneous and metamorphic Canadian Shield. Like nearby Cobalt and Timmins, Kirkland Lake was one of many northern towns with industry based primarily on hard rock mining, specifically on rich gold ore deposits in fractured and displaced veins extending thousands of feet below its forested surface. Miners like my father accessed ore bodies through deep vertical shafts. The work was difficult, dirty, and dangerous. Accidents underground were not uncommon. Occasionally they would involve rock collapse that produced the dreaded *air blast* within vertical shafts and horizontal drifts.

While mining activities were front-and-centre in the minds of Kirkland Lake residents, mines did not seem so in conversations. Rather, it was the weather of the various seasons, the winter season in particular. Winters were long and cold. Everyone talked about them. Citizens prided themselves on their ability to survive winter's length and intensity. After all, we were Canadian *northerners* despite the fact that well over 90% of Canada occupies more northerly latitudes.

First snowfalls arrived by Halloween and a white, almost monochromatic landscape persisted until April. I cannot recall Christmas being other than white. Nor can I recall many complaints about the winter season. Most residents welcomed its arrival. We boasted that our cold was *dry* cold. Cold could obliterate the flies far more effectively than could any bug spray. Cold turned off the rain and delivered to us a material with which children could fashion forts, snowmen, and missiles. It provided slippery surfaces for sleighs and ubiquitous rows of icicles that formed and hung off the edges of roofs, especially among houses that were poorly insulated. A switch to the winter season necessitated the change in wardrobe from shorts and swimsuits to leggings and boots.

Seasons as a concept constitute a period of time through which some recognizable and prominent characteristic repeats itself in a predictable fashion. We speak of seasons of plenty, seasons of life, and seasons of harvest. Polar regions have both a *light* and a *dark* season, with lengths of each increasing from one full day to six full months from the Arctic and Antarctic circles to each pole. Some areas of the tropics and subtropics define seasons in terms of precipitation, classifying them as either *wet* or *dry*. Places predominating in wet and dry seasons are common on the margins of equatorial rainforests in what are known as savannah grasslands. Here, the wet season is the hot season. By contrast, areas within the so-called Mediterranean climatic region (Greece, Italy, southern California, South Africa, and southwest Australia) have their wet season during their relatively mild winter. The relative constancy of light, moisture and temperature at the equator makes it difficult to define distinct seasons in that area. But by contrast, in the mid-latitudes, four somewhat distinct seasons are found (winter, spring, summer and autumn), with the length of each dependent upon latitude and proximity to large oceanic influences.

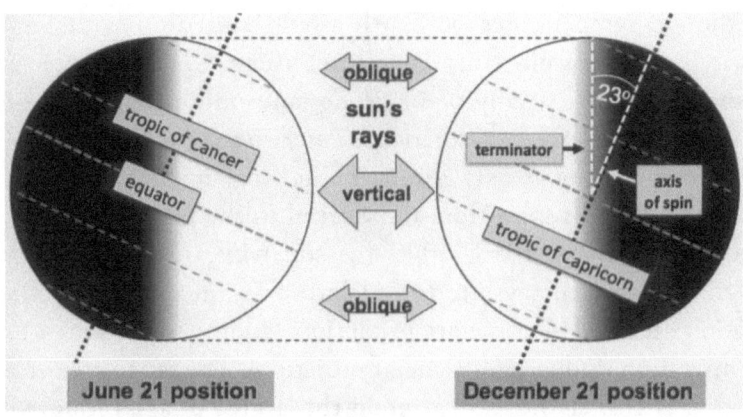

Two Positions of the Earth in the Sun's Rays[50]

We noted previously that seasons are related to the tilt of the Earth's axis of rotation relative to the sun. Tilt does not change; rather, it is the orientation of that Earth's axis in its orbit about the sun that changes.[51]

SEASONS AND THE NORTH-SOUTH DRIFT OF THE SUN

Among the year's 365 noon occurrences in the city of Honolulu, two noons (on May 27 and July 13) are described in local tradition by the phrase, *kau-ka la-ika-lolo*. Roughly translated, it means, *the sun rests on the brains*. These two dates are the only two instances when the sun at solar noon is directly overhead and when a person's noon shadow is said to disappear under foot.

Any person experiencing the sun directly overhead is said to be located at the *sub-solar point* (SSP). Three important facts relate to the SSP: (1) its *locations* on the Earth's surface; (2) its *movement* through these locations; and, (3) its *significance* to changing day lengths and seasons.

At any one instant, there can be only a single SSP, that is, only one place where the noon sun is directly above an observer, with rays perpendicular to the ground surface. If Earth had no axial lean, the SSP would always fall on its equator, migrating westward as the planet rotates eastward under it. All days at all latitudes would be 12 hours in length. And though temperatures on Earth would still drop with increasing latitude (because of planetary curvature), there would be little seasonal temperature change at any one latitude; and only people living on the Earth's equator would ever experience *kau-ka la-ika-lolo*.

But our rotational axis *does* lean, in fact, at an angle slightly in excess of 23 degrees away from the vertical to the plane of Earth's orbit. Consequently, as the Earth orbits the sun while rotating with a fixed axial tilt, its vertical rays are forced into an annual north-south-north migration (induced by planetary revolution), adding to the sun's westward daily migration (induced by planetary rotation). The range of north-south migration is entirely dependent upon the degree of axial lean, with the maximum migration defining the latitudes of the two lines called *tropics* (Cancer and Capricorn, latitudes 23.5° N and S) and, in addition, the latitudes of the two lines called *circles* (Arctic and Antarctic, latitudes 90 23.5, or 66.5° N and S).

In June, the vertical rays reach the northern-most latitude on the *Tropic of Cancer*. This is the instant that defines the *summer solstice*, the beginning of the summer season in the northern hemisphere. Six months later, they arrive at their southern-most latitude on the *Tropic of Capricorn*. This is the instant that defines the *winter solstice*, the beginning of the northern hemisphere's winter season. SSP transits of the equator north and south define the *equinoxes*, the vernal and autumnal respectively, March and September events that define the beginning of the northern hemisphere's spring and autumn seasons). Together, four seasons, all defined by the sun's behaviour, are created.

Locations beyond each tropic can never experience vertical sunshine (more latitude would experience *kau-ka la-ika-lolo* if axial lean were greater). On the other hand, all locations between the tropics (Honolulu, for example, just two degrees inside the tropics) experience vertical sun twice each year (for Hawaii, dates are May 27 on its trek north, and July 13 on its trek south). Since Hawaii is very close to a tropic, its two vertical sun dates are quite close together.

This continuous north-south shifting of vertical sun causes a corresponding shift in the sun's maximum radiation intensity as well as regular changes in the length of days. Along the equator, day length is virtually constant at twelve hours throughout the year and would remain so at any axial tilt. Annual variations in day length increase with latitude toward each pole, reaching 24 hours of continuous daylight at each circle and progressing to six months of continuous daylight at each pole.[52] Lengths of days in Toronto vary from a minimum of just under nine hours (December 21) to a maximum of just under 15.5 hours (June 21). This contrasts to Miami, Florida, at a lower latitude, where corresponding values are 10.5 hours and 13.8 hours, respectively, indicating less annual day length variation.

> *There is a time for everything,*
> *and a season for every activity under the heavens:*
>
> *Ecclesiastes 3:1*

Thus the world's seasons are the major consequence of SSP shifting, which in turn is the result of axial tilt. In addition, while it is true that our sun is closer to our planet in January than in July, and that total solar radiation received by our planet is greatest in January, it is nevertheless the factor of axial tilt, not planetary distance, which remains the principal reason for the four seasons. And because of axial tilt and the seasons that result, a more widespread distribution and variation of solar energy over the planet is produced than would be possible if axial tilt were zero.

Most of us are aware that temperature changes in Canada are slightly out of phase with SSP shifting, with maximum temperatures peaking in July (not June), and minimum temperatures occurring in January (not December). The phenomenon is called the *lag of seasons*, due to the fact that large quantities of solar energy are required to thaw surfaces and warm waters before the atmosphere can register significant increases in spring air temperatures. A similar delay occurs in the onset of autumn as excess energy packages stored in local land and water bodies require time to dissipate.

> *I see skies of blue, and clouds of white,*
> *bright blessed days, dark sacred nights*
> *And I think to myself, what a wonderful world.*[53]

THE USE OF PLANETARY IMAGERY IN SCRIPTURE

"The Earth is the Lord's, and everything in it" (Ps 24:1). As one might expect, planetary references abound in scripture, with just under 1000 scattered through fifty-one of the Bible's sixty-six books. As illustrative tools, they lead our minds from the realm of the visually familiar to contemplate what is for now unfamiliar and obscure, something beyond ourselves and otherworldly. Here we recall George Herbert's poem (see quote in *Introduction,* Endnote 6).

The idea of the Earth as ancient in itself helps one grasp something of what is meant by eternal. God, "the ancient of days," pre-exists Earth. That Earth's foundations were laid by Him (Ps 104:5) and, unlike Him, will eventually perish, testifies to His sovereignty as Creator and Sustainer of all things (Ps 102:25–26). Clearly, Creation is identified as distinct from its Creator. Clearly, the Creator transcends His Creation. Isaiah calls Earth "God's footstool" (Isa 66:1), again suggesting His sovereignty over it. He is the incomparable One (Isa 40:11–31) who never grows tired or weary and who is "mightier than the thunder of the great waters" (Ps 93:4). His signature on Earth is ubiquitous. Expressions of praise by the Creation in the form of rejoicing, singing, and loud shouts are widespread, natural, and spontaneous responses to its Maker (Ps 96:11–13; Isa 44:23; Isa 55:12).

We inhabit a world consisting of alternating periods of day and night, light and darkness. Darkness is the absence of light. Darkness holds secrets. It generates uncertainty and fear among us. Under the cover of physical darkness, thieves come to steal (Jer 49:9); God's people fled Egypt (Exod 12); In darkness, God's Son, with His earthly parents, escaped the wrath of an angry ruler (Matt 2:13); Peter escaped from prison (Acts 12); Jacob wrestled with an angel (Gen 32); and a period of strange, unexpected darkness came over the land at Christ's crucifixion (Luke 23:44).

The figurative use of light and darkness is common in scripture. Light is associated with life and goodness, while darkness is associated with evil and death. It is the fool that walks in darkness (Eccl 2:14). The Bible refers to the "chains of darkness" (2 Pet 2:4), contrasting its association with bondage to light's association with freedom.

Scripture describes darkness as more attractive than light (John 3:19). It also refers to the "power of darkness" (Col 1:13), but more importantly to the far greater power of God over darkness (2 Cor 4:6). The Gospel is described as "light" (2 Cor 4:4). Light is "sweet" (Eccl 11:7). God Himself is described as "light" (1 John 1:5) and as the believer's "light" (Ps 27:1). Contrasted to Satan (an angel of light) who uses light as a disguise (2 Cor 11:14) is Christ the "true Light" (John 1:9), the light that has come into the world (John 3:19) to give light to all who sit in darkness (Luke 1:79), suggesting that it is while sitting in darkness that one may learn lessons that could not be learned in the light. And as those called out of darkness into God's marvellous light (1 Pet 2:9), we are called to *be* lights shining in dark places (2 Pet 1:19).

The daily and annual cycles of the earth, sun, moon and stars are natural rhythms that appear frequently in scripture. They convert the linear progression of time into recurring time loops in the form of days, months, seasons and years.

While time demonstrates relentless progression, written into its very fabric is the theme of encouraging hope with fresh beginnings in abundance. Anyone who survives three-score years and ten lives through over 25 000 sunrises and new days, some 900 new moons and about seventy refreshing spring renewals. Each new morning and new spring is a visual reminder of the Gospel's theme of new beginnings, a message identified by a multitude of encouraging *"re"* words: *redemption* (recovering what was lost); *reconciliation* (reuniting what was separated); *repentance* (turning from, and reversing one's direction in life); and *resurrection* (restoration to life of what was dead). Resurrection is the ultimate fresh beginning.

In 1989, the song "If I Could Turn Back Time" appeared on the music charts with a message that stirred imaginations. Reflecting on some regretful conduct, the vocalist expresses her wish that time could somehow be reversed, that she could erase past wrongs, do it all again and thereby have a fresh beginning on a better relational path with her lover.[54]

Similar yearnings are shared by most of us. Christianity, with its themes of redemption, reconciliation, repentance, and restoration so central to its message, teaches that the past is anything but immutable. Clearly, however, it is not altered by efforts to do it all again in order to do it all better, but rather by receiving reconciliation from our God who, despite the wrong, like the actions of a loving parent of a small child, attends to that child, and somehow makes it all better. This is clearly illustrated in the parable of the Prodigal Son, who, despite the errors of his ways, is met, not with condemnation, reviews of his past follies, or with instruction to do it better a second time. Rather he is met with compassion, celebration and inclusion by his even more *"prodigal"* father, whose boundless grace startles us all.

> *But while he was still a long way off,*
> *his father saw him and was filled with compassion for him;*
> *he ran to his son, threw his arms around him and kissed him.*
>
> *Luke 15:20*

THE EARTH AS "HOME"

In 1970, James Lovell flew as commander of the near disastrous *Apollo 13* mission to the moon. Earlier, in the 1950s, over a decade prior to the beginning of the manned Apollo space program, he served as an American carrier-based fighter pilot. One evening, while practicing night manoeuvres over the Sea of Japan, an emergency occurred. In his book, *Apollo 13*, Lovell describes the harrowing incident with its litany of problems and anxious moments that required calmness and sound judgment—experiences that later proved to be valuable training for his mission to the moon.

As he attempted to rendezvous with two companion aircraft for their return to the rolling deck of the carrier, elements of his instrumentation suddenly failed. His radar jammed. His homing signal malfunctioned and his cockpit lights shorted out. Moreover, lights that delineated the deck of his carrier during nighttime exercises were not operational. Low on fuel, alone in a panorama of blackness, and desperate to locate his floating mobile landing strip, Lovell began to feel his only available *airport* was the sea surface itself.

But just then, a strange glow appeared below him. It presented as a long narrow carpet of phosphorescence that was faintly illuminating a portion of the sea surface. The source of the glow was green marine algae, known to most naval pilots. The incident was recounted in *Apollo 13*. In the scene, actor Tom Hanks, who played Lovell, reflects on the source and the significance of that mysterious faint green trail:

> *It was that phosphorescent stuff that gets churned up in the wake of a big ship. And it was . . . it was . . . it was leading me home. You know? If my cockpit lights hadn't shorted out, there's no way I'd have ever been able to see that. So, uh, you, uh, you never know what what events are going to transpire to get you home.*[55]

Longing for home was the theme of the folk song written back in the 1920s in which two slightly inebriated men on a train croon out the words, "Show Me The Way To Go Home."[56] Homesickness and the longing for home appear universal, so much so that one wonders if the longing is reflective of a deeper yearning for a more permanent dwelling: an *eternal* home.

The thought that this present *home* is only a foretaste of a far greater one is arresting. One wonders why we cannot immediately possess it if, in fact, a far greater one exists. Accessing this mysterious place requires a reliable source of light to illuminate the way. We recall that the light, like that supplied to James Lovell by phosphorescent algae, may only be recognizable when other seemingly stronger, yet distracting lights have been extinguished. Like Lovell, one never knows what events are going to transpire, or when or where they might appear to direct our way to this eternal home.

Of course, the concept of an eternal home may have no reality beyond our imagination and be nothing more than a warm, pleasant thought.

This planet and this life may be all we will ever know. Nevertheless, we must confront the persistence of what appears to be a universal yearning for something more than our present earthly home, better than we can ever hope for or imagine.

> *I need to believe*
> *that something extraordinary is possible.*
> *from the movie,*
> **A Beautiful Mind**[57]

> *Those who contemplate the beauty of the earth find reserves of strength that will endure as long as life lasts. There is something infinitely healing in the repeated refrains of nature—the assurance that dawn comes after night, and spring after winter.*
>
> *from 'Silent Spring'*
> *by Rachel Carson*
> **Conservationist and Biologist**

> *And I will give thee the treasures of darkness,*
> *and hidden riches of secret places,*
> *that thou mayest know that I, the LORD,*
> *which call thee by thy name,*
> *am the God of Israel.*
>
> *Isaiah 45:3 (KJV)*

3

MOON

O ye Sun and Moon, bless ye the Lord:
praise him, and magnify him for ever.

Benedicite (BCP)

The Moon near First Quarter Phase[58]
(NASA)

*What in this world would motivate someone
to freefall
from a height of 39 kilometres
to Earth
having travelled faster than sound,
then with open parachute
drop to Earth 9 minutes later?
another to struggle across the barren wilderness
of the world's largest ice shelf and frigid plateau
to an indistinct point,
its attainment known
only through mathematical calculation . . .
or another,
to climb through the "Death Zone"
to the top of the world's tallest mountain . . .
or another,
to journey through the vacuum of space
to Earth's only natural satellite?
I daresay neither fame nor fortune
renders sufficient payment.
Then if not these, then what?*

JES

In July 1969, three American astronauts onboard a cone-shaped space capsule lifted off from a Florida launch pad to begin a 400 000-kilometre journey to the moon. The purpose of the mission, named Apollo 11, was to land two on the moon and return all safely to Earth. On the ground, millions of people watched as the most powerful rocket ever assembled belched orange flame and huge plumes of white vapour as it fought the Earth's gravity to raise its human cargo and many tonnes of metal and fuel up and away from our planet. Stored onboard was a much smaller and more fragile lunar vehicle named *Eagle*.

The voyage was both complicated and dangerous. The pathway to the moon was not straight. Nor was it free of obstacles. Successful completion of the mission required precision timing of a series of rocket burns so as to effect critical mid-course corrections and ensure that their planned pathway to their destination was being carefully maintained. Jettisoning of rocket stages at precise times, correct orientation of spacecraft in flight, temperatures, pressures and oxygen levels—in fact, all aspects of *Apollo 11*'s behaviour had to be carefully maintained. To avoid disaster, all systems had to function as designed.

For about 80% of its outbound voyage, during which Earth's gravitational influence exceeded that of the moon, the spacecraft's rate of forward motion dropped. Eventually, as the effect of lunar gravity came to exceed that of the Earth, its rate increased. Throughout the long ride, stresses on men and materials were great. While previous Apollo flights had travelled to the moon, none had ever safely landed with a human cargo. Would the trajectory be correct? Would the engines function properly to ensure a soft landing? Would the engines re-ignite and burn properly to lift the capsule from the lunar surface? Would *Eagle* make a successful rendezvous with its companion to start their journey back to Earth? Would there be sufficient fuel for all return burns? Would the space capsule's angle of re-entry to the Earth's atmosphere be neither too shallow (which would cause it to skip like a flat stone thrown over water) nor too steep (which would cause it to burn up in frictional heat)? And finally, would its three parachutes deploy at the appropriate time to slow its descent to an ocean splashdown? Despite meticulous planning, uncertainties within the mission still remained.

Most of us know what happened. The functioning of systems was virtually flawless. On 20 July, a message was beamed from the lunar surface through the vacuum of space. The voice was clear: "Tranquility Base here, the Eagle has landed!" Instantly, a roar of applause expressing jubilation and release of tension went up from those at Mission Control. In fact, a whole world cheered. For the moment, all the voices that spoke of ventures into space as too costly and wasteful were silenced. Two of the three Apollo 11 astronauts emerged from *Eagle* to become the first humans to stand on the lunar surface. They had landed at a relatively cool spot, one that was experiencing morning and long shadows. But in the daylight glare, the sky was black and no stars were visible. They described what greeted them as "magnificent desolation."

What a journey! What a remarkable human achievement! What a testimony to the reliability of natural law to function out there as it does right here on Earth! Planning had been thorough. And things had functioned in accordance with their intended purpose. And what an appropriate place for *Eagle* to land—Tranquility Base, a flat piece of lunar real estate within a broad piece of terrain called the Sea of Tranquility. It was indeed a place of tranquility and of safety on the long and dangerous journey that was, at that point in time, only half over. Employing human ingenuity, careful preparations and nature's dependable laws, the return half of this historic journey was as flawless as the first.

> *God made two great lights—*
> *the greater light to govern the day*
> *and the lesser light to govern the night.*
> *He also made the stars.*
>
> ***Genesis 1:16***

For as long as humans have beheld the heavens, the moon has inspired imagination. Through the years, our nearest natural companion in space has been the object of much speculation and the subject of controversy. Early imaginings of its surface features resembling a mysterious *man in the moon* were fanciful. Later imaginings of a man *on* the moon seemed equally fanciful until the late 1950s, when solutions to complex problems associated with space travel began to be solved.

The moon has inspired the lover, the artist, the writer, the poet, and the scientist. It has also been thought of as influential in affecting human behaviour. Police departments and emergency units in hospitals report higher than average antisocial behaviour during nights of a full moon. Reasons are unclear. Research indicates that these spikes occur without visual sightings of the moon or knowledge of its phase.

With natural law appearing to be universal, the physical laws governing the behaviour of matter on Earth apply equally to the moon. With knowledge of the moon's mass and radius, scientists determined its surface gravity: a mere 17% of that on Earth. Gravitational force able to maintain astronauts on its surface is, however, insufficient to maintain a lunar atmosphere. Consequently, all visitors must arrive with their own oxygen. In the absence of an atmosphere, there is no sound propagation or protection from the sun's intense ultraviolet radiation. There is a total absence of surface water and vegetation; there is never a cloudy, windy, or rainy day, or a blue sky. Someone weighing 100 kilograms on Earth weighs only 17 kilograms on the lunar surface! Imagine how lunar gravity would influence the flight of a golf ball or reflect in the statistics from a lunar Olympic high jump competition.

A moon is a natural satellite of a planet. At present, over 400 moons are known to exist. Only three orbit the four inner planets, while about half trace circuits about Jupiter or Saturn. Neither Mercury nor Venus possesses a moon. We, of course, possess a single moon. More natural satellites probably exist. But since the largest moons are usually the first and easiest to discover, astronomers expect it is unlikely that diameters of any future lunar discoveries will exceed 2 kilometres.

Like all planets, all moons except one possess names. The exception is ours, which like *the* sun, is referred to as *the* moon. While our moon is not the solar system's largest, it has other distinctions. It is the most massive satellite relative to its primary, that is, the planet about which it revolves. Also, its diameter and proximity to Earth make it the most prominent object in our sky.[59] And, despite the fact that it is our one and only, certain features enhance its distinctiveness:

1. One half of the moon's total surface is constantly hidden from us:

The average period of revolution of the moon about its primary is about 29.5 days. Not only is this the longest orbital period among the solar system's fifteen largest moons, but this orbital period is identical to its period of *rotation* on its axis. Moreover, both motions of revolution and rotation are in the *same* direction, namely from west to east. In other words, the moon takes as long to travel about the Earth as it does to pivot about itself on its axis. These facts explain why the moon, while presenting all surfaces to the sun (through rotation), always presents the same side to the Earth (through a special *rate* of rotation), and why its far side (sometimes improperly called its *dark side*) can only be seen when spacecrafts transport any observer around to the moon's far side.

Evidence of the length of time the near side has continued to face toward its primary is the conspicuously lower number of surface craters on the moon's near side in comparison to the much larger number on the more exposed and less protected far side.

Some of us have reached the erroneous conclusion that we cannot see the far side of the moon because the moon does *not* rotate. This sounds somewhat reasonable until we imagine one of the moves one makes in square dancing: the *do-si-do*. When the caller calls my partner to perform a *do-si-do*, she must move about me, without pivoting about herself. To properly do a *do-si-do* with my partner, I stand in one place, stomping one foot in time with the music. The trick in her movement is that while she travels through one complete circle about me, she does so while facing the same direction in the room. So while she is revolving about me, she is *not* rotating about herself. Thus during one full circle about me, *without* rotating, both her front and back will face me sometime during each revolution.

Likewise, if the moon did *not* rotate while orbiting the Earth, it would perform a celestial *do-si-do* (revolving but not rotating) and its entire surface would eventually be seen through each revolution about our planet. So, in order for one side *never* to be seen, rotation *must* occur, but importantly, occur at precisely the same rate as its revolution *and* in the same direction. If my partner performed her movements in this manner, one half of her would always face me; but I would never see her other half. Try this experiment with these facts the next time you *do-si-do*.

How strange it is that our only moon has rates of rotation and revolution that are precisely the same. It is highly improbable that this set of circumstances is mere coincidence. If a discrepancy in rotation and revolution periods were to develop, even by mere seconds per month, all lunar surfaces would eventually come into view from Earth. However, all this has been proven not to be mere coincidence.

The reason for the precise match-up between the periods of lunar rotation and revolution relates to unequal mass distributions within the moon, resulting in a greater gravitational pull on one side of the moon than on the other. Simply put, the moon behaves in this manner because, due to gravity, it cannot do otherwise.

Recently, NASA created a series of 110 000 images of our celestial companion taken from its Lunar Reconnaissance Orbiter. Selecting only those images displaying the entire lunar disc in sunlight, it released to the public an animated sequence that clearly showed what is impossible for us on Earth to ever see, namely all surfaces of the moon, both the heavily cratered far side as well as the familiar near side perpetually displaying the familiar image: the *man in the moon*.

2. The moon's apparent size and shape are constantly changing:

Because of its elliptical orbit about Earth, the moon's distance from its primary is constantly changing. As a result, its apparent *size* varies, being largest when closest to Earth (at perigee) and smallest when farthest (at apogee). If this explains why the moon changes its size, what explains its apparent constant change in *shape*?

To answer this question, let us examine the geometry of Earth, our moon and sun in the accompanying diagram. The moon orbits the Earth some thirteen times for each Earth orbit about the sun. Thus, geometric configurations of sun, moon, and Earth undergo constant change. Changing configurations alter the appearance of the moon as seen from Earth in a repeating sequence of shapes called *phases*. The time required for a complete lunar cycle of phases (called a *lunation*) is about one month. Understanding the changing positions of the sun and moon relative to Earth, and the time periods involved in these changes is key to understanding phasing.

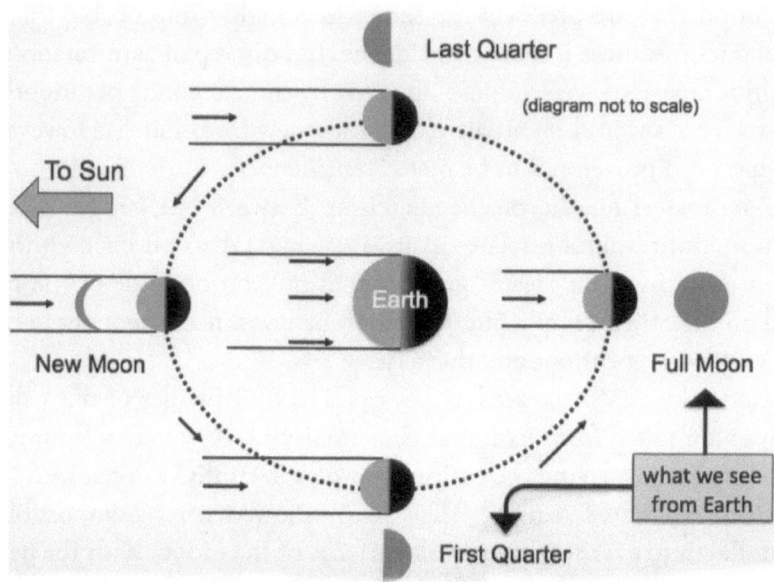

Four Moon Phases through a Complete Lunation[60]

At any one time, we are able to see only half of any distant sphere. At any one time, only half of a sphere can be illuminated by the sun. Only periodically is that illuminated full half facing us; just as frequently is the sun illuminating the side we never see. Phases result as the moon's illuminated half shifts from its near side to its far side and back. A configuration in which the moon and the sun are close to alignment on the same side of the Earth is called a *moon in conjunction*. A configuration in which the moon and the sun are on opposite sides of the Earth is called a *moon in opposition*.

When the moon is in conjunction, its far side is illuminated. Consequently, it appears at best as a very thin crescent in the shape of a letter C. This is the beginning of a lunation with a lunar phase aptly called a *new moon*. About one week into the lunation, the moon has migrated eastward through about 25% of its orbit. A right-angled configuration is now formed between moon, Earth, and sun during which only half of the illuminated half of the moon faces us. Through this time, it has changed from a C into a D-shape to become a *first quarter moon*.

Two weeks, or halfway through its lunation, the moon is in opposition. Now virtually the entire illuminated portion of the moon faces us. The D has slowly changed into an O, a *full moon*. Thus, for about two weeks, the moon has grown, or *waxed* in appearance. From this point on through the sequence, the moon *wanes* as less and less of the surface facing us is illuminated. The O becomes a *last quarter* (backward D) until finally, located in conjunction once again in the direction of the sun, it becomes *new*.

With conspicuous shape alterations occurring with such regularity, it is not surprising that the moon, like the sun, became an object by which time periods of weeks and months could be easily defined. The precision by which it migrates through its various phases makes it possible to accurately forecast the timing of monthly lunar phase events well into the future.

Of course, all this discussion of phases has been from the standpoint of an Earth observer. Observed from the moon, and in the same time period, a person would see our planet go through a phasing sequence similar to the ones we observe from Earth. But we would not see the same phase at the same time. For example, during a *full* moon, a person on the moon would see a *new* Earth. During a *new* moon, the same person would see a *full* Earth. This view of Earth from the moon would undoubtedly be the more spectacular scene since the Earth is much larger than the moon. Moreover, the full Earth would be seen, not as a white orb, but as a blue and white disc while in full phase.

Also, since Earth completes a full rotation every 24 hours, it would display its entire surface to lunar viewers in a single Earth day. And, as an added treat, if in view, it would never disappear from view, but would remain on permanent display and in a permanent position against the blackness of the lunar sky.

However, if observers occupied the moon's far side, Earth and its sequencing of phasing would never be seen. The good news for "far side" lunar observers is that since the moon rotates once every month, they would experience monthly sunrises, with the sun shining in a black cloudless sky for an uninterrupted half-month.

3. The moon's apparent size roughly matches the sun's:

The *apparent* size of any object depends upon its *actual* size as well as its distance from an observer. Big objects and close objects appear the largest to any observer. Although the sun is much farther from us than the moon (about 400 times farther), its actual diameter, coincidentally, is about 400 times greater. The net effect of these equivalencies is to make *apparent* sizes of moon and sun almost identical in our sky—each roughly the size of a pencil's eraser held at arms' length.

Since both the moon and Earth are opaque objects, they each project a shadow, or *umbra* downstream from the sun. Since the sun is so much larger than either our moon or planet, each umbra is cone-shaped. Given the relatively short distance between the moon and Earth, each is capable of occasionally passing through a portion of each other's umbra. Each time this occurs, observers on Earth experience the phenomenon called an *eclipse* (either of the moon or sun).

Since the Earth is larger than the moon, its umbra is larger in both length and width. This means that while the entire moon can fit into the umbra of the Earth and be eclipsed, only a very small portion of the Earth surface can reside in the lunar umbra to create a solar eclipse (even in optimal conditions). These facts explain why full lunar eclipses last a few hours, while solar eclipses last but a few minutes.

Now a slight correction must be made regarding the rough equivalency in the apparent sizes of the moon and sun. The issue relates to the fact that the orbits of our moon and our planet are *not* circular. Thus distances to the sun and to the moon undergo constant change. And distances to objects, we recall, help to determine apparent size. So if, for example, during a possible solar eclipse, the moon is farthest in its path about the Earth (smaller moon), and if at the same time the Earth is closest in its path about the sun (larger sun), the lunar disc will be unable to fully cover the disc of the sun during a solar eclipse. Conversely, with a closer moon at the time of farther sun, a larger lunar disc can readily eclipse the smaller sun and do so for longer than normal. Such distance conditions at the time of any alignment significantly alter the length and type of eclipses produced. More on the topic of solar and lunar eclipses can be found in the following chapter.

4. The moon's mass and proximity noticeably perturb world oceans:

From Isaac Newton, we learned that all matter attracts and that the capacity to attract varies with the amount of mass within objects as well as the distance that separates them. Both sun and moon influence the Earth gravitationally, although the moon's influence, because of the distance factor, is dominant. All mass on Earth is influenced. But the influence is most noticeable on the world's largest and more easily deformed fluid surfaces, namely oceans. The influence creates a rhythmic rising and falling of water over predictable time intervals. The phenomenon is called *tide*.

To understand the behaviour of tidal waters, let us imagine an idealized ocean surface covering the entire planet without continents to restrict the movement of waters. At any one instant, two bulges exist: one "under" the moon (the *sub-lunar bulge*) and another, about equal in magnitude (the *antipodal lunar bulge*) on the Earth's opposite side. In between, two low water areas are formed. These bulges (high tides) and depressions (low tides) remain permanently fixed relative to the moon as Earth rotates under them.

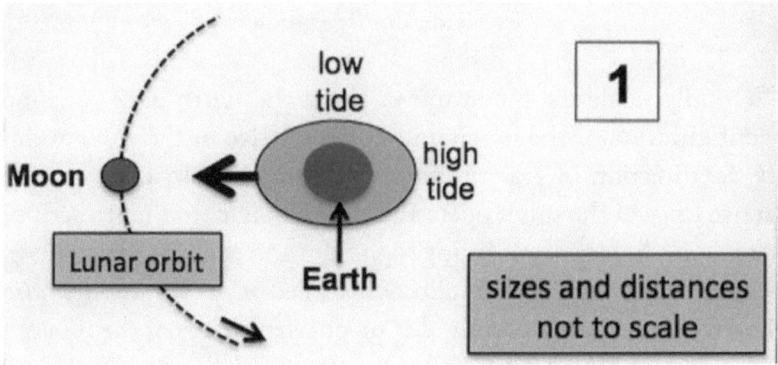

The Geometry of Ocean Tides[61]

Using Diagram [1], imagine an animation in which the Earth *rotates* on its axis, the moon *revolves* about the Earth, and the Earth *revolves* about the sun. Firstly, as the Earth rotates eastward once in 24 hours, the two high tides and two low tides, formed and fixed in position by the moon, will appear to move westward over the surface of the eastward-rotating

Earth. This means that each day, a given place would experience a high tide followed by a low tide once every 12 hours. However, since the moon is not stationary, but revolving eastward about the Earth monthly while the Earth is rotating eastward about itself daily, the time between successive high tides and successive low tides is extended slightly to about 12.5 hours rather than 12 hours.

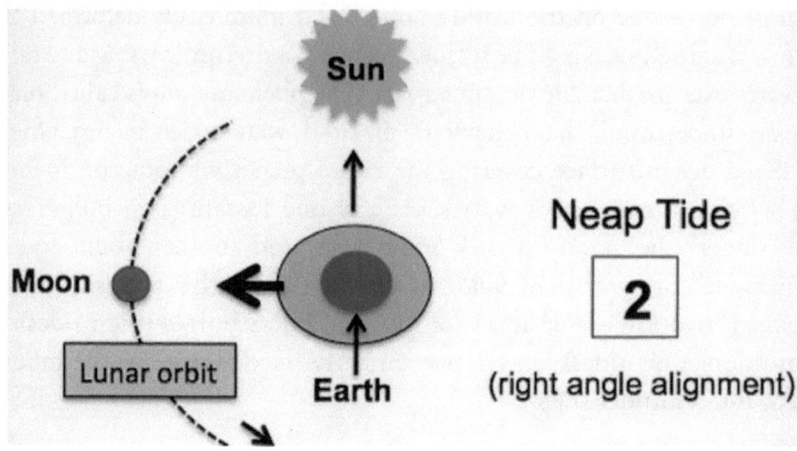

Neap Tide Configuration[62]

Secondly, since the moon moves about the Earth once each month, the configuration of the moon and Earth relative to the sun continually alters the direction of gravity's forces of attraction. In Diagram [2], the attractive force of the sun is operating at right angles to the attractive force of the moon, slightly diminishing high tides and slightly raising low tides, thereby diminishing tidal amplitudes. Called *neap tide configuration*, it occurs twice each lunar month, during quarter phases of the moon.

In Diagram [3], the sun and moon form a collinear alignment with the Earth, with gravitational influences that reinforce each other. This setup creates higher high tides and lower low tides, thereby increasing tidal amplitudes. Called *spring tide configuration*, this also occurs twice each lunar month, during full and new moon phases when the three bodies are collinear.

In summary, one can appreciate that the behaviour of waters at the seashore is dependent upon a multitude of factors operating concurrently.

With all factors considered, the highest high tides and the lowest low tides are created when the moon and Earth, together with the sun and Earth, are separated by the shortest distances (maximizing attractive force operating between objects), and when sun, moon and Earth are collinear (maximizing attractive forces operating in the same direction).

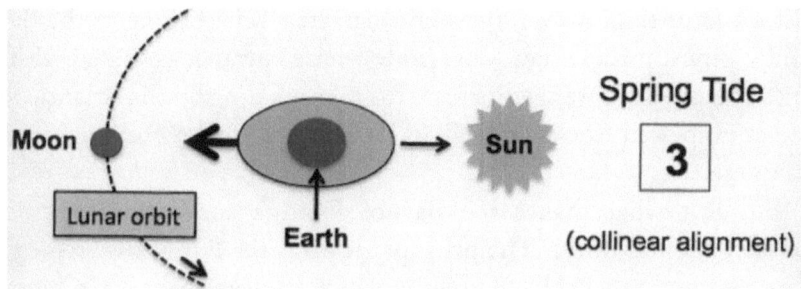

Spring Tide Configuration[63]

> **Welcome Assistance from Space!** On March 23, 2021, a massive, fully loaded container ship became grounded in the Suez Canal. Its positioning within the canal blocked all passage of ship traffic through this vital oceanic shortcut. Concern rapidly mounted that the problem would extend into many weeks.
>
> Fortunately, two lunar events occurred almost simultaneously: a *full* **moon** (March 28) that reinforced gravitational influences of sun and moon, and a *close* **moon** (March 30) that maximized lunar gravitational pull on Earth. These naturally occurring events combined on March 29 to raise tidal amplitudes, increasing volume of tidal water in the canal, lifting and refloating the ship during high tide. These influences, along with the assistance of tugs and dredges, resulted in the canal's re-opening to international shipping after only six days of total closure.

To complete our discussion of tides, a final factor governing tidal amplitudes must be inserted, namely the shape of the coastal container into which tidal waters are forced. Any study of tidal ranges at various oceanic recording stations reveals considerable differences in tidal amplitudes as well as times of maximum and minimum water levels. Amplitudes range from mild to extreme, with world averages in the range of 1 to 2 metres. Places where ranges exceed 10 metres include coastal France near the Rance River, Russia's Sea of Okhotsk, and England's Bristol Channel. However, the world's greatest tides belong to the Bay of Fundy, a mostly Canadian water body whose entrance is shared with the United States. Tidal ranges increase from its opening on the Atlantic to its head at Hopewell Rocks and Minas Basin. In optimal conditions, ranges top 16 metres.

But just what makes the Bay of Fundy's conditions so unique? Consider the following. The principal reasons for Fundy's extreme tides are related not only to the manner in which its water behaves in response to tidal forcing, but also to the influence of the bay's anatomy and its resulting natural period of oscillation.

Fundy's shape is an elongated, relatively straight bay whose water levels rise and fall every 12.5 hours in response to tidal forces from the sun and moon. But when one analyses tidal charts showing hourly water levels along the bay, there appears to be some additional player contributing, not the timing of highs and lows, but to the magnitudes of tidal ranges between highs and lows. Some ranges are greater than others. The additional factor relates to something called a *seiche*, a wave created by local atmospheric conditions of wind or pressure. Seiche frequencies depend primarily on the anatomy of the bay. Given its anatomy, a Fundy seiche will travel its length and back in approximately 13 hours, slightly longer than the oscillation period produced by the moon. Since the periods of oscillation induced by tidal forcing and atmospherics are almost equal, but not identical, it is only periodically that forcings completely overlap to reinforce and complement each other's actions at the same time and place. When this occurs, oscillation amplitudes can increase significantly to optimal conditions.

Most of us, including children, are familiar with the behaviour of a playground swing, which has a natural oscillation period based upon the length of the chains supporting it. When put into motion, a swing will oscillate at a rate determined by the length of its supporting chains. Any additional force applied to the swing, such as a push, will not change its natural oscillation period, but if applied at a time similar to its natural frequency, will increase its amplitude of swing. When such timing is applied to the swing, amplitudes can rise toward optimal conditions.

Concerning Fundy's basin anatomy, optimal conditions with proper timing are most achievable toward its northeast end at Hopewell Rocks and the Minas Basin.

SEEING BEYOND THE MOON TO A GREATER GLORY

With the moon occupying so lofty and unique a position in our heavens, its inclusion in the pages of holy scripture is not unexpected. Indirect references to the moon are found in the more than 280 references to the period of the lunar month scattered through over half of the books in both the Old and New Testaments. In many places, months are mentioned by number (Luke 1:26). In other places, a specific day within a month is mentioned. The ubiquitous and precise use of definite time periods helps to give events within the Bible temporal context and establishes them rooted in history.

In addition, over 60 direct references to the moon can be found in the Bible, with most in the Old Testament. As images, they are windows through which we glimpse something of the Creator and something of ourselves.

1. The moon as a trigger to wonder

Capturing something of the nature of an invisible God by means of a clearly recognizable object in the heavens is a valuable and oft-repeated pedagogical tool employed in scripture. The moon's capacity to teach profound lessons is linked to its capacity to evoke wonder among its observers as a handy visual aid. Once every 25 hours (not 24, since the moon is progressing eastward in its orbit), this object makes its appearance, rising somewhere in the east with a prominence and timing dependent upon its phase. We wonder why a full moon often appears with altered colour that lasts only a brief period after rising. We are curious as to why the shapes of moons, stars, and planets are restricted to spheres; why none is cubeshaped. We wonder if a Creator ever gets tired of applying the same geometric shape to so many celestial objects.

We imagine ourselves on the moon staring back at Earth as it rotates before us once each Earth day but, as earlier explained, never rises or sets in a lunar sky that is black during the two-week lunar sun-up. We enjoy the optical illusion created when a full moon at or near the horizon appears so much larger than it does overhead. We stare at the quarter phase and notice how light known as *earthshine* is of sufficient strength to reflect off our planet and partially illuminate the half of the lunar disc supposedly in darkness. We wonder what it would be like to stand on a body where days and nights are each two weeks long and where diurnal temperatures rise and fall well beyond the range of day-night temperatures common to our planet. We wonder why, from the moon, an observer facing Earth can experience a sunrise, but never an earthrise.

Periodically, the news media, knowing something of this fascination with our only natural satellite, remind us to enjoy the evening's *harvest moon*. Some of us even scan our calendar to find the unusual occurrence of two full moons occurring in a single month, the second being the socalled *blue moon*. Those of us with a math interest might wonder how often *a blue moon* occurs.

> *The known is finite, the unknown infinite; intellectually, we stand on an islet in the midst of an illimitable ocean of inexplicability. Our business in every generation is to reclaim a little more land, to add something to the extent and the solidity of our possessions.*
>
> T.H. Huxley[64]

2. The moon as a testimony to Divine Sovereignty

A book called *The Nautical Almanac for the Year 1983* sits on a shelf in my study. Despite its date of publication, it is a book of accurate predictions over lengthy time periods. It contains close to 300 pages of statistical tables relating to the behaviour of our sun and moon and certain stars and planets. It is a valuable navigational tool, fixing with celestial coordinates, the precise location of celestial objects for each hour of each day of the year. It gives useful information on times of twilight, sunrises, and moonrises. It is the perfect gift for all lovers of trivia.

Nautical almanacs are most useful to navigators and astronomers. With precision, my almanac predicted that in 1983 there would be three eclipses: two of the sun (June 11 and December 4) and one of the moon (June 25). It provided information on when each would begin and end, and from where on Earth each would be visible. Its statements did not say what would possibly happen, or probably happen. Rather, they expressed precisely what will, and eventually did happen.

The book is impressive for two reasons. Firstly, how can so many dates of special astronomical events be so accurately predicted so far ahead of their occurrences? Secondly, its degree of mathematical precision relating to timing of events in hours, minutes, and sometimes even in seconds is impressive. Simply put, all of its statistical data are reliable because the parameters such as force and mass that govern the behaviour of celestial bodies are known and quantifiable. Their behaviour is predictable because matter obeys fundamental laws of nature. So those on the island of Java who had the opportunity to witness the June 11 total solar eclipse in 1983 prepared for and observed the sun drift behind and become totally blackened by the moon for the predicted 5 minute, 11 second period. What had occurred was exactly what the almanac said would occur. People in North America watched two weeks later, on June 25, as 34% of the full moon's diameter (no more, no less) disappeared within Earth's shadow, as predicted.

By experience, we know that nothing behaves outside the sphere of natural law. If laws lead to erroneous predictions, it is because the scientist has overlooked some extraneous variable. The reliability characterizing behaviour within the cosmos is truly remarkable. It renders our lives secure within it. What we have come to know as ordinary, and in fact repeatedly take for granted, is nevertheless, because of its ordinariness and dependability, from the realm of the remarkable. As mentioned previously, the common tendency to restrict the miraculous to unique events—the sun and moon standing still in the sky (Josh 10:13) or Lazarus being raised from the dead (John 11:4)—must be rejected since that tendency excludes the infinitely more numerous *ordinary,* yet equally remarkable events that are seldom noticed. Both the unique and the ordinary event are miraculous in the sense that both inspire wonder and awe. Both give testimony to the omnipotence of a Sovereign God.

The celestial dance of objects in the heavens hints at a Master Choreographer who pre-existed all things, fashioned them, and sustains them. Sovereignty over His Creation means that at His will, He is able to maintain it, but also to suspend some or all of the very laws He established and periodically surprise us with a new dance step. Fortunately, for the sake of human occupancy on the planet, radical departures from the natural are not common. Nevertheless, novelty is a Sovereign's prerogative.

3. The moon as a testimony to both the temporal and the eternal

Anglicans are familiar with a group of songs in the *Book of Common Prayer* entitled *Additional Canticles.* One of these, "Surge, Illuminare," is based upon selected verses from Isaiah 60. As an appropriate song for the season of Advent, this canticle declares the arrival of Light:

Arise, shine, for thy light is come.

(BCP, page 28)

It is a reminder that what we see and experience is not all there is. Something more which lies beyond the visible and the temporal has made an appearance. What is visible has been acting the role of a metaphor, offering hints of something hidden (see C.S. Lewis quote in *Introduction,* Endnote 4).

The canticle testifies to the arrival of an eternal Light whose brightness can extinguish the brightness generated by the sun and reflected by the moon and yet itself cannot be extinguished. In its all-pervasive brilliance, in whose presence there can be no shadows, and therefore no night or waning moon, there is but constant Light.

These ideas are echoed in the extraordinary prediction recorded in Revelation 21: "an Eternal City having no need of the light of the Sun or the Moon, for the glory of the Lord who created light will be its Light." Psalm 72 is a comforting reminder that while the present celestial light is temporary, as is our ability to see it, God *The* Light will endure forever. Such a comforting thought is hard to grasp and maintain in a world in which everything, including the moon, changes and nothing endures.

> *Lighten our darkness, we beseech thee, O Lord . . .*
> *from the Third Collect, for Aid against all Perils*
>
> *(BCP, page 24)*

4

SHADOW

*Because you are my help,
I sing in the shadow of your wings.*

Psalm 63:7

Shadows over Lake Huron[65] **(JES)**

> *In faith*
> *there is enough light*
> *for those who want to believe*
> *and enough shadows to blind those who don't.*
>
> *Blaise Pascal* [66]

> *... in the shadow of his hand he hid me;*
> *he made me into a polished arrow*
> *and concealed me in his quiver.*
>
> *Isaiah 49:2b*

In October 1997, the United States launched a most ambitious mission, a seven-year journey to the planet Saturn.[67] Called the Cassini-Huygens NASA Space Probe, its pathway was far from direct. It first completed two loops about the sun during which it passed Venus twice and made one close approach to Earth. Then it swung outward following a smooth, arcing trajectory aimed at distant Jupiter. Arriving at, and eventually passing near this planetary giant, the probe trained its sights on and chased the even more distant Saturn, following a gravity-defined curving pathway before its eventual insertion into orbit around that planet in July 2004. The entire trip from launch to insertion into orbit took almost seven years.

Cassini-Huygens' journey is a remarkable story of navigational precision and rendezvous. It is also a testimony to the ingenuity of the human mind to devise tools that make it possible to safely guide an isolated speck of matter through fields of gravity and scattered debris, and through hundreds of millions of miles of virtual emptiness with few "gas stations" along the way.

The probe's indirect path to Saturn was necessary in order to gain the energy needed to travel such an enormous distance. It did so by tapping into, and draining off some of the kinetic energy of other moving objects on four separate flybys at critical distances and locations. The four planetary "slingshots" (each a form of gas station) provided gravity-assisted accelerations that catapulted the probe forward toward its final destination. Though circuitous, nothing along its route was haphazard or without purpose.

Nearing Saturn, loaded with scientific instruments, and with periodic instructions from its home base now some 1.5 billion kilometres away, Huygens separated from Cassini and soft-landed on Titan, transmitting back high-resolution photos via Cassini of Saturn's largest moon. Then, Cassini, negotiating the dangerous particle-laden rings of Saturn, and now captured by its massive gravity, began its many exploratory circuits, coming to within 200 kilometres of this celestial jewel, gathering scientific information while at the same time transmitting photographs of remote design and beauty residing in complete silence.

From its vantage point far above Saturn's gaseous surface, Cassini's cameras captured scenes impossible to view from Earth. Each photograph displayed unmatched clarity and detail. There were moons previously discovered, but now seen close-up, as well as five others newly discovered.

Amid the beauty contained within the serenity and form of this isolated island of matter was the largest shadow ever photographed—Saturn's shadow, projecting outward from its night side, and rendered visible against the background of its many illuminated rings. Passing through Saturn's cone of shadow, Cassini photographed its far side, producing a very unusual image. Light from the eclipsed sun, reflecting off the rings into Saturn's night side, made visible what would not normally be seen (see *Illustration* on back cover). Even with the probe's high speed, the journey through that cone of shadow took over 12 hours.

THE PHENOMENON OF SHADOWS

So much of human fun proceeds out of the nature of nature and from the simple laws of science. For example, we can stay upright on a bicycle because spinning wheels, like spinning gyroscopes, maintain their spatial orientation. We can ski because gravity is able to easily overcome the minimal frictional resistance offered by snow on sloping surfaces. We can soar in a hot-air balloon because air heated within the balloon is rendered less dense, and thus more buoyant than the air that surrounds it. The flight path of a baseball can be made to change when the pitcher, applying spin to the ball in a variety of ways, causes it to curve, sink or slide as it approaches the batter.

I recall the observations from a simple experiment made on the subject of shadows. It was the weekend and the family was eastbound on the 401 Highway to begin a day walking and exploring the countryside beyond the city.

The low morning sun to the southeast projected long shadows from the nearby tall hydro poles onto and across the roadway. The movement of our car intercepting and passing each shadow caught six-year-old Richard's attention. Without taking his gaze off the road, he said, "Daddy, look at the shadows." Referring to something I did not think noteworthy, he exclaimed, "They are all going the same way."

Recognizing this as a teachable moment, and desiring to enter into and encourage his interests, I replied, "Maybe what you have found is only true for *these* shadows. How do you know that the shadows farther down the highway will also point in the same direction?"

The question caused Richard to study the shadows more intensely. He watched patiently as our car drove through more of them. "Yep, another one! Another one! They all go the same way!"

With tenacity, I persisted on a slightly altered track. "Can you not find a single hydro pole shadow pointing in the other direction?"

After a period of silence, an answer came back: "Nope!"

As we continued our drive, Richard grew more and more confident that his theory regarding shadows was correct. Nevertheless, he remained watchful and open to the possibility that a shadow might eventually appear that would prove him wrong. (Good science always permits the data to lead. And the good scientist is always patient to investigate its lead). Of course, he found no exceptions. No shadow behaved differently. And so, confident his experimental results had led to a conclusion about how shadows from hydro poles behave in sunlight, we pulled the car off the road, parked, and ate some cookies.

The subject of shadows returned periodically over the course of that day. We searched to find shadows of differing colours (found none), searched for evidence that the colour of a shadow might be the same as the object making it (again, found none). We made shadows with our hands, altered our silhouettes to make them resemble the shapes of different animals (made many), laughed as we tried to outrun our own shadows (couldn't), and constructed a graph showing how shadow lengths and directions change as the morning sun approached noon and as the noon sun drifted toward evening. Like so many of the things of this world, shadows had become for Richard, as well as for his family, a simple and enjoyable toy.

What is a shadow? Shadows may be defined as a place where some physical quantity is diminished to levels below those quantities within immediate surroundings. For example, an area on the leeward side of mountains, known as a *rain shadow*, occupies a place of diminished precipitation relative to its surroundings. Similarly, areas of diminished light are places of light shadow. In both instances, some quantity has been removed and what is left is a remnant (or shadow) of what exists nearby.

In the case of the more ubiquitous light shadows, they occur wherever optically opaque objects as small as human bodies or trees, or as large as moons or planets, intercept visible light from some source, creating a region of diminished light downstream from the intervening object. These shadows can be seen best when they appear as a silhouette alongside a background of less diminished light. Shadows are their sharpest when the light source is strong, when that source shines on an object that is 100% opaque, and when no light from extraneous sources is available to bend into the shadow to provide borrowed light from elsewhere. Shadows produced by total or near-total absorption of light appear black or grey.

Shadows are useful in many ways. Undulations in land surface topography become more conspicuous because slopes inclined slightly away from the sun and absorbing slightly less sunlight appear somewhat in shadow, a situation common during times of low sun angle (see photo that begins this chapter).

This characteristic of diminished light-producing shadow helps us understand the use of x-ray as a diagnostic tool in medicine. As an imaging device, x-rays work because different body tissues absorb x-radiation at different rates. Because bone tissue is more opaque to x-ray than is soft tissue, a bone's downstream radiation shadow displays prominently on a photographic plate and may also reveal any bone pathology, if present.

Shadows are put to practical use in sundials. These simple instruments tell approximate time by means of a shadow cast by a vertically attached triangular device secured onto a horizontal surface that resembles a clock face. Sunlight shining on this stationary opaque instrument projects a shadow toward a number. In the northern hemisphere, the shadow pivots clockwise with the sun on the clock face to indicate the time of day.

Lengths of shadows falling on sundials change in response to time of day and season. With a number of adjustments for factors of latitude and longitude, sundials give good time approximations. Of course, sundials as clock-substitutes do not work on cloudy days or at night. However, they never need winding or electrical energy, and never begin that irritating blink after a power outage!

SHADOWS AND ECLIPSES

As we observed in the previous chapter, opaque objects in close proximity to light-emitting suns project shadows called umbras. Since the objects are in motion about their suns, umbras permanently sweep space in different directions from the dark side of the opaque object, producing some of the largest cones of shadow in all of nature.

But as is illustrated in the accompanying *Endnote* diagram, a second region of eclipse exists, called the *penumbra,* in which varying amounts of the sun remain visible. Both umbra and penumbra are projected into space thousands of kilometres from the dark side of the opaque object.[68] Since all planets and moons in the solar system are smaller than the sun, all umbras and penumbras are cone-shaped, with the former coming to a point in space and the latter ever-widening.

Lunar and solar eclipses are studies in three-dimensional geometry. In the chapter on the moon, it was stated that critical dimensions in the geometry of Earth, moon and sun include distances and diameters, and also rates of movement of Earth and moon with respect to each other and the sun. Knowing these variables renders the phenomenon of eclipses both regular and precisely predictable.

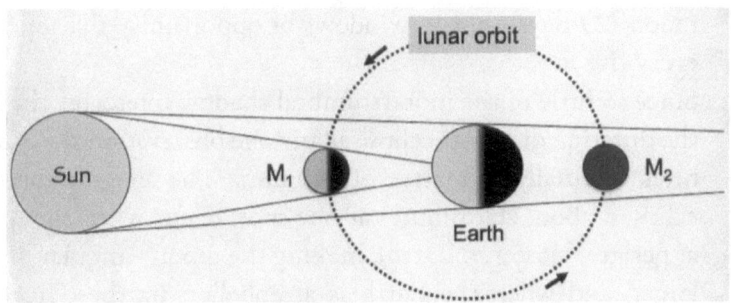

The Geometry of Solar and Lunar Eclipses[69]

1. Solar eclipses

Solar eclipses are spectacular visual events that most people take time to observe when opportunities arise. The following are significant facts about solar eclipses:

- Solar eclipses occur when the sun, moon and Earth are collinear, or near collinear, with the moon (M1) in conjunction (between the Earth and sun). Thus, the new moon is the phase associated with the solar eclipse.
- Since solar eclipses occur only when the moon is in conjunction, they are visible only to those who are experiencing daylight hours. Observers must use strong eye protection because viewing this eclipse type requires looking directly into the sun.
- When viewed from somewhere in Canada, an eclipse begins with a virtually invisible new moon approaching the sun's right limb (or edge) and advancing left to eventually cover the entire solar disc.
- If the alignment of sun, moon, and Earth is not precise, the lunar path across the solar disc will be such that the solar eclipse will only be partial.
- Since the moon's orbit is slightly tilted relative to the Earth's orbit about the sun, solar eclipses do not occur every month during each new moon. This is because most new moons in conjunction are not in perfect conjunction—that is, perfectly collinear—and so drift past the sun slightly above or below its centre. As a result, complete or partial solar eclipses occur, not during every new moon (29 days), but in windows of opportunity that open once every five months.
- Since so little of the moon's umbral shadow intercepts the Earth, the duration of a solar eclipse at any one observation site is usually brief, normally a matter of minutes. The longest total solar eclipses, about six minutes at one spot, occur when the moon is at perigee (closest to Earth), making the moon's angular diameter larger, and when the Earth is at aphelion (farthest from sun), making the sun's angular diameter smaller).

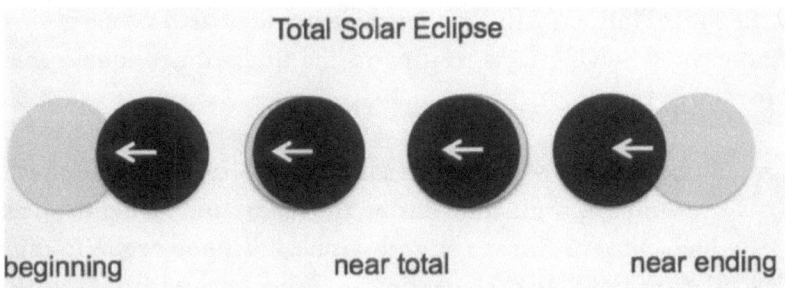

Migration of the New Moon across the Full Face of the Solar Disc[70]

- Probably the most attractive solar eclipse, and the most dangerous to observers, occurs when the moon (farthest from Earth at apogee) tracks through the exact middle of the solar disc at the time while Earth is closest to the sun (at perihelion). Unable to fully cover the sun at this time, the moon creates a spectacular *annular eclipse* of the sun during which one sees a bright ring of still-exposed (larger) sun surrounding a central black circle of smaller diameter.
- During a solar eclipse, an umbral shadow projected onto the Earth moves roughly eastward along a pathway called a *line of totality*. Thus, while total solar eclipses last only minutes at one spot, they remain in existence for hours as the end of their umbra progresses along the line of totality. Along this line, the complete eclipse is visible. On either side of that line, observers see varying degrees of partial eclipse, depending upon their distance from the line. This eclipse pathway, being narrow compared with the diameter of the Earth, means that the area in which solar eclipses can be seen is very limited. Thus, the frequency in which one may observe a solar eclipse from any one location is low. This is especially true with *total* solar eclipses.

2. Lunar eclipses

Lunar eclipses occur when the moon drifts through the Earth's cone of shadow. That is, lunar eclipses occur when the sun, moon and Earth are collinear, with the moon in opposition (Earth between the moon [M2] and the sun). Thus, only full moons can enter the Earth's cone of shadow. We note the following facts relating to the three-dimensional geometry of lunar eclipses:

- Since we face away from the sun to view a full moon, lunar eclipses are visible at some time during the night, not during the day.
- The eclipse begins as a brightly visible full moon begins to enter the Earth's invisible cone of shadow. When viewed from somewhere in Canada, darkening begins on the moon's left limb since it is approaching the area of projected Earth shadow from the right. As movement continues, darkening spreads and deepens across the entire lunar disc.
- If the alignment of sun, Earth, and moon is not precisely collinear— that is, if the moon is not perfectly *full*—it will not track through the central part of the Earth's cone of shadow. If this occurs, total lunar eclipses will be shorter, or, if the moon just grazes the cone's outer edge, the lunar eclipse will only be partial, with only slight lunar darkening occurring. On occasion, the moon just manages to track through the Earth's penumbra, in which case, observers may not realize that a partial eclipse is even occurring.

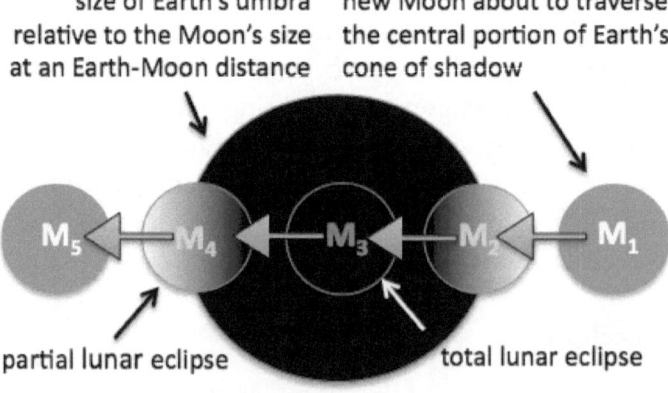

A Central Migration of the Moon through the Earth's Cone of Shadow[71]

- Since the moon's orbit is slightly tilted relative to the Earth's orbit about the sun, a lunar eclipse cannot occur every month at the time of each full moon. Like solar eclipses, they occur about once every five months in the same windows of opportunity afforded solar eclipses, separated in time by about two weeks prior to, or following a solar eclipse (since this is the amount of time it takes for a new moon to travel around to the opposite side of its orbit [from conjunction to opposition] to become a full moon).
- Since the Earth's umbra is so much wider than the diameter of the moon, the entire lunar disc is able not only to fit easily into it, but to continue to drift within it for an extended period of time. For this reason, if drift progression is through the central part of the shadow, the average lunar eclipse, when viewed from a single spot on Earth normally lasts a few hours rather than a few minutes.

3. **Eclipses in General**

   a. **Appearances:** A comparison of the appearance of the sun and moon during their complete eclipses reveals a striking difference. During the minutes of totality, photos of an eclipsed sun show a black orb surrounded by a diffuse ring of white light. This is part of the outer atmosphere of the sun visible only when the greater brightness of its central surface has been extinguished. By contrast, during the few hours of totality, photos of an eclipsed moon show a darkened lunar disc. Occasionally, lunar eclipses display a moon bathed in orange or blood-red light, a phenomenon created when light has been bent by the Earth's atmosphere into its own cone of shadow. Colours vary, depending on atmospheric conditions along the tracks of light at the time of the eclipse.

   b. **Frequency:** We have noted that solar and lunar eclipses occur in windows of opportunity during which shadows, which are always being projected by opaque objects within the sun's rays, are able, because of correct geometry, to fall on nearby objects. An open window means that a full moon (in opposition) or new moon (in conjunction) exists and resides on or near the Earth's plane of orbit. If so, there is time for at least one eclipse. But more often than not, these double requirements are not occurring simultaneously. The moon may be in opposition or in conjunction, but not on or near the Earth' plane of orbit. Or the moon may be on or near the Earth's plane of orbit, but not be in either opposition or conjunction. This explains why eclipses do not occur whenever full or new moons are observed. Instead, eclipses are restricted to seasons of optimal geometric conditions that are present about every five months and last for a few weeks.

c. **Eclipses observed from space:** Residing within the moon's cone of shadow during a solar eclipse, and looking in the direction of the sun, we see a blackened sun. If observed at the same time from space, would the shadow projected on the Earth surface be darkened sufficiently to be observable on that surface? With the advent of satellite photography, the answer was confirmed. The lunar shadow (its umbra truncated by the Earth) was clearly discernible as a darkened spot over North Africa during the total solar eclipse of March 29, 2006. First appearing over eastern Brazil, it inched eastward across the Atlantic, eventually arriving over North Africa. Here the absence of cloud cover, combined with the colour, dryness, and homogeneity of the Saharan surface, rendered the migrating shadow visible. Soon afterwards, it entered Turkey, having moved thousands of kilometres over the Earth's surface.

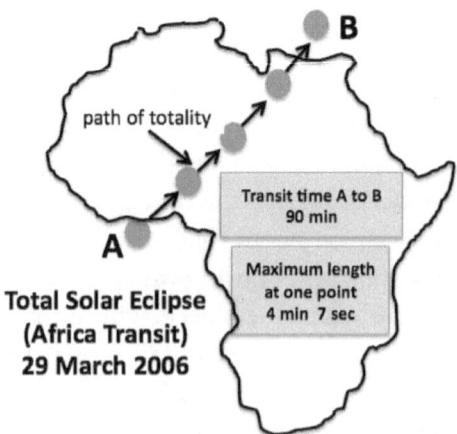

Path of the Lunar Shadow over the North African Sahara[72]

The diameter of the truncated lunar umbra projected onto the Earth's surface varies, depending upon the relative distances of moon from Earth and Earth from sun during a solar eclipse. At no time is this diameter large (typically in the order of 150 kilometres), a fact that explains the brevity of solar eclipses when viewed from one location. Like umbral diameters, truncated umbral shapes also vary, depending upon the angle at which the lunar umbra intercepts the Earth. At right angles, it is circular. If shadows fall on higher latitudes, projected umbral shapes are elliptical.

SHADOWS AS METAPHORS IN SCRIPTURE

In surveying common usage of the term *shadow*, both negative and positive images emerge, not only in the literal sense, but also in the figurative. The shadowy place, as a place of diminished light, obviously displays what is dark and gloomy. It conjures up the mysterious, possibly the hiding place of someone or something frightening or mischievous. Many of us who listened to the radio in the 1950s recall the linkage between shadows and mystery in the program *The Shadow*, in which a sinister omniscient someone somehow knew "what evil lurks in the hearts of men."

Nobody likes being overshadowed or living in the figurative sense within the shadow of someone else. But "overshadow" is the word used by the angel Gabriel as he addressed the frightened and bewildered young virgin named Mary:

> *The Holy Spirit will come upon you,*
> *and the power of the Most High will overshadow you.*
>
> *Luke 1:35*

Here, no negative sense of the image of shadow emerges. Rather the Spirit's overshadowing of Mary is an act conferring honour and favour on a chosen person while demonstrating divine presence, protection and power within her. Here the use of *shadow* enhances the mystery associated with the silent work of the Holy Spirit.

Possibly no more fearful concept of shadow exists than that found in the phrase, "shadow of death." The phrase, more accurately translated "shadow of darkness," is found in the familiar and popular Psalm 23.

The phrase is also the title of a painting by the nineteenth-century artist William Holman Hunt whose work is full of rich symbolism. The artist depicts Jesus with eyes raised upward and arms outstretched, seemingly joyful over what appears to be a satisfying day of carpentry. Behind him is His mother. Though her face is not shown, she is obviously staring, not at Jesus, but rather at His shadow, which is being cast onto a nearby wall. The projected image bears a strong resemblance to the image of Christ with outstretched arms on the cross. It foreshadows His death.

Despite their capacity to induce apprehension or sadness within us, shadows are also linked to relief and comfort. The image of shadow as *refuge* is known to everyone who seeks the protection of the shady spot, away from the intense heat of the sun. Unfortunately, shadows are shortest (namely at solar noon) when protection from the sun's most intense radiant heat is most sought after. The association of shadow with positive images of refuge and protection is particularly evident in the Bible, which refers to the shade afforded by objects like plants (Mark 4:32), clouds, and mountains. These images increase in significance when one recalls the limited presence of natural shade protection such as large and numerous trees in Bible Lands, especially in the more southern regions where desert landscapes predominate.

In a less concrete manner, other references, especially in Psalms reveal a God who in himself is able to make provision for His children, not only as a source of light, but also as a source of shade and shelter. Here, God is likened to a giant bird under whose wings the psalmist can find sanctuary (Ps 17:8; Ps 57:1). The same image is contained in the first verses of Psalm 91 where a more permanent dwelling in the shelter of the Most High (another form of shadow) provides gifts of rest and protection, even when more concrete sources of protective shade are absent. Here we see the most precious gift that God confers on His children who dwell in a place of tribulation, fear or uncertainty. Here we are reminded of the place of shelter Mary experienced when overshadowed by the Holy Spirit. This special sanctuary within a place of tribulation is not a physical entity, but God Himself (Matt 28:20, KJV).

Surprisingly, the sanctuary as described is a place of shadow. In such a dwelling, we find opportunity to give thanks, even to sing, as did Mary (Luke 1:46–55), for God's abiding presence with us *in* them, and possibly to give thanks, even *for* dire circumstances, since they aid us to more fully understand the travails of others.

> *Whoever dwells in the shelter of the Most High*
> *will rest in the shadow of the Almighty.*
> *I will say of the LORD, 'He is my refuge and my fortress,*
> *my God, in whom I trust.'*
>
> *Psalm 91:1, 2*

Elsewhere, the transitory nature of shadows renders them a suitable image to emphasize the transitory nature of life (Ps 102:11). The shifting nature of shadows stands in sharp contrast to the changeless character of God (Jas 1:17). The Old Testament law is described as "only a shadow of the good things that are coming" (Heb 10:1). A similar reference in Colossians 2:17, possibly the most encouraging of all images of shadows, suggests that this present world itself is but a shadow or sampling of what is to come, namely the truly genuine, characteristic of what will forever be permanent. Every 24 hours, we are reminded of shadow; each evening, we rotate into darkness as the Earth turns us into its own shadow. There we sit, awaiting dawn and the morning when we will temporarily emerge from darkness.

Finally, figuratively speaking, humans occupy *shadowlands*, a seemingly permanent world that can at best only approximate what is truly genuine. During our sojourn, lasting the years from birth to death, we experience understanding that is clouded by myopic and distorted vision (1 Cor 13:12).

The concept of shadowlands emerged in the 1989 film production of the same name. The Oxford scholar and writer, C. S. Lewis, played in the film by actor Anthony Hopkins, admits to serious doubts and confusion in the realm of Christian faith when confronted with the sudden illness and death of his beloved wife Joy and his deep grief that followed. In these shadowlands, appearance is an illusion that is easily mistaken for reality.

Though no adequate explanation is given in the Bible for the problem of pain and grief, there is assurance that one day shrouded clarity will vanish and shadow will be replaced by substance. In that day, reality will be neither distorted nor incomplete. The perfect will prevail and the partial will be entirely abolished (1 Cor 13:10). Then "we will know just as now we are fully known." And shadow and the night, uncertainty and confusion, like time and death, will be things of the past.

The steps of faith fall on the seeming void,
and find the rock beneath.

John Greenleaf Whittier[73]

5

ROCK

High up in the north in the land of Svithjod, there stands a rock. It is 100 miles high and 100 miles wide. Once every thousand years a little bird comes to the rock to sharpen its beak. When the rock has thus been worn away, then a single day of eternity will have gone by.

Hendrik van Loon[74]

Percé Rock off the Gaspé Peninsula, Quebec[75]
(JES)

*Crustal plates that move,
collide, and quake;
sea floors that migrate
under vast oceans of water
that deform the rock beneath;
hotspots in the Earth's interior
that periodically disgorge sub-crustal materials
onto its surface;
magnetic patterns frozen within rocks
that bear testimony within themselves
to the dynamic processes
that once produced them . . .
The geography of the rocky planet we occupy,
surcharged with beauty and mystery
overflows with geologic history
that is written and preserved
in the patterns and debris it leaves behind,
patiently awaiting discovery and the release
of its many buried secrets.*

JES

Those who travel north from Toronto and into the region of Muskoka pass a prominent break in land surface structure just north of Lake Simcoe. Over the space of a few kilometres, the landscape changes from expansive and gentle surfaces to a more rugged topography of abundant rock outcrops and lakes.

What has suddenly become visible is the rugged area of exposed rock known as the Canadian Shield. Representing some of the oldest rocks on our planet, the Shield is a vast repository of hard, erosion-resistant igneous and metamorphic rock that displays extensive surface prominence in numerous outcroppings throughout Quebec, Ontario, and Manitoba. Geologists tell us that these outcroppings are, in fact, residual stumps, remnants of high mountains that once belonged to the region that have slowly been altered by natural forces of gradation, worn away and transported elsewhere in particle sizes. Shield rock is but one of many massive rock packages that cover our planet, providing it with a relatively thin envelope of hardened material that is collectively known as the Earth's crust.

Our crustal envelope is solid because the melting point of rock is much higher than the temperatures that presently prevail on the Earth's surface. This may not have been so in the distant past during the time when our planet was completely, or partly molten. Though very old and traditionally regarded as immovable and stable, this envelope undergoes constant change by giant gradational forces from above it as well as from below. Fragments in a wide range of sizes presently form crustal *plates* whose margins present as sinuous articulating edges known as *faults*.

It is along these crustal plate margins that much widespread geologic activity common to crustal plates occurs. Activities include new plate formation, plate drifting, and plate destruction; crustal warping and mountain building; volcanism, sea floor spreading, and earthquakes. With new parts forming and older parts being destroyed at measurable rates, it is obvious all parts are not a common age. Given present rates of formation and destruction, estimates show that the crust will totally replace itself in some 200 million years.

Among geologically active world sites, the most active surround the giant Pacific plate along a lengthy perimeter known as the *Ring of Fire*. Countries situated on or near plate boundaries include Chile, Iceland,

Indonesia, Japan, and New Zealand. But human interest and appreciation of the dynamic nature of our crustal surface are largely restricted to its more cataclysmic events such as earthquakes and volcanic eruptions. By contrast, events such as mountain formation and sea floor spreading remain largely unappreciated as dynamic events since the processes that generate them, though relentless, are much slower and less dramatic.

MOUNTAINS AND MOUNTAIN BUILDING THROUGH CRUSTAL WARPING

Before the mountains were born
or you brought forth the whole world,
from everlasting to everlasting you are God.

Psalm 90:2

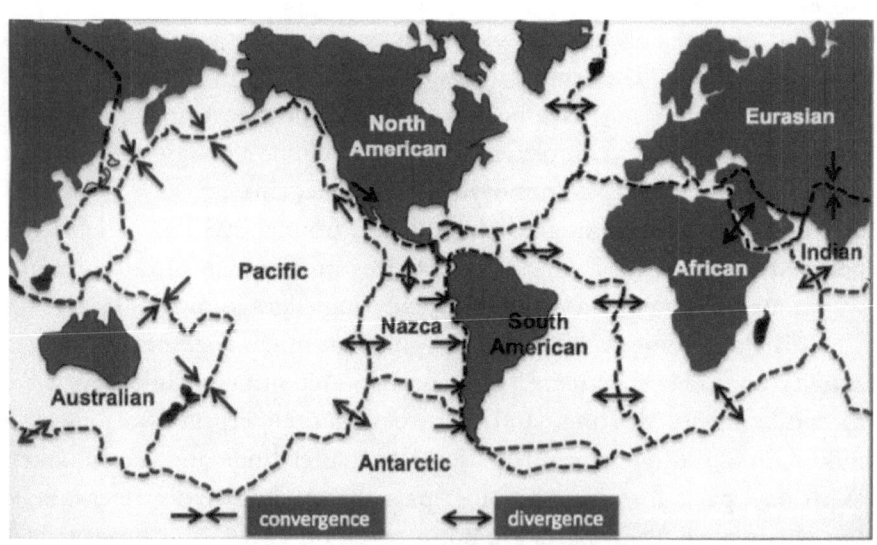

The Earth's Major Crustal Plates[76]

While the fact of crustal plate drift was suspected, the caution of many to accept it fully centred around plausible cause. Early hypotheses focused on sub-crustal material called *magma* and the effects of isolated regions called hotspots that are heated through the natural decay of radioactive materials and rock compression. Since these thermal pockets are isolated, the temperature regime within the magma is heterogeneous. Magma at different temperatures creates magma of slightly differing densities. Since magma is a fluid, slow convectional circulations are generated that are similar to, though so much slower than the convectional turbulence observed in a pot of soup that is warming on a stove. Over many millennia, sub-crustal currents, moving slower than a snail's pace and yet applying gargantuan forces to the massive solid plates overriding them, cause widespread drifting of plates and subsequent deformations and re-formations within individual crustal plate anatomy. Where warping is downward, extensive valleys and trenches are created, many of which end up below sea level. Among these can be found the deepest ocean water. Conversely, where warping is upward and widespread, prominent mountain ranges are created.

It is difficult to comprehend the magnitude of these unrelenting geologic forces that have been and are involved in the slow processes of mountain building and valley formation. Yet we are told that both North and South American plates, drifting slowly westward and colliding with the Pacific plate, warped and buckled on their leading or western edges to slowly create the majestic Western Cordilleran and Andean mountain ranges and their interior valleys. Similar orogenies are occurring as the northmigrating African plate drifts toward Europe and the Indo-Australian plate collides with the Asiatic plate.

These events are responsible for the raising up of the magnificent European Alps and the greatest assemblage of mountains above sea level, namely the mighty Himalayas. It is here through the regions of Tibet, Nepal, and Pakistan where all fourteen of the world's tallest peaks are located, each reaching beyond 8 000 metres above sea level. Highest of these is *Chomolungma* (Everest). At present, it is rising even higher by a few millimetres per year). In each example of mountain building resulting from plate compression, we note that the orientation of a resulting mountain range lies roughly perpendicular to the axis of plate movement.

Pushing a rug into a wall and noting the orientation of the folds of the rug relative to its axis of movement can clearly demonstrate this action.

In some regions of the world, mountainous structures form, not because rock has been bent and lifted, but rather because hot lava has been deposited on isolated surfaces, or because a surface has been partially eroded and transported away, leaving a residual mass of undisturbed material that is conspicuous only in relation to its degraded surroundings. Examples of the former process include various forms of volcanoes such as Mt. Fuji in Japan and Mt. Erebus in Antarctica. Examples of the latter process include mesas and their smaller residual cousins—buttes, conspicuous landforms common to Arizona's Monument Valley. Located in arid regions where vegetation cover is minimal, buttes and mesas create dramatic touristattracting topographies with tops that are often flat and sides that are steep.

As physical places, mountainous areas possess abundant human significance. They form boundaries between many countries. They are visually prominent, often mysterious and sometimes deadly. Their massiveness that appears imperishable suggests a permanency in a world of change. Their rugged features and relative inaccessibility make them places for human adventure, refuge, and security.

The tallest mountains regularly penetrate the clouds and reach to the heavens. Over the years, they have represented barriers that have restricted human migrations. Few people inhabit them; a handful of people climb them; and for a number of important reasons, commercial airlines avoid them. As places that are high and lifted up, they have for many been regarded as the dwelling places of the gods. Their slopes and summits are frequently the chosen sites for monasteries.

Mount Olympus, the tallest mountain in Greece, was considered in the ancient Hellenistic world the home of the Olympians, a family of gods and goddesses. Among people of Nepal and Tibet, belief is widespread that gods and demons inhabit the mountains and that permission is required to ascend to their domain. In addition, prayers and sacrifices are believed necessary to placate the various spirits to ensure that no misfortune befalls climbers. Not surprisingly, as occurred in the massive avalanche on the slopes of Mt. Everest in May 2014 that killed sixteen Nepali Sherpa guides, accidents and deaths are all too common. The misfortunes among the many who have dared to ascend to the loftiest of these supposedly divine residences have been interpreted as probable evidence of divine displeasure at the intrusions of unwelcome visitors into a holy realm of thin air and steep slopes.

EARTH'S MOUNTAINS AND ATMOSPHERE

The Earth's atmosphere is a thin envelope of gases that entirely surrounds the planet. If we liken the Earth to a basketball, atmospheric thickness would be analogous to a single sheet of thin plastic wrap about its surface.

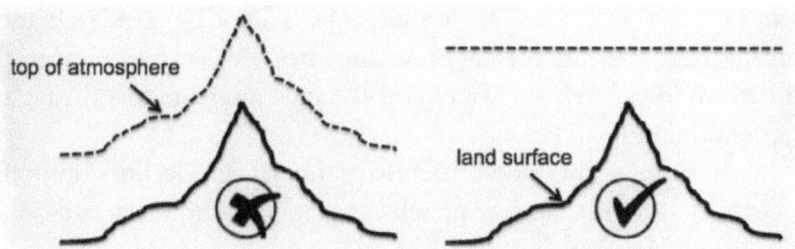

The Shape of the Atmosphere in relation to the Crustal Surface[77]

Given the fact that the atmosphere is not bent by mountains, but rather is pierced by them, less atmosphere exists at the top of a mountain than at its base. Not only does air density decline with increasing altitude, but it declines most rapidly at those altitudes close to sea level. For this reason, small changes in altitude at or near sea level cause the most noticeable changes in air pressure. Our ears "pop" on the longest elevator rides and in small aircraft that are the principal means by which most of us visit such altitudes. At the cruising altitudes for commercial jets, cabins must be sealed to accommodate excessive air pressure changes so as to ensure passenger safety and comfort.

At these altitudes, passengers sit in a micro-atmosphere whose pressure is *not* normal sea level pressure, but rather that which is common to a 7 000-foot altitude. Small cabin pressure reductions, noticed by few passengers, ensures that door and window seals are not subject to excessive stress and eventual failure. Nevertheless, reduced pressures cause water to reach boiling points somewhat below 100 °C, a fact that reduces the maximum temperatures at which hot beverages can be served. This link between the boiling point of water and atmospheric pressure's decline with altitude made it possible for Dr. David Livingstone to use water's boiling point to make rough estimates of altitude during his explorations of the African interior. This crude method was useful when much more precise methods were as yet unknown to nineteenth-century minds.

At the height of the world's tallest mountains, an altitude called the *death zone* by alpine climbers, air pressure has plunged to a mere 30% of its normal value at sea level and the boiling point of water has dropped to near 70 °C. It is at these altitudes where the effects on human physiology are most severe. Decreased air pressure lowers blood oxygen levels and air temperatures, while increasing breathing rates. Lowered air temperatures reduce humidity levels in tissues and enhance moisture loss through the lungs and mouth.

With changes in blood chemistry linked to declines in oxygen concentrations; with the ever-present dangers of pulmonary and cerebral edema; with the threats of frostbite and hypothermia from bitterly cold temperatures and storm-force winds; and, with altitude-induced dizziness, nausea and impaired judgment, it is clear that on the world's most elevated terrain, stresses on human physiology reach critical levels approaching and often exceeding thresholds of human endurance.

For those who expose themselves to such risks, survival in such places depends upon available supplemental oxygen, or minimizing the length of stay at the highest altitudes. Programs of preparedness for alpine climbers involving slow acclimatization to the highest elevations are vitally essential, and base camps for those seeking to climb to the world's highest peaks are wisely located below the so-called *death zone*. Unfortunately, this preparedness is hardly adequate for climbers caught in the death zone when progress is delayed because of the long line of climbers waiting to ascend through the most popular routes during the most popular summiting times.

Evidence of the natural decline in air temperature with rising altitude is visible in the snowpack at or near the tops of tall mountains. Within the lower atmosphere, air temperature drops on average some 6 Celsius degrees for every 1 000-metre rise in altitude. Thus, altitude is able to do to local climate and vegetation zones through only a few hundred metres of rise what latitude can only accomplish through horizontal distances of hundreds of kilometres. Such rapid changes with rising altitude explain why seasonal and some perennial snow can be present at the summit of the tallest mountains, even near the equator (as in Kenya, Ecuador, and Hawaii).[78]

My first-hand experiences with mountains are very limited. In Hawaii, I visited the slopes of Mauna Loa and the lip of the giant caldera of active Kilauea. But probably my most memorable foray into such regions occurred at Moraine Lake, a most popular tourist attraction situated in the Alberta Rockies close to Lake Louise. At a surface elevation of 1900 metres, the lake resides within *the Valley of the Ten Peaks* that forms a portion of the rugged Alberta-British Columbia border. This valley is one of a myriad of similar ice-excavated rock troughs fashioned long ago in the days when local climate permitted ice tongues to penetrate and scour surfaces at much lower altitudes. Now, after many thousands of years in which glacial melt rates have outstripped the rates at which glaciers form and advance, these alpine valleys lie exposed to the gradational influences of gravity, wind and water. The perennial ice and snow that once formed a continuous white blanket through the region is now but a shadow of its former glory, permitted by natural forces to occupy as residual fragments only the highest surfaces within the region.

The air was crystal clear as Nancy and I arrived at Moraine Lake. Billowy fair-weather cumulus clouds were scattered randomly overhead like cotton balls, displaying their characteristically well-defined edges against an unusually bright blue sky. A short pathway led from the roadway to the lake. As we approached it, a panorama of beauty opened before us.

The lake presents as a turquoise bowl of water, its colour reflecting the presence of suspended rock powder formed by local glacial scour. Mountains adjacent to this liquid jewel, their inverted and virtually undistorted images mirrored in the lake's still waters, rose some one thousand metres on three sides. Alluvial fans displayed their typical triangular shapes where tributary valleys meet the lake and where water-borne suspended sediment is suddenly deposited. A dense stand of conifers surrounded the slopes adjacent to the lake and reached up as far as surface slopes and temperatures would permit. The landscape was a monument standing as testimony to the slow and orderly processes that have generated these splendid natural patterns.

A short distance from the lake, we gathered alongside other tourists. A noticeable hush prevailed among those assembled. There were no signs telling us to behave in this manner. Neither were there honking horns nor idling engines to cause distraction. We stood in silence beholding this natural assemblage of tranquility, order, and beauty.

Our silence reflected the stillness of the place. Silence seemed the most appropriate and natural way to respond in the presence of such glorious majesty. It was as if the crowd was being spoken to. It was as if nature was delivering a sermon devoid of speech or language, and we were its assembled congregation with minds filled with questions and wonder. What laws imposed their influences on all this matter? What complex processes brought it all into being? *Who* brought all this into being?

What stimulates the human response called wonder? What prompts us to contemplate certain things with sustained silent attention? And why do certain things evoke a response of wonder in some of us and indifference in others?

Wonder is a means by which we engage emotionally with some aspect of reality. Engagements such as this are usually more common with those portions of reality that are less familiar, more complex and more cloaked in mystery. In contemplating the patterns and processes that saturate the world of nature, one cannot help but wonder. At times like these, the human mind is replete with questions. Such is the case when one contemplates the newborn baby, the organization and complexity of the systems within the human body, the various exposed strata within the truly grand Grand Canyon, the massive front of Antarctica's Ross Ice Shelf, the awesome force of rotating winds within the tornado, or the silent choreography of celestial objects as they perform their dance in the heavens with precision and with no need for rest or audience. When we wonder, we approach the realm of the ineffable. All indication points to wonder as an exclusively human activity that hints of more to reality than meets the eye.

MOUNTAIN BUILDING THROUGH VOLCANIC ERUPTION AND DEPOSITION

In the autumn of 1963, the crew of a fishing boat spotted smoke rising from the sea surface off the southwest coast of Iceland. Approaching what they thought was a vessel on fire, they soon found themselves instead sailing toward a geological maternity ward and a volcano in the violent process of being born.

For about a week prior to its birth, nature had foretold the arrival of this geologic infant with Earth tremors, rising water temperatures, and sulphurous fumes emerging from the ocean bed some 150 metres below its surface. In the weeks that followed, observers witnessed a spectacular performance by nature. Violent explosions could be seen and heard as vast amounts of liquefied rock burst forth from the Earth's interior, instantly boiling the surrounding water, eventually emerging at the surface as a column of black ash and rising white water vapour. After three months of activity, as deposits of rapidly cooled lava continued to accumulate on the seabed, and with uninterrupted quantities of building materials being delivered and deposited, a small island emerged to battle the erosive effects of the surrounding sea.

For a time, it was not clear if this fledgling newborn would survive in its inhospitable liquid surroundings. But the structure *had* survived the most critical stage in its birthing process and was now furiously depositing ash *above* the ocean surface where materials could cool more slowly and form a more erosion-resistant rock. In the end, after a process that lasted almost four years, the persistent infant prevailed. Destructive wave action was not able to eliminate what volcanism had furiously created. And so, with a surface of just under 3 square kilometres and a summit at 170 metres above the surface of the sea, the small, roughly circular volcanic island named Surtsey became a modest topographic feature on our planet's vast natural landscape.

Iceland, situated on the Mid-Atlantic Ridge, is one of the world's most geologically active regions. Located at a diverging plate boundary, it has birthed many volcanoes. While most have added to the overall topography of the island, the influence of others have been much more far reaching.

The massive eruption on April 14, 2010 under Iceland's Eyjafjallajökull Glacier is an example of the latter. Far below its cold surface, a geologic soup was brewing, brought to a boil by internal heat great enough to liquefy rock. As pressures increased, forces within the liquid came to exceed the strength of the crustal cover to contain them. On that day, after 200 years of dormancy within that mountain, the Earth's interior coughed and released its molten brew in a massive explosion. Liquid rock was spattered skyward hundreds of metres. In the intense heat, the overburden of ice within the glacier quickly melted, releasing torrents of water that had been sealed in ice for centuries. What did not rush to the sea found itself evaporated, then quickly condensing as white plumes of vapour pushed skyward by convective forces. Lightning flashes from the resulting atmospheric turbulence illuminated the night sky. White vapour and black soot rose in tandem to be transported, redistributed and diluted by the region's prevailing winds. For days afterward, the event made headlines as the ground continued to spew its contents into an atmosphere working hard to receive, scatter and dilute them. Thus, earth, water, wind, and fire combined in an impressive display of nature's might.[79]

Events associated with the eruption of Eyjafjallajökull were reminiscent of the widespread effects of similar eruptions: of Indonesia's Krakatoa in 1883 and of the Philippine's Pinatubo in 1991. Both generated an atmospheric mess whose effects were widespread. In fact, they were both global and sustained, increasing air turbidity and lowering air temperatures worldwide. In the 1991 and 2010 eruptions, air traffic through nearby heavily travelled air corridors came to a standstill. In it all, world communities were once again reminded that the disruptions to our planet caused by nature periodically dwarf those inflicted on it by human occupancy.

Volcanic eruptions that slowly *ooze* their brew from their craters normally distribute liquid rock locally. Volcanic eruptions that *explode* their brew dispense a much finer material upwards to higher altitudes, over wider areas, over longer distances, and for more extended periods of time. Greater transport of materials from more forceful eruptions is due to a number of factors. Firstly, giant explosions generate finer particulate, while the vast quantities of heat from explosive eruptions provide powerful air convection that lifts suspended materials to high altitudes where advective wind transport is the strongest and most persistent. Moreover, where convectional lifting is able to carry ash above normal cloud altitudes, rapid atmospheric cleansing through rainfall is not as likely. All this serves to increase the quantity, residency period, and transport of particulate matter in the atmosphere.

At present, volcanoes exist at different stages of development. So-called *active* ones display sporadic or continuous growth, either through quiet lava flow or through episodes of violent eruption. Three such examples are Sicily's Mount Etna, Hawaii's Mount Kilauea, and the dangerous Mount Nyiragongo situated at the eastern edge of the African Republic of Congo.

Active volcanoes that sustain relatively long periods of inactivity are classified as *dormant*. Dormant volcanoes like Japan's 300-year inactive Mount Fuji and most near the American west coast frequently appear in travel magazines. Their rugged beauty and symmetry make them both safe and popular tourist attractions.

Many volcanoes, like Mount St. Helens and others in the American northwest, alternate between activity and dormancy with unpredictable frequency. Still others, whose inactivity has extended over many millenniums, are classified not as dormant, but as *extinct*. Extinct volcanoes exist as diminished residual remnants, the results of the ravages of erosion, with no processes operating to replenish their extensive structural losses. Often atop many of these vestigial remains can be found dwellings, such as castles and monasteries. A linear pattern of eight aged volcanic stumps form conspicuous bumps near the south shore of the St. Lawrence River, extending eastward from Montreal's Mount Royal, through St. Bruno and Mount St. Hilaire.

> *The ancient mountains crumbled*
> *and the age-old hills collapsed...*
> *but he marches on forever.*
>
> *Habakkuk 3:6b*

Among prominent volcanic structures on the Earth's surface, two peaks have achieved notoriety. Each, like Mount Everest, can legitimately boast of being the world's tallest peak. Assigning this distinction to a single mountain peak is difficult since the published height of a mountaintop depends upon a clear definition of the base elevation from which height measurements are made. Normally height measurements begin at *mean sea level*. Measuring mountain peaks from sea level makes non-volcanic Everest the highest peak in the world, near 8848 metres. However, the peak of the dormant volcano Mauna Kea on Hawaii's Big Island at 4207 metres can also claim the same prize if measurements begin from its surrounding sea bed. Moreover, a third claim can be made for Ecuador's volcanic Mount Chimborazo. Sitting on crust close to the equator, where rotation has created a measurable bulge, its summit at only 6268 metres is the farthest point from the centre of the Earth. In fact, three other summits are also farther from that centre than Everest.

THE PHENOMENON OF SEA FLOOR SPREADING

A friend who teaches students in middle school had prepared a lesson involving a large colourful globe that displayed the world's continents and oceans. Seated around the globe, the students watched as she rotated it to locate and identify the world's seven continents and its four oceans. Then, with a beam of light representing the sun in the darkened classroom, she rotated the sphere to demonstrate how the motion of the Earth in the sun's rays produces day and night and how only half of the Earth can be illuminated at any one time. The children learned that all planets, as well as moons, experience day and night because they all rotate.

Then, from among the many curious students, a hand was raised and a question was asked. In seconds the attention of the class was fixed on the western and eastern margins of the Atlantic Ocean. Though far apart, yet with conspicuous shape similarities along edges, they appeared as if they had been separated.

Such thoughts popping into the minds of a classroom of inquisitive students are not unique. Earth scientists had played with them ever since mapping of the oceans and continents became sufficiently accurate enough to reveal coastal similarities such as these. When they eventually appeared, questions flourished. Are continents and oceans at present as they were in the past? Since continents change shape as sea levels change, at which sea level is the one that displays the best shoreline match-up? Are all crustal masses the same age? If smooth rounded rocks on a beach did not originate that way, maybe continents and oceans didn't either. Maybe the Earth's crust is not as stable and immovable as people believe, but rather is part of a slow, dynamic, and unrelenting process of change. With uncertainties abounding, and with firm corroborating evidence lacking, the idea of continents drifting remained an unproven hypothesis until the latter half of the 20th century.

But from whence came the corroborating evidence that eventually confirmed this dynamic process? Fortunately, nature provides its own evidence. And it came long after the events occurred, bearing witness to itself through widespread recoverable geological material preserved through time and through processes that are ongoing. The present serves as the key to the past, often in the most unexpected places. Nature writes its own history, this time within the once inaccessible ocean floor, accessed now with high-tech pressure-resistant submersibles, remote sensing equipment, and sophisticated diagnostic tools that can descend to great ocean depths to recover seabed samples. So, what was once mere imaginative hypothesizing and speculation soon became proven theory. The corroborating evidence surfaced from the emerging sciences of *radiometric dating* and *paleomagnetism*.

RADIOMETRIC DATING OF DRIFTING PLATES

Charts of the ocean bed reveal topography of deep canyons, extensive plains, isolated peaks and elongated mountain ranges. Chief among its mountain ranges is the world's longest, the *Mid-Atlantic Ridge*, which extends 16 000 kilometres (close to half the world's circumference) through the Atlantic seabed from north to south before bending into the Indian Ocean south of Africa's Cape of Good Hope. Along its margins can be found many of the world's major crustal plates.

Studies of this ridge and ones similar to it elsewhere show them to be giant submerged crustal rock factories from which vast quantities of hot upwelling magma emerge to cool, solidify, and become virgin rock. Studies of the seabed elsewhere display opposing processes where an equal amount of crustal material is being warped, folded, or reheated and destroyed. These opposing processes of crustal renewal and destruction are directly linked to the behaviour of convection currents, hypothesized years ago, that slowly circulate in continuous giant loops below the crust.

They form powerful conveyor belts that transport plates, compressing and bending crust in places, and snapping and separating it in others. Clear evidence was found within the Mid-Atlantic Ridge and the rocks on either side of it.

We note that since the newest rock is formed at a ridge and then conveyed away, age of rock must therefore increase progressively in both directions, east and west, away from the ridge. This fact has been verified through a careful analysis of rock samples from the ocean bed using the natural rates of radioactive decay within certain elements present within the rock. These elements are in the form of *isotopes*.

Decay takes time. Decay converts one isotope (called the radioactive "*parent*") into another isotope (called its "*daughter*"). This decay occurs at a known rate specific to each parent.

Careful analysis of a rock containing a certain radioactive isotope reveals the relative amounts of parent and daughter isotopes present in the rock. In general, the age of rock increases with the ratio of daughter-to-parent isotope in rock samples. Knowing the rate of conversion of parent into daughter, a rough age of rock can be computed. Radiometric dating applied to the sea floor of the Atlantic reveals the following:

- Oceanic crust lacks a single common age;
- Seabed crust is younger and thinner than continental crust;
- Crustal age in the Atlantic increases in both directions away from the Atlantic's central ridge;
- Parts of the floor on either side of the ridge and equidistant from it are approximately the *same age*;
- In a human lifetime, the Atlantic widens approximately 4 metres, with a growth rate roughly equivalent to the growth rate of a fingernail; and,
- Similar events are occurring elsewhere along active plate boundaries.

If these conclusions are valid and the sea floor shows age of rock increasing away from its mid-line, then we would expect to find ocean bed sediments deeper where they overly the older parts of the sea floor; that is, those parts farthest from the ridge. This is, in fact, what has been discovered. One can safely assume that if all sea floor had a common age, accumulated sediments would have a more uniform thickness over the entire ocean basin.

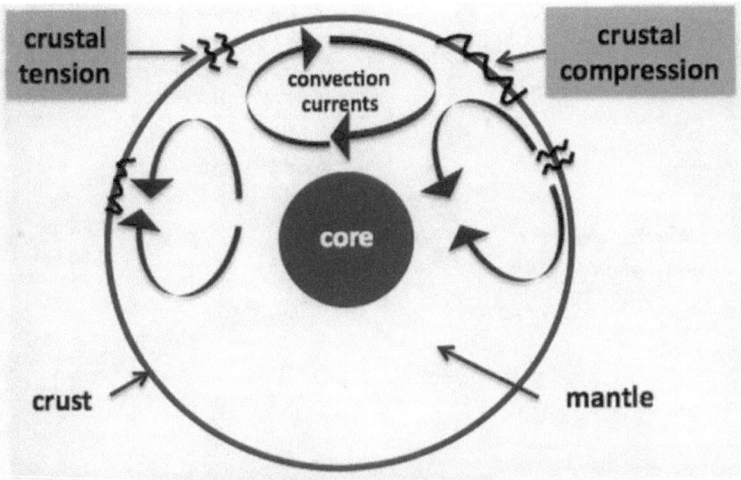

Forcing Mechanisms for Drifting Planetary Plates[80]

RADIOMETRIC DATING APPLIED TO PACIFIC ISLAND CHAINS

By far, the largest of the world's oceans is the Pacific. Islands within this liquid giant are numerous, with the greatest concentrations situated toward its west and southwest margins. Locations and patterns of these islands show that while some display random scattering through vast areas of ocean surface, many others belong to long and orderly chainlike groupings.

Whether isolated, randomly scattered in groups, or in some recognizable pattern, all islands point to processes that brought them into being. Among them all, it is the linear groupings of island chains in the Pacific Ocean that are most noteworthy since their orientations are roughly parallel to each other as well as to the axis of drift of the Pacific plate on which they are situated. Moreover, they are situated not proximal to, but far from plate boundaries where most geologic activity occurs.

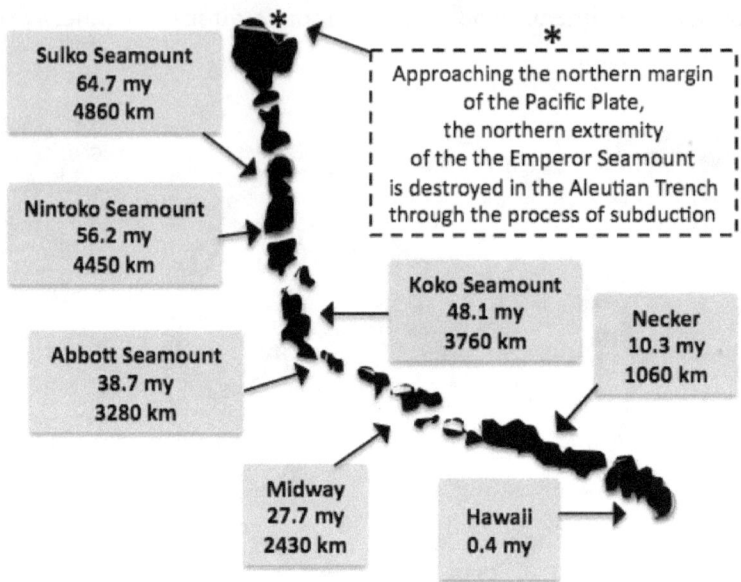

The Hawaiian Islands–Emperor Seamount Chain of the Pacific Ocean[81]

In terms of common island chain orientation, a northwest-to-southeast alignment is clearly evident in at least three long groupings that lie almost entirely between the tropics of Cancer and Capricorn: the chain containing the Gilbert and Marshall islands of Micronesia; the Tuamotu Archipelago and Line Island Chain in French Polynesia; and the Hawaiian Islands–Emperor Seamount Chain in the central and northwest Pacific. Let us focus our attention on the latter of the three.

Seamounts are submerged isolated volcanic mountains that rise from the ocean floor. The tops of the highest seamounts form oceanic islands. The Hawaiian Islands–Emperor Seamount chain is a series of underwater structures that became picturesque island atolls, shoals and reefs. This chain stretches 2 500 kilometres from Hawaii's Big Island northwest to Midway Island. Beyond Midway, the chain continues through another equally lengthy ridge, the Emperor Seamount, bending suddenly northward in the direction of the distant Aleutian Trench and the margin of the Pacific plate. The prominent elbow close to the Abbot Seamount represents a dramatic change in the direction of seafloor drift about 40 million years ago. At present, volcanoes are only active on Hawaii's Big

Island and on the volcanic infant, the still-submerged Loihi Seamount, to its southeast.

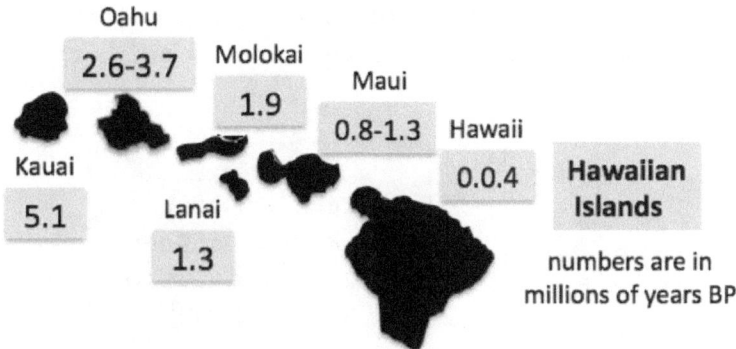

Ages of Hotspot Extrusions in the Hawaiian Island Chain[82]

Radiometric dating of the rocks at specific sites along this chain reveals progressive rock aging from the southeast toward the northwest, representing an age range of about 65 million years over a total distance of roughly 5 000 kilometres. In other words, for each additional eight-centimetre distance along the chain, age of rock increases toward the northwest by about one year.

What explains the chain and its orientation? Intrigued by active volcanism far from plate boundaries, geophysicists again relied on their original belief involving those localized sources of intense heat called *hotspots*.

To review, hotspots are relatively permanent and stationary regions found just under the crust. Because of their proximity to it, their heat is able to melt and disturb the overriding crust. When this happens, magma can extrude onto the crustal surface and harden. Long-term expulsion of magma results in substantial growth of conical structures on the seafloor that may, if extrusions are massive or sustained, rise above sea level to form volcanic islands.

Since the Pacific plate moves over a stationary hotspot, seamounts do not remain fixed over the source of magma that produced them, but drift with the plate toward the northwest. As a result, volcanic activity wanes on the newly created seamount as fresh portions of plate continue to drift into position to be melted over the hotspot. In this way, a sequence of volcanic structures are formed along a line parallel to the movement of the plate. Among the Hawaiian Islands, present activity centres on the Big Island where Kilauea, Mauna Loa, and the still-submerged Loihi Seamount contain the most active and youngest rock in the chain.

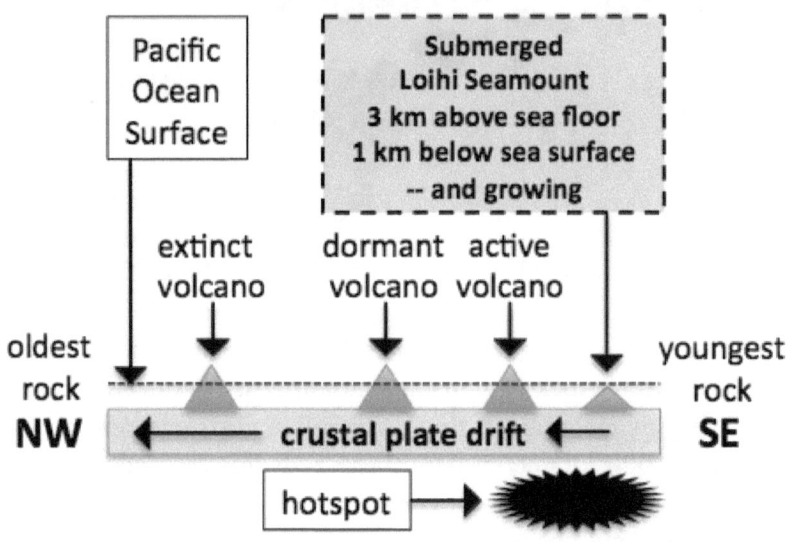

Progressive Deposition in the Hawaiian Island Chain[83]

Progressing in a northwesterly direction, the age of rock increases and volcanic activity wanes. Finally, at the extreme end of the Emperor Seamount, in the region of the Aleutian Islands, all evidence of past seamount formation beyond 65 million years is lost at the place of that seamount's demise, namely the subductive zone along the Aleutian Trench. Here, part of the Pacific plate plunges, melts, and disappears below the plate to the north. The extreme length of drift of the Pacific plate beyond the location of the hotspot now below Loihi Seamount means that a very long and orderly trail of accumulated and recoverable geologic history has been written, laid down, and preserved downstream from a visible display of similar structures presently in the process of formation.

SEA FLOOR SPREADING AND PALEOMAGNETISM

Of all the interesting toys in science class, two are among the most popular: the magnifying glass and the bar magnet. The magnifying glass can mysteriously bend and concentrate light. The bar magnet can draw certain metallic objects toward itself. With a magnifying glass, one is able to burn holes in wood and paper and examine tiny objects. With a bar magnet, one is able to induce magnetism in similar solids and make a second bar magnet.

Magnets exist in a variety of shapes and sizes. A compass needle made from steel is a miniature magnet; and our planet, with its magnetized core of iron, is a very large magnet. Whether small as a needle or large as a planet, a magnet is surrounded by an invisible three-dimensional magnetic field of influence, emerging from the magnet at one end to surround it before re-entering at its opposite end. For the Earth, opposing points called *magnetic poles*, distinct from its north and south *geographic* poles, are the only two places where the magnetic lines of force are vertical with respect to the Earth's surface.[84] This magnetic field, providing a thick wrapping over our entire planetary surface, serves as a valuable protective envelope of defense against the more harmful elements of solar radiation.

Compared with the Earth's geographic poles, whose locations wander slightly over time, magnetic poles migrate considerable distances in the same time period. At present, the South Magnetic Pole resides just off the coast of Antarctica, while its northern counterpart lies north of Canada's Arctic island archipelago. For the latter pole, its present location in the Arctic Ocean represents an 1100-kilometre migration northward since its initial discovery in 1831.

Unlike the North Geographic Pole, whose relatively permanent position directly under the North Star (Polaris) makes it relatively easy to locate, the North Magnetic Pole's more rapid wandering requires it to be rediscovered frequently. However, nature is merciful. Since magnetic needles follow the direction of lines of force, they naturally begin to orient themselves more vertically than horizontally when approaching the region where either magnetic pole penetrates the Earth's surface. Given that the magnetic field is oriented perpendicular to the Earth's surface at the spots where it enters and leaves the Earth's crust (see diagram), anyone searching for a magnetic pole need only determine where a compass needle reads a dip of ninety degrees to the horizontal. In places not over a magnetic pole, dip angle is less than ninety degrees. All dips that read zero degrees are located on the magnetic equator (not to be confused with the geographic equator).

Given its present course and rate of movement, the North Magnetic Pole, which has recently made its exit from Arctic Canada, is expected to locate somewhere in Russia if present drift rates and direction are maintained.

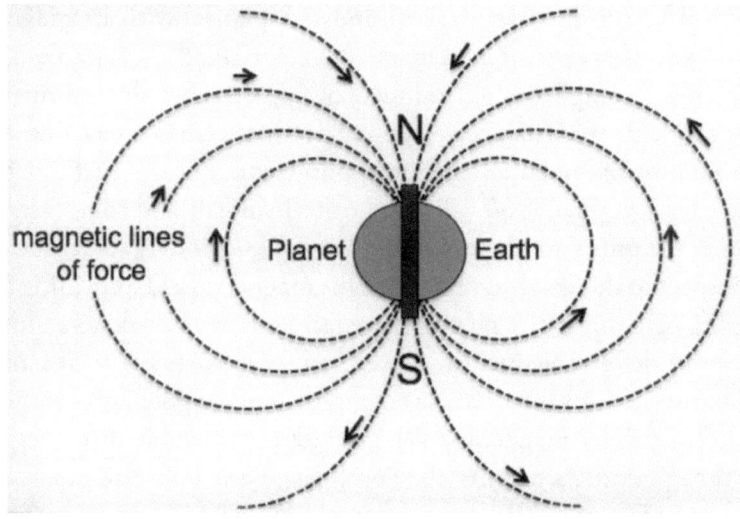

The Earth and its Magnetic Field: A Planetary Bar Magnet[85]

What is most confusing and poorly understood about magnetic poles, however, is not so much their wandering as their periodic and repeated reversals. They flip in orientation such that the North Magnetic Pole becomes the South Magnetic Pole, and vice versa. Studies of the reversal of the Earth's entire magnetic field reveal that it has undergone over 170 reversals over a period of some 75 million years. The flip-flopping of magnetic poles and field testifies to the apparent chaos that prevails in the complex motions of both the solid inner core and surrounding liquid outer core of the Earth.

What has made these flips so significant to geologists is the permanent and valuable record they leave behind in the symmetrical patterns contained within the spreading sea floor of the Atlantic Ocean. What is the pattern? How is it explained? And how does one explain its symmetry on either side of the Mid-Atlantic Ridge, or in other places where divergence occurs?

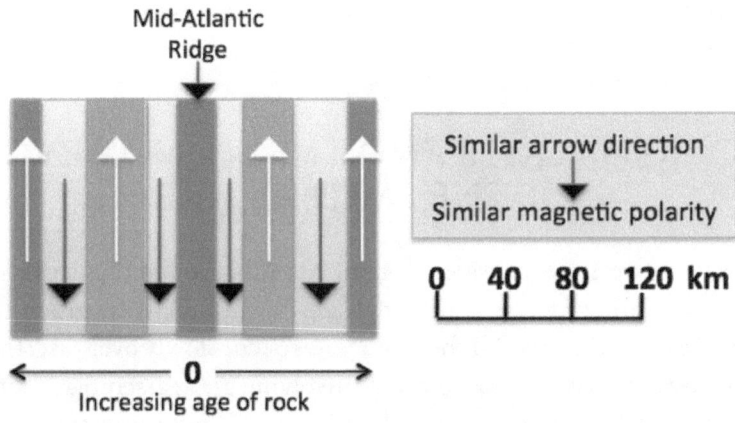

Flip-Flopping Magnetism in Sea Floor Rock Bands[86]

When iron-bearing minerals within rock are heated to very high temperatures, as happens within the Earth's interior, any magnetism they possess is destroyed. But when magma is extruded onto the Earth's surface and cooled, these same minerals, under the influence of the Earth's magnetic field, become re-magnetized and aligned parallel to the existing lines of force at the time of cooling. Once hardened, both alignment of lines of force and direction of magnetic polarity are frozen in the rock, regardless of any future change in rock orientation or location. Continued rock deposition during a period of similar alignment and polarity forms an identical pair of magnetically homogeneous strips on either side of the Mid-Atlantic Ridge.

When the Earth's magnetic field reverses and the north and south poles swap places, induced magnetism within newly cooled minerals continues, but with their direction of magnetic polarity reversed. Through millions of years, therefore, with repeated pole-reversals, a series of magnetic bands develop on the seabed. The bands are clearly recognizable by sensitive magnetic-detecting devices, called magnetometers, dragged over the sea floor. They present as a bilaterally symmetrical pattern with strips of rock of similar polarity on either side of the ridge. The widths of each strip express both the rate of sea floor spreading and the rate at which the magnetic field of the Earth undergoes reversal. And so, once again, in our orderly world, we observe natural patterns reflecting natural processes. And once again, the present shows itself a valuable key to unlocking the secrets of the past.

LOCKED PLATES AND THE PHENOMENON OF THE EARTHQUAKE

Up to now, we have considered giant assemblages of rock involved in various dynamic processes involving their formation, their growth, their drift and eventual decay. All these processes occur slowly over vast stretches of time. By contrast, among all events involving giant assemblages of rock, one occurs suddenly and with little warning. Though its effects cover a relatively small area, those effects can be devastating. The event is, of course, the earthquake.

In response to sub-crustal convection currents, plates are in continuous motion, coming in contact with each other along long and irregularly shaped fault lines. Movement past each other is not usually a smooth process. Plates often stick in localized places along fault lines. Since localized sticking does not interrupt whole plate movement, severe strain within rock is induced.

The length of time movement is impeded depends upon the ability of the rocks to sustain the strains of tension and compression at the contact points. If rock has little capacity to resist strain, it will readily crumble. Impeded movement of contact surfaces will be brief and the deformation of the rock in the region of the stuck surfaces will be minor. Subsequent readjustment of the rock to eliminate rock strain will be minimal, with possible tremors low in magnitude and often hardly recognizable. However, this is not the case with harder rock that can accommodate excessive strain.

Earthquake magnitude is described as the energy released when adjacent rock surfaces, unable to slide past each other unimpeded lock, bend, and eventually fail, finally snapping into new positions. The greatest sudden energy release is with plates whose rock surfaces are hard enough to resist vast amounts of strain over extended periods of time over long distances without failure. Since rock hardness is often non-uniform along any fault line, earthquakes do not occur at one time along an entire fault. Where failure does occur, the effects are often minor. But some are catastrophic, especially when the epicentre of the failure occurs close to the ground surface under heavily populated areas, or in ocean beds where massive water displacements can occur. Unfortunately, although rock strain can be known, neither timing nor magnitude of a rock failure or quake can as yet be accurately predicted.

Earthquake magnitudes have employed a measuring device called the Richter Scale. The scale, a series of numbers, is *logarithmic*. This means that energy release during a quake increases by a factor of 10 for each increase in magnitude number. Thus, during a 7.0 magnitude quake, 100 times more energy (10 x 10) is released than during a magnitude 5.0 quake. Similarly, a 9.0 quake releases 1 000 times the energy released by a magnitude 6.0 quake (10 x 10 x 10). While the logarithmic scale is useful in expressing quake magnitude, it is difficult to imagine differences in energy release between two earthquakes that differ merely by a single magnitude number.

Like many other events in nature, the frequencies of earthquake types are related to their magnitudes. The greater the quake magnitude, the lower the frequency of earthquakes of that magnitude. In other words, minor quakes occur far more frequently than major ones. Fortunately, earthquakes that exceed magnitude 8.0 are uncommon.[87] They happen when articulating surfaces containing fracture-resistant rock have been locked in a fixed position with minimal movement for an extended period of time. It appears probable that Richter Scale values of 9.0 may fall close to an upper limit of quake magnitude because rocks strained past this point may not have sufficient internal strength and elasticity to continue to bend and resist failure.

Monstrous quakes at this level of magnitude are known to have moved whole islands and have actually caused slight alterations in the period of Earth's rotation. Among the most violent quakes in recent history were the 9.5-magnitude Chilean earthquake in 1960, the 9.2-magnitude Anchorage Alaskan quake in 1964, and the 9.0 Japanese quake in 2011—all situated along the Pacific Rim. Within the region of the St. Lawrence and Ottawa Valley, quakes also occur, but fortunately for local residents, they have been low in magnitude.

ROCKS, MOUNTAINS AND EARTHQUAKES IN THE BIBLE LANDS

Our discussion so far in this chapter has emphasized the natural world's solid surface, with its patterns and its processes pouring forth a form of speech without words, expressing the handiwork of God (Ps 19:1). Let us consider these same elements in the world of Abraham, David, Jesus, and His disciples and examine how these features may illustrate something of the character, activities and sovereignty of God.

The Bible Lands of the Middle East are located in close proximity to the margins of three crustal plates: the massive African and Eurasian plates and the much smaller Arabian Plate. Residing in a complex confluence of active crustal fragments renders the region prone to periodic earthquakes, especially on the Palestinian border, and to the north in the Anatolian Peninsula (Turkey). Evidence of past volcanic activity is scattered along the western edge of the Arabian Plate in the vicinity of the Red Sea.

Many of the earthquakes that are recorded in scripture, and the shaking of the Earth that accompanied them, are associated with mighty acts of God. When God appeared to Moses and His people assembled at the foot of Mount Sinai, the whole mountain trembled violently (Exod 19:18).

At a place called *the Skull* at the Crucifixion, the ground shook in spasms seemingly bearing witness to the awesome event taking place a few metres above its surface and to its significance symbolized in the spectacular happenings of rocks splitting, tombs breaking open, a temple curtain ripping, and dead people emerging from tombs (Matt 27:51–52). A few days later at the Resurrection, another violent earthquake accompanied the removal of the stone at the entrance of Jesus' tomb (Matt 28:2). These events are considered antecedent to the prophesied eschatological shaking of the heavens and the Earth (Rev 16:18), when the act of what can *never again* be shaken will occur (Heb 12:26–28).

In general terms, the topography of the eastern Mediterranean, like the climate of the area, displays significant change over relatively short distances. Progressing inland from the sea, one encounters three distinct topographic strips aligned roughly north-to-south: a coastal plain that narrows toward the north; a more rugged region of rocks, hills and low mountains; and an extensive desert, particularly in the south. Dominating the centre of the middle region is a conspicuous landform, the Jordan Rift Valley.

This deep valley is the product of the collapse of a crustal block that has formed an elongated trench through the region. The trench, which begins in East Africa, runs northward 6 000 kilometres through the Red Sea, along the eastern border of the Sinai Peninsula, following the African–Arabian plate boundaries through Israel, Jordan, Lebanon, and Syria, all the way to Turkey. In it can be found the prominent chain of East African lakes as well as the Dead Sea, the Sea of Galilee, and the ancient city of Jericho.

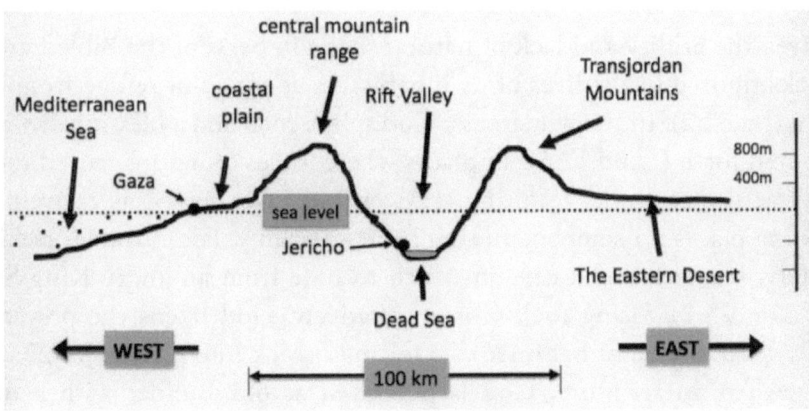

West-East Cross-section through the Bible Lands[88]

Rapid changes in climate and topography over relatively short distances within the Bible Lands mean that when natural imagery is employed for teaching purposes, there is a wide variety available to the teacher that is familiar to most of the learners. For example, the region's solid and exposed bedrock provides a familiar image to illustrate themes of steadfastness and permanency (Ps 62:7). By contrast, the shifting deposits of sands in Judaea, Sinai, the Eastern Desert, and the seashore, and the periodic earthquake provide readily recognized illustrations of instability (Matt 7:26), and elsewhere, of countless numbers (Heb 11:12).

IMAGERY INVOLVING ROCK, STONE AND MINERALS

For our purposes, let us clarify and simplify terms that are often used interchangeably. We shall refer to *rock* as large mixtures of minerals in consolidated form, *stone* as small fragments of rock, and *minerals* as distinct elements or compounds present in various concentrations in either rock or stone. All three terms refer to solid, inorganic, non-living entities of nature, the very repositories from which human life was first created (Gen 2:7) and to which all life returns after death (Job 34:15).

1. Rock

Given the aridity and lack of natural shade in parts of the Bible Lands, rocks figured in the lives of its inhabitants as places of refuge from the sun (Isa 32:2). In the wilderness, God split a rock and a blessing of water poured forth (Exod 17:6). In places where forces of nature caused rocks to fracture or erode, resulting crevices and caves served as convenient hiding places for someone fleeing from an enemy. For example, seeking safety, David found a cave in which to hide from an angry King Saul (1 Sam 24:2). Using rock more figuratively, God likens the power of His word to a giant hammer able to smash rock into pieces (Jer 23:29). Elsewhere in scripture, God is portrayed as our Builder with a rock quarry as His source of raw material (Isa 51:1). We are the work of His hands (Deut 32:18), bearing resemblance to Him just as quarried rock fragments bear resemblance to the parent formation from their source. God provides not only the materials that form us (Isa 51:1) but is also the reliable Foundation that supports us (Matt 16:18; Ps 40:2). He is identified as the Rock Himself (Deut 32:4) and the psalmist's rock and fortress (Ps 31:3).

Given that the hardness of rock is so well known, the meaning of the term *heart of stone* is clear to all. Clear also is how difficult it is for a heart of stone to be transformed into a heart of flesh (Ezek 11:19); we witness a process not humanly possible. Yet, according to scripture, to possess a heart of flesh is to be capable of knowing the One who created us (Jer 24:7).

Moreover, as individuals, we represent the building blocks by which God assembles a spiritual house (1 Pet 2:5). Here, in a figurative sense, we come to appreciate the distinction between *Rock* and *stone* and how God, as He did with dry bones (Ezek 37), is able to take something lifeless and cause it to live.

Comprising the people of God (stones) with God as its Head (Rock), both stones and Rock comprise His Church, the residence for both the Father and His children. It is described not only as a building but more intimately as an ever-expanding household in which believers, once foreigners and aliens, dwell with the One who, like an all-permeating Superglue, holds it all together (Eph 2:19–22). In Revelation, we are treated to a glimpse of our future home:

> *Look! God's dwelling place is now among the people,*
> *and he will dwell with them.*
> *They will be his people,*
> *and God himself will be with them and be their God.*
>
> *Revelation 21:3b*

2. Stone

Stone is an abundant substance that has a multitude of uses. Lifeless in itself, it is known both for its strength and durability. On tablets of stone on Mount Sinai, God inscribed His laws and commands for Moses and His people (Exod 24:12). Later, in Jeremiah, and by contrast, we read of God inscribing His laws not on hard stone tablets but rather more intimately in softened human hearts (Jer 31:33). In the New Testament, stones figured in the execution of the martyr Stephen at the hands of an angry mob (Acts 7:58).

A large stone, not sufficiently massive to prevent its mysterious removal, was used to seal the tomb of Jesus after His crucifixion and death (Matt 27:60). An association of a stone with permanency appears in the description of Christ as the "cornerstone." All stones in a construction find their place relative to the cornerstone. Scripture alludes to the critical and secure foundation (Christ) upon whom God's plan of salvation rests (Acts 4:11, 12).

Stones that are exceptionally rare and beautiful fall into the category of precious stones. In biblical times, precious stones and jewels were among the treasures that set the social standard for wealth and power. It is against this worldly standard that the Bible puts forth an altogether different image of what is truly precious: treasures, unlike stones, that are incorruptible (Heb 11:26).

It is here that we see how God's treatment of personal treasures differs from what is common among us. One involves extravagant giving; the other involves possessive hoarding. With parables about treasure buried in a field (Matt 13:44) and a pearl of great price (Matt 13:45, 46), the Bible likens the Kingdom of God to an attractive and unsurpassed treasure of infinitely greater value than those sought after within our natural world. It is God who possesses unparalleled wealth and power. Scripture portrays Him as abounding in riches and jewels.

The Heavenly City, the New Jerusalem of Revelation 21, is a city resplendent in beauty, with gates of pearl, and a wall whose foundations are "garnished with all manner of precious stones" (KJV), which include jasper and emerald. But God's most precious possessions are not among the inanimate objects contained within gates, streets or walls. Resident within the Holy City, and in this present world, are His most precious stones, namely His children, each a vessel of His mercy and honour.

Thus, to God, we are treasures of inestimable value, a fact made abundantly clear in the parable of the Prodigal Son in which the father, upon the return of the prodigal, lavishes his entire attention on his son's homecoming with grace, open arms, and celebration, but with no reference whatsoever to the inherited wealth his son had squandered.

> *A book of remembrance was written before him*
> *for them that feared the Lord, and that thought upon his name.*
> *And they shall be mine, saith the Lord of hosts,*
> *in that day when I make up my jewels.*
>
> Malachi 3:16, 17 (KJV)

It appears that the statement recorded in the Gospel of Luke that the heart is the residence of our most treasured possessions (Luke 12:34) is as true of God as it is of us.

3. Minerals

All rocks and stones contain minerals. Distributions of specific minerals vary in concentration from place to place. A mineral can exist in either elemental form (as in gold) or in compound form (as in salt). Some, like gold and iron, are classified as metallic minerals; others, like sulphur and potash, are non-metallic.

Human use of various minerals depends upon their physical, chemical or atomic properties. For example, since aluminum is strong yet light in weight, this metal finds extensive use in the aircraft industry. Use of sand to manufacture glass is possible because, when heated to a high temperature, some types of sand become transparent. Copper's use in electrical wiring is related to its excellent electrical conductivity as well as to the fact that it is a relatively cheap, malleable metal. The heat produced when certain isotopes of uranium split in a nuclear reactor renders this heavy element a highly efficient source of energy. And various special properties resident in certain minerals (iron, potassium, sodium, and magnesium, for example) are considered essential for human body health.

Depending upon issues of accessibility and profit, rocks containing a known mineral can come to be classified as *ores* of that mineral. An ore is a rock containing a useful mineral whose concentration deems its value when recovered significantly greater than its recovery cost. Through the years, it has been the level of technological development that has largely determined whether a useful mineral could be (1) physically accessed, (2) removed from an ore body, (3) processed, and (4) processed economically. During both Old and New Testament times, while technology allowed for extraction and processing of certain recoverable ores, and while primitive methods of refining, smelting, and alloy production were known, mineral production was limited. With the exception of iron and copper, few metallic ores were available for use.

Among the non-metallic minerals mentioned in the Bible, salt and sulphur (brimstone) are notable. Salt is abundant in easily accessible surface residue in hot, dry regions where excessive evaporation has caused dissolved minerals to precipitate out of solution. The result is a white salt deposit lethal to plant growth. Yellow sulphur is one of the few minerals that burns. Like salt, it possesses a lethal quality in its pungent fumes that are produced from combustion. While salt preserves, brimstone fumigates. Both are present in the southern region of the Salt Sea (Dead Sea) (Gen 19:24, 26), in land that is described as "a burning waste . . . nothing planted, nothing sprouting, no vegetation growing on it" (Deut 29:23).

Among the metallic minerals mentioned in the Bible are iron, gold, copper, and bronze. Acquiring various metals was either through local mining or through trade. Metals within the culture's many artifacts show a slow progression away from copper and bronze to iron as the society mastered the technology required to access and isolate various metals from parent materials and work with much harder materials.

The superior hardness of iron over bronze made it the preferred material in weaponry. Application of iron technology among the Israelites lagged behind their Philistine neighbours who, for military purposes, jealously guarded their secrets of iron processing (1 Sam 13:19) that somehow extracted iron from its parent rock.

Iron is one of the most abundant elements within the Earth's crust. But in ancient times, iron's high melting point made it difficult to extract from its parent material. Therefore, it was seldom used in its pure refined form. However, an important physical property of impure substances like poorly refined iron or petroleum is that each lacks a sharp melting point. Thus, when heated toward a liquid state, they behave somewhat like butter, softening before fully melting. Possessing relatively high malleability, iron is relatively easy to hammer into different shapes without causing the metal to fracture.

Due to its strength, iron is frequently employed as a standard by which the strength of other things is measured. For example, the limbs of

Behemoth, are likened to "bars of iron" (Job 40:18). Elsewhere, the sword of state, or sceptre, wielded by the strongest of the strong is described as "a rod of iron" (Ps 2:9).

Classified as one of the world's precious metals and esteemed the world over, gold combines very high value with relative scarcity. Though packaged in rock, gold is found in its native state as a reasonably pure metal. Average concentrations of gold in ores deemed recoverable are presently measured in ounces per tonne of excavated rock.

Chemically, gold is inert. Unlike aluminum that oxidizes, or iron that rusts, gold is resistant to forming compounds with other substances and therefore remains untarnished over time. Gold's physical properties include beauty, durability, and a malleability that allows it to maintain structural integrity, even when made into the thinnest of layers. When employed as a veneer on surfaces, gold can cover a relatively large surface when made wafer-thin. In ancient times, gold was frequently used in the manufacturing of fine jewellery and various artifacts for tabernacles and temples.

If iron represents a standard against which strength can be measured, gold is a standard against which *value* can be measured. But despite its virtually universal attractiveness, scripture teaches that its value is surpassed by other precious things; e.g., by wisdom (Job 28:15) or by God's law (Ps 19:10).

Gold is associated with the wealthy and powerful. It was one of the three gifts presented by Wise Men to a newborn King (Matt 2:11). A reference to the magnitude of King Solomon's riches describes gold as being as common as stones in the city of Jerusalem (2 Chron 1:15). Surpassing this expression of wealth is John's vision of the New Jerusalem, "a city of pure gold, as pure as glass" (Rev 21:18). Yet we are told that no amount of gold is sufficient to purchase human redemption:

> *For you know it was not with perishable things*
> *such as silver or gold*
> *that you were redeemed from the empty way of life*
> *handed down to you from your ancestors,*
> *but with the precious blood of Christ,*
> *a lamb without blemish or defect.*
>
> **1 Peter 1:18, 19**

Scriptural statements, as in the passage above, allude to a common human act called *misprizing*. Misprizing is the failure to assign something its proper value, either by assigning something too high a value or too little. At the heart of misprizing is the human tendency to choose, as did Judas, the wrong treasure. Within the pages of scripture, there are many examples pointing to the serious consequences of misprizing. The apostle Peter, in his thrice-denial of Jesus, chose personal security over loyalty to his Lord (Matt 26:69–74). Ananias and Sapphira selected money over honesty (Acts 5:1–11). A hungry Esau, acting on impulse, exchanged his inheritance for the short-term gain of a bowl of lentils and a piece of bread (Gen 25:29–34).

A story found in the Book of Daniel tells of three men who were thrown into a fiery furnace by King Nebuchadnezzar as punishment for disobeying a royal command to bow and worship the golden image he had made (Dan 3). The image, visually attractive and clearly visible to all, had precise physical dimensions: twenty-seven metres high by 3 metres wide. It stood in a prominent location on the Plain of Dura. Everyone knew where to find it. One could safely say the image was fully known and fully predictable, with no surprises, with characteristics common to gods we ourselves fabricate.

> *Do people make their own gods?*
> *Yes, but they are not gods!*
>
> *Jeremiah 16:20*

However, the image built by Nebuchadnezzar possessed neither breath nor speech (Hab 2:18, 19). It looked nice but did nothing. So long as its value lay merely in something concrete, something of material worth, something that would provoke envy in others, something of aesthetic value, its existence could be considered rather benign. If, on the other hand, it was an object to be worshipped, that was a more serious matter (Ps 115:1–8).

Though attractive, the image was impotent. Its greatness was inferior, even to the one who made it. There was nothing more to be known than its chemistry, its dimensions and its location. Within it dwelt no mystery. It could not evoke enduring human wonder.

The magnitude of the king's folly and the utter uselessness of the dumb golden idol were only realized when the misprized ultimate treasure appeared in the mysterious *fourth person* who came alongside the three men in the heat and flames of the furnace. Only then, when seen alongside this treasure, was the fabricated image seen as worthless. Only then did the treasure reveal His true greatness: by being to the captives both a Comforter alongside them in their miserable ordeal, and ultimately a Deliverer who in the end led them out of it to safety.

> *The books or the music in which we thought the beauty was located will betray us if we trust to them; it was not in them, it only came through them, and what came through them was longing. These things—the beauty, the memory of our own past—are good images of what we really desire; but if they are mistaken for the thing itself they turn into dumb idols, breaking the hearts of their worshippers. For they are not the thing itself; they are only the scent of a flower we have not found, the echo of a tune we have not heard, news from a country we have never yet visited.*
>
> *C. S. Lewis*[89]

6

WILDERNESS

*Wilderness puts us in our place.
It reminds us that our plans are small
and somewhat absurd.*

Preface to **Off the Beaten Path: Stories of Place**[90]

Twin Otter Resupply to a Remote Ice Island Research Station,
Arctic Ocean, July 1988[91]
(JES)

*The pressure ridges
massive and threatening,
testified
to the overwhelming nature
of the forces that were at work.
Huge blocks of ice, weighing many tons,
were lifted into the air and tossed aside
as other masses rose beneath them.
We were helpless intruders in a strange world,
our lives dependent upon
the play of grim elementary forces
that made a mock of our puny efforts.*

Sir Ernest Shackleton[92]

*The LORD your God
has blessed you
in all the work of your hands.
He has watched over your journey
through this vast wilderness.
These forty years
the LORD your God has been with you,
and you have not lacked anything.*

Deuteronomy 2:7

As one of five circumpolar nations, Canada has its share of lands and waterways classified as *Arctic*. Beginning in the south at the treeline, this region of tundra is vast in total area, sparse in human population, rich in both land and marine life, and awesome in natural beauty. In its northern half, Arctic mainland gives way to one of Earth's largest archipelagos, where three of the world's ten largest islands reside. With growing seasons measured in weeks, and where frost days occasionally collect even in July, the Arctic represents the vestigial remains of a land still emerging from the last ice age.

Beginning in the mid-80s, circumstances permitted me multiple separate forays into the archipelago portion of this vast wilderness. There, with the aid of choppers, icebreakers, Twin Otter aircraft, and snowmobiles, I travelled to remote calving sites for icebergs, scattered Inuit settlements, and remote weather stations. I descended an Arctic lead/zinc mine residing in permafrost, accompanied ice reconnaissance flights over the more navigable waters, and sailed through portions of the Northwest Passage. Among my most memorable experiences of wilderness, two are especially noteworthy.

In the summer of 1987, I had the good fortune to spend a few weeks at the Inuit settlement, weather station, and airport at Resolute Bay on Cornwallis Island. While there, a helicopter pilot doing logistical support for Arctic researchers invited me to accompany him on a flight to a few nearby islands. It was late July, and except for isolated snow patches where deep drifting had occurred, much of the snow cover on land surfaces had disappeared. In surrounding channels, sea ice that for most months fills these northern waterways was rapidly melting and countless puddles were scattered over ice surfaces that remained. In some places, linear ice fractures had opened to expose a dark sea surface. On a single ice slab, two lethargic walruses enjoying the noon sunshine appeared somewhat annoyed as our noisy machine passed 100 metres above their quiet resting place.

Our first destination was a remote sand bar on a river bend on Bathurst Island. The pilot brought the helicopter down close to piles of research instruments and camping equipment that were to be transferred to a nearby base camp. Realizing that the shuttle would significantly increase the chopper's weight and use up all available storage space, he informed me that the transfer could not be made with me onboard. I was to be left behind and be picked up a few hours later. Apprehension must have been written all over my face as the pilot completed the equipment transfer and made ready his departure. For he reached for a large leather holster, threw it to the ground beside me and shouted, "It's a .357 Magnum. Just in case!" Just in case? My eyes followed the aircraft as it flew low, down the meandering river valley. Then at a sharp bend in the river, it disappeared behind some hills. I strained my ears to hear what my eyes could no longer see. But soon, all was silent.

I glanced about me. The land was barren, with no people, no trees, apparently no animals or irritating insects, just the sun shining weakly in a cloudless sky, refusing at this latitude and at this time of year to set. I checked out the .357 Magnum lying on the ground, recalling the ominous name of the site where I had been deposited: *Polar Bear Pass!* It was my first experience of being totally alone in an isolated expansive wilderness. I picked up the holster then sat down against the vertical face of a large boulder to eat a granola bar, unsure of what I'd do if a polar bear visited the area to check out the visitor.

A second memorable experience of wilderness occurred a year later at a site many kilometres north of Polar Bear Pass. This time, I was a passenger onboard a Twin Otter to a remote research camp on a small drifting ice island in the Arctic Ocean some 600 nautical miles from the geographic North Pole. The island, originating from the terminus of a large ice shelf off northern Ellesmere Island, had entered the ocean's main circulatory system and was moving slowly westward within that ocean's dominant current. At the time, it was hoped the island would trace a path similar to other ice islands and complete a giant clockwise loop about the pole, repeating this trek over and over until it melted or broke apart, or until wind or current expelled it from that ocean and into warmer, more southerly waters. As it turned out, forces of wind and current were to soon nudge the island away from its predicted path and into the narrow channels of Canada's Queen Elizabeth Islands. There, it eventually fractured, melted, and quickly disappeared.

For the first hour, as the plane traversed a series of islands, I was able to follow its progress by identifying on my flight chart the corresponding shapes of islands below me. I was hoping that clear visibility would accompany us all the way to our destination. But alas, as the plane cleared the archipelago and droned along into uninterrupted ocean, cloudless skies gradually gave way to a low deck of stratus cloud. Slowly, it formed into a continuous layer of undifferentiated white below the plane that totally obscured the ocean/sea ice surface.

As the Twin Otter descended through this undercast, I wondered how the pilot, trusting his instruments, would ever find a small tabular ice island amid the densely packed assemblage of sea ice fragments. There were no identifiable landmarks and no local navigational beacons to direct us. I felt a distinct uneasiness about whether ceiling and visibility conditions over the ice island would permit a landing. I noticed that cockpit chatter had ceased. The horizon line before us had vanished.

Then suddenly, just when I was fearful that we had violated landing rules for ceiling and visibility, we broke through the cloud. To my amazement, our destination was directly below us: *Hobson's Choice*, a flat-topped ice island that formed a not-too-conspicuous topographic anomaly within its sea ice surroundings. Propelled by currents and wind, this 40-metrethick ice cube had become a mobile base and platform for important Arctic marine studies used alternately by both Canadian and Russian researchers. During its residency in Canadian waters, Canadian scientists occupied it. Approaching Russian waters, the Canadians would hop off and the Russians would take their turn.

After a few low-level passes over the island to locate a suitable landing strip amid huts, equipment and scattered melt ponds, our skis finally touched down on a bumpy ice and snow "runway." I recall thinking that if ever a landing should prompt wild and sustained applause for the pilot and his landing gear, this was one such landing. Emerging from the plane and standing in wet snow, I was somewhat shocked at the nature of our runway. It was actually a narrow, elongated rotting ice ridge. The ridge separated two parallel troughs, which were part of a series of similar linear depressions scattered over the ice island's corrugated surface that were filling with meltwater during the brief Arctic summer. Like many alpine lakes in the Canadian Rockies, all ponds were turquoise, a beautiful sight amid the monochromatic grey surroundings.

A light drizzle was falling. The air was still; the site was gloomy. Except for equipment scattered about and the faint sounds of distant machinery, this remote place seemed abandoned. As we awaited transport to the base camp, the haze through which we had descended dropped to sea level, eliminating all shadow and robbing us of those valuable clues that distinguish topographic rises from surface depressions. Within minutes, the horizon that had momentarily reappeared vanished again, and with it, that critical line of demarcation that separates sky and sea surface. Both had merged into one. Had our arrival been delayed mere minutes, a landing that day would have been impossible. Such are the unpredictable windows of opportunity afforded the traveller by the normally capricious Arctic weather patterns.

Eventually, two snowmobiles appeared and we were transported by towed toboggans back to base camp, retracing their outbound track that meandered around melt ponds and over the island's slightly elevated surfaces. Finally arriving near dinnertime at a small wooden shack (an oasis in the middle of this remote wilderness), we were treated to a delicious hot chicken dinner.

I was grateful for the warmth of both meal and hut since my clothing had become damp during the rather lengthy toboggan ride and I suspected I had become slightly hypothermic. The meal demonstrated a strange characteristic often experienced in places called wilderness: while they may frighten us and at times even threaten our well-being, in some strange way, they can also richly nourish.

Wilderness! Such places can be oppressively hot or bitterly cold. Most present as expansive places: as rainforest in Brazil; hot desert in North Africa; rugged mountain landscape in Nepal; immense ice sheets in the Antarctic and Greenland; seemingly endless regions in the world's oceans; and tundra in Canada's north. The name conjures up images of *wild*ness and the untamed, the antithesis of civilization. Charles Lindbergh experienced atmospheric wilderness during his 33-hour solo flight across the Atlantic. Roald Amundsen experienced a dazzling white wilderness with four companions in the uncharted desolation of Antarctica's Ross Barrier and Polar Plateau. And Apollo astronauts experienced a blackened sky, uninterrupted sunshine, and near-perfect vacuum wilderness on their journey to and from the moon.

For most of us, however, experiences of wilderness are vicarious, from a distance, through the window of a car or plane, sitting in a theatre with images flashing across a screen, or through imagination aided by word descriptions or pictures in books and magazines. At times, places we call wilderness arouse feelings of sentimentality and a certain degree of nostalgia, especially when we observe them from afar and contemplate the possibility of their eventual disappearance. We are attracted to their vastness, beauty, and mystery. We write about them. They capture the interest of the artist, the photographer, and the author. We imagine them as places of refuge, places yet to be scarred by the various marks of human habitation, a form of tonic for the human spirit.

To be within a wilderness is to experience a spatial isolation that provides our lives with a sense of scale and an appreciation of our context within a reality far greater than ourselves. In many instances, those who would not identify themselves as overly religious speak of their foray into a wilderness as a spiritual experience.

Yet not all responses to wilderness places are positive ones. Our approach to wilderness is with both respect and ambivalence. Anthropomorphizing such places, we frequently describe them as *cruel, indifferent,* and *unforgiving*. Though often immensely attractive and seductive in their beauty, they are also unwelcoming. They are places where vulnerability and loneliness are common experiences. Though at times one may refer to a busy central urban core as a form of wilderness, most mental images of wilderness display them as unoccupied, uncultivated, and desolate. They arouse in us feelings of abandonment, emptiness, and deprivation in which we are alone.

To most of us, wilderness represents a place to visit, not a place in which to settle and call *home*. We perceive that the hazards in wilderness places constitute elevated risk to personal safety and well-being. Visitors to high latitude wilderness confront the threat of hypothermia as rates of heat loss from the body can very easily exceed the body's rate of heat production. By contrast, those visitors to hot deserts face high sun exposure, punishing surface temperatures with little available shade, and body dehydration that can quickly render them *hyper*-thermic.

Within the rarefied atmosphere present in very high-altitude wilderness, in addition to the threats from bitterly cold temperatures, oxygen concentrations are at levels that readily induce conditions of hypoxia and potentially lethal cerebral or pulmonary edema. Of course, though often described like this, nature's behaviour is neither punishing nor unkind. Neither is it cruel, indifferent, or unforgiving. It is merely behaving itself, acting in accordance with natural laws that always function with remarkable reliability, both within wilderness and elsewhere.

While most forays into wilderness are planned and intentional, some are foisted upon us suddenly and by accident, leaving us unprepared and in a place we don't want to be. One of the most unbelievable experiences of an unplanned and prolonged exposure to wilderness occurred in the lives of Captain George Tyson and his party of eighteen people (men and women, adults and children, Americans and Inuit) who suddenly found themselves separated from their ship and marooned on a deteriorating ice floe in cold Arctic waters off the northwest coast of Greenland. They represented part of the Polaris Expedition to the North Pole that had been aborted soon after the mysterious death of their commander, Charles Francis Hall.

For an incredible 197 days, beginning in October 1872 and continuing through the entire winter season during which sunlight was either in daily short supply or entirely non-existent, these desperate individuals drifted southward past Baffin Island with wind and current in *Iceberg Alley* amid towering bergs and sea ice fragments. In constant exposure to bitter cold, they faced uncertainty, starvation, debilitating hypothermia, and death. About 100 days into their ordeal, Tyson wrote:

> *I have not been able to change [my clothing] for nearly three months . . . It is astonishing what men can endure . . . We survive through God's mercy and Joe's ability as a hunter . . . The wonder is not that one is sick, but that any are well . . . For the last six or eight days we have had something to lunch on—either skin or frozen entrails; today we have neither; and now we realize the value of those unsavory morsels, and feel the want of them more and more every hour. So do the most unappreciated "blessings brighten as they take their flight."* [93]

On more than one occasion, they scrambled from floe to floe as their rotting and fracturing ice platforms, responding to the destructive effects of warming temperatures and heavy seas, became too frail to occupy. Finally, on the last day of April 1873, having survived on food supplied by the waters surrounding them and made available through the hunting skills of Joe and the other Inuit, they were spotted and rescued by an astonished crew of a Newfoundland steamer off coastal Labrador. Mercifully and miraculously, all nineteen people escaped death.

A voyage that for 197 days in a cold marine wilderness appeared destined for certain disaster and death had ended instead in triumph and a renewed appreciation of life. What emerged from this seven-month 2400-kilometre drift were personal accounts that covered the spectrum of responses one would expect of those facing imminent death. Most noteworthy: self-sacrifice, when and where there was so little to share; determination to endure in the face of uncertainty and extreme adversity; and cooperation among people who, before the ordeal began, were strangers. Not seldom do noble acts of sacrifice and kindness emerge from those in tribulation and despair and great uncertainty.

While loss was the common element in their pathetic lives, it was clear that losses of security, comfort, shelter, and convenience were not identified as the most critical ingredients necessary to safeguard their future. Rather, the critical ingredient was *hope*. Loss of security and comfort could be endured, though at great sacrifice. Loss of hope could not. Hope seemed to emerge from some deep well within certain individuals, and the catalyst that unwrapped and exposed it was the situation of extreme personal deprivation.

Clearly, theirs was not a false hope. It blossomed when safety and predictability, convenience, comfort and ease had been stripped from lives, nudging the human mind in its internal wilderness to discover hitherto unappreciated blessings in an external wilderness that were very real, to employ hitherto untapped reserves of strength, and to incline itself toward positive future outcomes and away from debilitating despair. On the topic of hope, while still within circumstances of severe deprivation, Tyson comments:

> **Even now the storm rages without, while fierce hunger rages within; and though sometimes overcome with sad thoughts, as I think of family, children and friends at home, I am not without hope.**

> *God, in creating man, gave him [audacious] hope. What a blessing! Without that we should long since have ceased to make any effort to sustain life.*
>
> *If our life was to be always like these last months, it would not be worth struggling for; but I seem to have a premonition, though it looks so dark just now, that we shall weather it yet. Hope whispers, "You will see your home again."* [94]

In 2010, our world witnessed an ordeal similar to that of Tyson involving the search for, and rescue of thirty-three men trapped for sixty-nine days within a collapsed corridor of a Chilean mine. As with Tyson's party, the mine crew had been thrust into a wilderness experience both suddenly and through accident.

The site was a cavity 700 metres below the surface of South America's dry Atacama Desert. Knowledge that someone had survived the collapse, in fact, that *all* miners had survived, was not confirmed for some two weeks after the accident. However, when confirmation did come, a tide of euphoria swept through the community among those who, while maintaining hope against mounting odds, had kept long and faithful vigil.

Accurate directional drilling completed ahead of schedule succeeded in opening up a narrow cylindrical passageway to the miners. Implementation of the company's brilliantly crafted rescue plan was near flawless. With cameras present in the mine cavity, shaft, and at the surface, the world watched as one by one, and in a predetermined order, miners rode their specially designed shoulder-width tubular cage for a 15-minute ride upwards out of darkness and danger into light, freedom, safety, and the arms of loved ones.

As each emerged from the vehicle, the ecstatic crowd erupted in singing and spontaneous applause. Surprise mixed with joy as surface crew and family members saw the high spirits and healthy appearances of each survivor. Words such as *extraordinary, miraculous,* and *unbelievable* issued from the lips of spectators as many recalled the 1972 tragedy involving a plane crash in the frigid high-altitude wilderness of the Andes Mountains. Known as *El Milagro de los Andes*, sixteen of 45 passengers somehow had survived ten weeks before rescue, an ordeal whose length was coincidentally similar to that endured by the Chilean miners.

But now, with all miners plucked from a hot dark dungeon and safely on the surface, an emotional and proud Chilean president with his wife warmly greeted and embraced each man. Praising the success of the rescue team, acknowledging the tenacity and spirit of the miners, and observing that something most profound had transpired in the midst of the Chilean people, his comments fixed on the transforming power of a human drama that had thrilled and inspired a nation because life had emerged from a dark tomb.

One of the jubilant miners expressed the sense that a place of deprivation and growing despair had produced a strange awakening within them and their community. His sense was that there was one more than thirtythree persons present in their enclosed subsurface wilderness, a comment reminiscent of the biblical story of the three men in the fiery furnace (Dan 3). Another miner spoke of his experience as a taste of both heaven and hell. Resident in the minds of many was another incident long ago when one Life at the Resurrection emerged from a dark tomb.

In wilderness experiences such as those of Tyson's party adrift on a deteriorating ice floe, and the Chilean miners trapped within a dark underground cavity, there often occurs a distillation of human values in which mere survival counts more than bodily comfort and convenience. Moreover, when one is faced with uncertainty and the imminent threat of death, there emerges a sense of the existence of forces more powerful than those threatening our very existence.

To many, this represents vain hope in the face of death; a desperate attempt, when all else has failed, to grasp something that isn't really there. To others, this represents a reality that has always been there, but somehow fades in their fields of vision during times when life is more manageable and futures are more predictable. Wilderness experiences, specifically those that threaten survival, have a strange ability to reset our minds to reassess and frequently modify personal values and to believe audacious thoughts.

WILDERNESS IN THE BIBLE LANDS

As mentioned previously, the physical environments of the Earth are such that in some regions, a landscape can stretch homogeneously for many hundreds of kilometres with little visible change. Such is the case with the giant Antarctic plateau, the dense forests of Amazonia, and the rugged alpine region of the Himalayas. Such sameness over long distances contrasts sharply with those represented by the Bible Lands, where landscapes change rapidly over relatively short distances. Thus, a variety of physical landscapes (fertile valleys, flat coastal plains, rugged hills, isolated mountains, and desert wilderness) can be present almost within walking distance of each other and in a single small country.

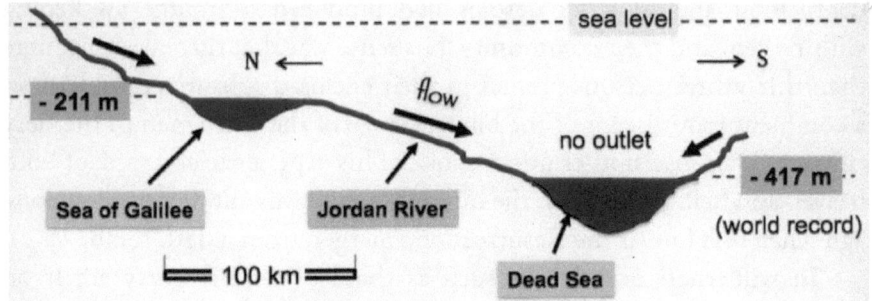

Cross-Section: The Jordan River Valley[95]

Such variety in surface features owes its land structure to factors that are geological and its surface complexion to a host of factors that are atmospheric. With regard to the former, proximity to the boundaries between three major crustal plates has exposed the region to major surface modifications, of which the Jordan River Valley is a principal example.

With regard to the latter factor, the region resides in a climatological transition zone within which conditions of moderate-to-high annual moisture change to moderate-to-severe aridity over relatively short distances. This is most evident as one traverses the region, not only from the Mediterranean shores eastward, but more significantly, from north to south from Galilee to Judaea. Thus, the most prominent and extensive wilderness within the Bible Lands is its southern desert region found in Judaea, the Negev and in the vicinity of the Dead Sea. These areas, residing on the periphery of the Saudi Arabian Desert to the southeast and giant Saharan Desert to the southwest abound in rock and sand, with sparse vegetation cover.

Israel's southern aridity is due to low rates of precipitation combined with relatively high rates of potential evaporation. Such conditions are adverse for maintaining permanent surface water. This is clearly evident in the region's scarcity of lakes and rivers. Moreover, with more water being withdrawn through evaporation than delivered through precipitation and surface stream inflow from other areas, and with significant volumes of water being diverted for irrigation and human consumption, a gradual decline in water levels over the centuries has made outflow from the Jordan River Valley to the sea and to the ocean impossible.

In the Dead Sea region, water levels have declined to well below sea level, exposing much of the deep trench in which this sea resides. Since water moderates temperatures, its scarcity anywhere tends to enhance temperature extremes. Moreover, warm temperatures accelerate evaporative processes and, with loss of water, salt concentrations within remaining water rise well above those found in oceans.

THE WILDERNESS IMAGE IN SCRIPTURE

With such a significant percentage of Bible Lands within arid and semiarid conditions, one would expect to find references to desert and mountain wilderness in the Bible. In these references, the wilderness represents a place of both negative and positive experiences. Desert wilderness is pictured as a place of danger (Deut 8:15), with venomous snakes and scorpions, creatures whose nocturnal nature renders them both frightening and unpredictable. It represents a place of discomfort, with unusually large temperature swings between day and night and with little provision in the way of food, drink, or protection from the desiccating influences of the sun. In addition, it is considered a place of demonic powers, the very site into which the Spirit led Jesus to be tempted by the devil (Matt 4:1–10).

But strangely, it is within the wilderness, the place of danger, discomfort, deprivation, demons, and death, where people had experiences of a different kind. For David, it was a place of refuge from King Saul (1 Sam 23–26). For Elijah, it was a place of safety from Jezebel, King Ahab's wife (1 Kgs 19:4) and his most fearsome enemy. For Jesus, it was an occasional sought-after place of solitude for meditation and communion with His Father. Moreover, it represented a rich environment from which to draw clear and valuable illustrations for His teachings.

Probably the best example of wilderness as a place of refuge is contained in the story of the Exodus of God's people from Egyptian bondage. But to a people who had been delivered from a place of bondage and instructed to move to a new place, a place flowing with milk and honey (Exod 3:8), it must have seemed to many, given their most unusual period of wandering, that their promised land of *"milk and honey"* lay behind them in Egypt and not ahead of them in Canaan.

Places of desolation are often described as *God-forsaken.* Yet, while ease and prosperity may have departed these places, it is the testimony of many that God does not. In fact, wilderness represents a principal venue in which many manifestations of God occurred. Here people beheld God's glory, namely the essence of His being (Num 14:22), and received His special instructions.

It was in the mountain wilderness of Horeb (Sinai) where God delivered the Ten Commandments to His people through Moses (Exod 19–20). It was in the desert where the Word of God came to John the Baptist (Luke 3:2). It was in an unnamed mountain wilderness where Peter, James, and John witnessed the glory of God when, for but a brief moment, the windows of heaven opened to reveal a radiant and transfigured Christ (Matt 17; Mark 9; Luke 9). And after His 40 days of temptation in a wilderness, Jesus found the comfort of a host of God's angels (Matt 4:11).

Accompanied, watched over, and provided for in their 40-year sojourn in the wilderness, the people of God were described as lacking nothing (Deut 2:7). In the absence of an adequate food supply, provision came from the hand of God in the form of a mysterious substance called manna (Exod 16). When water was lacking, God supplied it from a rock (Exod 17). The thought of lacking nothing appears in the first verse of the most popular psalm (Ps 23 BCP) that links ultimate human satisfaction with none other than the guardianship afforded by and the abiding presence of the ultimate Shepherd.

The presence in our world of physical wildernesses has its parallel in an inner wilderness that appears within the human spirit. Experiences within inner wilderness involve attitudes of abandonment, emptiness, and a paralysis of the will, with feelings that one is in a deep dark hole from which there is little hope of rescue or escape. Such experiences, found among even the healthiest of individuals and often at the most unexpected times and places, appear unavoidable. For some, feelings like these continue for extended periods, even to the point of suicidal death. The good news is God's capacity and desire to convert dry ground into verdant pasture (Ps 107:4–6), into fruitful fields (Isa 32:15), and into flowing springs of water (Ps 107:35). On this hopeful thought, the Bible speaks volumes:

- Scholars tell us that the word *wilderness* (from the Hebrew word *midbar*) contains the same root as that found in the word for *speech*. How wondrous is the thought that wilderness is a place of speech and that a recognizable and benevolent Voice can be heard in a dry and barren land, that it is God's Voice. How equally wondrous is the thought that the Voice heard by Elijah was a whisper heard over noises of mighty winds, quakes, and fire (1 Kgs 19:11–12).
- A quiet Voice when alone in a dark place may be solely for one's comfort. It may also be for instruction. This is encouraging since some "verdant pastures" can only be accessed when one is mentally within a dark place.
- While wilderness may be our present place of residence, God never intended it to be our permanent dwelling. Our rightful place is within an incomparable dwelling of abundance and companionship, of reciprocal and intimate residency, namely *God in us*, and *us in Him* (Rev 21:3).
- While wilderness is not our permanent dwelling, the reality is that some people's residency within a personal wilderness involving prolonged suffering may not end before death (Heb 11:36–40). In light of the goodness we ascribe to a loving God, this reality is puzzling. It seems that on this issue, at present, we are required to live faithfully in mystery.
- Prophetic scriptural teachings provide us with periodic glimpses of what will eventually be. Words describing the future place of wilderness in God's overall plan reveal it as devoid of all vestiges of negative imagery. The prophet Isaiah, in chapter 35,

envisions the wilderness itself as participating fully in rejoicing even with joy and singing. Within the new heaven and new Earth, wilderness, it seems, *will* be present. However, it will be a transformed wilderness. And wilderness as we presently know it shall be no more. Any attempt to describe this transformation will ultimately prove inadequate since God's promised blessings are immeasurably more than anything we may ask for or imagine (Eph 3:20).

> *The desert and the parched land will be glad;*
> *the wilderness will rejoice and blossom.*
> *Like the crocus, it will burst into bloom;*
> *it will rejoice greatly and shout for joy. (1, 2)*
> *Water will gush forth in the wilderness*
> *and streams in the desert.*
> *The burning sand will become a pool,*
> *the thirsty ground bubbling springs.*
> *In the haunts where jackals once lay,*
> *grass and reeds and papyrus will grow. (6b, 7)*
> *No lion will be there, nor any ravenous beast;*
> *they will not be found there.*
> *But only the redeemed will walk there, (9)*
>
> *Isaiah 35*

7
EARTH'S WATER AND ATMOSPHERE

... and the Spirit of God was hovering over the waters.

Genesis 1:2b

**Satellite Photo of Hurricane Dorian approaching Florida
Late Summer, 2019 (NOAA)**[96]

*Every day,
every passing second,
water is on the move.
The rivers flow,
the oceans perform their slow and elegant gyrations,
the clouds congeal and weep.
Each 3100 years,
a volume of water equivalent to all the oceans
passes through the atmosphere,
carried there [and naturally distilled] by evaporation
and removed by precipitation.
Yet
only a thousandth of 1 percent
of the planet's total water
resides in the atmosphere at any moment,
enough to deposit just one inch of rain
if it all fell uniformly
throughout the world.*

Philip Ball[97]

Among nature's many recipes, one appears to be both widely known and simple. It has only two ingredients: hydrogen and oxygen. When two atoms of hydrogen are combined with one atom of oxygen in definite proportions by weight, the resulting product is the virtually ubiquitous substance called water, chemical formula H2O, by far the most abundant liquid in existence on our planet. Given the pressures and temperature ranges most common over our planetary surfaces, it is possible for water to be found in all states of matter, not only as liquid, but also as a solid and a vapour. This would not be the case on bitterly cold Pluto where any existing water would be in solid form, or on cloud-shrouded Venus where, given its proximity to the sun, its very high temperatures permit water only as a vapour.

In its smallest quantity, water is contained within a single molecule consisting of three atoms. In its largest quantities, water resides in giant ocean reservoirs and ice sheets. Here, over 95% of all water is found. So great is its weight that it significantly depresses the solid crust that provides so much of its support.

Other important residences of the world's water include the atmosphere, in the form of water vapour; in subsurface deposits of groundwater and permafrost; on land surfaces in lakes, ponds, and rivers; and in solid form in surface glaciers. When subject to changes in pressure and temperature, it readily changes state through the natural processes of evaporation, condensation, freezing, sublimation, and melting. It comprises much of the weights of living organisms. Much of the human body is composed of water.

Whether it be solid, liquid, or vapour, water is a *fluid* in all three states of matter. That is, it has the capacity to flow, even as a solid. Most rapid flow is within wind in vapour form. Slowest flow is within ice sheets and permafrost as a solid, and in rock pores as a liquid. Never completely static, it circulates through these various residences, occupying periods of time that range from a few hours (as vapour in the atmosphere) to many thousands of years (locked in giant ice sheets or in stable rock formations).

When water freezes to form ice, its volume increases as its density drops.[98] With diminished density, ice floats in water, with a slight percentage of its volume above water.

Any conversion of ice into liquid, then further into a vapour, requires the addition of heat energy. This is why cubes of ice are added to drinks, since the melt process consumes heat taken from the surrounding water, thus cooling the drink. This is also why it is cooler to be in the shade of a tree than of a building.

Any reverse process, namely vapour conversion to liquid, then further conversion into a solid, releases heat energy. Thus, when atmospheric moisture condenses to form minute water droplets in clouds, a significant release of heat occurs. The amount of energy released is directly related to the amount of vapour that condenses to a liquid. This explains the enormous heat energy package generated, and the turbulence and air instability associated with thunderstorms and hurricanes, two atmospheric disturbances that produce large amounts of thick, towering clouds of temporarily suspended moisture.

As a chemical without additives, water has many significant properties. It is colourless, odourless, and tasteless. It is called a universal solvent because of its ability to dissolve many substances and form aqueous solutions. Its capacity to dissolve materials increases with water temperature but varies according to the solubility of the materials. Water's capacity to dissolve materials is apparent when we wash our hands, when sugar disappears in our hot coffee, or when water flows over rock surfaces. Moreover, since relatively large amounts of heat energy must be absorbed or released to either raise or lower its temperature, water serves as a critical planetary heat regulator.

Just how critical water is in maintaining stable temperatures can be seen in how things behave in its absence: in the high temperature ranges between night and day in deserts; in temperature patterns near the seashore as opposed to further inland; in rapid heating of car engines when liquid coolant has somehow been lost; and in human bodies exposed to severe dehydration in high temperatures.

Biblical references to water begin in its earliest pages. With water from four rivers flowing in abundance through the paradise of Eden, God turns the ground into fertile land, bringing life (Gen 2:10–14). By contrast, in Noah's time, a great flood of water brings death (Gen 7). God's people saw His miraculous provision of water for them in their escape from Egypt (Exod 14) and in their time of long wandering through the wilderness (Exod 17:5).

On numerous occasions, water is employed as a cleansing agent, used in foot washing (John 13:5) and in symbolic fashion in baptism (Matt 3). Water from a well was used as a source of refreshment and an illustrative tool by which Jesus moves a Samaritan woman to imagine a different water, a "living water" that, if consumed, would address the deep thirst of her soul forever (John 4:4–26). Verses later, believers are likened to human channels through whom "streams of living water will flow" (John 7:38). A similar reference to living water occurs in the latter pages of the Bible, where the water of life, clear as crystal, flows from the throne of God (Rev 22:1). Thus, biblical images of water appear in both the literal and figurative sense.

OCEAN WATER

We were a tiny speck in the vast vista of the sea—
the ocean that is open to all
and merciful to none,
that threatens even when it seems to yield,
and that is pitiless always to weakness.

Sir Ernest Shackleton[99]

A number of years ago, I enrolled in a training course: *Survival at Sea: Level 2*. The training included escaping from a submerged and inverted helicopter simulator, practicing climbing out of water using rope ladders and cargo nets, and learning ocean survivor techniques in life rafts and lifeboats. All trainees in water wore bright yellow supposedly "fits-all" immersion suits that covered the entire body, except for the face.

Initial instruction took place in a classroom and within the safe confines of a large swimming pool. Later, on the day when theory was to be put into practice, the classroom moved from swimming pool to ocean. Leaving the confines of Nova Scotia's Dartmouth Harbour, a group of a dozen apprehensive trainees travelled offshore some distance out into the cold and rolling Atlantic. The day was overcast, gloomy, and chilly.

Reaching our destination, we were given final instructions and then told to jump overboard. As our boat disappeared toward shore and its crew probably to the comfort of some cozy coffee shop, we and our two instructors became a community of insignificant human corks, bobbing about in two-metre swells, vulnerable to dreaded seasickness, but shielded from the debilitating effects of hypothermia by our conspicuous yellow immersion suits. With regard to safety, I would be relying on common sense, the natural buoyancy and thermal properties afforded by my suit, as well as on the knowledge and experience of our two marine instructors. With regard to my introduction to the ocean, this dunking represented baptism by immersion in a place of immense size, power, and complex surface motions.

Somehow I survived the abandonment and bobbing exercises on the rolling sea, the sardine-like confines of an inflated life raft (certainly no picnic for the claustrophobic), then finally the delightfully long ordeal sitting arm-to-arm with other wretched trainees in a totally enclosed motor-propelled lifeboat. Not a single trainee was able to handle the complex motions of the sea. And so a dozen stomachs, one by one, did what they had to do.

Someone has said that with the onset of seasickness, you are afraid you are going to die. But after an hour of the experience, you become afraid you are *not* going to die. How amazingly prophetic! The experience did little to encourage a stampede to enrol in *Survival at Sea: Level 3*!

While maps display four somewhat distinct and recognizable oceans, one can also consider that our planet has but a single ocean, since all these very deep puddles are interconnected, with all surfaces at approximately the same level, namely sea level. These surfaces constitute a dynamic liquid wilderness. Occasionally they are tranquil, behaving with apparent indifference to any human presence. On other occasions, they direct a vicious anger indiscriminately toward those who reside close to their margins or who dare enter a domain that can act with much cruelty and zero remorse.

But nature knows nothing of these anthropomorphic qualities of indifference, anger, cruelty, or remorse. Its actions are neither intentional nor malevolent. Nature's behaviour is always in response to natural processes and influences.

The ocean is perturbed by a variety of forces in nature. Each forcing mechanism distorts the ocean surface to fashion an ever-changing surface topography and sea-surface slope. Hence, at any one instant in time, there exists a variety of oceanic sea levels, with a single worldwide *mean* sea level (msl) being nothing more than a statistical average. Frictional effects of winds from above and periodic high-energy seismic disturbances from below and within the seabed create complex wave patterns of varying magnitudes.

Prevailing winds, whose strength and direction display constancy over time elevate sea surfaces in some places, depress them in others, transporting water long distances, sometimes through straits from one ocean to another. Regions of high pressure within the overlying atmosphere influence ocean surfaces by actually depressing them. Regions of low pressure have just the opposite effect. The combined effect is the creation of an atmospherically induced sea-surface slope (see Chapter 9's section on Iceberg Drift). Moreover, the combined forces of attraction of the sun and moon draw surface waters into the familiar, rhythmic, and predictable patterns whose undulations we know of as *tides* (see Chapter 3).

As each forcing mechanism exerts its influence, the ever-present influence of gravity attempts to wipe away ocean peaks and valleys to once again render surfaces featureless.

Sea surfaces influenced by winds, currents, air pressures, and tidal forces produce short-term modifications in sea levels locally. By contrast, another set of influences modify sea levels both globally and over the long term. Here, two influences predominate that are both related to long-term global temperature trends. Firstly, world temperature changes regulate ocean levels directly by affecting water *volume*, inducing expansion when waters warm and contraction when waters cool. Secondly, temperature changes regulate ocean levels indirectly by altering water *mass*, specifically mass that is stored in ice sheets on land. At present, global warming is resulting in water level rises from *both* increased mass *and* volume through thermal expansion and through water removed from land storage in ice.

Oceans cover approximately 70% of our planetary crust. Most water in solid form is locked up in the vast Antarctic ice sheet, which explains why the continent has partially depressed the crust. Smaller amounts of ice reside on Greenland and in scattered alpine glaciers in mid-to-high latitudes. Despite the significant volumes of water resident in lakes and the world's major rivers, total liquid water on land surfaces and in the atmosphere is extremely small when compared to amounts present in oceans and ice sheets.

With all this water, it may seem odd that our planet contains land surfaces. The fact that not all of the Earth's crust is covered by water is due to a combination of ocean volume and crustal surface topography. Like the ocean's surface, the crust is not perfectly smooth. Its convoluted and sharply undulating topography both above and below sea level includes soaring peaks, flat plains and deep depressions or trenches.

Because of gravity, ocean surfaces do not follow the undulating ocean beds below them. As a result, ocean depths vary significantly, becoming zero at oceanic margins and maximum in ocean trenches. In general, average depths of oceanic depressions far exceed average heights on land surfaces. In fact, the deepest oceanic depths significantly exceed the heights of the highest crustal mountains (see graph in Flood chapter). If Earth were a perfectly smooth featureless ball and all water were in liquid form, it is estimated that ocean volumes would cover the entire planet to a depth of a few kilometres.

OCEAN ORIGINS

From whence came the oceans? And why do other planets in our solar system not possess oceans similar to ours? Scientists tell us that H2O in the amounts present on Earth is most unusual compared to amounts elsewhere in space. This is not surprising when one considers the narrow temperature range in which water is able to exist in liquid form (between 0o and 100oC for pure water). Moreover, we are told that water in any form anywhere is quite rare, and that the volume of Earth's water has not always been as it is at present. Nor has its present very high liquid-to-vapour ratio always prevailed in its long history. The same is true for the liquid-to-solid ratio. In fact, in the early periods of the Earth's development as a planet, it contained virtually no water in liquid or solid form. Neither was there much atmosphere. What happened to change all this?

Scientific evidence points to an extremely hot Earth during its infancy when it was involved in a very prolonged process of planetary cooling. Cooling enables the eventual conversion of vapours into liquids and liquids into solids.

Given that different substances liquefy and solidify at different temperatures, it is clear that as Earth cooled, the heavier substances, such as metals and other minerals, liquefied and eventually solidified well before water vapour was even able to liquefy. We can imagine a slow natural distillation of the materials within the embryonic Earth as substances still in gaseous form (nitrogen, argon, carbon dioxide, and later oxygen), were released and retained by sufficiently strong planetary gravity to create an atmospheric envelope about a newly solidified planetary crust. Lighter gases such as hydrogen and helium could not be retained by the planet because of its insufficient gravity. But as surface temperatures cooled, water vapour was eventually able to liquefy and drop to the Earth as precipitation.

Rainfall must have been torrential and sustained. It filled the world's largest depressions to form our liquid hydrosphere, becoming interconnected oceans of various depths. Fortunately for us, cooling did not progress to the point at which atmospheric gases such as oxygen and nitrogen liquefy. Also fortunate was the fact that the presence of so-called greenhouse gases, such as carbon dioxide, methane and water vapour stabilized planetary temperatures, preventing their further decline and maintaining them above temperatures one might expect more appropriate for a planet 150 million kilometres from the sun. Nevertheless, water as liquid can still readily freeze or vapourize, but oxygen and nitrogen must remain as gases within the ranges of temperature and pressure common to our planetary surface.

Some of the many differences between the Earth's atmosphere and hydrosphere relate to their comparative thicknesses, densities, and pressures. Relative to the diameter of Earth, both envelopes are thin. At its greatest depth in the western Pacific, the ocean descends some 11 kilometres below its surface. By contrast, atmospheric thickness is much greater, but difficult to define since no distinct upper boundary exists. Air density decreases with altitude, but never really reaches zero. Initially, its decrease is rapid (50% of the atmosphere's entire mass resides below an altitude of 5 kilometres while 99% of it can be found below 31 kilometres). One might consider a proper measure of the thickness of our atmosphere to be approximately 42 kilometres since at this altitude, virtually none of the Earth's canopy of air resides above it.

Since liquids compress very little, there is only a slight increase in water density with increasing depth in water bodies. Here the variable displaying the greatest increase with depth is not density, but the pressure of water on water.

Since water is about 700 times denser than air at sea level, divers experience much more rapid increases in pressure as they descend in water than do parachutists as they descend similar distances in air. For the diver, these increases are equivalent to an additional Earth atmosphere pressing on them for each 10 metres of descent. At the greatest ocean depths within the Marianas Trench in the western Pacific, pressures on objects register a staggering 1000 atmospheres, far beyond what is needed to crush all but the strongest marine structures.

OCEANS AND SEAS

We occasionally call the world's largest puddles of water *seas* as well as oceans, although seas are more precisely defined as pockets of oceans. Some seas, however, are landlocked and *not* attached to an ocean. They resemble lakes. These include the Caspian, Aral, and the Dead seas. Regardless of size differences, both oceans and seas possess relatively high concentrations of dissolved chemicals (sulphates and chlorides) collectively referred to as *salts*.

Virtually all water in contact with ground is *saline* to some degree. Pure water exists only in its evaporated, distilled form. *Fresh* water contained in lakes and rivers differs from salt water not because of an absence of dissolved chemicals, but because relatively lower concentrations of chemicals present within fresh water still render it potable. To be called potable (drinkable), water must be capable of being absorbed into body tissue through a diffusion process called *osmosis*. Water that is swallowed can only enter body cells if its salt concentration is lower than the salt concentration within the cell. If it is higher, diffusion of water will be *from* the cell, through its semi-permeable wall and not into it. Thus, by ingesting salt water, cells actually lose their own water and begin a rapid dehydration. Dehydration is what also occurs in plants when roots are exposed to water that contains salt concentration in excess of what is contained in the plant cells.

Why are oceans and seas more saline than lakes and rivers? The answer relates to the nature of the evaporation process. The process is *selective*. When water evaporates from a surface, it becomes a distillate since dissolved substances are left behind. During the processes of condensation and precipitation, though small amounts of atmospheric gases are picked up on their descent, what falls is relatively pure water. Once in contact with the ground again, this water begins to dissolve more soluble substances through contact, and thus becomes slightly saline. Now in solution, these minerals are transported downstream through rivers to lakes and ultimately to the sea, still as relatively fresh water to be mixed with dissolved salts already present.

As with oceans, some evaporation occurs from the river water returning to the sea. However, the continuous transport and renewal of the waters into and through rivers and lakes prevents any appreciable buildup in water salinity along the journey. By contrast, oceans do not transfer their water into any other body of water, except sometimes, into another adjacent ocean. As hydrological *dead-end streets*, an ocean's only available exit from its hydrological cul de sac is upward through evaporation. Since the dissolved minerals delivered to the ocean do not evaporate along with the water, the salinity of ocean water undergoes slow but steady increases through time. At present, ocean salinity on average is 35 parts per thousand by weight. If one were to repeat the process with 1000 kilograms of water from a typical Canadian lake, the residue would amount to less than a kilogram of salt in 1000 kilograms of water. Thus, ocean water contains many times the salt content found in a typical Canadian lake. Among the Great Lakes, the freshest water is in Lake Superior. From that lake, salinity slowly rises through adjacent lakes downstream. Yet even at the terminus of the system, in the Gulf of St. Lawrence, Great Lakes water is still potable.

Ocean salinity is diminished locally wherever rivers or ice sheets discharge their freshwater contents into oceans. For example, the mighty

Amazon River's discharge is so great that Atlantic Ocean water is *fresh* for many kilometres beyond that river's mouth. Introducing large volumes of fresh water into an ocean environment is significant since salt water and fresh water densities differ. Such differences enhance important vertical mixing of ocean water as well as horizontal current flow, normally over long distances.

Despite what has been said, oceans are not the most saline bodies of water on Earth. Analyses of water salinity within inland seas such as the Caspian, Aral, and Dead seas reveal salinity values all in excess of ocean salinity. The reason is that all these water bodies share a common characteristic: they all reside in climatic regions that are warm and dry. As a result, the process of evaporation from their surfaces withdraws more water than the combined precipitation and inflow from streams deliver to them. Over time, water volumes and levels within these areas decline. With water levels declining to the point when basins no longer overflow to the ocean, concentrations of dissolved minerals begin gradual increases.

In the case of the Dead Sea, residing within a trough of a deep rift valley, water withdrawal through evaporation has dropped its surface elevation to the lowest in the world and increased salt concentrations to levels ten times average ocean salinity. Unless humans intervene to divert water into it to reduce salinity through dilution, the Dead Sea—with a surface dropping significantly each year and with salinity still rising—is expected to eventually disappear completely, as is the prediction for Utah's Great Salt Lake.

By contrast, the Mediterranean Sea, the Gulf of California, the Red Sea, and the Persian Gulf will not disappear in time. As with the Dead Sea, average evaporation rates from all four surfaces exceed precipitation and inflow from adjacent rivers. The good news is that the Mediterranean is joined to the Atlantic Ocean through Gibraltar, and the Gulf of California is attached to the Pacific. Trends toward lowered water levels in both areas are therefore offset by strong ocean *inflow* that continually replenishes lost water volumes, thus maintaining each surface at sea level. However, since these bodies receive water that is already saline, their salinities have come to slightly exceed those of the open ocean.

Similar conditions prevail in the Red Sea (whose water levels are maintained through inflow from the Arabian Sea through the narrow

Bab-al-Mandeb Strait) and in the Persian Gulf (into which Indian Ocean water enters through the Strait of Hormuz).

OCEANS, SEAS, AND HOLY SCRIPTURE

The ocean, vast, unending,
outstretching the eye's power to see its breakers
on some faraway shore,
hints to us of eternity.

Aubrey Podlich[100]

Given its geographic location, the Holy Land has direct exposure to seas but not to an ocean. However, this exposure is very limited. On its western edge is the Great Sea (the Mediterranean), linked to the Atlantic Ocean. On its southern extremity lies the Red Sea, linked to the Indian Ocean. In its eastern regions, two "seas"—Galilee (also known as Tiberius) and the Dead Sea—reside in a narrow north-south trench, joined by the 100-kilometre-long Jordan River. Located within Earth's deepest rift-valley depression, neither water body is an actual sea or a pocket of any ocean. Rather, each is a lake.

With low annual precipitation that prevails within the region, much of the landscape of the Bible Lands is arid or semi-arid, with aridity rapidly increasing southward from Galilee to Judaea. Most precipitation falls as rain, with the majority delivered in the winter months from November to March.

With high temperatures through the summer, surface evaporation is high and surface water in the form of lakes and large rivers is sparse. With the exception of small areas where nature's delivery of water is adequate, the region is dependent for its water supply on springs and wells fed by groundwater. In these areas, access to abundant subsurface water has historically been a most significant factor in the distribution of human settlements. Jericho, for example, one of the world's oldest cities, situated below sea level near the retreating shore of the Dead Sea, is located close to a highly productive and reliable natural spring.

Almost 400 references to the sea are scattered through some forty-six books of the Bible. The majority of these images are contained in the Old Testament. Biblical images relating to the sea rely heavily on its principal characteristics. The sea, enormous and mysterious, is described as a vast receptacle into whose depths God will hurl all our iniquities (Mic 7:19), there to lie out of sight and remembered by our forgiving God no more (Jer 31:34). Also noteworthy is that in John's vision of the new heaven and new Earth, there is still a river, but there is no longer any sea (Rev 21:1). God is sovereign over the powerful sea and at His will can calm it (Luke 8:22), dry it up (Isa 50:2), make it burst its bounds in flood (Gen 7), or destroy it.

Elsewhere, the restlessness of the wicked is likened to mud tossed up by a turbulent and angry sea (Jude 13). Doubters are likened to a wave of the sea "blown and tossed by the wind" (Jas 1:6). The prophet Isaiah looks ahead to the day when the knowledge of God will fill the Earth just as extensively as its waters now cover it (Isa 11:9). The supremacy of Christ over the awesome sea was demonstrated to astonished disciples on the Sea of Galilee when Jesus walked on water and then invited Peter to do likewise (Matt 14:22–33). This incident terrified the disciples who knew of the occasional fury and unpredictability of that lake. They responded with both *fear* (of the waves) and *amazement* (at Jesus' power over them).

> *Whoever can this be?*
> *He gives orders even to the winds and waters,*
> *and they obey him.*
>
> Luke 8:25 (JBP)

It appears that the One who calmed the raging sea had frightened them more than did the storm.

> *Mightier than the thunder of the great waters,*
> *mightier than the breakers of the sea—*
> *the LORD on high is mighty.*
>
> Psalm 93:4

EARTH'S WATER AND ATMOSPHERE

WATER IN CLOUD, FOG, AND MIST

We live and move and have our being *on* a solid crust and *within* a gaseous fluid atmosphere. While both crust and atmosphere are subject to change, it is in the latter where change is most apparent. Much of the change can be attributed to the presence of a single atmospheric ingredient: water vapour.

Dwarfed by the volumes of other atmospheric gases present, water vapour has significance far greater than its relatively minute presence would suggest. Evaporation from a variety of surfaces, particularly from oceans, introduces water vapour into the atmosphere. Of critical importance to the events of weather is the fact that evaporated water serves as a transport vehicle for the transfer of large quantities of potential energy into the atmosphere.

This energy, in the form of *latent heat* and consumed in the process of evaporation, is released into the surrounding air during cloud formation when vapour condenses back into liquid. The amount of heat released is directly related to the amount of water vapour that condenses. Release of large quantities of potential energy into the atmosphere through condensation, especially when insertions are both rapid and localized, tend to destabilize air, making it more buoyant, more likely to cool ,and more likely to release more heat energy to form cloud.

In the process of condensation, atmospheric moisture becomes visible as a white precipitate and can make its appearance in the form of cloud, fog or mist. Each has the capacity to play with sunlight, absorbing, filtering, scattering, and bending it to produce a multitude of visual effects, from rainbows and sundogs to spectacular sunrises and sunsets. Enjoyment of the visual displays from water vapour is virtually universal. The red sunrise or sunset is common when the sun near the horizon shines onto the bottom of a flat cloud deck, often resulting in clouds the colour of raspberries.

The most common form of visible atmospheric moisture is cloud. Satellite photos from space reveal that cloud over our planet's surface is widespread, displaying considerable variation in thickness from place to place, and from time to time at one location. Various cloud shapes and patterns testify to the influence of wind as the major factor in making and shaping them. For example, cloud associated with the area surrounding the eye of a hurricane forms a spiral in response to the circular swirl of winds that converge about the cyclonic eye. Cloud associated with a developing thunderstorm forms towering, vertically developed columns in response to the powerful updrafts from buoyant air that force rapid cooling and often make a column's vertical dimension exceed the width of its base.

As precipitate, clouds consist of countless tiny suspended droplets that form around dust particles acting as condensation nuclei. Droplets remain suspended in the atmosphere so long as coalescence does not cause them to exceed a critical mass. When critical mass is achieved, precipitate becomes precipitation that forms within the cloud and falls from its base.

Cloud altitudes range from a few hundred metres to heights of many thousands of metres. In general, the thickest clouds are found at the lowest elevations, with total suspended water declining with altitude. The planet's highest clouds, at altitudes exceeding 50 kilometres consist of extremely small water droplets that, because of very low atmospheric temperatures at this altitude, are in the form of very low-density ice crystals. Due to their high altitude and low density, they are only visible near the horizon during deep twilight, appearing as a bright oasis of blue in a darkened atmosphere. Their name, *noctilucent clouds* (meaning night-shining clouds), alludes to the fact that their height allows them to reflect sunlight well after sunlight has disappeared from the Earth's surface and the lower atmosphere. Their appearance is distinct from the much more dramatic, lively, and colourful displays that are formed at an even greater altitude close to the outer reaches of the atmosphere. Cloudlike in appearance, these ephemeral light displays, called *aurora borealis* and *aurora australis* (northern and southern lights), are the product of collisions of solar particles with very high-altitude atmosphere.

To some degree, the distinctions between cloud, fog, and mist are as amorphous as clouds themselves. In general, fog is classified as cloud at ground level, a type of condensed water vapour that surrounds us, reducing visibility, scattering light and creating glare. It is the only occasion when it is literally true that one's head *is in the clouds*. With heavy fog, immediate surroundings become a confusing monochromatic grey, eliminating a horizon.

Mist differs from cloud and fog in that it is a more localized phenomenon. In addition, its relatively lower moisture content makes mist more transparent than cloud or fog, rendering objects in it somewhat mysterious and lacking clear edges. Unlike fog, which can last for days, mist usually has a narrow lifespan, readily dissipating as temperatures rise, usually just after sunrise.

The fact that cloud thickness and density within it can greatly exceed the thickness and density of either mist or fog means that clouds can periodically block most light transmission through them. The results are clouds whose bases are differing shades of grey or, when thickest, almost black (as is common within a violent tornado funnel or severe thunderstorm). Given the amount of moisture suspended over us when daytime skies become their darkest, it is not surprising that heavy rain, lightning and thunder usually accompany ominous skies.

CLOUD, FOG, AND MIST IN HOLY SCRIPTURE

Clouds, fog, and mist provide ingredients that regularly alter the appearance of our visual world, forming and dissipating at times with considerable speed. Since *mist* tends to be ephemeral, it is an ideal illustration of whatever is short lived. The prophet Isaiah combines the characteristics of both cloud and mist to illustrate God's dealing with sin:

I have swept away your offenses like a cloud,
your sins like the morning mist.
Return to me, for I have redeemed you.

Isaiah 44:22

The sudden blinding of a man involved in sorcery is described as mist and darkness coming over him (Acts 13:11). The lack of permanency associated with mist renders it an ideal image for the transitory nature of human life:

What is your life?
You are a mist that appears for a little while,
and then vanishes.

James 4:14b

The ephemeral nature of mist is also used to describe short-lived fortunes made through deceit (Prov 21:6). False prophets are likened to "springs without water and mists driven by a storm" (2 Pet 2:17). False teachers are like clouds without water (Jude 12), in other words, deceptively empty. In the Book of Ecclesiastes, the word vanity (KJV), used to describe "all the works that are done under the Sun" (Eccl 1:14), can also be translated as mist. Cloud imagery is also associated with various appearances of God, arriving in a thick cloud (Exod 19:9). Elsewhere, clouds function as God's chariot (Ps 104:3).

Clouds are also associated with critical moments in the life of Jesus. At the Transfiguration when, for a brief instant, three disciples saw Him as never before, God spoke from a cloud (Matt 17:5). At His Ascension, Jesus disappeared into a cloud (Acts 1:9). At the end of the age, He will come again "on the clouds of the sky with power and great glory" (Matt 24:30). By contrast, clouds are associated with some negative imagery (Matt 27:45) as when darkness covered the land at His death.

WATER IN DEW AND FROST

O ye Dews and Frosts, bless ye the Lord:
praise him, and magnify him forever.

Benedicite (BCP)

It was one of those uncomfortable *3-H days* that southern Ontario residents occasionally endure in summer: hot, hazy, and humid. It was the kind of day that discourages strenuous work in the outdoors and turns faces toward relaxation and the backyard pool. As our family owned no pool, my refreshment was a jug of ice water and the shade supplied by a tree near the backyard deck. As usually occurs on 3-H days, the outside surface of the jug was wet with moisture. In meteorological terms, the thin film of air in contact with the cold container had cooled sufficiently and condensation called dew had formed on the jug. Had condensation occurred at a temperature below freezing, the dew would have been present in the form of frost.

Dew and frost differ from cloud, fog and mist in a number of ways. First of all, dew and frost contain much less condensed water vapour than do clouds, fog or mist. And secondly, while cloud, fog and mist form within the atmosphere at various altitudes with variable thicknesses, dew and frost form as localized coverings on ground surfaces with thicknesses normally measured in millimetres. Moreover, while condensation creating cloud, fog and mist can occur at any time in a 24-hour period, localized condensation associated with dew and frost is largely restricted to the cooler hours just prior to sunrise.

Night cooling normally continues until sunrise. Because the Earth's solid surfaces cool faster than the atmosphere, the time just prior to sunrise finds the ground cooler than the air above it. This is especially true after nights in which skies have been clear and winds have been calm. Clear skies enhance nighttime cooling and calm winds prevent air turbulence. Preventing turbulence keeps cooled air close to the ground and enhances the temperature drop near the solid surfaces on which dew and frost normally form.

During nights of very dry air, it is difficult to generate either dew or frost. This is because, in such conditions, dryer air requires a large temperature drop in order to create saturated air and cause the sparsely available moisture to condense. Since blankets of dew and frost are usually very thin, their lifespan is normally brief. On most days, they disappear as rising morning temperatures encourage the melting of frost or the re-evaporation of dew.

Regardless of the moisture content in air, the temperature at which condensation occurs in any air mass is called its *dew point*. In very humid air, such as is normally found in equatorial regions and in southern Ontario in the summer months, dew point temperatures are relatively high.

By contrast, in the dry air within polar regions and also in hot deserts, dew point temperatures are correspondingly low. Because hot air masses can store far more water vapour than cold air masses, it follows that when the dew point is reached in each air mass, far more water is condensed in the former than in the latter air mass. This explains many moisture phenomena, among them the following:

- At the Earth's equator, by volume, water vapour comprises up to 4 parts per 100 parts of the lower atmosphere. By contrast, water vapour concentrations in the surface air of Antarctica's bitterly cold interior are in the order of one part per million. The coldest parts of Antarctica possess the driest air in the world.
- Equatorial areas experience much more annual precipitation than do polar areas. This is because warmer air can hold and potentially release much more water vapour.
- Humidity levels in southern Ontario fluctuate seasonally, rising in summer and dropping in winter. To maintain comfortable moisture levels in our homes, most of us employ humidifiers to raise moisture levels in the winter, and dehumidifiers to drop much higher moisture levels during summer.
- Severe thunderstorms and hurricanes occur with the high dew point temperatures associated with warm moist air. Such disturbances depend upon the conversion of large amounts of water vapour into liquid water with the resulting release of vast amounts of latent heat. The most massive conversions can only take place when condensation occurs at high atmospheric temperatures, in other words, at high dew points.
- Snowfall rates occurring at temperatures near the freezing point are normally heavier than amounts in temperatures *well* below freezing. Though it seems that colder places receive more snow, it is probably because the snow that falls may persist with little further accumulation for the duration of the cold season, not because total snowfall amounts are much greater.

DEW REFERENCES IN SCRIPTURE

In the scriptures, dew is a useful image. Its usefulness relates to two important facts: firstly, locals are familiar with dew; and secondly, dew's various properties. The low annual precipitation in much of the Bible Lands makes inputs of moisture from dew, however small, very important. Given the rate that nightly temperatures drop in dry climates, especially under cloudless skies, dew events are relatively frequent and widespread. The prophet Hosea employs his knowledge of disappearing morning dew to illustrate the transitory nature of the people's love for God:

> *What can I do with you, Ephraim?*
> *What can I do with you, Judah?*
> *Your love is like the morning mist,*
> *like the early dew that disappears.*
>
> *Hosea 6:4*

Elsewhere, the action of the army of Israel descending on its enemy is likened to the silent manner and thoroughness by which dew descends to cover exposed surfaces (2 Sam 17:12). In the Book of Exodus, the appearance of a strange deposit of thin flakes like frost on the desert floor (God's mysterious provision of food called *manna*) follows the disappearance of morning dew (Exod 16:13–14).

Gideon's two strange requests for a sign that God would save Israel involved night deposits of dew: first, only on a fleece, and secondly, only on the ground beside the fleece (Judges 6:36–40).

Finally, in the story of Jacob receiving the blessing of his father Isaac while masquerading as his brother Esau, Isaac makes reference to blessings coming down from above as "heaven's dew" (Gen 27:28). A reference to dew similar to this is included in A Prayer for the Clergy and People in the Anglican *Book of Common Prayer*. The image testifies to the abundance of God's blessings:

> *And that they may truly please thee,*
> *pour upon them the continual dew of thy blessing.*
>
> *(BCP, page 13)*

WATER IN RAIN AND SNOW

> *"Music!" God shouted, "Let's have some music to dance by!"*
> *The sky, wishing to oblige, yet not wanting to admit it knew nothing*
> *about tunes, decided to make it rain.*
>
> *Aubrey Podlich*[101]

My four-year-old grandson stood beside me in the shower at the local swimming pool. After a few minutes, mist filled the large room and water in the form of small beads covered the surface of its tiled wall. Noting this as a teachable moment, and as Stephen watched, I placed my finger on the wall and slowly moved it downward, plowing through countless tiny droplets, an action that caused droplets to coalesce. At a critical point, the enlarging drops forming in advance of my finger seemed to get a life of their own. Needing no further push, they suddenly took off down the tiles by themselves, increasing in size and speed while carving out a vertical track as they devoured even more droplets, thus removing in their trails a large amount of beaded moisture from the tiles.

Watching with great interest, Stephen moved to duplicate my action. It took him little time to realize that by starting on a higher point on the shower wall, he was able to manufacture an even larger "raindrop" that accelerated as it descended. And so it was: in a very simple manner, Stephen and I had roughly duplicated nature's method of rainmaking. It was done through simple play, with curiosity our motivator and a swimming pool shower our lab and factory.

> *But more than anything, I think, I loved rain for the power*
> *it had to make indoors seem snugger and safer and a place to*
> *find refuge in from everything outdoors that was un-home,*
> *unsafe. I loved rain for making home seem home more deeply.*
>
> *Frederick Buechner*[102]

Nature's process of making rain begins with large quantities of water vapour condensing through sufficient cooling into countless suspended droplets to form cloud. Then in response to some stimulus, and at various points within the cloud, droplets begin to coalesce and gain weight.

Eventually, as each reaches a critical mass, increased weight causes them to drop through the cloud, accelerating as they fall. As they do so, they collect more droplets, grow even heavier until finally, they exit the base of the cloud, thus depleting a small portion of the cloud's moisture. Once out of the cloud, they are subject to the evaporative process that works to *subtract* moisture from drops and diminish their size. Thus, not all moisture reaches the ground.

Moisture subtracted from falling rain or snow through evaporation that fails to reach the ground is called *virga*. Virga is most common in regions where temperatures are high and humidity is low—two conditions that enhance evaporation. Occasionally, thunderstorms may contain virga. Some *only* contain virga. In such cases, so-called *dry* thunderstorms become dangerous. Forested surfaces not dampened by rainfall but subjected to lightning strikes often result in widespread forest fires, particularly evident in the North American fires of 2021.

Raindrops that reach the ground create a local rain event. Those most likely to survive their descent are the largest ones with the shortest distance to fall from the cloud base to the ground.

> *It always rains on tents. Rainstorms will travel thousands of miles against the prevailing winds for the opportunity to rain on a tent.*
>
> Dave Barry[103]

If raindrops develop through the incremental growth of coalescing water droplets tracking through and creating vertical pathways in cloud formations, it stands to reason that the factory that produces the largest drops, and therefore the most intense rainfalls must be the cloud with the greatest vertical dimension. Such a productive rainmaking factory is found in the giant thunderclouds whose tops can reach over 10 000 metres. And while the *vertical dimension* of a cloud is a good indicator of rainfall *intensity*, it is in its *horizontal* dimension where the *duration* of a rainfall event at any one location is expressed. Both horizontal and vertical dimensions are maximized in the giant bands of clouds associated with hurricanes, conditions that make hurricanes one of nature's most prolific and most violent rainmakers.

Depending upon temperature, humidity, and wind conditions, clouds can generate a variety of precipitation types, all from a single ingredient: H2O. These include: *hail* (ice balls repeatedly forced upward into freezing altitudes by powerful localized updrafts that prevent their release from the cloud base, thereby allowing for the accumulation of more and more precipitate); *drizzle* (fine rain that escapes the cloud base into calm air); *ice pellets* (normally small water droplets that freeze during their descent); *freezing rain* (very fine drizzle in liquid form that freezes into a thin, beautiful, but sometimes hazardous glaze on contact with cold surfaces); or *snow* (frozen hexagonal ice crystals that grow into an infinite variety of sizes and patterns and fall from clouds to form low-density pure white blankets on ground surfaces).[104]

Climatically, most of the eastern Mediterranean receives low annual precipitation, with rates decreasing rapidly toward the south and with most rain falling in winter months. With moisture amounts for agriculture close to critical levels in many areas, the arrival of rains are regarded as expressions of prosperity and divine blessing (Job 5:10; Isa 55:10).

Scripture speaks of rain of varying intensities, from soothing *gentle rain* (Ps 72:6) to *rushing rain* (1 Kgs 18:41) and to rain *in torrents* (Ezek 13:11). With increasing rainfall intensity, human responses move from welcoming to terrifying. In the latter case, the most famous deluge is the 40-day great flood when "the windows of heaven opened and water burst forth" (Gen 7).

> *As the rain and the snow come down from heaven,*
> *and do not return to it without watering the earth*
> *and making it bud and flourish,*
> *so that it yields seed for the sower and bread for the eater,*
> *so is my word that goes out from my mouth:*
> *it will not return to me empty,*
> *but will accomplish what I desire*
> *and achieve the purpose for which I sent it.*
>
> *Isaiah 55:10–11*

Metaphorically, God's words and teachings as vital sources of nourishment falling on His people are likened to "abundant rain dropping onto tender plants" (Deut 32:2). Elsewhere, scripture employs the image of "driving rain that leaves no crops" to illustrate the harmful effect of an oppressive ruler on the poor (Prov 28:3).

The immense variety of the natural scenes created by water suggests yet again a Master Artist from whose works emerges beauty far out of proportion to the quantity of material employed in the various processes.

WATER IN WIND AND STORM

> *O ye Winds of God, bless ye the Lord:*
> *praise him, and magnify him forever.*
>
> **Benedicite (BCP)**

What makes for a place of peace? For many, it is the permanent abode of quiet, beauty and the familiar. These ingredients are the solvents in which anxious thoughts dissolve and blood pressures decline. They form the seedbed that converts mental dissonance into order. In their presence, they are the catalysts that allow the human imagination to escape from, and rise above life's miry clay.

We all have our special places of peace in which quietness, beauty, and the familiar reside. They are our sanctuaries where the frantic pace of life slows and where we are permitted momentary respite to appreciate and ponder the ineffable.

In my list of places of peace is a trail that encircles an artificial lake near our home.[105] Recently, in early autumn, I visited it. Part of the trail, actually a wide pathway, was strewn with a fresh carpet of needles dropped from the canopy of pine and spruce trees that line and envelop it. Beyond the trees on one side was a large cornfield that had recently undergone a seasonal colour conversion from dark green to a golden yellow, the yellow one associates with ripening autumn wheat. Shafts of light reflecting off the corn stalks penetrated this dimly lit arboreal tunnel to illuminate portions of the ground. The long, now somewhat inflexible corn leaves fluttered in a light afternoon breeze and their swishing sounds were easily distinguishable from the equally pleasant melody generated by the breeze that ruffled the overhead canopy. For the moment, soft sounds of nature had drowned out those of human striving.

Human responses to the phenomenon of wind are mixed. We speak of the refreshing summer breeze that rustles leaves, lifts kites, dries laundry, billows sails, and brings comforting relief during hot, humid days. Occasionally, we are treated to demonstrations of nature as a sculptor, employing gusty winds as a vehicle to lift particles of sand, then selectively sort and redistribute them into the pleasant shapes in migratory desert dunes. Those of us who inhabit the colder climes regularly witness similar events when a powerful Hand transports snow particles to fashion streamlined winter drifts. Once again, natural pattern testifies to a causal natural process.

Human exposures to wind are not always pleasant. Positive responses of delight change to fear, apprehension, and even terror when wind speeds increase to destructive levels. Sustained high winds produce storms—those severe atmospheric disturbances that frequently darken skies and bring heavy precipitation. Over water, sustained gale-force winds generate heavy seas and destructive storm surges onto land. Giant waves accelerate metal fatigue and eventual failure in even the strongest marine vessels. Over land, especially in areas where airflow meets little interference from surface features, winds spawn the choking desert dust storms, the formidable sand storms, and the blinding disorienting blizzards common to polar regions. Here, descriptive adjectives that give wind negative anthropomorphic characteristics cease to allude to its gentleness, but rather express its malevolence and rage.

Without doubt, the most violent atmospheric disturbances are tornadoes and hurricanes. At present, though the causes of tornadoes are still largely a mystery, we know they develop in atmosphere over land, often in association with a cold front rapidly advancing against a humid spring/ summer air mass, sometimes arriving in families during a so-called tornado outbreak. They are primarily a warm-temperature phenomenon involving intense winds that form relatively rapidly and dissipate quickly. They emerge out of the base of low dark clouds, descending to Earth as rotating sinuous rope or funnel-like structures within very low central barometric pressure. In their mature and most violent stages, they lose their rope-like appearance and present as wider, more vertical cylinders of air and captured debris that extend from a low cloud base to the ground. Fortunately, the destructive influences of tornadoes are normally restricted to very narrow surface pathways. At any one place, these ephemeral storms normally last but a few minutes. But for those caught in their fury, tornadoes seem to last forever.[106]

While the tornado packs much of the strongest winds ever recorded, it is the atmospheric disturbance called the hurricane that possesses the greatest total energy, and the most widespread and the more sustained winds. Hurricanes are among our most violent atmospheric perturbations. While tornadoes are born over land and die over water, the reverse is true for hurricanes. The reason is that a hurricane's nutrition and energy come from massive evaporation from very warm sea surfaces, particularly those found in tropical waters where surfaces at their warmest typically rise into the mid-30s and higher. In the tropical Pacific, these storms are called *typhoons*; in the Atlantic, *hurricanes*; and, in the Indian Ocean, *cyclones*.

Regardless of the ocean in which they form, these storms have a common method of formation. Water vapour enters the atmosphere, carrying with it the potential energy of latent heat that entered storage in the evaporating process. When the water vapour condenses to form clouds, latent heat is released, destabilizing the atmosphere in the region of the storm.

Hurricanes evolve through a complex process of intensification: decreasing air stability, decreasing central air pressure, increased pressure gradients, and increased wind speeds, and finally rainfall in torrents. Beginning as mild tropical depressions, they develop strength during long passages over water, eventually progressing to tropical storm category and eventually achieve the status of hurricane when sustained winds exceed 100 kilometres per hour. Since it is the high moisture content that feeds the storm, and since moisture is more readily evaporated from sea surfaces that are warm, hurricanes deteriorate rapidly when they move from water onto land and when they leave the tropics and migrate into cooler higher latitudes.[107] Both these movements serve to diminish the amount of moisture available as storm nutrient.

From birth to death, these storms can travel many thousands of kilometres and have a lifespan of about two weeks. They last much longer than tornadoes, a much more local phenomenon whose lifespan is typically in the order of a few hours. Thus, unlike tornadoes, hurricane paths can be easily tracked and their prognoses can be predicted with moderate accuracy. Hurricane transit times over a single location are dependent upon their widths and rates of migration, but are usually in the order of one day. This single-day transit time was definitely exceeded in the case of Dorian, the second most violent Atlantic hurricane ever recorded. In early September 2019, a normal month for hurricanes, Dorian arrived over the Bahamas. There, its eye stalled in its progression northward, remaining almost stationary for over 48 hours, thus concentrating its fury on the islands below.

Satellite photos of hurricanes reveal a white rotating configuration of cloud with arms that spiral into a relatively clear central *eye*. Surrounding the eye is the *eyewall* where the storms strongest winds are located. From above, a hurricane bears a striking resemblance to a spiral galaxy. It is as beautiful as it is awesome. From below, however, the scene this disturbance generates is dark and chaotic.

When strong winds travel unimpeded over water for long distances, their kinetic energy has time to form heavy seas which, as they approach shores, produce powerful wind-induced bulges of water called *storm surges*. Surges are particularly destructive when they inundate low-lying settlements, especially where land gradients are shallow. In these conditions, widespread flooding combined with violent winds and heavy rain produce catastrophic damage. During Hurricane Katrina in August 2005, when water from the Gulf of Mexico breached protective levee systems, it poured into the low-lying coastal settlements of Louisiana and Mississippi.[108] Reported deaths (disputed by many) were mercifully below 2000 people (see Chapter 8).

In September 2021, 16 years later, Katrina's sister Ida delivered another catastrophic whack to Louisiana before advancing with uncharacteristically sustained fury northeast toward New York with high winds, storm surges onshore from the Atlantic, record rainfalls and flooding. Fortunately, Ida caused few deaths. By contrast, the 10-metre-high Bangladesh storm surge of November 1970 generated by onshore winds off the Bay of Bengal caused a reported half a million deaths.

But from what do winds originate? By what natural processes are they born and dissipated? Regardless of strength, winds trace their origin to the unequal heating of atmospheric particles. The result is the creation of air packages of differing densities and buoyancies. On television weather charts, density variations appear as high- and low-pressure centres that, when contoured on weather charts, resemble hills and valleys on a topographic map.

Unlike the permanency of undulating hills and valleys on land, high- and low-pressure regions in the atmosphere have relatively brief life spans. Both their intensities and their locations change rapidly over time. The reason for this is linked to the atmosphere's high fluidity; namely, its capacity to flow. Its natural tendency is to redistribute itself in such a way as to diminish and eventually eliminate spatial differences and imbalances in atmospheric pressure. The resulting movement of air from high pressure to centres of low pressure, not unlike water's tendency to move off hills and into valleys, creates the phenomenon known as wind.

The strength of wind is greatest in those regions where pressure gradients are their steepest, that is, where changes in air density are the greatest over the shortest distances. Strongest sustained winds are located within the wall of the hurricane's eye while the storm's lowest barometric pressure resides in the centre of the eye, a location in which winds become strangely calm and skies momentarily clear.

Winds disappear locally whenever air pressures over a wide region are equalized. However, there is never a moment when winds can disappear globally since the sun is continually generating new air packages of differing temperatures, densities, and buoyancies in different places.

WIND AND STORM IN THE SCRIPTURES

References of wind and storm contribute rich imagery to many biblical passages and serve as windows into biblical truth, particularly in relation to the character of God. Nature is not divine in itself, but rather is expressive of divine power and sovereignty *over* nature (Ps 29:10; Ps 107:29).

At times, winds or storms mark the presence of God (Job 40:6; Heb 12:18) and are, even in their raging, sources of praise to God (Ps 98:7–8). In Acts 2, the presence of God was declared by the sound of "a mighty rushing wind." In the Gospels, Jesus employs the mystery and unpredictability of wind to illustrate the mystery of the Spirit of God (Greek: *pneuma* = wind) whose activities, in complete unity with God's hidden plan, defy human understanding and control (John 3:8).

References to wind and storm in relation to people often involve negative imagery. The person plagued with doubt is compared to a wave of the sea, randomly tossed and driven by wind and storm with no clear direction (Jas 1:6). The variability of wind in both direction and strength is a snapshot of the inconsistency and instability of people whose beliefs lack firm roots in the Word of God (Eph 4:14).

Pronouncing the ultimate end of wickedness, the Bible uses similar imagery when it declares that wickedness will be swept away like straw or chaff before a powerful wind (Job 21:18). The cynicism of the writer of the Book of Ecclesiastes, expressed in the oft-repeated statement, "Meaningless, meaningless, all is meaningless," is applied to those whose myopic minds cannot conceive of anything beyond what is under the sun. The thought that so much human striving under the sun is pointless pursuit of a fickle wind (Eccl 1:14) is a clear indicator that the vain human striving for deep satisfaction under the sun is demanding something this realm was never programmed to deliver. As expressed by C.S. Lewis, "How could [one] ever have thought this was the ultimate reality?" (See Endnote 4.)

WATER IN RIVERS

All streams flow into the sea, yet the sea is never full.
To the place the streams come from, there they return again.

Ecclesiastes 1:7

Streams are nature's conduits that transport Earth's fluids from one place to another. Geographers speak of streams of air (wind), streams of ice (glaciers), streams of molten rock (lava), and streams of water (rivers). With the exception of wind, fluids move downhill in response to gravity. In the case of wind (as we have just observed), streams of air move in response to pressure differences within the atmosphere, with air particles moving away from high pressure into areas of lower pressure. As a result, air movements at one location, unlike flows of ice, lava, and river flow, are variable in direction.

Rivers of surface water are an integral part of the water cycle, a natural mechanism that begins when energy from the sun lifts water into the atmosphere against the pull of gravity and continues when condensation and precipitation return this moisture back to Earth. Most precipitation is in liquid form, and most falls into oceans (not surprising since oceans cover about 70% of our planet's solid surface).

Surface topography dictates both the pattern and direction of runoff, and a collection system for water eventually evolves in valley sites, usually as narrow ribbons of fluid separated by heights of land. As they flow, they act as agents of erosion, cutting landscapes, moving materials, and depositing them at lower elevations. Thus, the river and its tributaries are born. Tributaries form branching patterns similar to patterns elsewhere in nature: in the branching patterns found in trees, in lightning forks, and in the configurations of blood vessels in our bodies.

While these natural water conduits always flow downhill, their destination is not always the ocean. Many rivers contribute their flow into other rivers or lakes downstream. Wherever a lake's basin margins are sufficiently low, inflow may result in overflow outward from the lake container. This is what occurs along the entire Great Lakes system, where the outflow from each lake contributes water to an adjacent lake downstream, then to the St. Lawrence River, then to a final destination in the Atlantic Ocean. However, a conduit system of connecting river-lake flow and overflow is not always possible along the margins of basins, as with the Volga–Caspian and Jordan–Dead Sea systems. Insufficient water prevents containers such as these from overflowing their edges into the ocean.

The Volga River System[109]

The number of rivers within a region reflects the amount of precipitation a region receives, the porosity of the surfaces over which they flow and the amount of water that evaporates from those surfaces.

Reflecting very high annual precipitation rates, stream densities within the humid areas of the Congo and Amazon basins, and in countries like Burma and the Philippines, are very high. By contrast, stream densities are conspicuously low in the hot desert regions of North Africa and central Australia. In the driest areas of the world, where annual rainfall is low and where high temperatures encourage high evaporation rates, there is frequently a 100% depletion of river water volume, and streams only reappear after sudden and intense thunderstorms. These conduits, called *ephemeral* or *intermittent streams*, are most common in areas where rivers are short. The periodic disappearance of streams from land surfaces exposes dry riverbeds, known as *wadis*.

Disappearing streams, familiar to most people in Bible Lands, are often employed as useful imagery in scripture. For example, in linking the unpredictable loyalty of certain friends to the behaviour of these streams, Job leaves no doubt about their lack of dependability:

> *But my brothers are as undependable as intermittent streams,*
> *as the streams that overflow when darkened by thawing ice*
> *and swollen with melting snow,*
> *but that stop flowing in the dry season,*
> *and in the heat*
> *vanish from their channels.*
>
> *Job 6:15–17*

In areas of abundant moisture, rivers are normally large and permanent (Yangtze, Amazon, St. Lawrence, Mekong, and Mississippi). Moreover, water volumes in these streams tend to increase in a downstream direction as secondary channels contribute and concentrate their waters within the larger main channels. However, not all streams display discharge increases toward their mouths. If a river that has accumulated large volumes of water in a humid region begins to penetrate a less humid region where water losses through evaporation exceed water gains through precipitation, water volumes frequently get severely depleted and the river *decreases* in size downstream. Examples of these rivers, known as *exotic streams*, include the Nile, the Niger, the Colorado, and the Jordan rivers.

In many cases, natural depletions are augmented by withdrawals of water for human consumption and by enhancement of evaporation through the construction of dams. Dams widen rivers and thereby increase evaporation rates through a river's increased surface area. One of the most dramatic illustrations of the effect of natural and anthropogenic influences on stream volume depletion relates to the Nile River. Natural depletion occurs during this river's long transit through the eastern Sahara Desert. Construction of the large Aswan Dam (which increased evaporation rates because of river widening), combined with withdrawals of water for irrigation purposes, has added to overall depletion. Although slightly longer than the mighty Amazon of South America, the average discharge at the Nile River's mouth is a mere 2800 cubic metres per second, while that of the Amazon is a staggering 200 000 cubic metres per second (about seventy times greater). This is not surprising since the Amazon's entire route is through the world's largest humid rainforest.

Globally, small streams such as creeks and brooks greatly outnumber giant streams. This truth reinforces again a fact of nature that the frequency of occurrence of a natural phenomenon decreases dramatically as the size of the phenomenon increases. In other words, there are many small or ordinary things or events, but few giant or spectacular ones. For example, snow *flurries* are more common than snow*storms*, and minor earthquakes occur far more frequently than ones described as cataclysmic. This size-frequency rule is also applicable to ocean waves, volcanic eruptions, droughts, flood events in river valleys, and even to planet diameters and even total goals scored in NHL hockey careers. Given the serious floods along the Mississippi River in 1993 and again in 2008, we are all grateful that events of this magnitude are relatively infrequent occurrences.

Rivers are nature's organized method of transporting water. While performing this primary function, they also erode their valleys. The capacity to transport eroded sediment varies with stream volume and stream velocity. In general, stream velocity decreases toward the mouth of a river where rivers are normally wider because land gradients are normally shallower. Reductions in speed increase sediment deposition, altering stream anatomy with the formation of depositional features such as meanders, deltas, and natural elevated banks called levees.

The presence of shallow gradients along with larger volumes at or near a river's terminus means that increases in water levels have the potential for widespread flooding of adjacent land. When this occurs, a system that is highly organized becomes somewhat chaotic. Flooding is most severe on land with shallow gradients whenever the rate of delivery of water to the river system exceeds the capacity of the system to contain and move water within existing channels. But while floods cause damage, they also contribute valuable soil nutrient recharge within floodplains. This benefit to the soil of periodic flooding was recognized within ancient communities in Mesopotamia, Egypt, China, and India where occasional flooding was regarded as a blessing that replenished depleted soil nutrients.

However, the impacts of flooding on human life and property can be catastrophic. Probably no river has contributed to human misery more than China's Huang He. Dubbed *China's Sorrow*, it is estimated to have killed more people than any other river in the world (see Chapter 8).

History reveals a longstanding human love affair with rivers. River valleys possess a tranquil appearance and serve as sources of water and recreation as well as natural political boundaries and convenient means of transportation.

The geography of settlement sites shows proximity to rivers (especially at confluence points) to be preferred settlement sites. In our wisest moments, we have chosen sites well away from places where flood hazard is high. When site selections have proven less than wise, some forms of stream management schemes have been implemented to regulate flow through dam construction to diminish the threat of flooding. In some cases, however, poor choices for human habitation have proven disastrous. A most troublesome site selection involves the city of New Orleans, Louisiana, near the terminus of the 3 900-kilometre-long Mississippi River.

The mighty Mississippi draws water from thirty-one American states as well as from the southern portions of two Canadian prairie provinces. Its basin, moving toward its mouth some 18 000 cubic metres of water per second as well as roughly 800 thousand tonnes of sediment daily, is a giant funnel with a single outlet at the end of a growing delta projecting out into the Gulf of Mexico.

Within this basin, floods are common, not only because much of the basin is flat, but also because the quantities of sediment deposited over the centuries near the mouth of the river have actually elevated the riverbed above the level of the surrounding land. Under normal conditions, the river is contained within naturally deposited banks called *levees*. However, if river water during flood stage manages to breach the levees on either bank, it spills onto land whose surface is invariably *lower* than the river from which it escaped.

For protection, New Orleans, with much of its land below sea level, is ringed with artificial levees. The combination of heavy rains, strong winds, and a storm surge from Hurricane Katrina in August 2005 caused numerous breaches within these banks. Resisting containment, the river flooded 80% of the city. Because of its elevation relative to sea level, all water not passed on, evaporated, or absorbed within New Orleans had to be pumped out or seek new pathways to the sea (see Chapter 8).

Given the arid and semi-arid climates of the Middle East, long permanent streams are uncommon. Notable exceptions are the Nile, the Tigris and the Euphrates. As examples of *exotic streams*, these rivers have headwaters that occupy regions where climates are more humid. The inclusion of the Jordan River as an important waterway in Bible Lands is not because it is large with considerable volume, but because there is little else in the region of comparable size. Among the rivers of scripture, it is the Jordan that predominates in references and prominence.

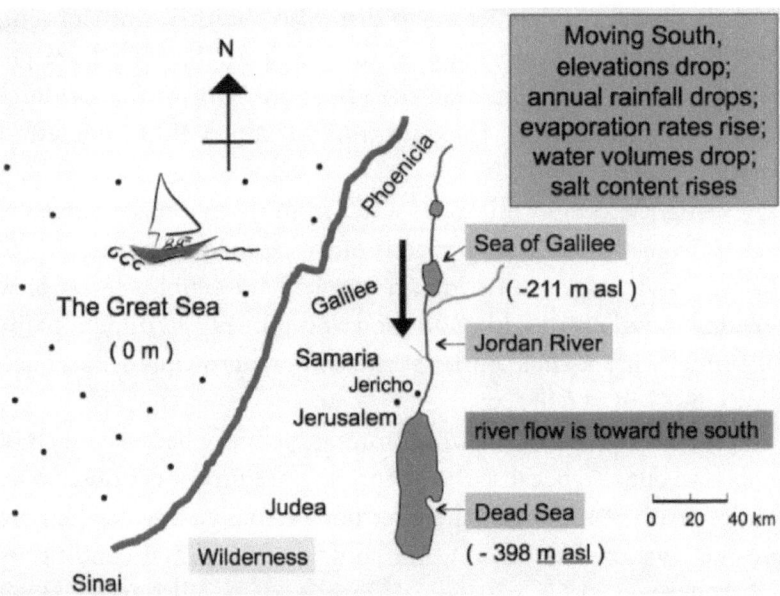

The Bible Lands[110]

The Jordan River System borders or flows through Lebanon, Syria, Jordan, Israel, and the West Bank. With serious shortages of fresh water supplies in the region, significant withdrawals of water from the river system by various nearby countries have seriously reduced downstream flow rates. Notably, south of the Sea of Galilee, pollution threatens the river's ecosystem. At present, the Jordan River System is listed as one of the world's 100 most endangered ecological sites. Cooperation among the local peoples to remedy a difficult situation has proven inadequate to date.

WATER IN THE CREATION OF LIGHTNING AND THUNDER

O ye Lightnings and Clouds, bless ye the Lord:
praise him, and magnify him forever.

Benedicite (BCP)

It was about 2:00 p.m., and the thick clouds darkened the skies to twilight. I had just settled my young campers onto their bunks for an afternoon rest in our tent when a sudden flash of light, followed immediately by a deafening explosion, broke the stillness. A few seconds later, accompanied by a powerful gust of wind, the heavens opened, and rain and hail poured down with a fury I had seldom seen.

Almost as quickly as it had arrived, the thunderstorm departed, and all became calm. Poking my head through the tent flap to examine our surroundings, I was startled by what I saw. The tall, stately white pine that had stood close to the entrance to our tent had been struck by lightning and had been ripped open. The energy within the lightning stroke had travelled through the length of the tree, instantly boiling its water and sap and shattering both bark and wood. My campers, terrified but uninjured, stood in silence beside their awestruck counsellor, trembling before what is, by comparison, a relatively minute expression of nature's awesome power unleashed in an instant and with little warning.

Listen to this, Job;
stop and consider God's wonders.
Do you know how God controls the clouds
and makes his lightning flash?

Job 37:14,15

What had happened, though terrifying, is not uncommon. Lightning is the sudden, prominent, and brilliant discharge of static electricity within the atmosphere that occurs when an imbalance in electrical charges between two places exceeds the ability of the intervening air to insulate and maintain that imbalance. The dramatic phenomenon, common to much of the low and mid-latitudes, has even been observed on other planets.

Estimates of rates of world lightning strikes are staggering, with the greatest frequency experienced in Africa's Democratic Republic of Congo. Lightning-imaging sensors onboard orbiting satellites tell us that individual bolts of lightning, about 1 to 3 centimetres in diameter, frequently occur on our planet each day. In Canada, the frequency of lightning storms is greatest in southern Ontario but rare in Arctic lands.

Most lightning is associated with land areas during the afternoon hours of the summer season and travel between cloud and cloud or between cloud and ground surfaces. Surfaces in the paths of lightning include places of prominence that represent targets of opportunity. Aircraft in flight, Toronto's CN Tower, and the Eiffel Tower in Paris have been struck repeatedly. Lightning has struck the space shuttle on its launch pad. Virtually all exposed surfaces are vulnerable. Lightning striking a sandy beach can convert a small amount of the sand into glass. Lightning striking forested areas is a frequent trigger for forest fires. Lightning that strikes people inflicts serious burns and, in about 20% of the cases, causes instant death.

It is friction associated with turbulent and abundant atmospheric water vapour that generates lightning discharges. The enormity of electrical discharges associated with lightning relates to the magnitude of its voltage (energy) and amperage (current). Total energy released within an average thunderstorm is considered comparable to an atomic bomb explosion.

With so much energy, it is not surprising that temperatures within a lightning strike often exceed 20 000 °C. Such temperatures (three times the sun's surface temperature) instantaneously superheat the air column that surrounds the discharge flash. This thermal work, completed in about 30 microseconds, results in instantaneous localized expansion of the air, heard as a violent atmospheric shock wave called *thunder*. Thus, thunder is the sound of exploding air from heat created by lightning.

If the lightning strike is close by, the sound of thunder is a startling sharp crack that is heard a split second after the flash. In fact, thunder heard close by is one of nature's loudest sounds. If the strike is far away, the sound is a low-intensity, low-frequency rumble, delayed because of distance, and sustained for a few seconds as it reverberates off various surfaces like hills, trees, and buildings. Time intervals between seeing the flash of lightning and hearing the sound of thunder increase at a rate of about three seconds for each kilometre of separation.

Given the magnitude of the explosions in thunder, it is not uncommon for them to be heard over distances in excess of 20 kilometres, depending on the temperature of the intervening air. Far off lightning strikes may not be heard for a full minute after the flash is seen. In addition, lightning strikes are not necessarily confined to the vicinity of the clouds that produced them. As a result, danger from lightning may spread many kilometres beyond the thunderstorm and appear within a clear sky. This explains the origin of the familiar phrase: *"a bolt out of the blue."*

Despite our sophisticated knowledge of the atmosphere, we can exercise little control over the pathways or intensities of thunderstorms. The good news is that nature does offer some hints of its impending action. While lightning discharges are sudden, the conditions that produce them develop gradually. The prominent, billowy, and towering cumulonimbus clouds so often associated with them also take shape gradually. Skies do not darken instantaneously. The first flashes of lightning and the first rumblings of thunder are usually some distance away.

The intensity of sight and sound are dampened, and the time lag between sound *after* sight affords the observer some time to prepare for what is to follow. Thunderstorms that arrive during the night are more surprising as cloud development cannot be seen. However, it is against the night sky that lightning flashes are brightest, most spectacular and more clearly defined.

Science informs us that lightning is much more than merely spectacular atmospheric light displays. Flashes have a critical role in the chemistry of atmospheric nitrogen by making it available for plant growth. Nitrogen, the most abundant gas in our atmosphere, is chemically stable. That is, it does not readily combine with other substances to form compounds. The reason lies in its strong molecular bonding. To facilitate alternate combinations with other chemicals, these bonds must be broken. To break bonds in molecules requires energy. The energy required to perform this task is provided in part by lightning, whose action permits the formation of various chemical nutrients in a form that plants can use.

> *But God made the earth by his power;*
> *he founded the world by his wisdom*
> *and stretched out the heavens by his understanding.*
> *When he thunders, the waters in the heavens roar;*
> *he makes clouds rise from the ends of the earth.*
> *He sends lightning with the rain*
> *and brings out the wind from his storehouses.*
>
> *Jeremiah 10:12–13*

Throughout history, especially prior to human understanding of the source and activity associated with this powerful atmospheric phenomenon, lightning was regarded and worshipped as a form of unknown and frightening deity. In Greek mythology, Zeus was acknowledged as god of sky and thunder and was usually depicted holding a weapon-like thunderbolt in his raised right hand. In Roman mythology, Jupiter was his equivalent. Of particular interest is the frequency with which gods of thunder appear in the mythologies of various disparate peoples, from Central America, Europe, and South Asia.

People of the Middle East were not unfamiliar with thunder and lightning. In scripture, lightning is used to signify God's presence. It is described as the arrow of God (Ps 7), the spear of God (Hab 3:11), even God's finger (Job 36:32), but never God Himself. Its near-ubiquitous presence on Earth alludes to God's omnipresence and illustrates our inability to hide from Him.

Psalm 29 has sometimes been referred to as *"the song of the thunderstorm."* Here, as elsewhere, a visible image is linked with something beyond the visible, a natural force with an even greater Force beyond it. The psalm acknowledges the greater power of the Creator, who is present even when the thunderstorm has disappeared. The link in the metaphor is with the voice of the Lord—thundering, powerful, and majestic, with the capacity to shake and shatter, and yet with the capacity to bless people with peace, with strength and wisdom. It is interesting to observe that the vision in the Book of Revelation concerning the final judgment has, as a fanfare, "flashes of lightning, rumblings, and peals of thunder" (Rev 16).

ATMOSPHERIC WATER IN THE CREATION OF THE RAINBOW

*Like the appearance of a rainbow
in the clouds on a rainy day,
so was the radiance around him.
This was the appearance of the likeness
of the glory of the LORD.*

Ezekiel 1:28a

Late on a sunny day outside a local fire station, a firefighter was lifted high above the ground in the bucket of an aerial ladder. With people watching, a lever at the end of his high-pressure hose was turned on and a powerful spray of water exploded from the nozzle. The spray formed a fine mist in the nearby air and, in an instant, a sequence of thin concentric bands of colour formed as a full 360-degree conspicuous ring against the wall of spray. With poorly defined margins, these bands created a continuous colour spectrum: red on the outside, followed by orange, yellow, green, blue, indigo, then finally violet on the inside. The action of sunlight passing through a patch of water droplets had produced what nature regularly manufactures without human assistance, namely a pleasing spectral display of arcing colour—a *rainbow*.

Rainbows capture the attention of both young and old. As in any moment of wonder, questions concerning this beautiful phenomenon abound. How do they form? What determines their shape and location in the sky? What process generates the colour? Can we ever see a naturally created rainbow displayed as a full circle in the sky as was manufactured with the firefighter's hose?

Many, if not most of us prefer to enjoy a rainbow rather than analyze one. We may prefer to allow the communicative qualities of an assemblage of rich colour to engage our imaginations and speak to us in a language devoid of words. However, since enjoyment is often enhanced through an understanding of patterns and processes, let us dip into a small sampling of information.

While our planet intercepts a wide variety of energy from the sun, very little falls within the category of visible light. Visible light comes packaged as a mixture of colours. And colour is a property dependent on its *wavelength*.

To manufacture the most common rainbow, nature requires two ingredients: sunshine and a transparent physical means of separating the colours within it. Among nature's materials that qualify, water droplets and ice crystals appear to be favourites. Because they exist as virtually ubiquitous substances in the atmosphere, they can perform their jobs of colour separation in countless locations simultaneously. In addition, glass in special shapes, such as prisms, produces smaller colour separations as well.

Nature's method of separating colours involves a process called *refraction* in which light is bent as it enters a transparent substance. Since the amount of bending of the energy entering the substance is determined by wavelength, the process of refraction becomes a method of distillation by which different wavelengths express themselves as separated visible bands of colour; in fact, a continuous spectrum of varying colour, from red light (longer waves) to violet light (shorter waves).

The process occurs in individual drops of water or in ice crystals. The resulting product of this natural process is the rainbow, seen most vividly when it is observed against the darkest backgrounds.

Nature is able to manufacture additional visible atmospheric effects through the process of light refraction and reflection. For example, a second colour spectrum is often formed outside a primary rainbow. Invariably, this spectrum is less conspicuous than its primary. Moreover, its colour sequence appears in reverse order, with red on the inside of the arc.

Many of us are also familiar with rainbows seen, not in opposition to the sun, but rather *in the direction of it*. Chief among these are *halos* (rings, often with visible spectral bands that completely encircle the sun or occasionally the full moon) and *sundogs* (false suns called *parhelia*, meaning *alongside the sun*). Sundogs can be found along a halo's luminous ring at low sun times, appearing as prominent colour bands displaced equal angles to the left and to the right of the sun. Like halos, sundogs are created with sunlight shining, not through water droplets, but through high-altitude ice crystals in high cirrus clouds. With halos and sundogs, there is no accompanying rain event.

At this point in the discussion, the role of geometry in our observing of any rainbow must be considered. (For those wishing to take this discussion further, see Endnotes).[111]

> *What skilful limner e'er would choose*
> *To paint the rainbow's varying hues,*
> *Unless to mortal it were given*
> *To dip his brush in dyes of heaven?*
>
> Sir Walter Scott[112]

RAINBOW IMAGERY IN SCRIPTURE

Rainbow imagery in scripture, though rare, is nevertheless of great importance. The first reference to a rainbow in the Bible occurs in the Book of Genesis immediately following the great flood (Gen 9). Additional references occur in Ezekiel (1:28) and Revelation (4:3). While the latter two references link the rainbow to a likeness of the glory of God, it is the reference in Genesis that links this same image to the *mercy* of God. It is all about God's covenant declared to Noah:

> *Never again will all life be destroyed*
> *by the waters of a flood;*
> *never again will there be a flood*
> *to destroy the earth.*
>
> Genesis 9:11b

The rainbow in the sky is installed by God as His reminder *to Himself* of His covenant of grace to Noah (as if God needs a reminder) (Gen 9:12–16). Its periodic but conspicuous presence in the sky, along with its shape, also serves as a visual reminder *to us* of God's mercy—His method of dealing with human sin. Imaginative minds have often seen in the rainbow's shape a resemblance to a bow, a threatening weapon of war. Others have commented that it is neither threatening nor a weapon since, as a bow, it is without string or arrows. Also, in its orientation, its arch is always directed upward toward the heavens and not downward toward Earth and humanity.

8

FLOOD

*The rain came down, the streams rose,
and the winds blew and beat against that house;
yet it did not fall, because it had its foundation on the rock.*

Matt 7:25

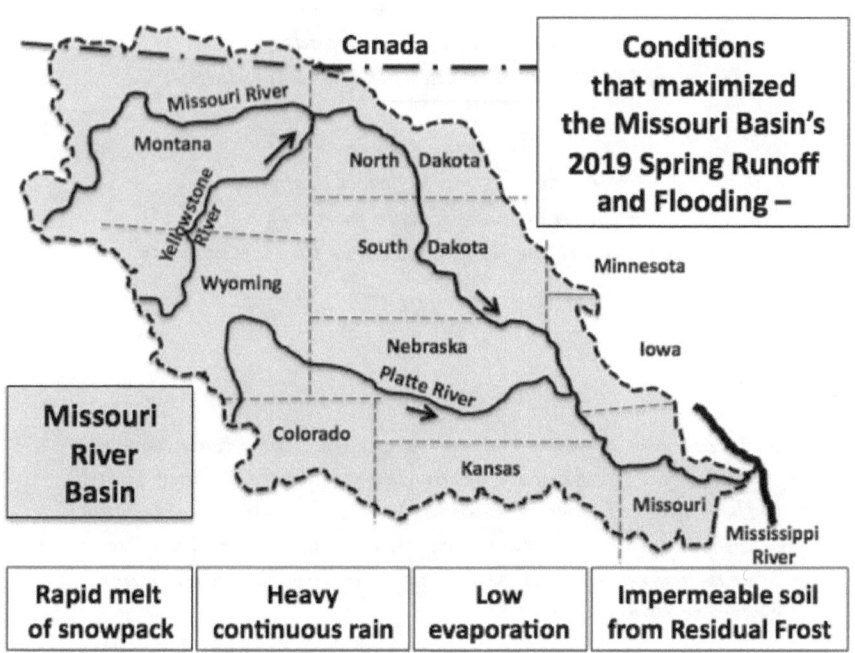

The Missouri River Basin[113]

Occasionally,
Mother Nature presents us with one of her superlatives
that appears to fall outside
its wide spectrum of natural variability.

Spectacular events come in many forms:
a record 24-hour snowfall;
a powerful and destructive sustained wind;
the longest ever drought;
an unprecedented volcanic blast;
the greatest ever earthquake.

The list seems endless.
Each time such an event occurs,
heads turn, people wonder,
and Nature's spectrum of magnitudes widens.

But among the events
that have proven the most destructive
to human life and property,
it is probably the flood that earns the first ranking.

JES

As the day of horror drew to a close, the ocean calmed. But where at the start of the day people were going about their normal lives or relaxing at exotic beach resorts, now millions of people were struggling with the reality of tens of thousands of dead or missing relatives, destroyed homes, and shattered lives.

written in the aftermath of the Indian Ocean Tsunami[114]

A few summers ago, returning home from vacation, our neighbours discovered that a burst water pipe had converted their basement into a shallow swimming pool. The incident, resulting in damage to their basement and its contents, appeared soon after in our local weekly newspaper. It began: *"Burst pipe floods home."* Although confined to a portion of a single dwelling, the incident illustrates the essential nature of the phenomenon known as *flood*.

A flood is a condition in which water within some form of container overflows its bounds and inundates places where it doesn't belong. On a small scale, like the one above, floods are annoyances whose effects are minimal and dealt with quickly. However, when they occur over extensive areas of land, effects on life and property can be highly destructive, costly, and even tragic.

Floods are facilitated by the fact that water is a fluid and that it possesses low viscosity. This means that it is not only capable of flow but is capable of flow with ease. Moreover, it is a liquid fluid that readily evaporates. This means that water is able to alter its place of residency, often over considerable distances via the atmosphere, and gain potential energy through lift. This it constantly does in massive amounts within a circulatory system called *the Global Water Cycle*.

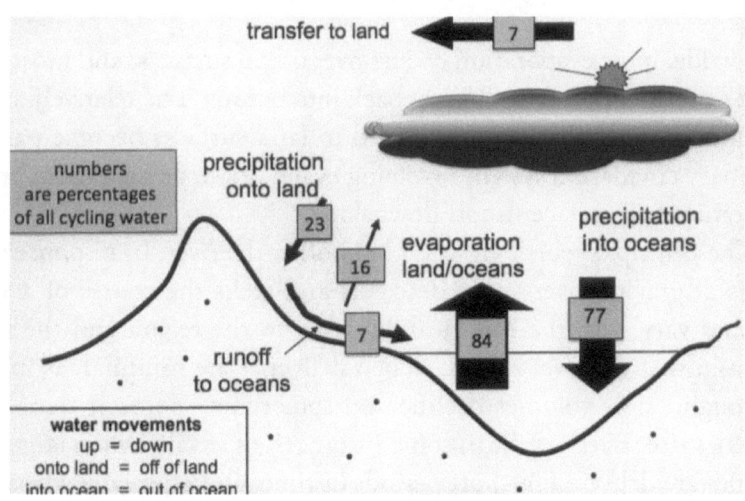

The World's Water Cycle
Percentages Transferred to Various Residences[115]

Each year, an average of 2 metres of water evaporates from the Earth surface. Since the amount of water residing in the atmosphere is believed to be roughly constant over time, it follows that the same amount of water must fall back to Earth surfaces annually as precipitation. It is clear, however, that while these figures describe conditions globally, they do not reflect conditions at any single place or at any single time. In fact, our world's water cycle displays great variations in the quantities of water circulating from place to place and from time to time. Precipitation amounts in Hawaii and rainforests far exceed those in dry areas like Antarctica and the Atacama Desert of Chile. Evaporation rates from warm oceans far surpass evaporation rates from cold ones. Moreover, while rainfall delivered to areas of southern Ontario displays minimal monthly variation, those amounts directed to monsoon lands show a definite seasonality, with the greatest fraction arriving during the region's warmest months. Thus, over the entire planet, the water cycle's delivery system reveals significant temporal and spatial variations, rendering flood conditions inevitable in some places, and drought conditions in others.

FLOODS ASSOCIATED WITH RIVERS AND THEIR MARGINS

Worldwide, most evaporation occurs over ocean surfaces, and most of the world's precipitation falls directly back into oceans. The relatively smaller amounts of water that are transferred to land surfaces become part of a secondary circulation system involving evaporation, precipitation, ground infiltration and surface runoff downslope.

The principal vehicle of surface runoff is the river. In response to the effects of gravity, river water descends and seeks the course of a valley. Volumes vary with the moisture delivered to the region and the size of the basin that the river drains. When deliveries are minimal, as in times of drought, river volumes decline and sometimes approach zero. When deliveries rise, rivers swell. In some instances, especially when large water volumes are delivered in short periods of time, and especially when water volumes are augmented by rapidly melting snowpacks, the river becomes unable to act as an efficient conduit to drain the landscape. Extensive rising and widening result in the phenomenon of river flooding of adjacent land surfaces, especially where soils are already at or near saturation levels and where adjacent lands, especially along flood plains, possess low surface gradients.

In river valleys with a history of frequent flooding, efforts to mitigate the severity of flooding, especially near populated regions, have been implemented. For example, on the Grand River System in southern Ontario, construction of dams along the system's main tributaries has greatly reduced floods along most of the waterway. Dam construction mitigates the threat of flood by restricting flow during times of excessive river discharge and storing excess water upstream in artificial lakes. These reservoirs are permitted to slowly drain during periods of diminished basin flow.

In general, most rivers will experience the phenomenon of flooding at some time. The most extensive flooding occurs on rivers that traverse the flattest land over the longest distances. Severe flooding has often occurred along the Amazon, Mississippi and Nile rivers. In this century alone, a sampling of places that experienced serious flooding include: Central Europe (2002); Mumbai, India (2005); Louisiana (2005); Indonesia (2007); Queensland, Australia (2010); China (2010); Brazil (2011); Japan (2012); Alberta, Canada (2013); Northern Colorado (2013); and the Missouri Basin (2019).

Natural events such as snowstorms, hailstorms, hurricanes, earthquakes, and floods are often identified qualitatively with adjectives: moderate, severe, or devastating. A more quantitative method identifies a natural event in terms of the percent probability of recurrence of an event of similar magnitude. For example, a river not known to produce devastating flooding may be labelled a *1000-year* event. The 1000-year label, alluding to the frequency of an event of similar magnitude, is called that event's *return period*. A 1000-year event, for example, may occur at any time before or after the predicted return period, since the number is a statistical average. In general, return periods increase in length with the severity of an event. Thus, it is reasonable to say that with a return period of 1 000 years, a flood of similar magnitude has only a 0.1% chance of occurring in a single year *in that location*. Among the most unfortunate places experiencing the greatest frequency of major flooding—thus a brief return period—is China's Huang He, *China's Sorrow*.

THE HUANG HE: A CASE STUDY OF CATASTROPHIC RIVER FLOODING

The Huang He or Yellow River flows eastward from the mountains in western China toward the Yellow Sea. Through the years, this 2 900-kilometre-long liquid conduit, along with its longer partner, the Yangtze, and their tributaries, have been associated with some of the most devastating valley floods our world has witnessed, accounting for the highest recorded death tolls from river flooding on Earth. In 1887, floods and their aftermaths killed an estimated two million people. In 1938, close to one million people died. But it was during the 1931 floods and their aftermaths that deaths attributed to the Huang He and Yangtze floods were reported to have reached a staggering four million people. This is probably the world's single greatest known natural disaster. Figures included deaths from drowning, exposure, hunger, and disease.

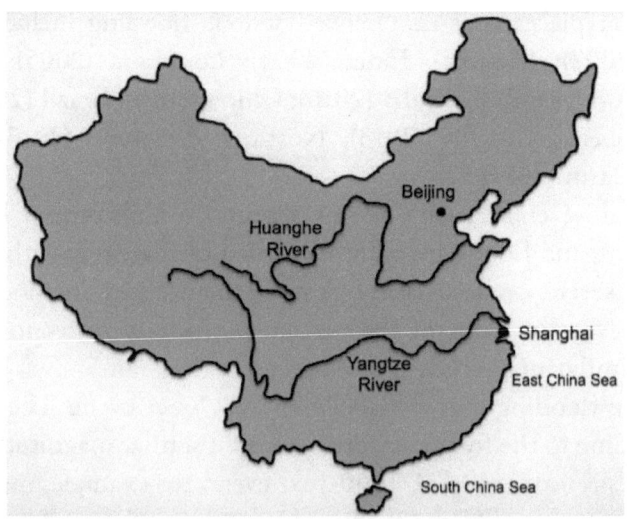

China's Two Principal Rivers[116]

While many of the world's rivers have claimed countless lives through flooding, the Huang He's reputation is unparalleled. The reasons for this wretched distinction are linked to three clear causes: two that are environmental, and one linked to population distribution and numbers:

1. **Massive accumulations of sediment from upstream sources that have severely altered downstream river anatomy:**

   Midway along the course of the Huang He, west of Beijing, there exists a giant windblown deposit known as the Loess Plateau. Believed to be the largest formation of its kind in the world, the plateau is a massive accumulation of fine silt believed to have been eroded and transported by wind from distant arid surfaces to the west. Being very fine and largely unconsolidated material, Loess readily succumbs to the cutting action of lively river water, especially during peak flow periods. Estimated annual load transport of sediment is very high. As the river descends to lower and flatter terrain further east, its flow rate drops, its width widens, and its capacity to maintain the silt in suspension declines. The result is that for the last 25% of the river's course toward the sea, a relentless rain of yellow silt imported from upstream falls onto the riverbed. Over many centuries, this thickening accumulation has succeeded in elevating the riverbed higher than the surrounding land. Fortunately, the structural integrity of the river during normal flow rates is maintained by the natural levees also formed through stream deposition. During peak runoff periods, however, such is not the case.

2. **A river basin exposed to seasonal summer monsoon precipitation with annual quantities that frequently far exceed average values:**

   Being on the northern extremity of the Indian Ocean summer monsoon, the basin of the Huang He does not receive its precipitation evenly throughout the year. Instead, most is concentrated in the summer months. In addition, during times when the pulses of summer monsoonal winds are particularly severe, summer precipitation into the region can far exceed normal values. On such occasions, river levees are easily breached, allowing water and its suspended load to pour from the river *down* onto surrounding land. Here flooding can be extensive because land gradients are so shallow.

3. **Overlap of some of China's greatest population densities with areas of the river basin most prone to the severest flooding:**

> Serious environmental conditions facilitating serious flooding along the Hwang He would not by themselves earn this river the title *China's Sorrow* if it were not for the fact that China's urban and rural population densities are among their highest precisely where the flood hazard is most severe.

FLOODS ASSOCIATED WITH OCEANS AND COASTAL LANDS

Valley sites along the margins of rivers are not the only regions that are visited by floods. Natural floods also occur along the line that separates oceans from continents. Unlike river flooding, oceans do not spill their contents on surrounding shorelines because of localized precipitation. Relative to the volume of water contained in oceans, the amount of water that even the heaviest rainfalls contribute locally would represent far less than a cup of water in a large lake and would do little to alter ocean volume and sea level. Instead, floods from oceans are the direct result of massive *displacements* of ocean water. Forcing mechanisms contributing to significant ocean water displacement include regular tidal forcing (induced principally by lunar gravity); unexpected tsunamis (triggered by giant sub-oceanic earthquakes); and periodic wind-induced storm surges (wind setup from local hurricanes and strong onshore winds).

The degree to which ocean water is able to inundate coastal lands is dependent on the magnitude of each force, its duration, as well as on the gradient of the coastal lands affected. The largest displacements ever recorded have occurred when more than one forcing mechanism combine their influences to reinforce each other simultaneously. Among all influences, however, it is the tsunami, which ranks as the most destructive of all forcing mechanisms for coastal flooding.

COASTAL FLOODING GENERATED BY EARTHQUAKE-INDUCED TSUNAMIS

1. Indian Ocean Tsunami

On 26 December, 2004, at 8:00 a.m. local time, as most people in Canada were finishing Christmas dinner, a major human tragedy was about to visit the opposite side of the world. Far under the Indian Ocean, a geologic drama was unfolding involving two crustal plates: the Indo-Australian plate drifting slowly northward and the massive Asiatic plate standing in its way. But, as frequently happens over time, the articulating surfaces between these plates had become locked. Gradually, enormous strain developed as these locked surfaces resisted the relentless and uninterrupted plate drift northward. On Sunday morning (local time), the strain on the crust came to exceed the rock's capacity to bear that strain, at which time the rock experienced a sudden catastrophic failure. In response, the bed of the Indian Ocean snapped violently, and a significant portion of the seabed rose vertically, forcing its heavy liquid burden upward. Instantly, at the epicentre of all this tumult, in the waters of the Indian Ocean off the northwest tip of the island of Sumatra, a seismic wave (or *tsunami*) was born.

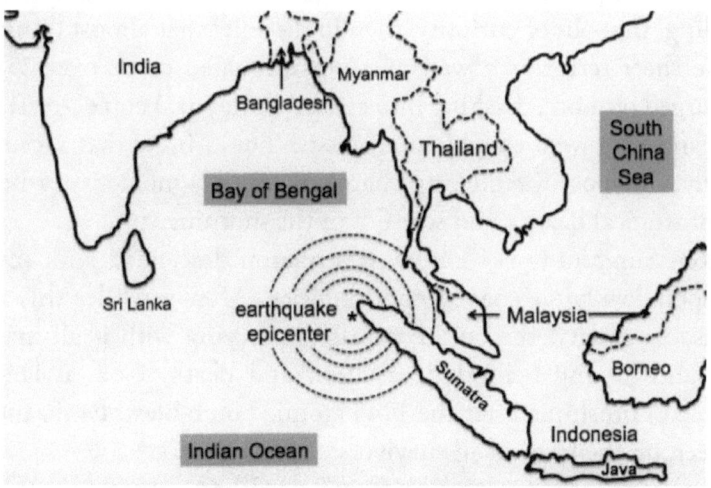

Major Regions Impacted by the Indian Ocean Quake and Tsunami[117]

The resulting geologic snap was one of the fifth largest in all recorded geologic history. It was as if a giant hammer had struck the Earth. Islands adjacent to the fracture jerked into new positions as seismic instruments recorded a violently quaking planet. Millions of cubic metres of water shifted to accommodate a newly shaped oceanic bowl. Our planet's geographic poles shifted whole centimetres. The shape of the Earth was altered; its speed of rotation increased. The result was a microsecond reduction in day length.

What had happened? Why this sudden monstrous crustal perturbation? The answer is, again, that nature was merely acting normally, behaving in accordance with the laws and forces to which it is continually subjected.

Planetary quaking is what our planet does on a regular basis. Fortunately, most quaking is of low intensity. The 2004 Indonesian earthquake and tsunami was significant, not because of its occurrence, but because of its magnitude, its location, and because its destructiveness spread into fourteen nearby countries.

Transferring its energy to the water, the quake generated a massive surface wave that radiated outward in all directions with a speed proportional to the depth of the ocean. As it approached land, ocean depths decreased and wave speeds dropped. Also, the shape of the wave changed as its trough impacted the ocean bed, with lengths decreasing and heights growing significantly. People near the shore watched the drama unfolding, first out of curiosity, then in disbelief that almost immediately became sheer terror as a wall of water estimated to be over 25 metres high surged onshore, crashing into coastal lowlands. People, trees, houses, boats, and cars were caught in a massive liquid brew that raced inland virtually unopposed, rendering chaotic what only moments earlier was a place of tropical beauty and serenity in the morning sun.

From Sumatra to Sri Lanka, destruction descended with incredible fury upon low-lying coastal communities. After a while, this time in response to gravity, the ocean retreated, carrying with it all manner of debris and leaving behind devastation and death. Coastal landscapes resembled Hiroshima after the 1945 atomic bomb blast. Panic and shock were seen on the faces of all survivors.

By the seventh day, the estimated dead had surpassed a staggering 240 000. Many people had disappeared, either buried in deep rubble or lost in the depths of an angry ocean. Injuries were too numerous to count. In the aftermath, in an environment devoid of familiar features, adequate food, clean water, medicine, and shelter, and sadly replaced with pain, suffering, loss, and violent death, fears mounted that the horror wasn't over, and that deaths from malaria and cholera would soon exceed those from the tsunami and quake combined.

2. Pacific Ocean Tsunami

Seven years later, on 11 March, 2011, another massive plate failure occurred, this time in the bed of the western Pacific just offshore from the island arc of Japan. The rock failure, jerking the land eastward whole metres, generated the most violent earthquake ever experienced by the Japanese, and the world's fourth largest ever recorded. Given the magnitude of the quake (9.0 magnitude) and its shallow epicentre, this seismic event triggered a powerful tsunami. With the epicentre so close to Japan's coast, it was only minutes before it came ashore.

The tsunami provided little time for people to move out of harm's way, and its effects were devastating. As a wall of water with estimated heights of 38 metres rushed inland, cars, entire houses, boats, and trees were picked up, mixed together and devoured, swept long distances inland, and then carried out to sea in a massive backwash. People young and old, rich and poor alike, unable to flee the advancing wave, disappeared within the churning maelstrom. In a matter of minutes, order had been converted into a chaotic mess and little could be found where things were supposed to be. People who somehow survived in the immediate vicinity of the onrushing water stared in shock at the magnitude and extent of the tragedy and the speed with which their properties had been radically devoured.

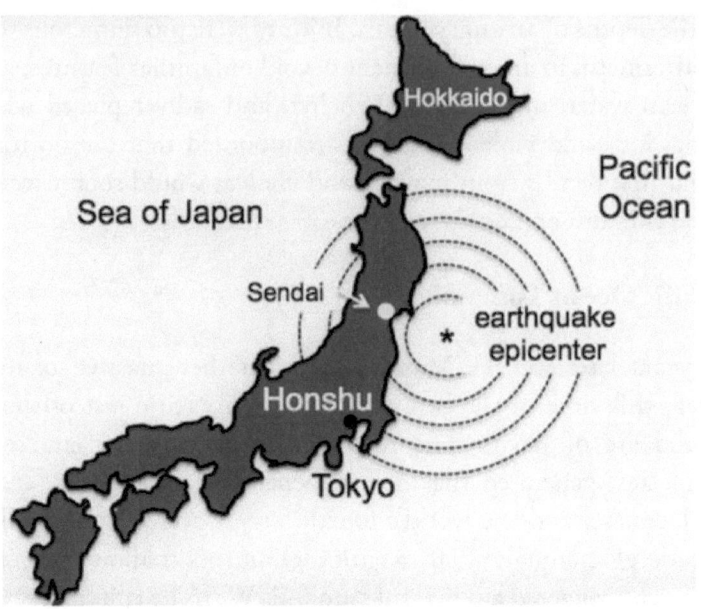

Birthplace of Quake and Tsunami of 11 March, 2011[118]

For days afterwards, aftershocks large enough to qualify as major quakes in themselves struck the region. People searched for survivors. But as hours changed to days, searching for survivors changed to recovery of bodies and to rummaging through debris for precious recognizable memorabilia.

With the utter ruin that was left after the departing wave; with fertile coastal farmland contaminated with high concentrations of salt water from the sea; with tens of thousands of people traumatized, homeless and hungry; with economic shock waves reverberating through world stock markets; and with the fears and uncertainties generated by the release of harmful radiation from one of Japan's damaged nuclear power facilities, the original 9.0-magnitude earthquake was proving to be just the first act in a nightmare that would not soon end but rather would endure past the long and arduous tasks of rescue, relief, and recovery. With the triple disaster of quake, tsunami, and seriously damaged nuclear power plant, the March 2011 disaster had become the world's most expensive catastrophe. Losses topped a staggering $235 billion. By 2014, estimates for Japan's final recovery from the disaster came to exceed $300 billion USD.

COASTAL FLOODING GENERATED BY HURRICANE-INDUCED STORM SURGES

1. Katrina

While tsunamis as flood-inducing agents influence sea surfaces from below, violent hurricanes perform the same task from above. In the last chapter, brief mention was made of Hurricane Katrina, that, in August 2005, passed over south Florida and entered the very warm waters of the Gulf of Mexico, intensifying while making its way toward the Louisiana coast. Adding more thermal energy along the way through a most vigorous evaporation process, Katrina made landfall close to the mouth of the Mississippi River in Louisiana as a fully mature Category 5 superstorm, Laden with vast amounts of evaporated water already converting back into thick cloud and precipitation within a darkening spiral, Katrina set in motion the series of predicted vicious atmospheric events that would deliver an atmospheric chain reaction both to Louisiana and Mississippi with the release of massive amounts of latent heat, followed by increased instability of the atmosphere, sustained torrential rain, powerful destructive onshore winds triggering a storm surge, and severe widespread flooding, especially in low-lying coastal communities, It became one of the strongest storms ever to travel through the Gulf and added credence to fears that storms of this magnitude increasing in both frequency and magnitude.

The *location* of Katrina's path and eventual landfall along low-lying shorelines was as critical to its destructive capability, as was its *strength* as a Category-5 storm. The reason for this is to be found in the structure and behaviour of a hurricane. Like tornadoes, hurricanes rotate, and do so counter-clockwise in places north of the equator. Rotation means that winds about its spiral arms can be from any direction, depending upon the portion of the giant spiral impacting a location.

Katrina was advancing northward. Winds within the spiral to the east of the eye were vigorously moving air northward. The combination of a northward-moving system and a wind from the spiral *toward* the north gave the east side of the spiral its strongest onshore winds, intense rainfall and the powerful storm surge. The situation was made even worse because Katrina made landfall on a portion of coastline that could least handle such a crisis, namely the low-lying lands of the Mississippi delta and those areas of New Orleans at or *below* sea level.

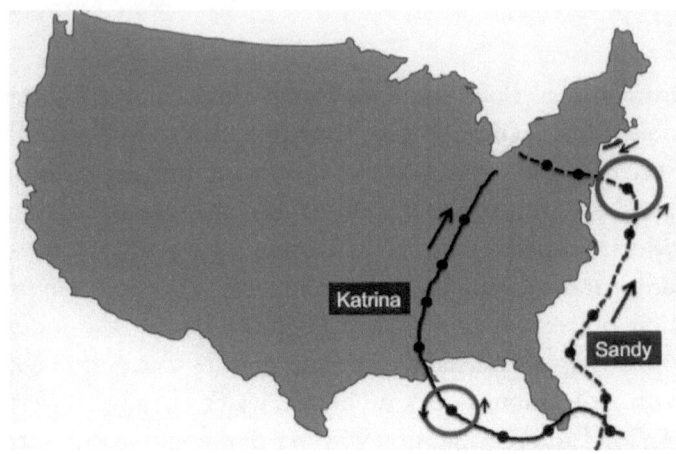

Two Violent Hurricane Tracks[119]

Katrina caused massive damage to local infrastructure and necessitated the resettlement of many of the area's residents. Over 1800 people were confirmed dead. In New Orleans, over fifty levees were breached by Katrina's storm surge and over 80% of the city was flooded. Offshore, it destroyed some islands. Estimated property damage resulting from Katrina topped $100 billion, making it the costliest American hurricane to date. As predicted, Katrina's continued passage northward over land led to its demise since it had been detached from the warm energy-generating marine environment that provided its moisture and latent heat.

2. Sandy

Arriving close to the end of October, Sandy was a late entry to the 2012 American hurricane season. Like Katrina, it began in the Atlantic as a tropical depression. But unlike Katrina, Sandy migrated northward, tracking parallel to the US coast some distance offshore. Then, as predicted, it suddenly veered northwest toward the mainland, delivering hurricane-force winds and heavy rainfall to the densely populated urban centres in and around New York and New Jersey. The result was a storm surge that brought severe flooding onshore to that country's greatest concentration of people. It became known as *Super Storm Sandy* for the following four reasons:

1. Sandy was massive in size and slow moving. These two characteristics maximized the hurricane's area of influence and its time at any single site.

2. Sandy's location as it bore down on the American coast maximized the strength of the storm surge, this time created off its northern flank. Hurricane-force onshore easterly winds hit the coast near the eastern end of the narrow Long Island Sound. Water funnelled westward through the Sound into an increasingly confined space on Long Island's northern flank, making overflow and severe flooding of adjacent lands inevitable. Ironically, many of the surfaces inundated by Sandy were part of the land reclamation program that has seen the gradual southward extension of Lower Manhattan Island.

3. Meteorological phenomena classified as depressions, storms, and ultimately hurricanes are all atmospheric disturbances involving low atmospheric pressure. Lowest central pressures are normally associated with the most severe weather events. Sandy broke existing records locally with some of the lowest barometric pressures ever recorded in the US.

4. The arrival of Sandy in the New York–New Jersey region on October 29 coincided with the timing of a full moon. During this lunar phase, sun, moon, and Earth are close to being collinear; that is, aligned in a virtual straight line in space. While the gravitational attraction of both sun and moon influence our oceans continually, a collinear alignment ensures that their separate multiple forcing mechanisms were reinforcing each other at the same time (see Chapter 3). In the area of the New Jersey shore, collinear alignment increased high tides by an estimated 20%.

With wind, rain, and storm surge combining along its entire path, Sandy was responsible for the deaths of over 250 people (half of those Americans). It affected the lives of people in seven countries, from the Caribbean through to Canada, and made its presence felt in almost half of the US states. It flooded subway tunnels, grounded thousands of commercial flights, cut off electrical service to millions, and left thousands of people homeless. Preliminary estimates of total damage topped $60 billion in the United States alone.

ANTICIPATED FLOODING FROM GLOBAL WARMING

While floods from disturbances over and under oceanic water bodies can have a serious impact on both life and property in coastal areas, their effects are both temporary and relatively local. Recently, however, a far more serious but less dramatic threat of flooding has arisen whose impact is expected to be both long term and more widespread. The agent strong enough to generate floods of this magnitude is global warming, a naturally occurring form of climate change that now appears induced, or at least augmented, by human influences.

The world's continents and islands get their shapes and sizes largely from the amount of water present in the oceans that surround them and from the forces that temporarily redistribute this water spatially. On any world map, the location of lines that delineate the edges of these land surfaces represents the average position of global coastlines over time. Since total ocean volume has been relatively constant through recent history and since forcing mechanisms from gravity and atmospheric disturbances create only temporary dislocations, world maps have been able to treat coastlines as largely fixed through time.

But what happens when shorelines are subject not only to a *redistribution* of ocean water over the Earth's crustal surface, but also to a long-term net change in total ocean water *volume*, a condition that is expected to endure? Historically, ocean boundaries have migrated in response to sea level changes. When sea levels drop, continental areas expand. The reverse occurs when sea levels rise. The major contributor to changing water volumes is long-term alterations in world temperatures.

Altered sea levels are linked to global warming for two major reasons. Firstly, warming causes a thermal expansion of water, increasing world sea levels because the same mass of water occupies a larger volume. Secondly, warming enhances glacial melt, thus contributing additional volumes of water to ocean basin that are now in storage on land within large ice sheets. Long ago, during so-called ice ages, cooler global temperatures are believed to have significantly *reduced* ocean levels and *increased* land areas through an increase in ice volumes over continental lands. This resulted in the recession of shorelines globally, and the creation of land bridges: most notably between Siberia and Alaska, and between the European mainland and the British Isles.

In recent millennia, world glaciers have receded, restricting residual ice sheets to higher latitude and altitude locations and raising global sea levels to present values. Given the magnitude of ice still resident on land surfaces (mostly over the Antarctic continent, but also over Greenland), the potential for additional widespread increases in sea levels through the melt process is significant and worrisome.

At present, annual ocean level rises are measured in a few millimetres, with volume increases being contributed by both volumetric expansion and glacial melt. Sources of meltwater are at the present time primarily from mid and high latitude glaciers and from the margins and surface of the Greenland Icecap. With the exception of ice shelves surrounding its lengthy Palmer Peninsula, Antarctica's massive ice sheet, most notably in East Antarctica, appears relatively stable, at least for the present.

While the combined effects of ice sheet ablation and volumetric thermal expansion are small in comparison to the total volume of water already resident in the world's oceans, its impact on humans becomes significant because of how present land surfaces are positioned relative to sea level. We note, for example, the threat to very low elevations in the coral atolls in the equatorial Pacific, and to the extensive low coastal plain surrounding the Ganges River Delta in heavily populated Bangladesh.

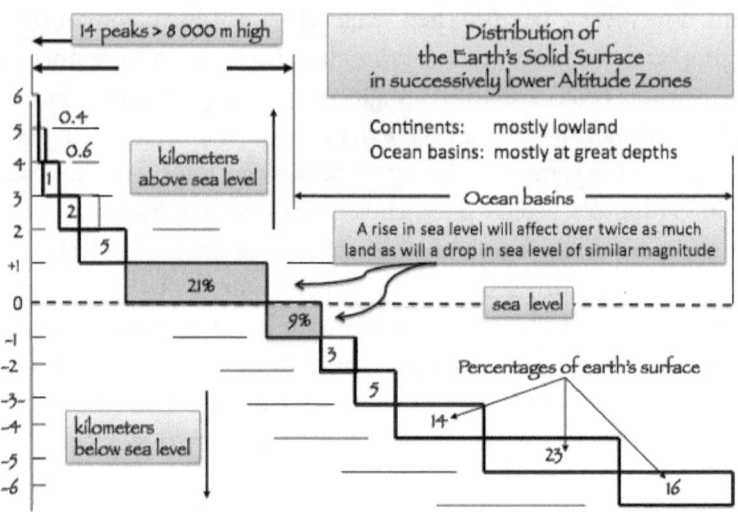

Distribution of Earth's Solid Surface in Successively Lower Altitude Zones[120]

The accompanying graph plots the percentages of the Earth's crustal surface at various altitudes relative to present-day sea level. From the graph, we note the following significant facts:

- More crust resides below sea level than above sea level.
- While most crust below sea level is *far below* sea level, most crust above sea level is *just above* sea level. Therefore, small increases in ocean volumes due to global warming must be considered more significant than decreases from cooling since large world populations are located close to present-day sea levels.

THE EARTH: PROCLAIMING THE WORK OF GOD'S HANDS

Whether flooding originates from waters in oceans or rivers, whenever waters burst their bounds and inundate their margins to destroy life and property, a sober mood falls upon all who witness the nature of nature. We wonder about a world whose life-giving waters are able to provide both serenity and refreshment, yet that are also able to behave with unexpected fury, invade our residences, and capture our people, doing it all with apparent indifference.

Destruction on this scale has a habit of sifting our fundamental values and righting priorities that have become overturned and skewed. Events of great magnitude bring to the surface feelings and questions we largely ignore during times when our lives are not threatened. We feel a sense of powerlessness as we contemplate the destructive power that nature is able to formulate and deliver. We fear oceans that with little warning, can suddenly invade the space we consider permanently and exclusively ours. Let's face it; nature, as we have seen in these circumstances, is merely behaving itself. While it follows a most orderly process in always behaving according to natural laws, the net effect is often an incredibly chaotic mess.

We question to what degree our technology can immunize us to hazards we are unable to control and to what degree better planning of human settlement locations could reduce human exposure to specific hazards from both land and sea. We wonder about the uncertainty of life and the apparent randomness of death. We wonder if anything, or anyone, or anywhere can be made completely safe.

Most of us find the answers we give to such questions inadequate. We wonder if all of life runs on things like chance and luck and whether there is any truth to the doctrine of the sovereignty of God over all things. We wonder about the nature of an all-knowing and all-powerful God of goodness who seems at certain times indifferent to human suffering, and who appears on occasion to be anything but good. Some of us believe that if God created the world, surely He could have done a better job.

One person, at a time of personal pain and grief, expressed his anger at God in a comment that questions just who is to be judged on the Day of Judgment if, in fact, there actually will be such an event. He envisioned, "a creator god would be answerable *to us* for these things at the day of judgment—*if he dared to turn up.*"[121] In light of the realities within our natural world and those involving discord among humans, these questions and opinions are as legitimate as their answers are elusive.

The Bible is clear on two important points concerning our world. Each relates to the nature of nature and the degree to which we are able to impose control over it. Firstly, we have assigned to this world a responsibility for our personal safety and security that it was never meant to bear. No component of this present world is utterly safe and predictable. In the light of this fact, the answer to the oft-repeated question, *what can we do so that this tragedy will never occur again?* should be clear. In this world, while elaborate and costly measures can be implemented to reduce human risk, it can never be totally eliminated. The words of Psalm 46 testify that it is the Creator, not any aspect of His Creation, who is ultimately trustworthy. The chapter also hints that, while to God we possess infinite worth, an agenda greater than our personal one may be what we as individuals have to contend with in this world:

> *God is our refuge and strength, an ever-present help in trouble.*
> *Therefore we will not fear, though the earth give way*
> *and the mountains fall into the heart of the sea,*
> *though its waters roar and foam*
> *and the mountains quake with their surging . . .*
> *The LORD Almighty is with us;*
> *the God of Jacob is our fortress.*
>
> *Psalm 46:1–3, 7*

Secondly, as was discussed earlier, the natural world in which we live is anything but natural. The processes and events we describe as thoroughly *natural* are *not* thoroughly natural. That is, at present, they do not function in accordance with their original purpose. It is as if a foreign and discordant note not included in the original composition has somehow been inserted into a beautiful song. It is jarring to the ear, troubling to the human spirit and seemingly inconsistent with a loving God.

But the true measure of what is *natural* is the state of reality way back in that idyllic Garden. At the time of the Creation of all things, God established what is *natural*. Elements of nature were never intended to destroy human life. Nor were they ever intended to induce in us fear or apprehension, disappointment or sorrow. Rather, elements of nature were designed to enhance life and were intended for our good, for our joy and our satisfaction, and for uninterrupted joyful life with the One who created us. What proceeded from the creative mind and hands of God was a benevolent world, not a malevolent one, a *good* world functioning in complete accord with the original purposes of its Craftsman.

And if one is to believe the words of the Bible, there will come a day when the raging seas, quaking plates, and violent winds that periodically cause untold death and sorrow will be no more. The poetic words contained in Isaiah 11:6–9 serve as a window through which one is permitted a preview of a restored world and a glimpse of what the truly natural will look like, with neither influences of *harm* or *destruction* present: a world that at present exists only in our imaginative yearnings:

> *The wolf will live with the lamb,*
> *the leopard will lie down with the goat . . .*
> *The cow will feed with the bear,*
> *their young will lie down together . . .*
> *The infant will play near the cobra's den,*
> *and the young child will put his hand into the viper's nest.*
> *They will neither harm nor destroy on all my holy mountain,*
> *for the earth will be filled with the knowledge of the LORD*
> *as the waters cover the sea.*
>
> Isaiah 11:6–9

FLOOD REFERENCES IN THE BIBLE

Ranking in the number one spot for biblical flood references is the devastating deluge in the story of Noah and the Ark, an event that has captured the attention of researchers in fields such as history, theology, geology, and archaeology and has been the subject of much controversy and little consensus. Regardless of how one interprets the story, and whether one accepts its historicity, this image testifies to the power of God, who is able to use cataclysmic events (Gen 6–8) to accomplish His purposes. It also testifies to His provision for survival amid cataclysm, using the buoyant forces of water to prevent the ark from being overwhelmed, and that ultimate safety rests not in this present Creation, but in its Creator.

Scattered elsewhere through the Bible are many expressions of flood imagery found within both similes and metaphors. By contrast, the image of overflowing abundance is frequently the picture used to express the extravagance and magnitude of God's provision for His people. Examples include an overflowing *cup* (Ps 23:5) and overflowing streams from a rock in a wilderness (Ps 78:20). God's provision of enrichment is likened to the enrichment of soil when fresh river water and sediment spread over its floodplain (Ps 66:12). Elsewhere, flood imagery displays negative results: entangling cords of death in "overwhelming torrents of destruction" (Ps 18:4). A far more comforting image is God as Lifeguard, delivering His children from the hands of His powerful enemies.

> *He reached down from on high and took hold of me;*
> *he drew me out of deep waters.*
> *He rescued me from my powerful enemy,*
> *from my foes, who were too strong for me.*
>
> **Psalm 18:16, 17**

In the story of The Wise and Foolish Builders in Matthew 7 and Luke 6, Jesus likens the building of one's life to the construction of a house: that stability and permanency of both are primarily dependent upon firm foundations.

This mini-parable presupposes that threats to one's life are as real as threats to one's dwelling. These threats, presented metaphorically as physical forces from wind, rain, and flood, have great destructive capability. The parable teaches that the structural integrity of any dwelling to withstand such onslaughts does not lie principally in the dwelling's structure, but on something external to it (Luke 6:48).

The application to human life is clear. Establishing a stable and reliable base on which to develop our lives is comparable to a wise builder who, in light of the inevitability of nature's storms and overwhelming floods, chooses solid rock rather than shifting sand as suitable and necessary foundational support for his dwelling. With all due respect to the lesson in the story of *The Three Little Pigs*, the destructive "huffing" and "puffing" forces of this world are not rendered ineffectual simply because of the strength of a structure's building materials (bricks preferred over straw and sticks), but rather because of the adequacy of something external to itself, namely the structure's Foundation (on Christ the Rock).

> *The rain came down, the streams rose, and the winds blew*
> *and beat against that house; yet it did not fall,*
> *because it had its foundation on the rock.*
>
> *Matthew 7:25*

9

ICE AND SNOW

*O all ye Ice and Snow, bless ye the Lord:
praise him, and magnify him forever.*

Benedicite (BCP)

**Glacial Ice Flow over Mountainous Terrain,
Ellesmere Island, Nunavut
(JES)**

*Water is a tangled mess of molecules
that romp around,
catching each other's hands and releasing them again,
squeezing together and recoiling.
And then, when it freezes, all the dignity returns.
The molecules line up formally,
obeying careful rules for where to stand.
They also hold each other at arm's length,
which is why ice is less dense than water,
and why ice cubes float.*

Gabrielle Walker[122]

*And among these myriads of enchanting little stars,
in their hidden splendour
that was too small for man's naked eye to see,
there was not one like unto another;
an endless inventiveness
governed the development
and unthinkable differentiation of one
and the same basic scheme,
the equilateral, equiangled hexagon.*

Thomas Mann[123]

High in Canada's north, in the region of the Mackenzie Delta, there stands a series of prominent conical mounds known as *pingos*. As some of the few thousands that occupy cold regions, these miniature mountains, sometimes referred to as topographic *pimples*, evolve from groundwater that migrates into near-surface pockets and freezes. The resulting volumetric expansion that occurs when water converts to ice causes an imperceptibly slow vertical heaving of the soil surface cover. Eventually, this uplift forms an isolated hill or near-offshore island that continues to grow as new water is imported and freezes, reaching average heights of some fifty metres above the surrounding flat surfaces. As a core of ice with a thin covering of soil, pingos represent one of the many features that reflect the complex processes within a region of the Earth known as the *cryosphere.*

The cryosphere, the environment of perennial ice and snow, owes its existence to low atmospheric temperatures that persist through much of the year. On our planet, the incidence and persistence of low temperatures increase with increasing latitude and with increasing altitude above sea level.

The temperature regime on Earth is such that ice and snow are rendered perennial where latitudes are greatest, non-existent where latitudes are minimal, and seasonal at the transitional intermediate latitudes during the low sun season of winter. Since temperatures also drop with increasing altitude, the presence of ice and snow at any latitude is made more probable when the altitude factor is added. Thus, near the summit on Tanzania's 5 900-metre Mount Kilimanjaro near the equator, there is a small snow and ice remnant.

Russia's Vostok Station in Antarctica holds the world's record for the coldest recorded surface temperature. Situated some 700 nautical miles from the South Pole, and far from the moderating influences of the Southern Ocean, it sits firmly in cryosphere at an altitude of 3500 metres above sea level. In its brief "summer," occupants enjoy temperatures that struggle to reach -30 °C despite a sun that refuses to set for a period of roughly four months. These bitter summer temperatures contrast to those plunging below -80 °C during long dark months of winter! And that's not counting the effect of wind chill!

While Antarctica enjoys a perennial cryosphere, ours is seasonal. Each year, beginning in late July over the northern hemisphere, and in response to the movement of our planet about the sun, the season of winter emerges from its perennial storehouses and begins its rapid migration toward lower latitudes and altitudes, giving to other places a taste of perennial cryosphere. In Canada, like a giant blanket, it enters northern Nunavut in August, overtakes the southern Arctic by September, penetrates the northern prairies in October, and finally arrives in our most southerly regions sometime in November. As noon solar altitudes drop, and daylight hours decline, daytime temperatures descend into negative values.

Winter conditions continue until further movement of the Earth about the sun causes increases in solar altitudes, in solar radiation, in daylight hours, and corresponding increases in average air temperatures. It is then that processes reverse and winter begins its hasty retreat, chased poleward and into higher altitudes by an advancing spring, a warmer sun, and an awakening landscape.

Winter represents a period of time in which nature shows off its artistic talents with water. Under certain atmospheric temperature conditions, it condenses fine droplets of water, which descend through warm air onto cold surfaces, creating a thin frozen glaze on road surfaces, power lines, trees, and windshields. It extracts large volumes of heat from rivers, lakes, and ponds and converts their liquid surfaces into a solid. High above our heads, it takes atmospheric moisture and mixes up an impressive batch of snowflakes, carefully fashioning each one through the application of unique design to a common geometric shape. With no apparent weariness at such redundancy, and with the aid of gravity, it randomly scatters them onto ground surfaces. Then, with a dash of wind, it redistributes this accumulated mass into smooth undulating drifts. Nature's grand recipe for exquisite beauty, employed repeatedly with countless variations on countless occasions, delights our hearts, except in those moments when they impede our travel, damage our property, or threaten our safety. As with a brilliant chef, its own delight is as much in the presentation as it is in the preparation of all its fashions.

In places like southern Canada, where winter arrives the latest and departs earliest, the coldest season of the year is not as long and not so severe. Here is where those features formed when nature plays with water are least enduring, since longer summers delay frost events while earlier springs hasten the ablation of all that winter creates. But what is nature capable of whenever her activities within cold regions progress with *minimal* warm-season interruptions? The answer is abundantly apparent when one leaves the domain of seasonal cold and journeys to the domain where cold is virtually endless, namely in the perennial cryosphere.

In 1953, as a young woman of British royalty prepared for her coronation as queen, Sir Edmund Hillary left New Zealand, crossed the equator, and ventured into the perennial high-altitude ice and snow of Nepal. There, along a pathway leading to the summit of Mount Everest, with ice screws, ropes, and ladders, and a single Sherpa guide, he came upon the tangled array of massive ice blocks, dangerous snow bridges, and crevasses at the Khumbu Icefall. To assemble this magnificent mess, nature needed centuries of almost uninterrupted time.

Earlier, in 1841, the British explorer James Clark Ross sailed south into our planet's quintessential domain of ice and snow. As his two ships approached the uncharted waters off the Antarctic continent, Ross came upon a massive volcano rising almost 4000 metres above the sea and belching red flame and black smoke. Beside it lay a companion dormant peak. Nearby he spotted a thin white line that stretched unbroken across the horizon as far as the eye could see. The line turned out to be a 1000-kilometre-long wall of ice rising vertically about 70 metres out of the water, capped with a thin topping of non-metamorphosed snow. It was the terminus of the world's largest ice shelf.[124] Soon after, Ross wrote:

> *This was a sight so surpassing everything that can be imagined ... that it really caused a feeling of awe to steal over us at the consideration of our own comparative insignificance and helplessness, and at the same time, an indescribable feeling of the greatness of the Creator in the works of His hand.*[125]

The shelf, about the size of France, and one of many marine extensions of the world's largest ice sheet, is a flat-topped white wilderness from whose edges are calved the world's largest tabular icebergs. Such is the nature of landscape within the domain of perennial snow and ice where uninterrupted, over many millenniums, nature has the time to further modify and refine its frozen artwork, a process that is never allowed to progress to this extent in more moderate climes.

What is it like to behold this majesty, this splendour? And what does it say about a God who meticulously fashions it piece-by-piece over vast stretches of time, and doing it all mostly in remote places where only the most ambitious seekers among us will ever stand in its presence? Does grandeur arrest us not only because it possesses intrinsic beauty, but also because it represents a window into something far greater than itself? The thought is alluded to in the provocative quote over the entrance to the Scott Polar Institute in Cambridge, England. It reads: "He sought the secrets of the pole and found the hidden face of God." For many, Creation's design bears solid testimony to both the existence and the nature of a Designer.

> *Then the LORD spoke to Job out of the storm. He said:* . . .
> *Have you entered the storehouses of the snow?*
>
> *Job 38:1, 22a*

A few decades ago, with covetous eyes directed toward the eventual recovery of suspected rich hydrocarbon deposits lying in relatively remote Arctic acreage, a number of major oil companies embarked on a massive oil exploration project in Canada's north. One particular focus of exploration was off the Tuk Peninsula, in the shallow waters of the Arctic's Beaufort Sea. To facilitate access to possible oil-bearing formations below the sea's shallowest waters, the industry had constructed a series of artificial islands from sand dredged from the sea bottom to use as drilling platforms. In the summer of 1984, I visited the offshore to study the technology associated with these islands, built within the realm of Arctic permafrost.

The largest of them was an isolated conical mound of dredged sand poured onto a single spot on the sea surface until the accumulating mass broke the surface to rise a few metres above sea level. From the air, this expensive sandbox resembled a circular heap of brown sugar surrounded on all sides by white icing. It enclosed a surface of sufficient size to support a drilling rig, a helicopter landing pad, adequate storage facilities, and crew accommodations. Blue surface melt ponds on the surrounding ice field testified to the ablating effects of the brief summer melt season. On its windward side, the island's shoreline presented as an assemblage of raised sea ice fragments. Driven by onshore winds and under relentless pressure, massive ice blocks had rafted one on top of another, scouring the seabed and invading the beach to create an ever-shifting random assortment of sand-laden rubble.

The ice movement was slow, almost imperceptible. Low-frequency groans interrupted by periodic loud snapping sounds were constant reminders of the dynamic nature of an ice surface responding to the fickle forcings of wind, tide and current. Dissipation of much of this energy at the island's peripheral beaches rendered all enclosed property safe. This artificial island, one of four types created in the region, was proving the appropriateness of its name: *sacrificial beach island*.

Soon after my arrival, and with suitable clothing and footwear, I ventured through the surrounding rubble field and onto the less disturbed ice surface beyond. I was assigned an Inuk guide. He proved to be strong, kind, and wise. He carried a high-powered rifle and wore a cap that displayed the crest of the Calgary Flames.

For approximately four hours, we wandered the ice surface in temperatures that were surprisingly mild, meandering to avoid the tallest pressure ridges and skirting numerous melt ponds and leads. Apart from the persistent drone of machinery at the distant drill site and the low-frequency groans emanating from the ice, the seascape was relatively quiet. The curious, beautiful, powerful, and amazingly patient polar bears that frequent the area were not present. No seals or walrus were visible. The ice surface that separated us from the ocean below seemed firm and stable. To the north, more dynamic ice stretched toward the horizon in giant fragments separated by leads and open water. I stood in a wilderness of ocean, ice, and snow with a single companion who knew his surroundings far more than did his visitor, very much aware that caution and constant vigilance so vital for human survival here could never be relaxed.

My wanderings with my guide were not without conversation. In response to my periodic questions, this soft-spoken and gracious Inuk shared a wealth of knowledge. For example, he mentioned a very different artificial island much further north of the one nearby, created by spraying sea water onto already existing sea ice, also in remote shallow offshore waters. As ice produced through much more rapid freezing thickened, the whole mass would slowly sink and eventually impact the shallow sea floor. After additional spraying to ensure this thickened "ice island" was stable enough to support all necessary drilling equipment, all was ready for use.

Attentive to the sounds and appearances of happenings around us, my Inuk guide observed much of what passed by me unnoticed. He was like "Radar" O'Reilly from television's *M*A*S*H*, the corporal who was always the first to alert others of the approach of yet another stream of Medivac choppers.

It was he, and not I, who detected the all-important change in the wind. Without my noticing, winds had shifted to the offshore and had increased in strength. In response, the ice regime was now straining to accommodate a new pattern of atmospheric forcing. Previously static, it had begun to migrate away from the island and areas of open water were appearing along its margin. Moreover, the massive pan of ice on which we stood had slowly rotated so that my appreciation of direction had diminished. Elsewhere, ice chunks were slowly being squeezed, lifted, and reassembled into giant ridges. The entire surface topography and visual appearance of the ice within our area were being slowly altered, and it was imperative that we return promptly to our island. Without my guide's knowledge of and sensitivity to his environment's dynamic nature, our return would have been difficult and dangerous. I cannot imagine a better four-hour introduction to the nature and behaviour of Arctic sea ice than the one I shared with my gracious, intelligent, and experienced Inuk guide.

Within the expansive storehouses of the snow, frozen water in a variety of forms is virtually everywhere. Most forms develop from accumulated snowfall. Some forms arise when surface seawater and subsurface groundwater freezes. Most forms are visible and somewhat mobile. One, namely permafrost, is almost all subsurface and immobile.

1. Permafrost

Beechey Island is a 5-square-kilometre desolate hump of rock and gravel situated on the northern margin of the Northwest Passage off the southwest tip of Devon Island, 15 degrees from the North Pole. Actually, it is presently not an island since it is joined to Devon Island by a smooth and very narrow spit of deposited sand. Within sight of its bleak northern shore stand four weathered gravestones. Three of these markers identify the resting place of the first crewmembers who died on the ill-fated Franklin Expedition that departed England in 1845.[126] The fourth contains the remains of a man who met his death on a search for the other three. All graves are shallow. Some 140 years after their deaths, their bodies were exhumed for autopsy. Given the age of their remains, though significantly discoloured, they were surprisingly recognizable, with hair, flesh, bone, and clothing fibre intact. Major body decay had yet to commence.

Much farther north, along Nares Strait which straddles the 80th parallel of latitude, near the desolate shores of northwest Greenland, is the burial site of Charles Francis Hall, one of the many men who joined the search for the lost Franklin Expedition. Hall died in 1871. About 100 years later, because his death had been sudden and unexpected and deemed suspicious by many, his shallow grave was located, and his body exhumed for autopsy. Though more decayed than were the human remains on Beechey Island, sufficient tissue had survived the ravages of time and could be analyzed.

Arctic burials such as these occur in ground that is refrigerated, with bodies in a perpetually frozen condition. Refrigeration, especially in the coldest regions, severely reduces an organism's rate of decay. Even after so many years, the suspected higher-than-normal lead concentrations in the bodies of William Braine, John Torrington, and John Hartnell, men who accompanied Franklin, could be confirmed and suspected as a possible cause in their premature deaths. With regard to Hall's death farther north, the presence of toxic levels of arsenic in bone, fingernail and hair samples added credence to the theory that he had not died a natural death, but rather had been poisoned, possibly deliberately by a member of Hall's expedition.

The Arctic's earthen refrigerator that delays the decay of human remains is *permafrost*: permanently frozen ground. Permafrost is virtually ubiquitous throughout polar regions and in the world's highest altitudes. Categorized as sporadic, then discontinuous, then continuous with increasing latitude, permafrost is present because summers are too cool and brief to entirely destroy the ground frost that accumulates over the much longer and more severe winter period. And so, while the warmth of summer manages to melt surface frost to a depth of a few centimetres, deeper layers remain solid and undisturbed. The near-surface layer, alternating between seasonal freeze and thaw, is called the *active layer*. Obviously *not* permafrost, its thickness varies with the relative lengths of the summer and winter periods.

The world's most extensive permafrost occurs in the northern hemisphere through Siberia and northern Canada. Deepest permafrost is found in eastern Siberia, where depths greater than 1000 metres have been recorded. Nature finds it difficult to exceed these thicknesses since the warming effects on frost generated by the Earth's internal geothermal heat from below become progressively more significant with increasing depth.

Permafrost provides excellent foundations for human structures so long as it remains frozen. Its stability enhances safety in mining operations, especially where ore bodies are sedimentary and unconsolidated. Such was the case at the Polaris Mine on Little Cornwallis Island, with its shallow ore body stabilized by permafrost. However, with mining operations generating significant quantities of heat underground, it became necessary to pump refrigerated air underground in order to maintain mine temperatures below freezing. Imagine air conditioning as a necessity in the high Arctic!

Sections of permafrost have been excavated in many northern settlements as refrigerators for the cold storage of meat from musk oxen, fish, seal, walrus, and caribou. Over many millennia, it has provided excellent natural refrigeration for the preservation of now-extinct animal species. Occasionally, whole woolly mammoth carcasses have been found, with hair, tusks, and even stomach contents still intact.

On the other hand, permafrost can pose problems, especially in areas of human settlement. Special engineering is required in settlements built over permafrost to prevent serious ground shift and collapse since structures such as utility piping and house foundations, as well as buried oil and gas pipelines inject large quantities of heat into near-surface permafrost, increasing the thickness of the active layer and thereby threatening permafrost stability.[127] To cope with these issues in towns such as Inuvik near the Mackenzie Delta, and elsewhere, houses not raised above the ground are constructed on insulated foundation pads without basements, and with utility pipes inserted in above-ground insulated corridors called *utilidors*.

At present, a serious concern relates to the widespread influence of global warming on permafrost, a climatic trend that is more pronounced in the Western Arctic than elsewhere. This concern relates not merely to the destabilizing of slopes as permafrost melts, but also, and more importantly, to anticipated giant outgassing of stored carbon in the form of methane. Methane is a greenhouse gas (reported to be about twenty times more powerful than carbon dioxide), which, when released, is expected to behave as a positive feedback mechanism to further enhance global warming. With positive feedback, what happens accelerates future happenings of the same event. In other words, warming accelerates further warming.

2. Ice sheets

Within the region of perennial snow and ice, the ice type containing the largest amount of water is the land surface phenomenon known as the *ice sheet*. Ice sheets like those that cover virtually all of Antarctica and most of Greenland contain the greatest reservoir of fresh water on Earth.

The parent material for an ice sheet is snow. Ice sheets, like the one that covered most of Canada and Europe during the last ice age, develop whenever and wherever snowfall amounts over a year exceed the amounts that melt. The residual snow that survives the cold season then becomes the surface upon which snowfall from the next snow season accumulates. Eventually, over many similar years, the downward pressure of snow upon snow causes a slow fusion and metamorphosis of snow particles into ice. The resulting conversion formed by pressure of new snow on accumulated snow is called an *ice sheet*.

The world's most massive ice sheets, over 4 kilometres thick in places, bury all but the highest topographic features. They contribute such an enormous weight to the surfaces upon which they rest that they slowly deform and depress them, punching them down into the Earth's crust, just as a boat loaded with cargo rides lower in the liquid medium that supports it. Canada, structurally depressed during the last ice age, is presently still in the process of slow isostatic rebound, with landscapes rising in response to glacial ice loss. This phenomenon is clearly evident in raised shorelines along the Hudson Bay coast.

Because the thicknesses of the world's largest ice sheets are so great, their surfaces are at altitudes where perennially low temperatures ensure minimal annual melting. So great is the volume of water presently locked up within the world's ice sheets that if they totally melted, the resulting release of water would raise world sea level an estimated 70 metres, significantly altering the shapes and slightly diminishing the sizes of continents. Regions most sensitive to sea level rise include extensive coastal plains at or just above present sea level, some of which are the most densely populated places on the planet. Collectively, these places presently contain a population of over half a billion people. Fortunately, present sea level rise is slow with annual increases measured in millimetres.

To the army of scientific detectives, an ice sheet represents a vast repository of buried historical information that is deposited, locked up, and preserved within its various strata. Clues to what transpired in the past reside not only within ice chemistry, but also in the foreign materials that have migrated to and been buried within it. These materials include an assortment of airborne pollen, samples of atmospheric gases, volcanic dust, fossils, evidence of ancient viruses, a few aircraft, and the remains of some unfortunate explorers.

What there is at present testifies to what occurred on its surfaces in the past. In 1991, hikers in the Italian Alps discovered the preserved remains of a man. Modern dating techniques indicate he had been dead for an estimated 5300 years. In the Greenland icecap, eight World War II aircraft were discovered buried in approximately 80 metres of ice and snow 50 years after they crash-landed in Greenland in 1942. The bodies of Robert Scott and his four companions who died on their return journey from the South Pole in early 1912 lie entombed and preserved some 20 metres below the Antarctic ice surface. Sealed within what is a giant conveyor belt, their graves are slowly deepening and being delivered to the edge of the Ross Ice Shelf where, after an extended and unintended stay of a few hundred years, they will be rudely expelled from the continent they came to explore. This same fate awaits Sir Douglas Mawson's two companions, who died late in 1912 while on the Australasian Antarctic Expedition to King George V Land, near the South Magnetic Pole.

Experts tell us that the longest historical records buried within the deepest ice deposits in Antarctica speak to events that reach back hundreds of thousands of years. Access to this wealth of information is through ice coring, whereby long cylinders of ice are cut, extracted, and refrigerated for future analysis. Information from the least disturbed ice over the centuries provides the most reliable data. In general, age increases with depth. What emerges is a veritable treasure chest of information from the past: temperature records from the ice itself; imported pollen and volcanic dust from far away; atmospheric composition from ancient times; and much more.

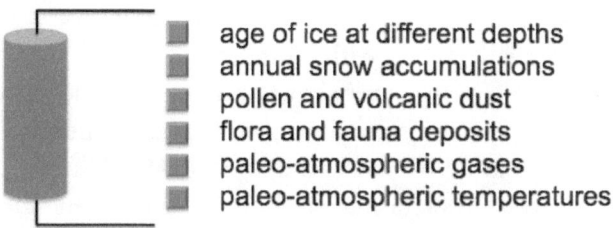

Earth History Revealed through Ice Core Analyses[128]

The ability to interpret data at an acceptable degree of accuracy is possible through the use of sophisticated scientific instrumentation. What emerges through painstaking studies are the secrets of the snows from preserved ice contained in visible, microscopic, and isotopic residues, as well as *paleo-calendars* with which to date these events. Samples of the atmosphere trapped in layers of snow deposited thousands of years ago reflect atmospheric composition near the times of deposition and entrapment.

If left undisturbed by massive movements or melt, depth is a useful indicator of age. Information correlated with ice cores from Greenland serves to verify Antarctic data and also reveal interesting anomalies. Like aged trees with their annular rings, the thickest ice sheets are *old enough* to contain lengthy historical records and *permanent enough* to keep records relatively free of gaps during which the voices of wealthy information generators fall frustratingly silent.

3. Glaciers

Like sea ice, ice sheets flow. But unlike sea ice, flow direction is one way. In response to gravity, flow is normally whichever way is downhill and away from centres of greatest ice concentrations. When flow is confined to narrow valleys, the result is a river of ice called a *glacier*.

As with rivers of water, different glaciers flow at different rates. Moreover, different parts of the same glacier display differential flow, a condition that causes ice to audibly groan, to snap unexpectedly and open, forming jagged and dangerous surface *crevasses*. Crevasses are most common wherever a glacial stream is forced to abruptly alter direction, either horizontally (to the left or right) or vertically over a convex slope (one in which slope decreases with increasing altitude).

Records of human treks over alpine and high latitude icefields include many tales of sudden and sometimes tragic plunges into hidden jagged crevasses made invisible by snow bridges formed by drifting. Normally, if possible, ice near protruding land surfaces is given wide berth by travellers since the strain while negotiating immovable obstacles such as rock outcrops usually generates chaotic fields of hazardous and irregular crevasses. Such chaos in an ice stream is most prominent at or near a glacial terminus since this is where the most accumulated straining and fracturing of glacial ice can be found.

Average glacial flow is normally slow, but occasionally rapid enough to be noticed, especially in the summer season and in locations where surface gradients are steepest. Glacial tops move faster than glacial bottoms. Middles flow faster than sides. One of the fastest rivers of ice is that of Greenland's galloping *Jacobshavn Glacier*, advancing in places at an average rate of a metre an hour.

A glacier whose terminus reaches a body of water is called a *tidewater glacier*. Here, it may continue beyond the shore to become a floating *ice tongue* or, if wider, a more extensive *ice shelf*. It is at the leading edges of these ice shelves and tongues where *ice islands* and *icebergs* are calved and born. The prolific tidewater Jacobshavn Glacier alone discharges to the sea an estimated 7% of Greenland's total ice volume, most of which becomes floating ice fragments, the largest of which begin their journeys southward in Baffin Bay toward Labrador.

Unfortunately, rates of iceberg calving presently exceed rates at which ice is being conveyed to the various shelves. As a result, despite glacial advance, the position of most calving fronts is in retreat in the direction of their places of origin. If such rapid ice ablation persists, glacial fronts will eventually lose their distinctive role as tidewater glaciers and no longer birth floating ice cubes.

4. Icebergs

> *It appeared a mountain of alabaster resting calmly upon the bosom of the dark blue sea... I stood in the presence of God's work! Its fashioning was that of the Great Architect! He who hath built such monuments, and cast them forth upon the waters of the sea, is God, and there can be none other!*
>
> *Charles Frances Hall*[29]

Icebergs rank as some of nature's most impressive objects, with fragments ranging from piano-size *growlers* and room-size *bergy bits* to masses the size of small countries. The largest icebergs are southern hemispheric, flat-topped giants of incredible mass that originate along the margins of Antarctica's many extensive ice shelves. The largest ever observed broke off the western end of Antarctica's Ross Ice Shelf in March 2000 and, before it began to fragment, it had a surface area exceeding that of the island of Jamaica.

Born in ice that formed from thick snow deposits on land, icebergs live and eventually die as foreigners within the hostile environment of the sea. Regardless of size, they float. Their buoyancy is related to the fact that, because of its crystalline structure, ice has a lower density than water. In other words, if one imagines two equal masses, one of water and one of ice, the ice mass will have a volume roughly 10% greater than the water mass. Given that ice and water densities differ by only about 10%, icebergs float with only about 10% of their mass exposed (slightly more in the denser salt water). In shallower waters, they often become grounded and immobile as keels intercept the ocean bed.

Primary forces dictating iceberg drift paths include winds, currents, and water depths, with drift paths more predictable with current than with wind. Of secondary importance to drift paths is the atmospheric pressure field over iceberg-infested waters. Locally, where pressures are relatively high, the atmosphere depresses water surfaces under them creating a seasurface topographic valley. Where adjacent pressures are relatively low, water surfaces rise to form a shallow liquid mound. The resulting ephemeral pressure difference creates a localized sea-surface slope. Icebergs that encounter this temporary surface condition respond to these liquid hills and valleys, drifting downhill from regions of low atmospheric pressure and toward regions of relatively higher pressure.

The Phenomenon of Icebergs Explained![130]

Icebergs drift quietly and slowly. Because of frictional drag in water, wind-forced icebergs travel a mere fraction of the wind speed, often at the speed of someone out for a casual stroll. Whenever icebergs are free of land, seabed, and sea ice obstructions, they normally migrate long distances in currents, usually toward warmer climes. Subjected to increasing water temperatures and wave action within a marine environment, they fall prey to melt and fracture. Where icebergs fracture, newly exposed surfaces are sharp and jagged. When their ablation is through melting, surfaces are smooth and rounded. But during their relatively brief sojourn at sea, they serve as mobile art studios, where, with sun, wind, and water as her tools, Mother Nature displays talent as the matchless Sculptor, carving out residual peaks, concave beaches, cascading waterfalls, and shallow turquoise freshwater mini-lakes formed from ice-cold meltwater accumulating within the berg's surface depressions.

Inevitably, processes of melt and secondary calving destabilize bergs by altering their centres of gravity, causing them to perform slow but spectacular flips. This fact, combined with icebergs' tendency to fracture abruptly without warning, makes these structures dangerous surfaces to occupy. To the delight of all observers at safe distances, countless crystalline surface reflectors scatter sunlight in all directions, enhancing iceberg colour, brilliance, and beauty.

Icebergs inspire awe and respect in all who observe them. As testimonies to the nature of nature, they represent not only transient beauty but also potential trouble for both humans and property. Oil rig crews working in so-called *Iceberg Alley* off the coasts of Newfoundland and Labrador regularly practice emergency procedures to avoid iceberg collisions. Procedures include: careful berg *monitoring* (especially when berg numbers peak during April and May); *towing*; and when a collision appears unavoidable, costly *suspension of all drilling operations*; and occasionally *rig abandonment*.

The rupturing of the *Titanic's* massive hull and the subsequent rapid sinking of this "unsinkable" ship on an April night in 1912 awakened a sleeping world to the destructive capability of icebergs. Both berg and ship were on maiden voyages through cold North Atlantic waters, the former on a slow drift southward and the latter on a swifter passage westward. When recently milled steel impacted ancient metamorphosed ice, human ingenuity and technology proved no match against nature's might.

> *And as the smart ship grew*
> *In stature, grace, and hue,*
> *In shadowy silent distance grew the Iceberg too.*
> *Thomas Hardy*
>
> **(from *Lines on the loss of the Titanic*, 1912)**

Though little is known of that iceberg, speculation is that the impact of the state-of-the-art ocean liner with this floating ice mass was probably analogous to a pound of butter encountering a hefty NFL lineman. Over 1500 lives were lost, principally through a lack of lifeboats, the debilitating and lethal effects of hypothermia, and a captain who sailed his so-called unsinkable ship through Iceberg Alley at a relatively high speed, at night, during the height of the local iceberg season while grossly overestimating the strength of his ship relative to that of the berg. In the end, the iceberg, not the ship, proved to be *unsinkable*!

Recent analyses of atmospheric conditions at the time of the collision have given clues as to why the ship's night watch did not spot the iceberg sooner than it did. While the night sky was clear, there was no moon. But also, meteorological reports for that night indicated that a strong air inversion prevailed over the region.

An *air inversion* is an abnormal thermal atmospheric condition at ground level. Normally, air temperatures drop with increasing altitude. But in air inversions, they rise instead. So-called *steep* air inversions (*rapid* rises of air temperatures with increasing altitude) significantly distort the visual field of an observer, changing the shape of objects, generating the occasional mirage, and altering the apparent distance to one's horizon. Evidence of the strength of the inversion the night of the disaster is contained in eyewitness reports of *lazy* smoke and steam from the *Titanic* seemingly unable to rise very far above the stacks of the stricken vessel (a common sight when smoke from house chimneys is expelled into a steep inversion). Those in urban areas, within valleys, especially before dawn, know that such conditions impede airborne pollutant dispersal, creating diminished air quality and visibility.

Research abounds concerning the effects of global warming on the sizes and numbers of icebergs that stream south from Baffin Bay toward Newfoundland.[131] At present, warming air temperatures are causing reductions in both the thickness and extent of the Greenland ice sheet through surface melt. In places, melt rates exceed rates of ice formation. There is also firm evidence of greater ice loss because of increased iceberg production at the ice sheet's margins. This fact is most apparent within a few of the most northerly ice shelves along Antarctica's long and prominent Palmer Peninsula. Ice melt and berg production are linked because meltwater that percolates in cracks to the base of glaciers acts as a lubricant, enhancing slippage downward toward the shelves and tongues where iceberg calving occurs.

While iceberg production is increasing because of warming temperatures, it also appears that their average residency within their ocean environment is decreasing. There are three reasons for this trend. Firstly, enhanced glacial movement induces greater mechanical fracturing of the ice mass. This results in more numerous but smaller ice fragments. Reducing iceberg sizes through fracturing increases melt rate because of increased ice surface exposures.

Secondly, ice fragments enter a marine environment that is, at present, warmer than normal. Increasing water temperatures significantly increase melt rates. Thirdly, a sea ice cover whose extent and permanency has historically given protection against the destructive effects of wave action has greatly diminished over the last few decades. Open water facilitates wave action that, in turn, promotes more rapid fracturing of icebergs, making for even greater exposure to the melt process.

5. Sea ice and pack ice

Previously mentioned, the parent material for icebergs is traceable to land ice formed from metamorphosed snow that eventually migrates to, and is deposited in the sea. Sea ice, however, has a less spectacular origin. It is simply the product formed when an ocean surface freezes. Freezing begins as heat is released from the ocean surface into the atmosphere and as water temperatures drop to their freezing point. Freezing then proceeds downward. But ice insulates. As it thickens, heat transfer from water, through surface ice cover, and into the atmosphere becomes impeded and slows. Thus, sea ice formation eventually cuts off further sea ice formation. As a result, sea ice (formed by ice accumulation on water surfaces) can only attain thicknesses of a few metres, while ice sheets (formed by snow accumulation on land) can attain thicknesses that approach a few kilometres.

The anomalous presence within the Arctic Basin of sections of naturally formed sea ice much thicker than a few metres is explained by the fact that once formed, it is subject to redistribution processes involving compression, deformation, fracturing, and rafting of ice on top of itself. The thicker ice formed in this manner is called *pack ice*. Pack ice is often noisy ice. In areas of dynamic ice re-formation, sudden snaps and low-frequency groans are clearly audible.

The greatest concentrations of sea ice are found in the oceans that surround Antarctica, in the Arctic Ocean, and in the Arctic Archipelago of Canada's north. In each hemisphere, ice coverage displays significant changes from winter to summer, with the critical months of maximum and minimum coverage being March and September respectively in the Arctic, and September and March in the Antarctic.

Recently, in what appears to be more than merely the product of natural variability, a trend toward reduced ice coverage and thinner ice over the Arctic Ocean has captured the attention of ice experts. In fact, in September 2012, the Arctic Basin recorded its lowest summer minimum ice coverage ever, rendering the Siberian side of the basin and the Northwest Passage virtually ice-free. If present faster-than-predicted warming trends continue, sea ice in the region may well convert from perennial ice to seasonal ice within decades. At present, total ice-free conditions are unlikely.

Such rapid alteration in Arctic ice conditions is dramatic and somewhat worrisome. Its widespread demise is expected to decrease average reflectivity of sunlight over the surface of our planet, further enhancing local sunlight absorption. However, widespread sea ice melting, unlike widespread glacial ice melting, will only raise sea levels indirectly. The reason is clear. When sea ice forms, it uses water already in oceans. Thus when it melts, the net increase in ocean water is zero. By contrast, there will be a net increase in water levels whenever the release of meltwater from ice and snow stored on land exceeds the amount of water *put into storage* as snow and ice *on* land. Such a condition is easily maximized during a prolonged period of global warming.

6. First-year and multi-year ice

Ocean surfaces freeze, but due to its salt content, the process begins at a depressed freezing point of about -1.8oC. However, nature says an emphatic "no" to the inclusion of salt crystals in ice crystal formation. Having been rejected from the ice crystals, salt takes up residency *between* crystals, forming concentrated pockets of brine. High salt concentrations within brine pockets impede their freezing. In response to gravity, these liquid pockets make their way downward through the ice as their lower edges melt and their tops refreeze. Eventually, if ice survives multiple summers of melt, brine pockets may descend all the way to the bottom surface of the ice and be expelled. As this process continues, the chemistry of sea ice undergoes a slow distillation as salt concentrations drop and sea ice freshens.

Ice whose life begins and ends in the same year (as is the case for all ice formed in the Great Lakes) is called *first-year ice*. However, if summer melt is incomplete and the ice survives through repeated warm-season melts, distillation can continue and the ice can freshen to the point that its waters become potable. Such ice is given the name *multi-year ice*. The physical properties of this older ice are related to continued reduction in salt content, rendering it distinct from first-year ice. Changes resulting from the metamorphosis of first-year into multi-year ice include altered colour, along with greatly increased hardness and durability. Given its concrete-like hardness, multi-year ice represents a serious hazard to marine transport.

Higher amounts of the fresher, harder, and bluer multi-year ice have been more common in portions of the Arctic Basin than in the waters surrounding Antarctica. This is related to the fact that the Arctic Ocean, unlike the Southern Ocean, is virtually surrounded by land, a condition that impedes ice migration toward warmer climes where more rapid decay is likely.

Thus, it is in the Arctic Basin and its adjacent waters where, in its brief summer, partial melting is able to create an array of turquoise puddles and interconnected channels. In places, so-called *plunge pools* act as conduits that allow puddles and streams to drain vertically through the ice and into the ocean below. At present, the percentage of sea ice in the Arctic Basin that is older, harder, fresher, and more resistant to decay is diminishing rapidly. What multi-year ice remains is presently restricted to the Canadian side of the basin since the dominant current flow within the basin (the Trans-Polar Drift) is away from Russia and toward Canada.[132] At present, the oldest Arctic sea ice is a thin remnant found along Greenland's north coast off Cape Morris Jesup.

The majority of us are arrested when we contemplate the nature of nature, when we discover that an ice sheet is a vast storehouse of preserved historical information, meticulously deposited but accessible for future recovery and interpretation. The repeated refrains in the patterns and processes of ice and snow express incredible beauty, obedience to natural law, and extravagance.

But again, why is wonder triggered when we contemplate nature's ubiquitous designs? Might they be the product of an invisible Designer? Yet the critics may be right when they assert that it is God, not the human, who is the construct, who is made in the image of humans because we cannot imagine any other cause. But, on the other hand, maybe the human propensity to wonder, and *keep* wondering, is an indication that there actually *is* a Designer who, like a Master Artist and Architect, writes

His signature and leaves His fingerprints on all His designs. Indeed, we wonder at a Creator whose works are so awesome that we, with myopic vision, are prone to enjoy the works with little appreciation of the Artist who fashioned them.

SNOW AND ICE AND HOLY SCRIPTURE

Bible Lands, located closer to the equator than to the poles, are not noted for snow and ice landscapes. Nevertheless, they may occur seasonally, particularly in the region's higher altitudes, where slightly lower temperatures make for slightly more enduring winter snowpacks. Best conditions for persistent snow within the area are present on the slopes near the prominent summit of the 2800-metre Mount Hermon.

Since snowfalls within Bible Lands are not common, it is not surprising that scriptural references to snow are few in number. In fact, there are only about two-dozen in all. Each reference to snow is an illustrative tool emphasizing one of its chief characteristics, namely its dazzling whiteness. For example, to illustrate the measure of the thorough cleansing God affords to penitent sinners, the psalmist declares that His washing will render them *"whiter than snow"* (Ps 51). Implicit in the linking of the image of snow to thorough cleansing from sin is the manner in which each snowflake is fabricated: though each identical in its hexagonal framework, each is nevertheless distinct since patterns formed on different hexagons are all unique. The whiteness of snow and its linkage to purity also appear in Daniel's vision of God, whose clothing appeared "as white as snow" (Dan 7). It appears at the Transfiguration, where Jesus' garments are described as "exceeding white as snow" (Mark 9 KJV), and at the Resurrection when the angel of the Lord appeared with clothing, again "white as snow" (Matt 28). In Proverbs 25, snow is seen as a delightfully cool refreshment and a welcome respite from the heat often associated with harvest time. A rather different image of snow is found in Job 24. Here the transient nature of human life is expressed in the suddenness with which snow disappears in the presence of heat and drought. Later on, in the same book, we recall that through a series of questions, God directs Job to contemplate various elements of the Creation (see Chapter 1) that include "the storehouses of the snow" (Job 38:22).

Moreover, we recall that God's deflection of Job's primary focus away from his own personal ills and toward a greater story than his own becomes a turning point in Job's life. A new perspective transforms his worldview, a transformation that radically alters his perception of himself in the grand scheme of things. This altered mindset is reminiscent of the radical change wrought in human perception when Ptolemy's concept of a geocentric universe was smashed by the later Copernican view in which the sun, not the Earth, was seen as the central body of the system. Job's response to God (Job 42:5) is again testimony to the revelatory nature of the Creation (Rom 1:20) and its power to speak of God's glory displayed in His handiwork (Ps 19:1).

Yet, God's question to Job concerning "the storehouses of the snow" alludes to an area of the world not frequented by many. At present, except for those who inhabit the margins of these storehouses where the approaching winter season drags its characteristics into their domain, appreciation of the patterns and processes of winter is from a distance. For most of us: strange cryogenic mounds that swell the Earth's surface; images of white landscapes and monstrous ice sheets as big as continents; rivers of ice that flow like thick molasses; massive floating ice shelves the size of countries; majestic icebergs, perennially frozen sea surfaces, and ground as hard as concrete: all this is difficult to imagine.

FOUR EXPLORERS WHO ENTERED THE STOREHOUSES OF SNOW AND ICE

History records the names of a number of brave and adventurous souls who went beyond imagination.[133] They prepared for, journeyed to, and for many months placed themselves well within that domain. Each entered what was largely unknown. Some entered wisely; some entered ill-prepared, with little knowledge of what to expect and with a variety of motives. The most ambitious entered before atomic-powered vessels were able to ram their way through the toughest of sea-surface conditions; before orbiting satellites could provide near-instantaneous data on their precise locations and on atmospheric and surface conditions; before permanent stations had been established on the continent; and, before aircraft could deliver multiple resupply packages to expedition members on demand.

Though they were greeted with the storehouse's vastness and beauty, the price of admission was high. Some endured, survived, and returned for a second trip. Others did not, succumbing to some of the worst environmental conditions this world has to offer. The following four men represent a small sampling of those who entered the perennial cryosphere at the world's highest latitudes.

1. Sir John Franklin

From fragments of information gained through early nineteenth-century explorations, there emerged growing evidence that a navigable route (a Northwest Passage) existed somewhere through the many channels of the Canadian Arctic Archipelago. In 1845, with two ships and a crew of 128 men, John Franklin ventured forth on his third foray into the Arctic to confirm the existence of a yet undiscovered central 500-kilometre stretch of waterway. This was the passage's *"missing link."* On two previous overland trips to the region, Franklin had confirmed the existence of the entire western section of the sea route, while others had confirmed the existence of an eastern portion.

Somewhere along King William's western shores, in Victoria Strait, the forward progress of this British expedition ended. Both ships mysteriously vanished and all crewmembers were lost. Fragmented evidence of the expedition's fate included a few graves, written messages, scattered human artifacts, disarticulated bones, and equipment and personal possessions strewn over the region's barren landscape. Not a single member of the Franklin expedition was ever found alive. Attempts to assemble a comprehensive story of the tragedy from the paltry remains and from the testimonies of nearby Inuit proved largely futile.

Despite repeated efforts to locate his ships, Franklin's abandoned vessels had just disappeared. For over sixteen decades, their whereabouts remained a mystery.

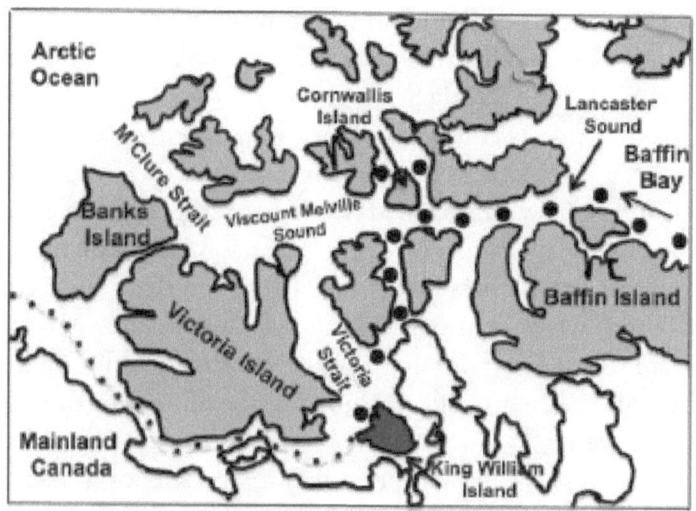

Franklin's Journey of 1845[134]

When finally discovered with modern equipment and from information provided by local Inuit, the ships were found—upright and largely intact in shallow waters, south of, and surprisingly close to their last known positions. To date, Franklin's grave has never been found.

While ice entrapment stopped the expedition's forward progress, it did not explain why everyone perished. There is evidence of possible contamination of canned food exposed to their improperly soldered joints. A theory, also relating to lead and solder, points to possible contamination of the water supply in the pipes onboard *Erebus* and *Terror*. Supporting evidence for such a theory lies buried within the ships and must await their recovery to be confirmed. In addition, much has been said about the reluctance of expedition members to learn survival techniques and the lifestyle of local aboriginals who, despite their own hardships and tragedies, had managed to eke out an existence and survive in one of the coldest and barren parts of Canada.

What is most certain is that Franklin had sailed south into a major bottleneck where old ice from the north, transported through Victoria Strait, must negotiate an ever-narrowing passageway farther south. Moreover, the possibility that Franklin was in possession of inaccurate and incomplete charts of the King William coastline might have led him to believe that King William Island was, in fact, a peninsula of the larger Boothia Peninsula to the east, and not an island at all. If so, he may have concluded that Victoria Strait as a way forward for his ships was his only option. If this is true, it was a most unfortunate error, given that Victoria Strait is known to contain some of the most formidable multi-year ice conditions within Canada's northern waterways, a condition in sharp contrast to the somewhat milder ice regime in the more easterly channels of Rae and James Ross straits (straits on King William Island's eastern shores, whose existence at the time was unclear). In fact, these straits were the ones eventually travelled by Roald Amundsen, who, in 1906, became the first to successfully sail the entire Northwest Passage from east to west.

In the years that followed Franklin's disappearance, much time and money were spent on multiple voyages sent out to solve the Franklin riddle—approximately thirty voyages in the space of the three decades after 1848. Curiously, the benefits of these later voyages lay not in piecing together much of the Franklin mystery. Rather, they lay in new knowledge gained about Canada's northern geography: its lands, its peoples, and its waterways, and with an added bonus that not one, but multiple passages exist through Canada's northern archipelago.

2. Lieutenant Adolphus Greely

In 1881, the American explorer, Adolphus Greely, set sail to do geographic exploration and atmospheric studies on northern Ellesmere Island and to establish a base and living quarters at the outpost of Fort Conger. Three years later, of the twenty-five members of his party who entered the storehouses of the snow, only six, including Greely, returned alive.

In terms of fulfillment of principal objectives, however, the expedition was successful. Exhaustive meteorological data were collected. Parts of the far north were explored and mapped. And a *Farthest North* was claimed for the United States, a mere 392 geographic miles from the North Pole. Unfortunately, however, due to severe ice conditions, a resupply vessel promised for the summer of 1882 failed to arrive. Also, in the summer of 1883, a vessel dispatched to rescue the marooned men was crushed and later sank in the ice just south of Cape Sabine. With the growing likelihood of spending a third winter at Fort Conger and facing dwindling provisions originally intended to last for only two years, Greely made the fateful decision to leave the relative comforts of Fort Conger and head south.

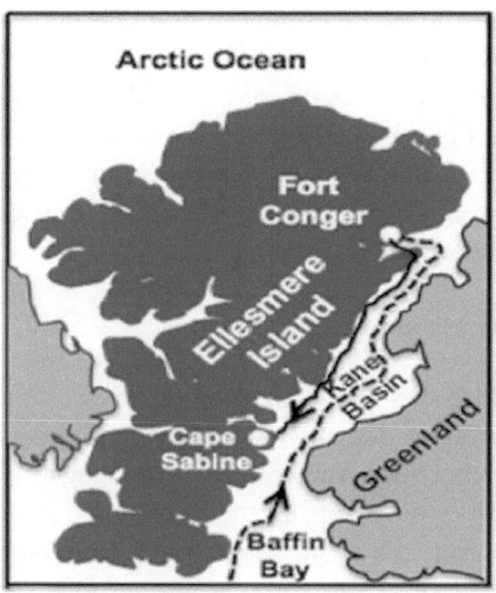

Greely's Journey of 1881[135]

After a 51-day journey, initially by boat, and then on ice floes, the party finally arrived on the rocky shores of Cape Sabine. Here, in late October 1883, in bleak surroundings (the sun absent for 110 days), with minimal food supplies, and with men isolated and starving in a dark, bitterly cold, and unfamiliar place, a human tragedy began to unfold. It was not until June 22, 1884, two years beyond its scheduled arrival date, that a relief vessel managed to reach Greely's camp. Confronting the rescuers was a scene of indescribable misery. Pitiful survivors, almost unrecognizable, lay moribund, awaiting the grave while many who had recently perished from hypothermia, starvation, or drowning, lay unburied. One man, recently executed for his crime of stealing rations, lay among them. Despite attempts to conceal the evidence, many of the bodies displayed unmistakable signs of cannibalism.

Reflecting on the expedition to Ellesmere Island and into the remote domain of snow and ice, Greely's account was filled with the unexpected. Despite the prolonged sufferings of his men, his was a story of praise for a small band of starving individuals who, despite inexperience with the North, had fulfilled all principal objectives of their expedition and who, despite the threat of imminent death, had demonstrated noble human qualities in a place where it was so much easier to die than to endure, and where God seemed conspicuously absent. Yet Greely spoke of numerous acts of self-sacrifice, concern of one man for another, and survival instincts that had often been tempered by compassion for the weak. In other words, he spoke of the emergence of goodness in a place of prolonged and unbelievable suffering.

3. Sir Douglas Mawson

During the "golden age" of polar exploration over a century ago, a number of men dared to enter the windiest, coldest, and most remote realm of snow and ice: Antarctica. Among them was Douglas Mawson. In early January 1912, Mawson set off on the *Australasian Antarctic Expedition*. Arriving via his ship *Aurora* at Antarctica's Commonwealth Bay, he set out to establish a base of operations at nearby Cape Denison to explore the region surrounding the South Magnetic Pole.

Almost immediately, it became abundantly clear that Mawson had chosen to enter the Antarctic at what is likely the world's windiest location. Commenting on hurricane-force winds that sustained monthly averages for the next six months in excess of 90 kilometres per hour, and periodically exceeding an incredible 300 kilometres per hour in raging gusts, a member of the expedition facetiously wrote:

> *It really looks as if there must have been a large surplus of bad weather left over after all the land had been formed at the Creation, a surplus that appears to have been dumped down in this small area of Antarctica.*[136]

Early in November 1912, organized teams of men set out from Cape Denison in different directions to explore and chart the 3 000-kilometre Antarctic coastline south of Australia. With Mawson were two companions,

Belgrave Ninnis, a military man, and xavier Mertz, a Swiss lawyer and mountaineer. With seventeen dogs and with food and equipment packed onto two sledges, they edged eastward, battling the fierce katabatic winds that streamed incessantly from Antarctica's interior toward the coast, traversing a surface strewn with hidden crevasses. Despite conditions, after five weeks of arduous travel, they had managed to trek and sledge close to 500 kilometres.

Then suddenly, almost without sound, tragedy struck. The first hint that something was amiss came when Mertz, who was leading on skis, was observed anxiously scanning the area. Mawson, riding his sledge behind Mertz, stopped and turned. There was no sign of Ninnis. He had simply vanished.

With rising panic, Mawson and Mertz immediately ran back along their tracks to discover a deep hole some 4 metres wide in the snow surface. On the far side was a set of tracks; on the near side, there were none. The bridge of snow that had adequately supported Mawson and Mertz a few moments before had collapsed under the more concentrated weight of Ninnis.

Desperately, and with fears rising, they peered into the yawning abyss, called out repeatedly and listened for life. After the pitiful moaning sounds of a dog ceased, all was silent. Ninnis was gone, along with six of the expedition's best dogs, a sledge that was carrying the bulk of their food supply and most of their equipment. Immediately, the expedition's principal objective switched from casual exploration to survival and a hurried scramble back to their base at Cape Denison before their ship departed.

Mawson and his lone companion figured that with their remaining food, supplemented by eating their dogs, they could survive for about five weeks. By then, with good weather and favourable surface conditions, and by ruthlessly dumping all extraneous equipment, they hoped to make base. Halfway along on their return journey, however, Mertz began to feel ill with severe stomach pains that he attributed to the dog meat, particularly dog liver. His general health declining rapidly, and just three weeks after the death of Ninnis, Mertz died. Now Mawson, all alone in a wilderness of bitter cold and wind, faced his own probable death.

> *Cold makes the Antarctic alien – but winds make it more deadly. The worst, and most dangerous, are katabatic winds, flying rivers of air, cold and heavy, falling down the frozen slopes from the polar plateaux and increasing in speed, with gravity, to assault those parts of the coast where they find outlet. They reach gusts of above 200 miles an hour and can blow consistently for days and not drop their force below 80 miles for many hours on end. Such winds lift gravel and hurl rocks and heavy objects out to sea; they blow men from their feet and their breath encases eyes, nostrils, mouths in ice.*
>
> *They are the worst winds in the world, a greater menace than cold. Born in rare high solitudes, they pick up snowflakes, ice crystals and frozen pellets, compacted like hail, all of which, blown in the wind, become abrasive material that can polish rough metal to brilliant sheen and scour the wood from between the grains when they are left exposed for a winter. Cold and wind can reach the sheltered parts of a man's body and cause deadly frostbite, adding to his peril.*[137]

Mawson's solo journey back to his main base at Cape Denison is a story of remarkable determination amid extreme hardship. Miraculously, despite his own rapidly deteriorating health and after more than one neardeath plunge into jagged and hidden crevasses, he managed to reach his destination in one month. During that journey, in complete isolation, he had much opportunity to reflect on recent events. He wondered why the decline in Mertz's health was so precipitous. Facing starvation, he had resisted the strong temptation to cannibalize his companion's body. Often his thoughts drifted toward just giving up and allowing death to provide an easy exit from suffering and despair. Given his plight in the place one writer aptly called *"an accursed land"*, one wonders what motivation inclined him toward endurance. Commenting on significant changes in him, one of Mawson's friends wrote,

> *A noticeably chastened man, quieter, humble, and I think very much closer to his God . . . He told me that there was*

> *some other power he had borrowed on that journey which was superior to the willpower that pulled him through. His faith steeled him; he drew his personal strength from his faith.*
>
> Eric Webb[138]

Although the precise object of Mawson's *faith* is unclear, those of faith frequently face critics who doubt its genuineness, seeing it as an example of "*foxhole religion*," an escape into unreality, done in desperation when no other options are available. Others suggest just the opposite, that, during times of extreme personal danger, we see more clearly what constitutes the *essence* of reality since impediments to faith are swept away.

> *We came to probe its mystery,*
> *to reduce this land to terms of science,*
> *but there is always the indefinable*
> *which holds aloof yet which rivets our souls . . .*
>
> **from** *This Accursed Land*[139]

4. Sir Ernest Shackleton

Among those Antarctic explorers who sought the virgin wilderness of the South Pole during the Golden Age of polar exploration, three names dominate. Roald Amundsen, on his second trip to the Antarctic continent, entered with four companions and dashed south to where all meridians of longitude converge and the only spot from which all directions point northward. He returned unscathed with the sought-after prize for Norway of "*first to the South Pole*." At the same time, Robert Scott's second trip to the Antarctic aimed to trace a different route to the same pole. Scott not only lost the race with Amundsen by one month, but he and all four of his companions perished close to base camp on their return journey.

Ernest Shackleton's experiences in Antarctica are all remarkable. In total, he journeyed south on four separate occasions from his home in Ireland. But on each journey, his principal purpose was thwarted. On his first trip, accompanying Robert Scott over the Ross Ice Shelf, sickness forced him to return home prematurely. On his second trip, this time as leader of his own expedition, he penetrated the vast hitherto uncharted Antarctic plateau to a mere 97 geographic miles from the South Pole before a severely depleted food supply forced him to turn back. On his third trip, heavy sea ice in the Weddell Sea prevented him from even setting foot on the southern continent, while his fourth trip was abruptly terminated when a massive heart attack ended his life. Of these four expeditions, it is the third trip, sometimes referred to as his *"successful failure,"* that many would agree was his most remarkable.

Its lofty name was the *Imperial Trans-Antarctic Expedition*. Its ambitious objective was the complete crossing of the continent. It consisted of two groups: Shackleton's party, which would approach the continent from the Atlantic side through the Weddell Sea to traverse the continent; and the Ross Sea party, which would approach from the Australian side of the continent to establish supply depots to support the latter stages of Shackleton's trek.

However, Shackleton's crossing never really began. His ship *Endurance* left Britain in early August 1914—coincidentally, on the first day of the First World War—and sailed to the Antarctic coast via the island of South Georgia. Soon after the ship entered the Weddell Sea, it became trapped in heavy pack ice that prevented it from reaching the continent at Vahsel Bay. With the surrounding ice now in control of the ship's direction of drift, and with the powerful strength of the ice threatening to crush it, Shackleton and his crew began a slow, forced, wide clockwise rotation about the Weddell Sea that lasted for a gruelling 282 days.

Eventually succumbing to the pack's giant crushing strength, *Endurance* began to list badly, whereupon Shackleton ordered the doomed ship abandoned. Fortunately, the three weeks it took for *Endurance* to drop out of sight afforded ample time for the offloading of valuable equipment onboard.

For over four months, as a form of consolation, the ice that had crushed their ship now provided the crew with a solid surface upon which to construct a camp. But as their ice surface continued north into lower latitudes, its stability declined through melting and fracture. At this point, the men had no choice but to abandon both ice and ship and take to the three lifeboats that had been salvaged from their sinking vessel. After one week in choppy open water, they arrived on the desolate shores of Elephant Island off the northern tip of the Antarctic Peninsula. With complete indifference, the Antarctic continent had expelled twenty-eight men before any had placed a single foot on that greatest of all ice surfaces. And so, from departure from South Georgia until arrival at Elephant Island, Shackleton and his crew had not touched land for 497 days.

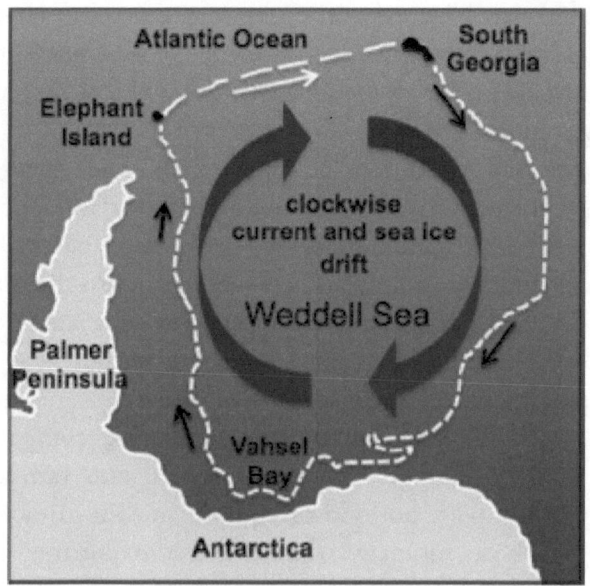

Shackleton's Two-Year Southern Ocean Circuit[140]

While there was much relief at having arrived at Elephant Island, there was also much concern. The chances of being discovered and rescued at this location were considered poor. For one thing, it was known that ships seldom visited the region. Moreover, no one was expecting the expedition to be anywhere near Elephant Island. Fully realizing these troubling facts, the resourceful Shackleton promptly devised a rescue plan. In the largest of his three lifeboats, with a crew of five, he would embark on a hazardous journey of 1300 kilometres eastward through the chaotic waters of Drake Passage to the known whaling station of Stromness, near the point where the expedition had been launched on South Georgia Island. He knew that without flawless navigation to locate "a needle in the proverbial haystack," his boat and crew would miss South Georgia (if indeed they survived their journey) and be deposited by the prevailing winds in one of the emptiest areas of ocean in the world, with no remaining strength in body or vessel to battle the opposing winds and currents for a second approach.

But flawless navigation is precisely what this small group of desperate men possessed. For 16 days, they battled waves and fierce weather, surviving at one point a terrifying encounter with a towering rogue wave of monumental size. Near exhaustion, they reached the island with a boat in pitiful condition. But again, their landing received mixed reviews since landfall was made on South Georgia's southwest coast, *not* on the side of the whaling station.

Given the sad condition of both vessel and crew, Shackleton determined that their only option was a daring overland journey through the island's uncharted mountainous ice fields. And so, leaving a party of three in uncertainty, he and two others set out to cross the island. Thirty-six hours later, after glissading down a long steep glaciated slope, holding onto each other like children on a toboggan without the aid of their ice axe to partly control their speed and direction, an unrecognizable Shackleton, with his two equally unrecognizable companions, stood before the station manager, in filthy, ripped, and tattered clothing, with energy spent, with no food or equipment, but miraculously alive. Reflecting on those moments that ended the journey across South Georgia, and ruminating on life when so many comforts of life had been stripped away, Shackleton wrote:

> *At the bottom of the fall we were able to stand again on dry land. The rope could not be recovered. We had flung down the adze from the top of the fall and also the logbook and the cooker wrapped in one of our blouses. That was all, except our wet clothes, that we brought out of the Antarctic, which we had entered a year and a half before with well-found ship, full equipment, and high hopes.*
>
> *That was all of tangible things; but in memories we were rich. We had pierced the veneer of outside things. We had "suffered, starved, and triumphed, grovelled down yet grasped at glory, grown bigger in the bigness of the whole." We had seen God in his splendors, heard the text that Nature renders. We had reached the naked soul of man.*[141]

Philosophically, in words reminiscent of the mysterious fourth person in the Bible story from the Book of Daniel, Shackleton reflected on his experience crossing South Georgia. With similar thoughts echoed independently by each of his two companions, he commented:

> *When I look back at those days I have no doubt that Providence guided us, not only across those snowfields, but across the storm-white sea that separated Elephant Island from our landing-place on South Georgia. I know that during that long and racking march of thirty-six hours over the unnamed mountains and glaciers of South Georgia it seemed to me often that we were four, not three.*[142]

The obvious locational contrast between the fourth person's presence with Shackleton and his threesome through frigid mountainous South Georgia, and the fourth person's presence in a blazing furnace is seen by many as representing God's abiding presence with His children, regardless of time, location or circumstances (Ps 139:7-12; Dan 3:25; Matt 28:1620 KJV).

The rest of the story tells of Shackleton's attempt to mount a rescue of his entire crew. His return to his three companions on the island's south side was quick and easy. However, attempts to rescue the larger party on Elephant Island were long and frustrating, given the ice conditions that prevailed in the approach to shore. Nevertheless, 129 days after leaving the group, amid doubts they would ever be reunited, it happened. Soon after, Shackleton returned his entire party of twenty-eight men safely back home.

Months later, Shackleton faithfully returned to retrieve the Ross Sea party. All but three men had survived. As for the string of depots that were successfully laid by that party, they remain in their places, undisturbed, buried in the snows of the Ross Ice Shelf. At present, this massive shelf is transporting its string of depots at roughly 800 metres per year toward its terminus, there to be eventually and unceremoniously expelled into Antarctica's surrounding waters along with the bodies of Scott and his four companions, and the bodies of Mawson's two friends.

One wonders why anyone would choose such hazardous forays into extreme danger within the "storehouses of the snow." On the topic of possible motives, writer Elspeth Huxley suggests the following:

> *The skein of action is raveled up from many threads. Fame and fortune are generally given first place. Also on the list are love of country, lust for adventure, devotion to a cause, and obscurer forces like an urge towards martyrdom.*
>
> *Certainly there is curiosity: desire to know what lies over the next hill, at the top of the highest mountain and at the bottom of the deepest sea, on the moon, on the planets and beyond the stars. All such motives are mixed up together, and the analyst who tries to sort and label them is generally wasting his time.*[143]

10
IMAGO DEI

O ye Children of Men, bless ye the Lord:
praise him, and magnify him forever

Benedicite (BCP)

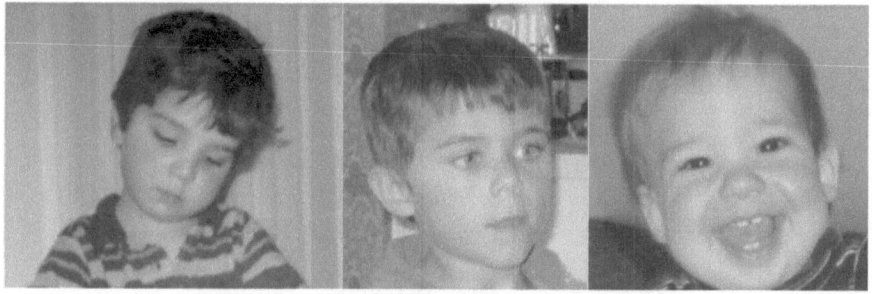

Grandsons Jonathan, Stephen, and Andrew
(JES)

*For, after all,
put it as we may to ourselves,
we are all of us from birth to death
guests at a table
which we did not spread.
The sun, the earth, love, friends,
our very breath are parts of the banquet . . .
Shall we think of the day
as a chance to come nearer to our Host,
and to find out something of Him
who has fed us so long?*

Rebecca Harding Davis[144]

*So God created mankind in his own image,
in the image of God he created them;
male and female he created them.*

Genesis 1:27

*The Son is the image of the invisible God . . .
For God was pleased
to have all his fullness
dwell in him . . .*

Colossians 1:15, 19

OUR WORLD: GOD'S VISIBLE LANGUAGE: A QUICK REVIEW

In the previous chapters of this book, our minds feasted on a world abounding in rich physical imagery. *About us* and *below us*, on our own planetary orb, we probed Earth's solid, liquid, and gaseous elements and noted the frequency with which this imagery is employed in scripture as illustrative aids to grasp profound biblical truths. And *above us* in the vastness of space, we discovered visible expressions of order, greatness, and extravagance. In it all, nature silently spoke, grabbing our attention and encouraging our wonder.

We beheld what we could see; we imagined what we couldn't: arresting beauty; origin and design; age and distances; patterns and processes, in scales of matter from the macroscopic to the subatomic, all reflecting cosmic history scattered throughout its geography, all hinting of something more, something far greater than self, expressing truth everywhere. We wondered about our world's capacity to increase mystery by offering more questions than answers.

An astronaut likened our planetary sphere to a Christmas tree ornament hanging in space without visible support. An astronomer imagined our sky as a celestial ballroom with suns, moons and planets participating in a well-choreographed dance with movements governed by precise natural laws beyond themselves. Another astronomer, observing in planetary orbits a harmony in the heavens, expressed them in terms of chords and notes on a musical scale fashioned by a brilliant Composer.

Numerous artists perceived God as the Ultimate Artist with nature as His canvas. Theologians described Creation as *"the first of two books"* written by the finger of God. And a British explorer, beholding a massive Antarctic ice shelf, called it a sight surpassing the imagination, thus generating an indescribable feeling of the greatness of the Creator. Sounds something like Job's experience with God when God, seeming to ignore Job's troubles, captured his mind with questions about various elements from His visible Creation, His *"visible language."* And what was Job's reply to God's visible and persuasive language? *"My ears had heard of you but now my eyes have seen you."*

IMAGO DEI: OUR SPECIAL STATUS IN THE CREATION

In the Bible's very first chapter, with virtually no extraneous information written, we read that the cosmos proceeded out of the mind of God who spoke it into being. To everything He applied universal order and governance. In a time period described as six days, an orderly progression of beginnings was established, with humans introduced last in the sequence. And at the end of each creative act, with obvious exultation, God declared it all "very good."

In that first chapter, it is clear that God pre-existed His Creation. While the cosmos had a beginning, the Great "I AM" didn't. Also, it was clear from the beginning that humans were to enjoy special status within a unique familial relationship with their Creator, as God's children, made "in His Image" (*Imago Dei*) and "in His likeness" (Gen 1:26). In addition, only into their nostrils did He breathe "the breath of life" (Gen 2:7). And into their lives, He inserted special identity, inestimable value, and clear purpose. Established in and surrounded by the beauty of an idyllic garden residence, they lived in close friendship with the One who had created them. Endowed with moral character and freedom of choice, they were assigned specific responsibilities alongside their Maker, with goodness, beauty, and truth clearly established as absolutes.

IMAGO DEI: AND YET A MARRED IMAGE

The so-called human "Fall" represented a colossal tremor that reverberated throughout the whole of the created order. Discordant notes of disobedience, deception and shame, fear and secrecy, guilt, alienation and blame had inserted dissonance into Creation's harmonious order. The consequences were somehow universal and, for the time, seemed both permanent and irreversible.

The good news is that these consequences were neither. Human actions violating divine law were countered by God's grace, unmerited favour, ultimate redemption, and restoration (Is 43:1–3a) promised through the atoning death of Christ on the cross (Rom 8:22–24; Col

1:21–22). Moreover, although God's likeness has diminished within us, it has not been entirely erased. Vestigial remains of God's image and likeness remain permanently stamped upon us as recognizable remnants that neither the Fall nor the passage of time has entirely obliterated.

But what does *"in His likeness"* look like? We know that it maintains close company with truth, goodness, or beauty. Markers of His likeness among us include expressions of gratitude and joy; light and peace; harmony, satisfaction and empathy; honesty, loyalty, and exultation; humility, self-sacrifice and generosity, mercy and hope, all ingredients of a state of mind that leads toward a *heart of "gladness"* (Heb 1:9) both in the one who gives and the one who receives.

During the infamous morning of 9/11, 2001 when four high-jacked passenger jets were converted by terrorists into guided missiles to deliver intended death and destruction to critical urban targets, all American airspace was immediately shut down and all operating aircraft flying to it or over it were ordered to land at the nearest airport. Of 238 aircraft diverted to Canada, over 30% landed at airports in Newfoundland and Labrador. Of these, slightly over 50%, comprising about 6600 passengers on 38 aircraft arrived at *Gander*, home to a population roughly equivalent to the number of total arrivals.

To the relief and surprise of the arrivals, they had landed in what came to be called an *"oasis of kindness"*. "Arrivals" did not seem the appropriate descriptive term for them; and neither did the term, "visitors". Rather, from the warmth and the high degree of preparedness by which they were received, they felt more like "guests", sometimes even like "family" of the hosts eager to receive them. Receiving total strangers with spontaneous welcome and generosity was normal, automatic, simply *the right thing to do*. Friendliness and generosity such as this had long ago been written into their genetic code and into the mental posture of a people who, because of Gander's somewhat remote geography and proximity to a frequently hostile ocean, were well versed in the value of community as a vital means of survival. One can say that the people of Gander were well-prepared for friendly responses to their visitors. Need of others close by promoted community-building and prompted spontaneous acts of kindness, even to strangers, even when numbers exceeding 6000 newcomers literally descended on their community uninvited, all at once and with virtually no advance warning.

Many arrivals enjoyed free accommodation offered to them in private homes. Many were received as guests in local churches, in school facilities and in nearby summer camps. All were looked after. Those who preferred more privacy were directed to hotels. Together with their hosts, the visitors attended community functions, picked blueberries and explored the countryside in and around Gander.

It is clear that vestigial remnants of God's likeness abounded in the people of Gander as evidenced in their preparation for their guests' arrival, their unconditional and wholehearted acceptance of everyone and with no apparent mention of personal inconvenience. Passengers who were part of that unscheduled 9/11 stop in Gander Newfoundland had experienced it as a most unusual place, truly an "oasis of kindness" filled with unexpected blessings from hosts practicing image-bearing, possibly not even aware that that's what they were doing.

It was not surprising that many people, both among those who were part of this story, and those who had heard or read about it, saw obvious similarities to the *Parable of the Good Samaritan* from Luke 10:25-37: assuming additional responsibilities for the sake of another; sacrificially attending to the care of one in need, with no payback required; faithfulness in providing necessary extended care, regardless of personal costs. In that story, Jesus is *the* Good Samaritan. But rather than an image-bearer of the invisible God (as we are), He Himself IS the Image (Col 1: 15-16).

And so, on a smaller and more personal scale, what are some of these vestigial remains of God's image and likeness in persons I have known? Firstly: four brief snapshots of image-bearing from family; secondly, from four seasons in my life (childhood; parenting; career; and grandparenting) from various folk who exemplified image bearing in a variety of circumstances, places and times.

- in Albert, my father-in-law, whose decisions reflected fundamental life principles over personal convenience, made the ultimate sacrifice as an air navigator in 1944; and wife Ivy who, like many other mothers, bore her grief with *strength, grace, wisdom,* and

humility, raising three children as a war widow with endurance and limited means, all sacrificial acts repeated by countless others;
- in Mary, who used her gift of hospitality repeatedly to welcome guests into our home, seat them at her table, and treat them to delicious delicately prepared foods;
- in a moment of *joy* and *exultation* at a hospital nursery window when Nancy first beheld the face of Stephen, our first grandchild;
- in the *satisfaction* in grandsons Andrew and Jonathan, while rearranging sand on a PEI beach to *create* castles and roads with pails and shovels.

1. Evidence of "Vestigial Remains" from Childhood

What does image bearing look like in everyday life? Individual lives develop as a unique set of inherited genes in combination with a unique set of experiences. For me, the initial venue was a northern Ontario mining town. It was during a World War and the ending of the Great Depression, the times of my earliest memories. Our dwelling was a small flat above a corner store. Those were the days of ration books; telephone party lines; newspapers from Toronto always arriving one day after publication; serious childhood diseases like measles, whooping cough, and mumps; repeatedly darned wool socks; and countless episodes on our Philco radio of *The Green Hornet,* soap operas whose stories went on forever, and *L for Lanky* (an exciting drama of the war based upon the role of a Lancaster bomber crew).

On Saturdays, with a few pennies, I would go to the Grand Theatre, watch its double feature, buy popcorn, and cheer as the Lone Ranger battled evil forces without ever dirtying or wrinkling his clothes. For my Saturday night bath, I sat in a two-foot-square grey galvanized tub in the middle of the kitchen floor in water warmed over our wood stove. We picked blueberries in August while swatting mosquitoes, set up outdoor lemonade stands from old orange crates (selling cups for two cents each), and sawed, split, and piled our wood supply of poplar and birch for the winter. It was a *good* and simple life.

Those were the days when it was more likely that stuff would be fixed rather than replaced, when leftovers were common fare at dinner, and when a couple of pennies would buy a bagful of candies at Gordie's Confectionery. I made airplanes from folded paper and assembled airplane models from balsa wood purchased from a hobby shop. I constructed cars from discarded spools of thread propelled by elastic bands. My dad taught me to make whistles from poplar branches and crude hockey pads from bamboo strips squeezed into pieces of felt. Sticks, string, and elastic were the resources from which I made bows and arrows and slingshots. Like many others, what limited financial resources could not buy, we managed to make, or do without.

In my early years, it became apparent that I was predisposed to left-handedness. For me, to throw a ball, hold a fork, or write with a pencil with my left hand was as normal as breathing. However, when I entered first grade, someone decided that it was unnatural to print with one's left hand and that it would be advisable that I switch. To date, I still throw a ball and hold my fork with my left hand, and still have difficulty making a pair of scissors cut properly.

Concerning *daily bread,* my stay-at-home mom, like most mothers at the time, was resourceful and imaginative in her food preparation, managing to produce great meals on a meagre budget. Among the meals of the week, her greatest efforts were directed toward Sunday dinner, our big escape from leftovers. Each meal included multiple dishes; each resembled an elaborate art form. I don't recall her using recipes. As a culinary artist, she measured ingredients qualitatively without recipes, with *"just a dash of this"* or *"a pinch of that."*

Concerning our bread-winner, my father assumed the role of family head, gleaning a meagre living from a store he purchased in the years just prior to the war. Like many others in our town during the latter part of the Great Depression, this small business failed, whereupon he joined the Canadian army. Following the war, he managed to find work in one of the town's gold mines. His authoritarian leadership within our home was a mixture of firmness and kindness, with very rare use of corporal punishment. In discipline, I recall his smiles more than his frowns, his facial expressions more than his words, but his watchful eyes as much as his powerful hands.

On the subject of his eyes, one of my fondest memories of him captures the usual manner in which he dealt with issues of discipline. He was sitting in his favourite chair reading the *Northern Daily News*, with his ever-present *roll-your-own* cigarette drooping from his lips (his cigarettes were mostly paper with almost no tobacco). Playing close by, and doing what I clearly knew was wrong, I turned to see if he had noticed. He had. In that instant, I saw my father turn his face toward me, pause just long enough to let me know he had noticed my misconduct, and then in a deliberately slow motion, with no words uttered, yet with a slight smile, close his eyes and slowly turn his head away. I often wonder about the package of lessons contained within that simple yet effective means of discipline. Shining through it all was a clear expression of a father's grace in the presence of a child's disobedience, as well as a father's attentiveness and quiet enjoyment of a child just being a child. His most important lessons could only be communicated with acts and not with words. How truly strange are the subtle and incidental means by which one learns important lessons of life. I had a *good* mother and father.

On the subject of my father's hands, the most appropriate descriptive adjectives include rough, powerful, large, and yet gentle. One day when I was quite young, I somehow incurred his anger while playing in the small yard adjacent to our flat. He beckoned me, but instead of complying, I started to run away (something I rarely did). To my surprise, he chased me (something he rarely did). Running as fast as I could toward the back of our house, I came upon the set of wooden steps on either end of a slightly elevated porch. In my haste, my foot caught the edge of the top step and I fell forward, sliding both hands along the rough wood planks of the porch surface. The pain of hands covered in multiple slivers was immediate. As I lay screaming, I recall his pair of hands lifting me and quickly transporting me home. There, with his arms about me, he and my mother slowly removed each sliver, one by one. Here was power and goodness embodied in people I cherished the most.

Within our rather conservative and traditional home, respect for family name and for various authorities was assumed. I don't recall these topics ever being discussed. For my older sister and me, life revolved around our home, our church, and our school. First impressions of church were not particularly positive. It seemed otherworldly. I got the impression that church was all about sitting still and being nice.

Sitting on a hard pew in our local church and trying to be quiet was my first lesson on the length of eternity. It was definitely not my idea of fun. On frequent occasions, my mind would rush to my rescue and transport me to some other place where something exciting was happening. I imagined myself as a Maple Leaf forward, stick-handling through the entire Black Hawk team to score the winning goal in the Cup finals. My mind was my instant playback and escape mechanism providing exciting entertainment I could summon at will.

I could not understand the apparent pleasure of those kind church ladies who felt it their duty to regularly pinch my cheek and ruffle my hair. I was certain that since Jesus was once a young boy, he must have had similar thoughts and annoying experiences while attending synagogue. In fact, it was the stories of him walking on water, calming the fury of a storm, standing up to bullies, and wrecking furniture in the temple, rather than those depicting him as *gentle, meek,* and *mild,* that captured my attention and admiration. I remember a particularly embarrassing event at the annual talent show when my sister and I sang a song, something about fishers of men. Somehow, it didn't go as practised. Like a record unable to advance beyond a defective groove, we got stuck in a melodious loop, and were unable to end the song.

Sunday was the day for family visits. With no car, we always walked. Visits to the homes of friends and relatives seemed endless. However, I enjoyed two: the home of my godmother and that of a family friend—Aunt Sadie. Without doubt, in first place was the home of my godmother. The attraction was her son's all-metal electric train, with its transformer, set of tracks, passenger cars, and cool engine. Any kid who owned an electric train set immediately became the most envied boy on the block, for he now owned the ultimate toy. How I yearned for one to be under my tree at Christmas.

I was confused as to why Aunt Sadie was *Aunt* Sadie since she wasn't a relative. She was always kind and took a keen interest in my interests. Chief among the latter was her living room floor. It was far from level. It had a pronounced warp. On each visit, I would take along a bag of marbles, sit on that floor and play the same game—a game of problem solving involving marbles rolling in response to gravity and the floor's contours. I would place a small target against a wall and then position myself a distance away. The trick was to determine just where to place each marble so that, when released, it would roll and pass through a hole in the target. No small challenge, given the topography of Aunt Sadie's floor. To add more challenge, I would occasionally alter the target's location on the floor. With my experience, I could well have become a putting coach for aspiring golfers who need the same skill to negotiate the undulating and challenging surfaces of golf greens.

But there was a second object of interest at Aunt Sadie's—that of her sofa. Reason? It offered me the possibility of a significant cash grab. As a result of casual exploring, I had found a few pennies deep down between two sofa cushions. In those days, the discovery of a few pennies was tantamount to winning the lottery and represented for me a week's haul in candy at Gordie's. Given the fact that I would find more pennies on subsequent visits (which I was always allowed to keep), I suspect Aunt Sadie deliberately planted them in that sofa, as I was convinced my father did in our chesterfield at home.

My first school teacher was Miss Barkell. Like many teachers who teach Grade One, Miss Barkell was a saint and a mother-substitute during weekdays. Her love for her children was obviously not triggered by our behaviour. Her patience appeared to emerge from a bottomless reservoir.

Way back when, someone had come up with the idea that kids should scribble crayon wax on paper. The activity was called *colouring* and kids were supposed to like it. But colouring carried with it an important rule: all scribbling had to be contained within clearly defined areas! Lines that formed the picture of the tree, the snowman, or the face of the clown were mysterious boundaries limiting where crayons were permitted to wander. Similar limitations applied to printing within the coloured lines in my notebook. To my recollection, nobody ever asked why. It was just one of many rules that formed part of the fabric of living, like the rule about elbows on tables, chewing with mouths closed, and wearing socks that matched. I was grateful for the fact that so many letters of the alphabet can tolerate a wide range of shapes and still be recognized for what they are supposed to represent.

Prior to my ninth birthday, my father got a job in Toronto, and our family left familiar surroundings, venturing south by train to a new flat. Toronto was unbelievably big and busy, with a telephone book difficult to lift and thicker than even our old Eaton's catalogue. Gone were the blueberry patches; the really cold winters that froze my long underwear into solid boards on the outdoor line; my friends on my street; the wooden sidewalks; our popular radio station, CJKL; and the Grand Theatre. Gone was my cat *Minoo* and our wood stove where Minoo had his afternoon nap; the electric train set belonging to my cousin Albert; and, of course, Aunt Sadie's magic floor and revenue-generating chesterfield. I remember how noisy the big city seemed, but by contrast how silent the crowds were on buses and streetcars. Compared with the chatter between strangers back in my hometown, it seemed odd that so little talk between passengers occurred in that huge place farther south.

Our new dwelling was situated on a busy downtown Toronto street. Since the nearest Presbyterian church was some distance away, my father decided on the Anglican church nearby.[145] His decision was somewhat surprising, given his opposition to any liturgical form he considered too elaborate. This opposition I later discovered emerged out of a concern that the substitution of liturgical *form* for theological *substance* was all but inevitable and that without vigilance, the worship of aspects of the Creation would come to replace the worship of its Creator. As it turned out, however, despite his cautionary note, my father's insistence that we attend an Anglican church proved to be a definite positive in my life and in my family's.

To someone accustomed to a small church, my first exposure to the inside of St. Paul's was shocking. The sanctuary resembled a vast cavern. Surrounded on all sides by colourful stained glass windows, tall stone pillars, and banks of long unpainted grey zinc organ pipes directed my gaze heavenward. This seemed important because someone had already determined that the direction to heaven is *up*. Expressing theology in architecture, the Lord's Table, and not the pulpit was the church's principal focus. Behind it stood a large, white-marble carving of the Last Supper. A massive Bible lay open on the wings of a large metallic eagle. Throughout the sanctuary, dim lighting served to reinforce the element of mystery that is so much a part of the Christian faith. And the arrangement of the many church pews was in the form of a cross. It was obvious that those involved in the architectural planning and construction of this magnificent place of worship had done their theological homework.

Despite all its unfamiliar appearance, St. Paul's came to represent order and safety for a young guy now contending with much uncertainty in a new environment within a monstrous city. In every way, architectural integrity within the church's design prevailed. And architecture reflected traditional Christian theology. It was architecture saturated with scrupulous detail, artistic flare, and significant meaning. Though I didn't fully appreciate it at the time, the glory of that visible structure somehow bore subtle yet powerful testimony to the greater glory of the invisible God.

Given its central urban location, but primarily because of its size and beauty, St. Paul's was a popular site for special services, most notably weddings, funerals, and memorial services. One Saturday, motivated by sheer curiosity, and with nothing better to do, I wandered into that crowded church to investigate what was happening. A reporter covering the funeral service of a prominent Torontonian caught sight of me and, also, with nothing better to do, asked me a few questions. Nervously, I attempted a few answers. The following Monday, in a Toronto newspaper, an article appeared that erroneously identified me as yet another person who took the time to pay his respects to one of Toronto's beloved citizens—an altruistic spin on an impulsive act by an inquisitive kid!

A few weeks after our arrival at St. Paul's, I was invited to audition for the 20-voice boys' choir. The invitation to be a chorister was completely unexpected. To the surprise and delight of my parents and myself, I was accepted. Each week, I was required to be present for three practices, attend catechism class, and sing at two Sunday worship services. My monthly salary of $3 was far more than I had ever gleaned from dear Aunt Sadie's chesterfield. I was given my own hymn book, prayer book, and anthem book, and assigned a box in our choir room in which to store them. I was outfitted with choir robes consisting of a new black cassock and white surplice. Then I was shown my place in the front row on one side of the large church chancel and immediately in front of its four-manual Casavant organ.

At the time of its installation in St. Paul's, it was considered the largest pipe organ in Canada and the third largest in the world. This splendid instrument made nearby pews and portions of my anatomy vibrate whenever notes in the lowest octaves were played. I was certain it could be heard all the way to Kirkland Lake. I quickly learned that music can be *felt* as well as heard. Soon I was singing hymns and various psalms and canticles from the *Book of Common Prayer*, as well as selected anthems from the works of Bach and Handel, Mozart and Purcell.

I was proud to be part of something out of the ordinary. I confess, however, that I did not comprehend much of the content of what was sung:

I waited patiently for the Lord,
and he inclined unto me, and heard my calling.

Psalm 40:1 (BCP)

Jesus lives, henceforth is death but the gate to life immortal.

Hymn 606, v.2, by C.F. Gellert
(Anglican Hymn Book)

The people that walked in darkness
have seen a great light.

Isa 9:2 (KJV), from Handel's Messiah

I had little understanding of what it all meant. In my learning, *form* was to precede *substance*. Information bits were to precede integrated packages of understanding. For now, the emphasis was on attentiveness, on memorizing tunes and words, on enunciation, sound and timing, rather than on meaning. And throughout that time period, I made new friends and learned some of the most valuable lessons of my life, lessons that somehow found their way into some mental storage bin, there to lie dormant and in embryonic form to be saved as bottled influence for future withdrawal and contemplation. I was disciplined in a manner that complemented the discipline received at home. The focus was on the acquisition of life's building blocks.

As a young chorister, I was encouraged in the pursuit of excellence, in following directions, in punctuality, perseverance, cooperation, and accountability. I was taught that behaviour matters, that responsibilities to others often must take precedence over personal wants. Expectations and standards were high. Sloppiness was not tolerated. I was required to memorize numerous passages of scripture and began to understand the depths of something called *grace*. I was introduced to the best in classical music. Much of these foundational lessons managed to survive many years within my mental storage bin and helped to bring stability and balance to my life.

There are rich benefits in preparing long hours for and being part of events, some ordinary, and some that are truly grand and larger than self. In the category of *truly grand*, one was powerfully illustrated during an evening presentation of Handel's *Messiah* sung before a packed church. I sat amid an ocean of voices since an additional choir had joined ours from an Anglican church nearby. Directly in front of me in the church chancel sat the orchestra: with violins, trumpets, and shiny copper kettledrums about to issue forth sounds sequenced by musicians in formal dress. Standing in her place of prominence among the four soloists was our lovely soprano. She was every choirboy's choice if ever the church decided to choose a *Miss St. Paul's*. Behind me at the mighty organ sat Dr. Charles Peaker, our organist and choirmaster, who laboured many hours preparing us for special services.

Dr. Peaker's 20-voice boy choristers were the beneficiaries of the wisdom and musical skills of an outstanding musician and leader who knew, appreciated, and enjoyed the antics, restlessness, potential, and lively imaginations of young rascals whose natural tendencies could never be totally disguised beneath white collars and freshly pressed robes, and whose minds regularly planned and executed their own form of entertainment while appearing to be listening intently to sermons from our rector.

At the practice prior to that special evening, this kind and generous father figure, who watched our every move and whose ears could somehow differentiate between individual voices, had reminded each boy that all that was required of us was to watch our conductor and follow his guidance. He promised that if each of us complied, a strange blending of voices would somehow transform individual musical contributions into a harmonious and pleasing sound. Of course, he was right.

Jerry Salloum

As Sir Ernest MacMillan, the famous composer and conductor took his place to conduct choir and orchestra, and as choristers and musicians awaited his first command with his baton, something in that momentary silence I did not understand at the time stirred within me. Before any note from orchestra, organ, or chorister issued forth, Sir Ernest paused to deliberately look at each of us. There were no thoughts of breakaways in the hockey game and no impulses to exchange coded messages with buddies across the wide chancel.

Messiah began with a brief overture, followed by a tenor solo from Isaiah, chapter 40: *"Comfort ye my people, saith your God . . ."* As voices and instruments added their unique sounds to deliver a unique story and message, a glorious composite sound radiated out in all directions within that cavernous place, just as Dr. Peaker promised would happen. It was the beauty of some of the best music this world has to offer. It was the Word of God inserted within a musical score composed by the brilliant and highly esteemed George Frideric Handel.

We sang mostly in four-part harmony, but also in unison, with voices at times like thunder, and at other times in whispers. We had been reminded that God's speech is sometimes like thunder and sometimes like soft whispers. And I was privileged to be part of it all. In the end, *form* had *not* replaced *substance*. Rather, *form* assisted in the appreciation of *substance*.

Decades later, something of the profundity of these childhood experiences as a chorister began to be realized as unprocessed fragments of past lessons surfaced in my memory. Ideas planted within me years before were now maturing. In it all, I discovered something partially hidden. I came to see St. Paul's Anglican Church not only as a place of fun, challenge, and acceptance, but also as a giant repository of sounds and symbols inserted within long-established liturgy and magnificent architecture, assisting worshippers to grasp the profound messages contained in the teachings of scripture, while stimulating our imaginations to journey beyond the realm of the visible toward meaning within deep mystery. Pastor Galen Guengerich adds the following thoughts about the contributions of church to our lives:

> *We're here not so much to make spiritual progress each week, though that's wonderful when it happens. Rather, we mostly*

> *come for the consistency—for what remains week after week: the comfort of the liturgy, the solace of the music, the reassuring sight of familiar faces, the enduring presence of ancient rites and timeless symbols. We are here to remind ourselves of values that unite us and commitments that keep us heading in the right direction. We're here to choose again what we chose before.*[146]

Might there be at the heart of the cosmos a glorious melody wafting through its vast emptiness, its individual notes in perfect harmony, a melody that the ubiquitous cacophonous clutter within this world has succeeded in dampening, but has never fully extinguished? Might it be that those sweet notes sung at St. Paul's that evening, though glorious in themselves, are but samplings of an even more glorious archetypal Melody, fashioned by the Master Composer by whose touch, all things are rendered beautiful and *good*?

2. Evidence of "Vestigial Remains" from Parenting

As young parents, my wife Nancy and I spent many enjoyable hours with our two sons. Needless to say, their arrivals into this world radically altered our lives, precisely at a time when the effects of so many mega-events (marriage, graduate studies, and the start-up of new careers) required much attention and accommodation. Our formal education seemed of little significance in preparing us for parenting. To some degree, we relied on instinct and common sense and the fact that, in truth, we had never really graduated from childhood ourselves. The good news is that God is merciful. Our kids, endowed with a great ability to eat, coo, and cry, mercifully had a large capacity to also sleep—to sleep quietly, at any time, in any place, and seemingly in any position. Moreover, each day saw delightful additions to their growing repertoire of responses. Laughter was added to smiling; walking and eventually running replaced crawling; and babbling evolved in the direction of recognizable words, phrases, and sentences.

Somewhere among all these additions, there emerged an insatiable desire to play. Without doubt there is no need to teach children to play; they're wired to play. Moreover, there is definitely no need to schedule play. Play simply happens! As with head, arms, and legs, ability and desire to play comes with the kid.

The minutes of each day constituted the temporal space in which they executed play. The den, the sandbox, the playground, the beach, the back seat of the car, even the bed (our boys' first trampoline)—all were preferred available venues for play. Toys facilitated play. And play generated new toys.

Toys assisted our children to create, alter, and control things in their space and time. They afforded them opportunities to imagine and pretend. Like their father years before, if they lacked a toy, they manufactured one. The stick became a sword; the lid from the garbage can became a shield; the can became a drum; the new refrigerator's discarded box became a fort; and the green beans, originally spread randomly on their dinner plates, when systematically rearranged, became a pile of logs. The organization and use of the stuff in their world was theirs and not the world's to determine. Who would guess the refrigerator freezer would serve as the perfect hiding place for grandma's toothpaste?

Fortunately, play is not extinguished with age. For many, the most fulfilling work contains the element of play. Thus, with age, play is merely modified, possibly becoming more cerebral and less physical. This is apparent in the writings of the imaginative and witty G. K. Chesterton into whose seminal mind popped the following suggested use he imagined for his bedroom ceiling:

> *Lying in bed would be an altogether perfect and supreme experience if only one had a coloured pencil long enough to draw on the ceiling.*[147]

Undoubtedly, the responsibilities associated with childrearing were some of the most demanding of our young lives. No parent is immune from interruptions in personal schedules, from the constant need for self-sacrifice and from those endless nights of uncertainty while attending a sick child. However, most can say that, in retrospect, the season of parenting contained many of their most cherished moments and profound lessons. There were the times just after we had acted in a manner unbecoming of a loving parent when we experienced the undeserved forgiveness of our children. There were the times when, falling asleep on my shoulders, my young one presented me with a demonstration of the meaning of *faith*, namely *trusting in and resting on the strength, wisdom, and provision of another without understanding it all*. But among all the cherished moments and profound lessons issuing from our children were the ones that involved glimpses into the delightful manner in which children think and attempt to make sense of their world.

One such moment was generated by our two-year-old one weekend morning. Making a solid effort not to disturb his sleeping parents, but at the same time anxious to begin his day with action, this young guy crept quietly into our bedroom. Resisting the temptation to use our bed as his trampoline, he crawled between us as we pretended to sleep, his face mere inches from mine. There he stayed still for less than a minute. But after what must have seemed to him an eternity of waiting, he decided to find out if his father was still asleep.

But just how does a two-year-old determine if Papa is asleep? Answer? Perform an experiment! So, climbing carefully onto my chest, and placing his small forefinger ever so softly on my eyelid, he pushed it open, moved forward, and peered intently at what lay inside. I guess he had concluded that an eyeball that is asleep looks somehow different from an eyeball that isn't. For a few moments, with faces touching, we stared at each other. Then, as I struggled to delay my laughter as long as possible, he, with obvious joy and a triumphant screech, shouted, "Mommy, Baddy not seep! Baddy wake!"

> *A two-year old is kind of like having a blender,*
> *but you don't have a top for it.*
>
> *Jerry Seinfeld*[148]

The world into which our kids were born knew nothing of personal computers, video games or flat-screened *smart* TVs with multiple remote controls and channels numbering in the hundreds. It knew nothing of texting or blogging, or tweeting, or downloading, or selfies or emoji pictograms. And their parents knew less. Our children's first impressions of television were of a large, heavy box with defective horizontal and vertical holds that necessitated, for "improved" reception, frequent re-bending and alignment of our improvised, conspicuous, and ugly coat-hanger antenna. This television set, a hand-me-down from parents, produced poor quality pictures on three channels in black and white. It was not surprising that it played a relatively minor role in afterschool entertainment. Instead, usually before supper, imaginative and energetic play was the main activity. It would frequently involve unexpected ambushes, attacks, mock battles, laughter and rolling about on the living room rug. It did not take long to realize that the most enjoyable times with our kids occurred when play contained the ingredients of *spontaneity, surprise,* and *repetition.* It was out of this realization that the game of *Kaboom* was born.

Kaboom fed our kids', as well as their father's, insatiable appetite for play. It quickly evolved from nothing into a popular game. Few evenings could pass without some time spent playing this game. Each little guy would take his turn on my lap with feet pressed against my chest and hands firmly in mine. The game started when I initiated a vigorous bouncing while belting out a tune from the musical, *Can-Can.* Then, bouncing and music would abruptly stop. A period of silence and tense anticipation would follow as each boy waited for what he knew was certain to follow. Then, without warning, precisely what was expected would happen. My knees would part, and with his hands tightly held, he would plunge through my legs. The game would end with a vigorous attack of tickling as he lay laughing on the floor. Invariably, tickling would be followed by repeated refrains of *"More Daddy! Do it again, Daddy!"* or *"One more time, Daddy!"*—statements that convinced me that they liked the game at least as much as their father did.

As a fun, active, and noisy game, Kaboom had no equal and never failed to generate delight in our children. Despite the fact that all events in the game were known, and their sequence was always the same, their timing could never be accurately predicted. Periods of inaction and silence would end suddenly in an explosion of activity. It was this combination of a familiar routine of the predictable with the sudden insertion of the surprise, the unpredictable, and the change in tempo that helped to explain the game's popularity in our home.

Humans love the certain, the *known,* the anticipated, and the refrains that repeat. With them comes a measure of security. However, life needs a second ingredient. Our fondness is also for the *surprise* (so long as it is not the sort that generates pain and sadness). Surprises that smash and destroy a portion of the fabric from which we draw security generate apprehension, insecurity, and anxiety, not pleasure. By contrast, surprises inserted within a life of security that somehow strengthen that same fabric generate fun, joy and laughter. The injection of a dash of freshness into human life brings delight.

Neither of our two sons was ever taught the importance of either the predictable or the unpredictable. They were born with a need for what is secure and certain as well as a longing for risk, adventure, and surprise, a need for endless repetitions of the familiar and a thirst for periodic unexpected novelty. These needs appear universal and are not restricted to the young.

Given the importance in the Bible of the themes of God's constancy and trustworthiness *(the same yesterday, today, and forever)* that appear alongside his unpredictability *(I am about to do a new thing)*, I sense that the game of Kaboom originated not with me, but rather, long ago with a God who seems to have a fondness for play. It represents a principal avenue toward understanding. Moreover, my hunch is that it is one of His favourite games. It seems to me that the central activity of heaven will be delightful play with our heavenly Father. I surmise that the playground for this play will be the entire expanse of the cosmos! Just imagine the game of hide-and-go-seek with the entire cosmos as our hiding place!

Within parenting, there are moments when issues arise in the lives of our children that generate uncertainty and require wise counsel from "headquarters." Two such moments within our family surfaced around bad language and smoking. That day is inevitable when a child returns home from school and asks the meaning of a word heard in the playground that, if uttered in the presence of grandma, would abruptly curl her hair. The site was the dinner table. One evening, out of the blue and with his mouth full of mashed potatoes, our littlest one turned to his mother and innocently asked, "Mommy, what does #$%^•∞ mean?"

As if some mental dam had suddenly burst, other words in the same category as #$%^•∞ surfaced. "Why did Allan call me that? Are those bad words?" Our eldest immediately followed with a list of his own. Dad coughed and looked at Mom, who wisely purchased some valuable seconds to seek wisdom from on high by filling *her* mouth with more mashed potatoes. Then, when she was certain that her response would be orderly and measured, and realizing that kids frequently put forth questions whose full answers fall beyond their capacity to comprehend, she calmly addressed the issue. In this instance, as in others, her approach was both unexpected and nothing short of brilliant. Separating off words relating to God as ones we ought not to use improperly, she surprised the kids with a radical idea: "Okay guys, . . . for the next minute at this table, . . . but only for this minute, . . . you can say . . . any 'bad' word that comes to your mind!"

Our kids, though delighted, looked at each other in disbelief. Question marks suddenly appeared over their heads. I held my breath. "Ready? Go!" Richard and Robert sat momentarily dumbfounded, wondering if they had heard their mother correctly. In fact, neither had ever heard his mother utter anything worse than the odd *"Balderdash!"* or, in extremely frustrating moments, *"Oh, phooey!"* Nevertheless, with permission granted, the stream of words began. Whether it was the novel approach to the issue, or the calm manner in which it was executed, the method proved most effective in terms of securing the hoped-for outcome. The end had justified the means. Surprisingly and thankfully, interest in such language declined rapidly.

The issue of smoking surfaced a few years later. One day, at about nine years of age, our eldest son asked me if he would be permitted to smoke. Avoiding the issue of whether it is *good* to smoke, and choosing to focus on *how* to smoke, I replied, *"Certainly! It's really easy. Get your brother and maybe he can try it as well . . . all three of us . . . Yes . . . Maybe Mom, also??"*

Appearing somewhat startled at a response they were certain would be a definite "No," both boys showed great excitement as they contemplated involvement in what was considered *grown-up* behaviour. And so, to prepare for the Big Event, we walked to the local corner store and purchased a package of cigarettes, some matches, and three of the fattest and cheapest cigars we could find. As their mother shook her head and quietly contemplated a mop-up operation (a Plan B if Daddy's Plan A failed), the three of us set out as men-on-a-mission. Our destination? Our small backyard woodshed.

There we sat in a circle on pieces of firewood and prepared to begin our great adventure, with door and window closed. Excitement was in the air! They agreed with me that we should start with the cigars. Each kid got one and proceeded to copy his father by ceremoniously unwrapping his cigar, biting off the tip of the tapered end (for no known reason), then spitting it out. We all agreed this was cool behaviour, just like what we imagined big guys would do. Then, the Big Moment came when the Master, who had never smoked a cigar in his life, demonstrated how to light it and draw smoke. The two boys copied their dad. In seconds, smoke filled the woodshed.

Including the prep time in the shed, the whole affair lasted less than ten minutes. As smoke drifted about us, the mood of the kids "went south." And so did the mood of their father. Smiles turned to frowns and chatter diminished. My nine-year-old began to cough. My six-year-old said he felt sick. And my eyes began to water. "This is cool," I uttered as I feigned pleasure. Looks of revulsion and disillusionment appeared on faces that just a few seconds earlier had beamed with eager anticipation. At that moment, trying to sustain the experiment as long as possible without uncontrollable coughing or laughter, I said," So now, guys, let's try the cigarettes. Who's first?" "Not me!" coughed my eldest. "No way!" groaned my youngest. Both had had enough. And so had Papa.

As they stumbled hurriedly from the shed and into fresher air, they met their mother who was nearby, feigning indifference to the whole affair, but realizing quickly that no Plan B would be needed and that my scheme to address the smoking issue had been no more outrageous than her scheme to address the issue of bad language. Their comments were brief but telling. *"That was gross! Cigars taste awful! Yuck!"* As I walked triumphantly past my wife, happy that my plan to address the smoking issue had been as successful as her plan to address foul language, her word for the experience was a barely audible and terse, *"Disgusting!"*

And so, once again, by God's grace, an unconventional method of parenting had proved effective in terms of achieving its desired objective. A desired end (namely, *discouraging* the habit of smoking) had justified a rather dubious means (namely, *encouraging* the habit of smoking). Choosing to focus on *how* to smoke, we somehow managed to address the more important issue of whether it is *good* to smoke. Of course, I have recounted two of our more successful acts as parents. There were other occasions when our methods were colossal failures. Such is the up-and-down, hit-and-miss nature of parenting.

Puppies, fresh basil, sunsets, a field of golden wheat swaying in a gentle autumn breeze, and chocolate cake: who does not have a very positive attraction to these elements of life in the natural world? Change the list to bed bugs, roaches, maggots, and rats, and it would be difficult to find much positive attraction at all. While there is seldom universal agreement on what we regard as unpleasant, certain categories of things regularly score high in their ability to generate widespread negative human responses. Typical of these responses are irrational fear, loathing, aversion, and the thought that Noah ought to have been less thorough and far more discriminating and selective when he gathered up the occupants for his ark. Many are convinced his cargo of animals ought *not* to have included *slithering snakes*.

For Nancy, "dislike" is too mild a word when used to describe her feelings toward snakes. Revulsion and disgust are more appropriate terms. She refuses to touch them or even to talk about or look at them. And she is not alone in her loathing. I am not too fond of them myself. A few years ago, Hollywood capitalized on the widespread fear of snakes by releasing two movies about these reptiles—one about a giant anaconda prowling about in murky Amazon waters, and another about hundreds of deadly snakes that slither out of their confinement on a commercial jetliner and proceed to terrorize its passengers. The film's producers made no attempt to hide their subject matter within the movie titles.

Needless to say, my wife saw neither movie. Nor did I. One morning, as she sat reading and relaxing on the slope of a long hillside, our younger son, who was playing a short distance away, suddenly stumbled on a rather large garter snake. Picking up his prize carnivore, and certain he would delight his mother with his acquisition, this fearless four-year-old started up the hill for an on-the-spot *show and tell*, holding one end of the snake in his hands with the other end stuffed in his pocket.

I was a short distance away, anticipating an encounter I would gladly have paid good money to see. Anxiety, not delight, was rapidly rising in her as our son and his treasure approached. As his enthusiasm mounted, he began to run. "Mommy, Mommy, look! Look, Mommy!" The second last thing Mommy wanted to do at that moment was *look*. And the *last* thing Mommy wanted to do was to remain seated. Nevertheless, not wanting to transfer her fear of snakes to our little one, she got up, slowly folded her chair and, with as much courage and control as any mother over the centuries has ever mustered, she began a calm and casual retreat up the hill. Struggling to maintain her composure, and with a noticeably restrained voice that clearly demonstrated her knowledge of high-level diplomacy, I heard her manage a statement that went roughly like this: *"Very nice, darling . . . Thank you for showing me . . . I think you should take him back where you found him . . . His mommy is probably looking for him right NOW!"* A slight emphasis on the words *"right NOW!"* was clearly evident.

A bit bewildered by his mother's lack of enthusiasm for an acquisition he considered a treasure, our young one turned, paused to examine his prize again, then shuffled back down the hill. With the mini-crisis averted, her final reaction to the event was a clearly visible shiver that the French call *un frisson*. As for me, the brief drama on the hillside generated more than a chuckle.

> *Fathers and mothers, husbands, wives, children, or the company of earthly friends, are but shadows. But the enjoyment of God is the substance. These are but scattered beams, but God is the sun. These are but streams, but God is the fountain. These are but drops, but God is the ocean.*
>
> Jonathan Edwards[149]

3. Evidence of "Vestigial Remains" from a Career

In my early years at university, in terms of academic and career choices, my friends were more fortunate than I. While looks can certainly be deceiving, they appeared more satisfied than I with their various academic choices and confident of their future plans. With only minor alterations in their programs, they moved toward clear goals like guided missiles locked onto distant targets.

As for me, there was no *locking on* because there was no distinct target. Attending university as an undergraduate was merely an act of maintaining academic momentum established in earlier years, but with no clearly defined goal. As a result, and without realizing it, I passively applied to my life the goals of others, wandering in and out of various faculties and schools within that giant academic city, the University of Toronto, seemingly with neither compass nor rudder as navigational aids.

Eventually, having completed premedical school and a potpourri of subject fields within the Faculty of Arts and Science and the School of Theology, I finally stumbled into teacher training in the Faculty of Education. There, my circuitous wanderings through various halls of learning abruptly ended. And they ended with surprising satisfaction. They had demonstrated the truth in a quotation from the English novelist Thomas Hardy: *"By experience, we find out a short way by a long wandering."*[50] As the decades that followed bore evidence, those long wanderings were to reap a host of unexpected benefits in my professional life as a teacher. My academic potpourri and wanderings had proven to be the ideal foundation for a career in that encyclopedic subject known as Geography, more specifically, Earth Science.

My long career as an educator began in high school teaching, then later as a university lecturer, then as a lecturer in a *lifelong learning* program, then finally as an ordained Anglican minister. As a high school teacher, I was privileged to know an outstanding pedagogue named Lou Pickering, who had been my science teacher in high school. And now he was my colleague. He taught Physics and Biology and possessed that rare quality that motivates and moves students to reach for things slightly beyond their grasp. His classroom was his playground, and his toys were all the gadgets common to any science class. He displayed inquisitiveness about the natural world that was both provocative and infectious. He had a gift for generating a form of mental itch in his students that encouraged frequent scratching. He had that spark that could challenge passive indifference to things academic.

Lou's natural talent could awaken and ignite the curiosity one requires to explore mystery, the curiosity so often but so unfortunately anaesthetized by elements within the world in general. He had the skill that moves a student's transient isolated thoughts into lasting integrating wonder. It was Lou who introduced me to a special way of acquiring understanding, namely *the scientific method,* a systematic way of solving specific problems within its field that ironically generates more questions than it answers.

> *Asking yourself these deeper questions opens up new ways of being in the world. It brings in a breath of fresh air. It makes life more joyful. The real trick to life is not to be in the know, but to be in the mystery.*
>
> *Fred Alan Wolf*[51]

From the beginning, Lou became my mentor, model, and personal friend. Together, we discussed theology, parenting and teaching methods. For many years, I watched and attempted to emulate the techniques of this highly respected man. In the classroom, he was considered tough but warm. He was good. His standards were high. Yet few thought them unreasonable. Not surprisingly, he championed that great teaching tool called *the question*.

Lou refused to function as a dispenser of knowledge. Instead, he would lead his students to mental takeoff points with carefully crafted questions, and then stand aside to permit imagination and natural curiosity to move them to ponder mystery, the stuff lying just beyond their ever-present limit of vision. How he challenged his students was how he challenged me. Like my father Eddie and my choirmaster Dr. Charles Peaker, Lou had become for me what certain friends were to Sir Isaac Newton, namely giants upon whose shoulders he was privileged to stand and be enabled to see farther.

It is vital for teachers to remain learners. And some of the most profound learning comes through unexpected sources at unexpected times. As illustrations of this are two brief stories, one involving the young son of friends and another involving a senior high school student.

Daniel's Story *(But I don't know who Pardon is!)*

The occasion was a study group dinner, and Daniel had just come from the kitchen, where he had been checking out the dessert. There he had discovered a box containing a large white cake smothered in creamy icing and slivers of coconut. Standing close to me and on tiptoes, he whispered, "Jerry, who brought the cake?"

With much conversation at the table, I missed his words and replied, "Pardon?" My reply puzzled him. And so he repeated his question, whereupon I, leaning forward, repeated my one-word reply.

Slowly, this five-year-old, looking somewhat baffled, stared at me. Then, after a few moments of deciding the best reply to my response, he then replied, *"But I don't know who Pardon is!"*

Daniel's response was as much a delight as a surprise. Who would have thought that Pardon would be interpreted as a person's name? Daniel did. Yet his interpretation of what was said was entirely reasonable. Why can't Pardon be a person's name? It certainly can. Why couldn't Pardon be a noun? Daniel had asked a question, "Who brought the cake?" And I had replied, "Pardon."

Those moments with this bright and curious five-year-old illustrated some important pedagogical truths: words are symbols; words have assigned meaning; meanings of words can change depending upon their use in sentences; meanings are often ambiguous; and ambiguities often result in discrepancies between what a teacher intends to teach and what a student learns. There were many similar instances where I enjoyed and learned from this young and delightful guy named Daniel. I have used this incident many times as an illustrative pedagogical tool, teaching that what is said may not be what is understood.

Margaret's Story *(I used to love the moon; but now I hate it!)*

My classroom was the arena in which I had the joy and privilege of facilitating learning among my students, learning with them, but also learning from them. Together with those who learned best by seeing and those who learned best by hearing, we dabbled in elements of ice, land, air, and water, and the celestial space that surrounds them, attempting to appreciate the detailed configurations, patterns, and processes that abound in our world.

Every so often, during some special moment, a student would grasp something profound about the nature of nature. Some refer to these times as *eureka moments*, moments often accompanied by some form of emotional response. They are commonly moments of joy, satisfaction, and surprise when something hidden is suddenly uncovered and exposed. Fortunately, these moments are as much the experience of the intuitive students who love to appreciate things wholly, as they are of the analytical students whose enjoyment begins with the appreciation of fragments. A senior student named Margaret enjoyed both.

One afternoon, at the end of class, Margaret approached my desk. We had just completed a detailed study on the behaviour of the moon as Earth's natural satellite. Bright and inquisitive, Margaret had experienced many eureka moments. However, at the end of the lunar unit of study, she did not appear filled with much satisfaction. She appeared on the verge of tears. I asked if she could tell me what was troubling her. She managed a quiet statement that startled me. Expressing herself politely, she replied, *"I used to love the moon; but now I hate it!"*

Needless to say, I was somewhat shocked. Was she joking? What had prompted such an unexpected response from a student who exulted in mulling about the physical world? What had I communicated? What had I missed?

The following day, when she was able and willing to reflect on her words, I got the explanation. It was yet another time a student, without intending to do so, had taught the teacher. Simply put, my lessons on our only natural satellite had drained the moon of much of its romance, and Margaret was left frustrated and disappointed. She wanted to enjoy the moon, not dissect it. To dissect it was tantamount to sacrilege: disassembling a work of art into its fundamental components and attempting to appreciate something whole that was now in fragments. The academic acts of systematically categorizing lunar movements; assigning special descriptive vocabulary to them; understanding various lunar phases; working out eclipse frequencies; and calculating the moon's mass, density, surface gravity, and orbital period—to her, this was all very interesting. But somehow, the exercise that frequently ended with neat mathematical expressions was incomplete. Somehow all this was acting not to enhance enjoyment but rather to diminish it.

But even more significant was this young student's sense that descriptions of the moon and explanations of its behaviour were subtle hints to her that we were about to tamper with and ultimately destroy its mystery. The whole exercise had been too cerebral, too cold and sterile, too much head and not enough heart, too much quantification and not enough dreaming, questioning, and wondering, too much simplification of a reality we all know is immensely complex. Confronting mystery that remains mysterious when the exercise ends—rather than tackling problems that we consider solved when the exercise ends—was critical to this young student. The enjoyment of the whole was necessary to her enjoyment of the parts.

Graciously, Margaret had pointed out a serious flaw in my approach to my subject. I had taught something I never intended to teach. This was a eureka moment *for me*. Moreover, I had taught something I didn't know I was teaching. Somehow I had inadvertently conveyed the impression that what was said with words and illustrated with numbers, graphs, and diagrams, was all there was to say on the subject of the moon. We had dabbled in an act that philosophers call *reductionism*, an oversimplification of things complex.

I had hinted, though I probably never said, that elaborate *descriptions* of phenomena constitute *explanations* and answer the question, *Why?* I sensed that Margaret was not so much upset about what had been done in this unit of study as she was about what had been left *undone*. Her words to me were a polite reminder that although detailed analyses are valuable exercises, many aspects of reality are far too grand to be merely quantified and infinitely too complex to be appreciated in fragments. She reminded me that science does not provide explanations but, rather, elaborate and valuable descriptions of phenomena. To explain, one is required to address issues of meaning and purpose, topics that I repeatedly tackled with parishioners as a church pastor. For Margaret, it was satisfying when lessons ended with even more mystery and questions.

In learning, the mind does with thoughts what the body does with foods. It ingests slowly, incrementally taking in a rich assortment of mental nutrients, and then waits as these nutrients are chewed, swallowed, digested, transformed, then somehow assimilated along with other nutrients into some integrated package of mental growth.

But eating doesn't eliminate appetite. In like manner, rather than satiating appetites, sound learning creates more appetite for more learning.

Every act of unpacking what is hidden leads somehow to a sense that far more unpacking is required and that what is hidden will always exceed what is disclosed. Thus, learning should not fully destroy mystery; rather, it ought to increase it and hopefully encourage humility when enjoying fresh nourishment. I grew as an educator because of students like Margaret.

> *The diversity of the phenomena of Nature is so great, and the treasures hidden in the heavens so rich, precisely in order that the human mind shall never be lacking in fresh nourishment.*
>
> *Johannes Kepler*[152]

4. Evidence of "Vestigial Remains" from Grand-parenting

Stephen is my eldest grandson. He is one of the delights of my life. One day, when he was very young, Stephen crawled up onto my lap as I worked at my computer, wiggled into a position of comfort in front of the screen and stared at the array of colours and shapes appearing before him. Observing his obvious interest, I clicked onto some colour photos of the heavens. Stephen's eyes widened as an animation of a full moon becoming a last quarter moon flashed before him. He sat transfixed as additional images of planets and galaxies faded in and out of his field of vision. As each image took shape, there emerged from somewhere deep within him a barely audible expression of delight. Inhaling deeply, then in a soft whisper, he would greet each picture with the repeated refrain: "Oooooh, . . . Looka dat! . . . Looka dat, Gampuh!"

This was the language of joy expressed very simply by a child as he beheld a fragment of our wondrous cosmos he had never seen before. His immediate response to beauty was applause and wonder: *"Oooooh."* Moreover, it was an automatic and immediate invitation to me to enjoy what he was enjoying: *"Looka dat ... Looka dat, Gampuh!"* How interesting it is that, even at the tender age of three, he was declaring that enjoyment is maximized when it is shared.

More than my appreciation of those snapshots of the heavens was my joy in Stephen's delight. Unaware of anything else around him, he appeared totally engrossed in these images. His response was pure enjoyment of something for what it is. His joy in the natural world was what enabled him to play for an entire morning by the seaside, oblivious to all activity around him, digging in the sand with his plastic shovel (just like his two cousins), then filling, emptying, and refilling his pail with samplings of the beach and ocean. Later, his joy was to wander with me through the sand and rocks in Fundy's exposed seabed at low tide and retrieve samples containing the mineral quartz. Nobody had ever sat him down to teach him to *exult*. It seems that exultation would be resident in anyone made in God's image since, after each day of Creation, God Himself exulted in it and called what He had created *very good*.

> ***The soul is healed by being with children.***
>
> ***Fyodor Dostoyevsky***[153]

Our delight in children arises in part from their capacity to exult, to rejoice, and to revel in the moment. Going for a walk with a child can be frustrating if we assign a greater importance to the destination than to the journey. Journeys are opportunities for serendipitous discovery and for rejoicing in those discoveries. This fact was most evident one day when Stephen and I walked to a nearby park. The route to the park was a relatively straight path down the street. But to Stephen, this mattered little. His was a wandering path made circuitous by curiosity with discoveries.

The journey, not merely the destination, was his delight. A host of things strewn along his pathway formed a gallery of attractions. There was the pebble delicately perched on the edge of the sewer grate that, when tipped by his finger, caused great glee as it went *plunk* in the black abyss below. His appetite to duplicate the funny sound of a stone hitting water was insatiable. There was the dandelion that had to be carefully dissected and examined. There was the irresistible mud puddle that beckoned him as flowers beckon bees. And of course, there were the two twigs that became boats (one his and one his grandpa's), twisting their way down the rain-soaked gutter toward the sewer grate where they would abruptly disappear into darkness.

What was Stephen demonstrating in all this? What was he seeing? To me, he was revealing what life looks like when one, unencumbered by a set agenda, is able to enjoy whatever discloses itself in the present. My agenda was getting Stephen to play on large pieces of molded plastic in the schoolyard. But he had time to catch an elusive grasshopper and examine it; to rattle a stick against fence boards and enjoy the sound; and to locate the letter S in a cloud. Each response to pebbles, flowers, and puddles, to sticks, grasshoppers, and clouds was spontaneous delight. His pleasure was in the moment, in making things happen and to share his experiences with others. Each response was filled with *wonder*.

> ***I will give you the treasures of darkness, riches stored in secret places,***
> ***so that you may know that I am the LORD.***
>
> ***Isaiah 45:3***

Wonder? Wonder is one of our most precious mental capacities. It is that tool by which we venture beyond knowledge into the world of mystery. Wonder is that *wonder*-full mental activity that is activated when we pass that limit of vision, that mental horizon beyond which light is replaced by darkness or shadows. To wonder is to stand before something we sense is buried treasure, to reach for, but never fully grasp. To wonder is to contemplate something greater than ourselves and to realize that our knowledge of it is incomplete. To wonder is to open the door to the possibility of surprise. A fully known world, like a fully-fabricated god is a world that does not require wonder, a dreary world without surprises in which nothing is unexpected. In such a world, there are *no* eureka moments. *Wonder* is fuelled by hope, the sense that eventually, we will move from *seeing in part* to *fully knowing* as we are at present *fully known* (1 Cor 13:12).

But this creates a problem. Does it mean that in heaven, there will be no experiences of wonder and no *eureka moments* since, as the Bible says, we will *fully know? Everything?* Personally, though my mind is unable to resolve this issue, I am inclined to believe that, in the presence of the One who made it all, and without the limitations of time and space, experiences of *eureka moments* and the enjoyment of surprises will somehow *never* disappear.

For now, I have long since stopped wondering about pebbles going plunk in sewers. The same is true about rattling a stick against a fence; or grasshoppers; or Christmas with tinsel, trees, and truckloads of gifts. But since my vision is still limited and buried treasures still surround me (both the more amorphous philosophical treasures wrapped up in my mind, and the more concrete treasures within the natural world), I am still filled with wonder. I wonder about what happens when atmospheric conditions convert mild tropical disturbances into violent Category 5 hurricanes. I wonder whether present perturbations in global climate are a result of natural variability or indicative of long-term change. I wonder why polar bears and emperor penguins don't seem bothered by snow blindness. I wonder how that housefly landing upside down on the ceiling never makes a mistake. I wonder if my toast, falling from the table, actually lands jam-side down more often than not. I wonder what it will be like for me in the seconds following my death. I wonder about the God capable of making something out of nothing. I wonder about that incredible moment in the garden when Jesus Christ, dead for three days, unexpectedly appeared before a distraught woman named Mary and softly uttered her name.

Wonder is God's gift that moves us toward making sense out of a world steeped in mystery. Wonder is our attempt *to get it all together.* In mulling over the heavens and the Earth, one must wonder. To capture the essence of each parable of Jesus, one must wonder. In questioning whether an omniscient god can ever experience surprise, one must wonder.

Wonder is what we do whenever we contemplate the truly beautiful. What makes something truly beautiful is the degree to which it behaves in accordance with its original purpose as defined by God. And what makes something or someone truly beautiful is the degree to which that something or someone testifies to what is beyond, to a greater glory, a glory greater than Handel's *Messiah*, greater than the cosmos. Hmm, I wonder why God never tires of making big things, small things, ocean waves or billowy clouds, star clusters, binary stars, or pebbles, or drops of dew, or pomegranates, or the human eye. I wonder if in wondering we approach the essence of that mysterious practice we call *worship*. Come to think of it, is worship even possible *without* wondering?

> *The Sun, with all those planets revolving around it and dependent upon it, can still ripen a bunch of grapes as if it had nothing else in the Universe to do.*
>
> **Galileo Galilei**[154]

A person entranced by wonder is pulled out of the normal voice-in-your-head self-absorption and finds [himself] awed by something greater than [self]. There's a feeling of radical openness, curiosity, and reverence. There's an instant freshness of perception, a desire to approach and affiliate.

David Brooks[155]

In the category of grandchildren, Nancy and I are blessed to count three. In God's scheme of things, grandchildren afford us opportunities to recapitulate elements of the past, to enjoy some of life's earlier experiences again, to slow the pace of life, and to review lessons learned. We gladly lay aside other responsibilities to immerse ourselves in the delightful minds of our grandchildren, to attempt to travel in their world, at their pace, hear their comments, pray for them through their struggles, attempt to answer their questions, and watch as they, through the exercise of their imagination and curiosity, observe, construct, and modify a small portion of their surroundings while developing early impressions of the world that surrounds them. Unmatched are the times when our young ones crawl onto our lap and ask us to read them a story, usually a familiar one they have heard many times before.

On one occasion, during some of those hallowed moments just before bed and prayers, as young Jonathan sat close by, I began to read yet again the story of *Horton Hatches the Egg*. Well aware that no error in my reading would go unnoticed, I would periodically and deliberately alter individual words or skip a line to elicit an immediate correction from an alert and attentive listener. About halfway into the story, I stopped reading and, after a brief silence, I suggested that Andrew, Jonathan's four-month-old brother who was sleeping nearby, take his turn reading.

At first, Jonathan completely ignored my unexpected proposal, probably assuming that it was yet another example of Grandpa being silly. On the third attempt, he turned, looked curiously at me, and said, "*Grandpa, Andrew can't read,*" whereupon I continued reading. A few moments later, assuming that story time required far more action than that generated between the covers of the book, I interrupted the story once again and asked, "*Are you sure Andrew can't read? How do you know?*"

With a slight hint of annoyance that I would persist with such silliness, and without bothering to turn to address his grandfather, Jonathan' reply was terse: *"Because Andrew has no teeth!"*

What? Because Andrew has no teeth? Isn't this also silliness, an attempt to be funny? Or is this the developing mind of a scientist in embryonic form? The conclusion that ability to read should be somehow linked to the presence of teeth in one's mouth is the product of a scientific mind. It is an attempt to investigate, and possibly create some form of theory and relationship between two known facts. Fact one: "Andrew can't read!" Fact two: "Andrew has no teeth!"

The scientific world is full of all sorts of similar attempts to hypothesize causal linkages between things that appear at first glance unrelated. Often these attempts lead nowhere. But sometimes they bear much fruit, resulting in valuable and surprising discoveries. For example, who first latched onto the idea that the rising and setting of the sun is due to the behaviour of the Earth in daily rotation about an axis, rather than to the movement of the sun about the Earth? Who first stumbled onto the seemingly outrageous idea that the rhythmic rising and falling of water at the seashore is linked to the invisible gravitational influence of a celestial lunar object 385 000 km away rather than to some characteristic resident in the nature of water? Who would have first thought that human conception would be linked to an event occurring nine months before birth? And who first conceived the idea that the birthplace of ideas is within the human cranium, not within the human abdomen?

Continuing my reading with my grandsons, I ruminated on the delightful thought that one day, this childlike scientist, now talking, thinking, and reasoning like a child, would move on to discover linkages between variables never before considered related, linkages that would eventually prove causal, and that each new discovery would move human understanding one important step forward.

Praying for our three grandsons, I asked that their *moving on* would never result in the loss of *childlikeness* and those God-given gifts of humility, curiosity, laughter, wonder, and the enjoyment of adventure and play. My hope, shared by my wife, is that their playing in the rich fields of God, having been made in His image and in His likeness,

(Gen 1:26) will continue well into eternity and be the natural central ingredient of the *Abundant Life* begun here on Earth in their present home, and later as God's *New Creation* in the world to come when time will be no more.

> *At that time the disciples came to Jesus and asked,*
> *"Who, then, is the greatest in the kingdom of heaven?"*
> *He called a little child to him,*
> *and placed the child among them.*
>
> *Matthew 18:1–2*

POSTSCRIPT

(1)

O thou from whose unfathomed law the year in beauty flows,
Thyself the vision passing by in crystal and in rose,
Day unto day doth utter speech, and night to night proclaim
In ever changing words of light, the wonder of thy Name.

Frances W. Wile (1910)[156]

(2)

Throughout the pages of this book, we have observed the God who has chosen His visible Creation as one of His principal vehicles by which to convey something ineffable, namely knowledge of Himself. But as to the reason for choosing a language that *speaks without words*, much speculation abounds. In the introduction to his book, *The Sacred Journey*, author and theologian Frederick Buechner addresses this mystery and offers a plausible reason:

> *Life itself can be thought of as an alphabet by which God graciously makes known his presence and purpose and power among us. Like the Hebrew alphabet, the alphabet of grace has no vowels, and in that sense [God's] words to us are always veiled, subtle, cryptic, so that it is left to us to delve their meaning, to fill in the vowels, for ourselves by means of all the faith and imagination we can muster.*
>
> *God speaks to us in such a way, presumably, not because he chooses to be obscure but because, unlike a dictionary word whose meaning is fixed, the meaning of an incarnate word is the meaning it has for the one it is spoken to, the meaning that becomes clear and effective in our lives only when we ferret it out for ourselves.*[157]

(3) CONTEXT

What has come through the words and paragraphs of this book are glimpses of a God expressing Himself in all He has created: extravagantly, yet mysteriously, in patterns and processes, and with order, design, imagination and extravagance. However, His glorious nature has not been expressed *solely* through His *Creation*. For example, he speaks also:

1. ***Through His Incarnation.*** God visited our planet from another realm, becoming visible in the form of Jesus Christ: "In the fullness of time, God sent forth His son, born of a woman" (Gal 4:4); "The Word became flesh, and made his dwelling among us. We have seen his glory, the glory of the one and only Son, who came from the father, full of grace and truth" (Jn 1:14); "Emmanuel . . . God with us" (Matt 1:23); "the image of the invisible God" (Col 1:15a). The strange event called Christ's transfiguration (Matt 17) represents the moment when three of his disciples saw their clearest image of divinity in Jesus when His raiment shone with ineffable light.
2. ***Through His inspired Written Words.*** Just as the heavens and the Earth declare God's glory visibly without words, and the Incarnation declares God's glory visibly and historically in the flesh, so it is with the Holy Scriptures that declare His glory *with* words. These words are God's revelation to His children, His self-disclosure, separating off what is ours to know, from what are, at least for now, God's *secret things* (Deut 29:29).

But that's not all. In addition to His natural world, His incarnate Word and His written words, are hints of His Glory revealed through the Holy Spirit (Paraclete: [Greek] Comforter; the One alongside), and through a host of image-bearing family members, personal acquaintances, even strangers. With all these spiritual aids, we stand on this side of a semipermeable wall separating our temporary world of time and space from another world: our future eternal home called heaven (1 Cor 13:12).

Passage from the temporal (as mortals) to the eternal (as immortals) is cloaked in mystery. In the Book of Acts, we read of Stephen, a faithful follower of Jesus Christ who, at his death by stoning, and about to enter his eternal home, looked *up to heaven* and said to the crowd, "Look, I see heaven open and [Jesus] standing at the right hand of God" (Acts 7:56). *Heaven open? Jesus Standing?* What a welcome! What a gracious act of honour bestowed by Jesus who stood to receive Stephen at the moment of his glorious homecoming! Definitely a flashback to the prodigal son's welcome home by his exceedingly prodigal Father (Lk 15).

ENDNOTES

Preface

1   C. S. Lewis, *The Four Loves* (London: Geoffrey Bles, 1960), 30.

2   George Herbert, "The Elixir" (first stanza), *The Temple* (ed. Nicholas Ferrar, 1633).

Introduction

3   This iceberg, calved from the face of a nearby tidewater glacier, sat grounded amid frozen sea ice in Slidre Fiord, North Ellesmere Island, in April 1989. Severely fractured, it readily succumbed to the degrading effects of summer sun, wave action, and increasing water temperatures and soon completely disappeared not far from its place of birth.

4   C. S. Lewis, *Miracles* (London: Collins/Fontana, 1960), 104.

5   The apparent path of the sun in our sky is a circuit along the perimeter of an imaginary disc. Its movement along this perimeter is caused by the Earth's rotation about its axis. Thus, to complete a single circuit takes 24 hours.

   At the Earth's equator the *plane* of this disc is oriented perpendicular to the horizon line. As one moves from the equator to either pole (a change equivalent to 90 latitudinal degrees), the plane of the disc pivots a corresponding 90 degrees. Thus, at either pole, the sun's circuit is a pathway not perpendicular to, but rather parallel to the horizon. This fact makes it possible at very high latitudes for uninterrupted daylight conditions for a portion of the year, followed by twilight and uninterrupted night conditions. Light conditions such as these are impossible at lower latitudes.

6   George Herbert, "The Elixir" (3rd stanza), *The Temple* (ed. Nicholas Ferrar, 1633).

7   Annie Dillard, *Pilgrim at Tinker Creek* (New York: Harper Perennial, 1974).

Chapter 1: Cosmos

8   Such a profound thought of the Creation rendering testimony to its Creator is probably what gave birth to an old canticle still used periodically in the liturgies of the Roman Catholic, Anglican and Lutheran churches. The canticle is the *Benedicite* (meaning *"good word"*). The Benedicite personifies elements of nature ("Sun and Moon," "Stars of Heaven," "Winter and Summer," "Ice and Snow," "Light and Darkness") as a cosmic choir, each with distinct parts to *sing*, but collectively unified and endowed with the capacity to offer gratitude and praise to its Maker and Benefactor. As such, the canticle is an anthem, not *to* nature, but rather *by* nature to the God *of* nature who is sovereign over all. Of course, the words of this hymn allude to a cosmos that by its very nature needs neither words nor promptings, or an audience present to become vocal.

9   Messier-31, a spiral galaxy, seen from Earth through the Milky Way's constellation Andromeda, is 2.5 million light years away from Earth. It is estimated to contain some one trillion stars! It is the Earth's closest galactic neighbour. Though appearing as a fuzzy blur to the naked eye, the shape of Messier-31 is visible through binoculars. Because the orientation of the plane of the disc is at an oblique angle to our line of sight, we observe its shape as elliptical, not circular. Credit: NASA.

10 Planet Uranus, one of our solar system's giants, is 15 times the mass of the Earth. Ranked as one of the four largest planets in our solar system, Uranus revolves with an axis almost parallel to its plane of orbit. As a result, its axis of rotation and its poles almost point to the Sun twice every orbit. Orbiting Uranus is a family of 27 known moons.

11 Planet Uranus orbits the Sun once in every 84 Earth years, while Neptune takes approximately double that time to do the same thing. This means that Uranus will come close and pass Neptune near the end of its second orbit about the sun (in about every 170 years). At the closest distance between them, their gravitational influences on each other are maximized. A close approach near the time of Neptune's discovery facilitated its detection when a disturbed visible object (Uranus) clearly testified to the presence of an invisible one (Neptune).

12 John Herschel, *A Preliminary Discourse on the Study of Natural Philosophy* (1831), 14–15.

13 C. S. Lewis, *Till We have Faces: A Myth Retold* (London: Geoffrey Bles, 1956), 308.

14 Bruce Prewer, retired minister, The Uniting Church in Australia; used with permission.

15 In 1996, NASA launched the Mars Global Surveyor (MGS). Ten months later, this piece of technological ingenuity was successfully inserted into orbit about the red planet to study and to map the Martian surface and to analyze its gravity, atmosphere and magnetic field.

On 22 May 2003, due to a timely alignment of planets Earth and Jupiter relative to the satellite's location, MGS was able to capture with its high-resolution camera both Earth (139 million kilometres away) and Jupiter (1 billion kilometres away) in a single photograph. Due to the length of transmission distance, the image relayed back to Earth took some 14 minutes in transit. Unlike the photos of Earth taken by lunar orbiters showing a much larger and colourful planet, this image displayed two planets both at far greater distances. They were barely recognizable objects in an ocean of black space.

Never before had such visual perspective been achieved to provide an image of planetary insignificance within the vastness and virtual emptiness of space. What a visual aid in helping humans to comprehend the profundity of the biblical statement contained in Psalm 8:4!

16 Over 99% of the mass of our sun consists of hydrogen and helium, with all other elements combined contributing the remaining mass. Hydrogen, by far the most abundant element, exceeds helium by a ratio of 10 to 1.

This preponderance of just two elements is not unique to our solar system but is believed to approximate the composition of the entire universe.

17 The total energy released by the sun each second is called its *luminosity*. The total amount of this energy the Earth is capable of intercepting is dependent upon its distance from the Sun as well as upon the Earth's diameter. For every two billion units of solar energy released, our planet receives but a single unit. Spatial distribution of this unit on the Earth's surface varies with latitude.

18 Calculating the circumference of the Earth with rudimentary instruments is a daunting task. Eratosthenes' method was both simple and brilliant. The level of accuracy he achieved (which, of course, could only be verified many years later) was partly due to the fact that a few wrongs sometimes come close to making a right.

19 Philip Ball, *Life's Matrix: A Biography of Water* (Berkeley: University of California Press, 2001), 276.

20 Circles and ellipses are examples of conic sections. Imagine a cone-shaped solid sitting on its flat base. Now imagine cutting through the cone along a plane parallel to that base. The perimeter of that cut, like the shape of the base of the cone, will describe a circle. If the plane of the cut had been made at a slight angle to the horizontal base, the resulting perimeter would describe an ellipse. In geometry, the conic section called a circle is considered a special form of an ellipse.

21 Is something true just because the Church, or anyone else says it is? Galileo's objections to the Church's pronouncements on subjects in which it appeared largely ignorant were shared by many of his contemporaries. The Portuguese explorer, Ferdinand Magellan, with his knowledge of the world and navigation, is reported to have commented a half-century earlier, *"The church says the Earth is flat, but I know it is round, for I have seen the shadow on the Moon, and I have more faith in a shadow than in the church."*

22 Galileo Galilei, *Dialogue on the Great World Systems* (1632).

23 Galileo Galilei, *Letter to the Grand Duchess* (1615).

24 Galileo Galilei, *The Authority of Scripture in Philosophical Conversations* (1632).

25 Alexander Pope, *Epitaph for Newton in Westminster Abbey* (1730).

26 With a large nucleus consisting mostly of ice, Halley's Comet begins to partially vapourize as it nears the sun. Vapourized particles stream off the comet creating a tail (or coma) that, under the influence of the solar wind, always points away from the sun. Thus, the orientation of the tail is not aligned with the direction of the comet. The relatively massive nucleus of Comet Halley means it possesses both a long lifespan and a significant visual prominence among the family of visible comets within our solar system.

27 Isaac Newton, "Letter to Robert Hooke" (5 February 1675–76), in *The Correspondence of Isaac Newton, Volume 1, 1661–1675*, ed. H. W. Turnbull (New York: Cambridge University Press, 1959), 416.

28 Joseph Spence, *Anecdotes, Observations and Characters, of Books and Men* (1820), Vol. 1, Section 1259 (1966 edition), 462.

29 Isaac Newton, *The Principia: Mathematical Principles of Natural Philosophy* (1687).

30 Newton, *Principia*.

31 Newton, *Principia*.

32 Whether they be arcing streamers or curtains of green or yellow light, auroral displays are most dramatic during periods of maximum solar activity. Peaks generally follow the sunspot cycle of 11 years.

33 Through a vacuum, light travels its fastest, namely 299 792 458 metres in a single second. Through air, its speed declines. Through glass, speed declines even further.

34 With its high-altitude location and its ultramodern technology, the Hubble Telescope revolutionized space observations by allowing astronomers to see much further and with superior clarity. Scheduled to exceed Hubble's capabilities is the James Webb Space Telescope. Costing an estimated

10 billion USD, it is expected to become operational by the year 2021. Scientists report it will be 100 times more powerful than Hubble.

35 The common view of a miracle is an event that goes beyond the category of the unusual, since it is seen as contrary to what we know to be natural. Events such as these, being totally unexpected, cannot be understood in any usual manner since the laws on which we normally rely for explanation seem not to be operative. But confining miracles to the category of the "un-natural" may be too restrictive. Why would God need to suspend familiar laws in order to display the miraculous? Why are not the *usual* and highly reliable workings of His laws considered equally miraculous? Many would argue that the regular, dependable and highly predictable workings of the natural world are nothing but one miracle after another.

36 For more on the topic of miracles, especially the suggestion that they function as "foretastes" of what is to come, see Philip Yancey, "Miracles: Snapshots of the Supernatural" in *The Jesus I Never Knew* (Grand Rapids: Zondervan Publishing House, 1995). Also, C. S. Lewis, *Miracles* (London & Glasgow: Collins/Fontana, 1947).

37 G. K. Chesterton, *G. K. Chesterton* (Saint Thomas Aquinas, Garden City, NY: Doubleday Image, 1933), 174.

Chapter 2: Earth

38 A view of the Earth from Apollo 11 on 19 July 1969. Credit: NASA. Earthrises viewed from the Moon are only possible while *in orbit* about that object. Since the orbital period of astronaut Michael Collins' Command Module was once every two hours, he observed an earthrise every two hours. An earthrise *from the lunar surface* is impossible to observe since the identical periods of lunar rotation and revolution fix the Earth in a relatively permanent position in the lunar sky. This also means that anyone standing on the opposite side of the Moon will never see an earthrise.

39 Edgar Mitchell [US Apollo 14 Astronaut], *Looking Back at Earth Quotes*, http://www.eyesturnedskyward.com/earth.html

40   Charles Walker [US Space Shuttle Astronaut], *Looking Back at Earth Quotes,* http://www. eyesturnedskyward.com/earth.html

41   The relative distances of each of the planets from the sun are approximated by an arithmetic sequence of numbers called Bode's Law. Start with the numbers 0 and 3. Double 3, then create additional numbers each twice the value of the previous one. In this manner, create a sequence of 10 numbers. To each of these add 4 and then divide each by 10. The resulting sequence, by sheer coincidence, approximates the actual distances of objects from the sun (from Mercury to Pluto, no longer classified as a planet) when all distances are expressed relative to the Earth-Sun distance of (1). The Bode number of 2.8 corresponds not to a planet, but to the multitude of orbits within the asteroid belt lying between Mars and Jupiter. The actual distances of each object, relative to the Earth-sun distance (expressed as one unit) are listed in the bottom line of the chart. Note that for the inner planets, calculated distances closely match actual distances. However, beyond Uranus, as clearly observed in the following chart, Bode numbers increase far more rapidly than actual distances, and thus become of little value in expressing relative planetary distances.

sequence	0	3	6	12	24	48	96	192	384	768
add 4	4	7	10	16	28	52	100	196	388	772
divide by 10	0.4	0.7	1.0	1.6	2.8	5.2	10.0	19.6	38.8	77.2
planet distance	0.39	0.72	1.00	1.52	?	5.20	9.54	19.2	30.1	39.4

42   A single rotation on Earth takes 24 hours. By contrast, a single rotation on Venus (whose day is *longer* than its year) takes 243 Earth days. On Jupiter, a full rotation takes under 10 hours, while our sun, not a solid body, spins at a rate that varies with latitude (once in 25 Earth days at its equator; once in 35 days at either pole). Facts concerning days on Earth include the following:

The beginning of each day: The tradition of beginning each day at midnight dates back to the Romans. The tradition of beginning days at sunset was started by the Jews.

The number of days in the week, their names and sequence: The Creation Story recorded in the Book of Genesis covers a period of seven days, the seventh being the day of divine rest. This seven-day period happens to roughly correspond to the interval between quarter phases of the Moon. A third appearance of the number seven is found in the light anomalies seen wandering at different speeds through the multitude of fixed stars within the celestial canopy. Counting the Moon and sun as wanderers, these objects numbered seven. With little knowledge of the nature of these wanderers, but correctly assuming that the slowest one was the farthest, ancient minds arranged them according to their perceived distance from Earth, from farthest to closest. Each was assigned a special name, after one of the many gods of polytheistic Rome. From the list, came the sequence of the days of the week, beginning with Saturn's Day.

Wanderer	Hours ruled by each planet							
Saturn	①	8	15	22	5	12	19	2
Jupiter	2	9	16	23	6	13	20	3
Mars	3	10	17	24	7	14	21	etc.
Sun	4	11	18	①	8	15	22	
Venus	5	12	19	2	9	16	23	
Mercury	6	13	20	3	10	17	24	
Moon	7	14	21	4	11	18	①	

From the accompanying list, however, it is clear that the sequence of wanderers based upon perceived distance does *not* correspond to the order for the days of the week, given that Sun's day does not directly follow Saturn's day, nor does Moon's day follow directly after Sun's day. To understand how our sequence of days is linked to the perceived order of wanderers, consider the following explanation while referring to the above chart:

Wanderers were assigned rule over individual hours of the day. Rule passed in order from Saturn through to the moon. Since there are 24 hours in which to exercise rule, but only 7 wanderers, Saturn who ruled hour 1 would also rule hours 8, 15, and 22 in the first day. Jupiter and Mars were assigned hours 23 and 24 of that same day, which meant that the sun would rule the first hour of the second day. The rule for naming days was simple: The name of each day was the name of the wanderer that ruled the *first* hour of that day. Thus, Saturn's day, was followed, not by Jupiter's day, but by Sun's day. Sun's day was followed, not by Venus's day, but by Moon's day, etc. A reference to five of the seven wanderers is clearly evident in most French equivalents: *lundi, mardi, mercredi, jeudi, vendredi.*

43 In the daily progression of the Sun across our sky, its highest point is the instant of noon (solar noon). At this instant locally, its energy intensity is maximum for the day and the sun, without overcast conditions, appears its brightest. Since, for convenience, our clocks are set according to standardized time zones, and not in exact accordance with the time of solar noon, the time of the highest and brightest sun seldom coincides exactly with 12:00 noon on our clocks. In other words, solar noon is seldom exactly at clock noon.

44 Though not generated by either moon or stars, spectacular colours of red preceding sunrises or following sunsets are the result of preferential filtering and scattering of incoming sunlight by our atmosphere. Filtering and scattering of sunlight is maximized during low sun periods when, because of their orientation, sunlight paths cut through more atmospheric distance and hence, more interference, to get to our eyes.

45 Knowing that twilight varies with latitude, is there any change in twilight periods from month to month at a single latitude? The answer is "yes," but only slightly. Thus it is less noticeable. Twilight is slightly longer during solstice periods in June and December, and slightly shorter during equinox periods in March and September. This is related to the fact that at any one latitude, rising and setting paths of the Sun around solstice times are less vertical with respect to the horizon than are paths near equinox times.

46 Joseph Addison, "The Spacious Firmament on High," third stanza, Hymn 602, in *The Book of Common Praise* (Anglican Church of Canada, revised 1938). [Its words reflect the central theme of Psalm 19 in which nature is seen as bearing testimony to God's glory.]

47 All systems that count progression of time count off years from some agreed-upon temporal base line. Among those progressions are

numbering systems specific to individuals. We number our years of life from our year of birth and wedding anniversaries from our year of marriage. Personal packages of time lie within a more widespread system that recognizes as its base line a past event significant to a large number of people. For much, though by no means all of the world, that event is the birth of Christ. This single historical event is the temporal base line from which the Christian calendar numbers its years. Years before Christ's birth are counted back in time, using the notation BC (meaning before Christ); years after His birth use the notation AD (from the Latin, *anno Domini*, meaning "in the year of our Lord").

By contrast, Jewish calendars number years, not from the birth of Christ, but from the time of Creation. For convenience, reference is still made to the BC/AD distinction, but with alternative names: BCE (before the Common Era) and CE (of the Common Era). With a date of Creation set at 3760 BCE, the year 2006 CE was for Jews the calendar year 5767. Among Muslims, years are numbered from the prophet Mohammed's emigration to Medina in AD 622.

At the time of Christ's birth, the local population used a Roman calendar that dated years with the notation AUC (*ab urbe condita*), from the founding of the city of Rome. Conversion from AUC to AD did not occur until AD 533. The conversion was later found to contain a significant miscalculation in the probable timing of Jesus' birth, considered now by most scholars to have occurred closer to 4 BC than to AD zero. This makes His birth closer to the planetary conjunctions that are dated in and around 7 BC.

Western calendars begin on January 1. Jewish calendars begin at sundown on Rosh Hashanah, a variable date related to the behaviour of the new moon and falling somewhere between early September and early October of each year. The so-called "church year," though similar in length to a calendar year, begins on Advent Sunday, about a month prior to the celebration of Christmas.

Christmas Day is fixed as a date (December 25), and therefore can fall on any day of the week. This date is not linked to the actual birthday of Christ, but rather had its origin in the ancient Roman Feast of Saturnalia at the winter solstice, which celebrated the "return" of the sun. By contrast, the date of Easter varies. The day of celebration must be a Sunday, the first one following the first full moon on or after the vernal (spring) equinox. Defined in this manner, Easter must occur sometime within a time window between the end of March and the middle of April. Dates of Easter for Eastern Orthodox Christians differ for a number of reasons, but primarily because their dates are calculated using the Julian, not the Gregorian, calendar.

If one counts back 40 days before Easter day (not counting Sundays), we arrive at the day called Ash Wednesday, which begins the period in the church year known as Lent. While the date of Christmas determines the timing for the four Sundays of Advent, the date of Easter fixes the season of Lent.

48   The word "parabola" is derived from two Greek words: *para* (meaning "alongside," as in "paramedic" or "paramilitary") and *ballo* (meaning "I throw," as in "ballistics"). The normal flight path of a baseball is a parabola, as are the shapes of the cables that support suspension bridges and the trajectories of some comets that pass close to our sun only once. Even the surface of a liquid that is vigorously stirred within a circular bowl momentarily assumes the shape of a parabola. Unlike an ellipse, which has two foci, a parabola has only one focus.

As one might expect, the words "parable" and "parabola" are etymological cousins, having roots in the same two Greek words. This etymological similarity provides us with a visual aid in comprehending something of the nature of parables in scripture. In a parable, the focus is some element of divine truth, represented in story form in metaphorical language by objects such as a mustard seed, a coin, or a pearl, or two men arriving at the temple to pray, or an unmerciful servant not doing unto another as he was done unto. Each parable represents a vehicle by which concrete and familiar images are used to convey imaginative lessons about things *hidden since the creation of the world.* Parables testify to the fact that although much knowledge is obtainable through human striving, some knowledge is obtainable only through revelation. Unlike problems whose solutions can be found through logic, research, and plain trial and error, deep mysteries require disclosure in another way. God's clear prerogative is to reveal what He chooses, to reveal them in the way He chooses, or to keep hidden *secret things* (Deut 29:29).

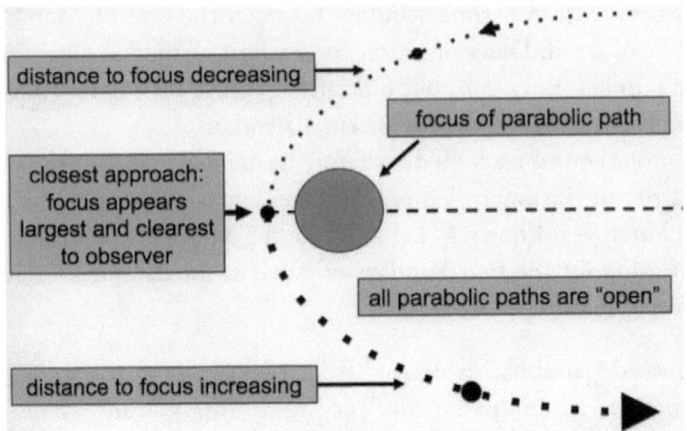

A Typical Parabolic Pathway

Scripture identifies Christ as the One *in whom are hidden all the treasures of wisdom and knowledge* (Col 2:3). Given this, His frequent use of parables to disclose the mysteries of the Kingdom is not surprising. Each represents a partial unwrapping of a treasure, hitherto concealed, in order that we progress toward what is described as *the full riches of complete understanding* (Col 2:2). With parables, like the geometrical parabola, we are taken on a directed journey and drawn toward a focus, a nugget of truth, approaching closer and closer to it, yet never fully arriving. And then, the God of all truth, choosing to permit us to know only in part, and aware of our tendency to misunderstand, nudges us forward with undiminished patience on another approach, sometimes on different paths to the same nugget, and sometimes on new paths to entirely undiscovered ones. Thus, through struggle, a long, wandering, and some stumbling, and in close association with God, we assemble a partial picture of reality and come incrementally *to know the mystery of God, namely Christ* (Col 2:2), as antecedent to eventually *knowing fully just as now we are fully known* (1 Cor 13:12).

[49] It is somewhat incorrect to speak of the Earth orbiting the sun. It is more correct to speak of both bodies orbiting a common centre. This common centre is called a barycentre, the centre of mass and balance of the two moving bodies. Its location is always somewhere on a line between the two bodies. Stars orbiting each other are called *binaries*.

To understand the concept more fully, first imagine a set of barbells with weight distributed equally at each end of a long rod. Now imagine someone lifting this apparatus and throwing it in such a way that it tumbles on itself. Since the end weights are equal in mass, a slow-motion camera would capture the entire apparatus pivoting about a barycentre. In this special case, the barycentre is located along the rod equidistant from either mass.

Now if one mass were increased and the other diminished, the barycentre would slide away from this central place and be displaced in the direction of the larger mass. The greatest displacement would occur with the greatest difference in masses between the two bodies. In this analogy, the two masses pivoting about each other represent the Earth and the sun, with the long rod an invisible line between them. Since the sun is more than 330 000 times the mass of Earth, their common centre of pivot is highly displaced, so much so that it resides well *within* the body of the sun and, in fact, very near its centre. Despite all this, though incorrect, yet for convenience, we choose appearance over reality and say that Earth orbits the sun.

50 We note from the diagram showing the two positions of the Earth in the sun's rays that it is only between or directly on the two tropics that the noon sun can shine vertically. At all other latitudes the sun's rays shine indirectly. Indirect sunlight generates reduced radiation per unit time and per unit area.

We in Canada experience the greatest annual radiation in our more southerly latitudes. At any one place, greatest radiation values are daily during the noon hour and monthly during June. We also benefit from the fact that during the summer months, the total number of daylight hours reaches its maximum value. Thus, in the same season that sun angles are maximum in Canada, we benefit from our maximum number of daylight hours and thereby enhance total incoming summer radiation. However, during our winter months, an opposite situation prevails. At this time, reduced daylight hours combine with low sun angles to make for significantly reduced total incoming daily radiation.

Since rising and falling radiation patterns are in harmony with sun angles, seasons of the year are not the same in both hemispheres. Summer in Canada occurs at the same time as winter in Australia. Spring in Argentina coincides with autumn in Europe. Rising and falling temperatures in both hemispheres are readily apparent from satellite photos from space with snow surfaces expanding and contracting in response to seasonal temperature changes.

51   Though four distinct seasons exist in Canada, each officially beginning at either a solstice or an equinox, and thus each approximately 91 days long, variations in individual lengths of seasons are evident if one uses temperature as the criterion. In south central and eastern Canada, the transition seasons of spring and autumn pass rather rapidly, with winter weather persisting from November through to late March and summer frequently lasting from mid-May into mid-September. On Canada's west coast, lower annual temperature ranges are common, with Pacific air masses moderating both summer and winter extremes. In Arctic Canada, especially in the extreme northern portion of the archipelago, July temperatures struggle to get above 10 °C in a summer that usually fails to last beyond six weeks. Here, seasons are as much defined by light conditions as they are by temperature.

52   At low latitudes the number of daylight hours varies little with season. Variations increase progressively toward each pole. Icelanders, for example, experience much longer daylight in June than do Floridians. The reverse situation occurs in December. What is also noteworthy is the rate at which daylight hours change from most to least at any latitude. In Toronto, for example, hours of daylight change very little during the month of June (when they are at their maximum) and through the month of December (when they are at their minimum). Changes are most rapid on the equinoxes: hours decline more rapidly in September and increase more rapidly in March.

53   George David Weiss and Bob Thiele, "What a Wonderful World." Performed by Louis Armstrong in *What a Wonderful World*, ABC Records, 1967, song. [The song also featured in the 1988 film, *Good Morning, Vietnam*.]

54   Diane Warren, "If I Could Turn Back Time." Performed by Cher in *Heart of Stone*. Geffen Records, 1989, song.

55   *Apollo 13*, directed by Ron Howard (Hollywood, CA: Imagine Entertainment, 1995), film. [Spoken by Commander James Lovell, played

by Tom Hanks, responding to the question from television reporter Jules Bergman, "Is there a specific instance in an airplane emergency when you can recall fear?"] Also recorded in story form: James Lovell and Jeffrey Kluger, *Apollo 13* (Houghton Mifflin, N.Y.: 1994), 66–69.

56 James Campbell and Reginald Connelly, "Show Me the Way to Go Home," 1925, song.

57 *A Beautiful Mind*, directed by Ron Howard (Hollywood, CA: Dreamworks/Universal, 2001), film. [Spoken by Alicia Nash, played by Jennifer Connelly, to her husband John, played by Russell Crowe.]

Chapter 3: Moon

58 The moon near quarter phase, December 19, 2012 (Credit: NASA). Virtually half of any celestial object is illuminated by the sun at any one instant. That line that separates the illuminated and dark portions is called the object's *terminator*. We are forced through the Earth's terminator twice each day, because of rotation, during each sunrise and sunset event. A person standing on the more slowly rotating moon would be forced across its terminator only twice each month.

Two significant features of any terminator are its *distinctiveness* and its *shape*. The existence of a twilight zone on any object surrounded by an atmosphere renders the transition from light to darkness gradual. As a result, terminators on such objects are less precise. Such is the case for the Earth, but not so for the moon. Moreover, the existence of high mountains and deep valleys on any object renders the terminator's *shape* less uniform. In our photo, valleys near the terminator, but in the sun side, may be deep enough to lie in shadow. Conversely, mountains near the terminator, but in the dark side, may be tall enough to catch sunlight. Thus a terminator possessing irregular shape is a clear indicator that it resides on a surface that has significant topographic irregularities.

59 On December 12, 2008, near the end of a television newscast, the resident meteorologist commented on that evening's full moon. It was exceptionally bright. When asked to explain the event, he alluded to a single factor, namely the moon's close approach once each orbit, which increases its apparent size and renders it brighter. His explanation was

correct. However, given the amount of time available to someone who is asked at the end of a newscast to put forward an explanation that includes far more than a single factor, his answer was incomplete. As a result, the full significance of what was happening that evening was largely missed.

So, what happened in the sky on December 12, 2008 that caused some people to look up and wonder? Simply put: not one, but a pile of coincidental happenings. The moon's brightness, affected by a number of natural conditions, had been maximized because virtually all the conditions causing increased brightness had come together at about the same time. It was, as the Bible once described, a "fullness of time" event, an event filled with natural, though unusual coincidence. So what were these coincidental events?

- The moon occupies an elliptical orbit about the Earth. Being rather oval in shape, its distance to the Earth undergoes constant change. On each 27-day circuit about us, it traverses a point of closest approach (*perigee*) and then, about two weeks later, a point of farthest approach (*apogee*). At perigee, the size of the moon, though hardly detectable to the casual observer, is slightly larger. As such, it is slightly brighter. The December 2008 perigee event occurred on December 12.
- The elliptical orbit of the moon is not constant in shape. Rather it experiences continuous alterations. As such, some perigee distances are shorter than others.
- The December 12 lunar perigee was the shortest for the year and one of the shortest on record.
- Full moons are the brightest of all lunar phases. This is so because at the time of a full moon, the illuminated half of the moon faces the Earth. The celestial geometry of sun, moon and Earth create a full moon condition once in slightly over 29 days and dictate that such a moon will be highest at midnight and visible throughout the night. The December 2008 full moon, above the horizon all night, occurred on December 12.
- We are all aware that though the Sun traverses our sky each day, the position of its arc from sunrise to sunset varies with season. In the winter, the arc is lowest. In the summer, it is highest. Likewise, all moon phases undergo a seasonal shift in their arc across our sky. With regard to the full moon, it scratches out its highest arc if it is

full on December 21, the very date when the sun's arc is lowest. The December 12 full moon, nine days off this mark, appeared almost directly overhead in southern Ontario at its highest point.
- That portion of the sky that is directly overhead possesses the greatest visual clarity.

This is so because light from objects located directly above us pass through the shortest atmospheric distance and, therefore, the least energy-robbing atmosphere. Thus, with all other factors being equal, December full moons should be the brightest of all full moons for the year. However, atmospheric clarity determines just how clear that clearest full Moon will be. Clarity depends upon the amount of moisture and particulate matter present within the atmosphere and, of course, the absence of cloud cover. Over southern Ontario on December 12, 2008, skies were clear, winds were northerly and cold, clean air with low humidity was flooding the region. As a result, the atmosphere through which moonlight shone on the night of December 12 was relatively "clean."

And so, with a full moon, a close moon, a high moon, and a clear atmosphere through which to see it, the night of December 12, 2008 featured a *fullness of time event*. No event was un-natural. No event was unique. Rather what occurred was simply *unusual*. The series of concurrent normal events had been coincidental.

[60] In the diagram, it is clear that through a single lunation, moons though not equally prominent can be visible during the day or night. Moons at or near full phase are seen during the night. Those at or near new phase are seen during the day. Day moons are less conspicuous occurrences, not only because their light is diminished by sunlight, but also because day moons are never near full moon phase.

[61] Tides are not restricted to water. Though less noticeable, they occur within the crust of the Earth as well as in its atmosphere. Moreover, tides are not restricted to oceans. Though not as obvious, tides also occur in smaller bodies of water such as lakes. In lakes, however, factors other than gravitational influences are more significant. One such factor is local wind, which, when strong and sustained for many hours over a lake surface, generates the phenomenon of wind set-up. Wind set-up redistributes surface water and significantly raises water levels

62 Neap tide configurations lower daily tidal amplitudes. These naturally low amplitude tides (highs not so high, and lows not so low) can be further enhanced if, during neap tide configuration, the moon is at its farthest distance from Earth (diminishing lunar influence) while, at the same time, the Earth is at its closest distance to the sun (increasing solar influence).

63 The Earth-moon and Earth-sun distances maximize the magnitude of spring tides if this configuration occurs with the moon at perigee (closest distance to Earth) and the Earth at perihelion (closest distance to sun). The former occurs once every 27 days while the latter occurs once a year in early January.

64 T.H. Huxley, "On the Reception of the Origin of Species," in *The Life and Letters of Charles Darwin, Including an Autobiographical Chapter*, Volume 2, ed. F. Darwin (1888), 204.

Chapter 4: Shadow

65 A sudden mid-January thaw has allowed wind and wave to fracture Lake Huron ice and pile it into a chaotic near-shore rubble field. Its irregular surface topography, though only slightly elevated in places, is clearly visible in the late afternoon sun because of the shadows each ice fragment projects. The contrast with the more uniform lake surface is obvious. At any instant, shadow length reflects height of ice.

66 Blaise Pascal (1623–1662) in *Pensées* (1669).

67 Saturn, the second largest planet in our solar system, bears little resemblance to the Earth. Though greater in mass, it has a lower density; so low in fact that, if thrown into a giant ocean of water, it would float! Though not the only planet possessing rings, it is the only one whose rings can be seen from Earth with just a minor optical aid.

Saturn, like its three giant companions Jupiter, Uranus, and Neptune, is a gas planet with no clearly visible solid surface. Its atmosphere, consisting mostly of hydrogen gas and some helium, is so thick that the weight of its upper portions compresses its lower portions into a liquid.

Compression also generates considerable heat. For this reason, the planet, remote from the sun, actually releases into its surrounding space more radiant energy than it receives from the sun.

A single journey of Saturn about the sun takes almost 30 Earth years. This it does with a tilted axis of rotation similar in magnitude to Earth's. Like the ring structures on our other three planetary giants, Saturn's rings lie on the plane of the planet's equator. Rings consist of orbiting fragments of matter of various sizes, from tiny grains of sand to much larger rock and ice fragments. Ring thicknesses are minuscule in comparison to ring diameter. Nevertheless, their collective mass is more than sufficient to cast a perpetual thin shadow over Saturn's surface. And Saturn's size is more than capable of projecting a prominent, wide black shadow across all rings.

Over the space of a 30-year orbital period, the appearance of rings changes dramatically. This confused early observers until these changes were linked to Saturn's changing orientation relative to Earth. During times when our line of sight takes us over or under the plane of the rings, the rings present themselves as separated wide bands elliptically shaped. At other times, when we see them edge-on, the rings shrink into a narrow single band. Of course, the best photographs of Saturn's rings are those taken not from Earth, but rather from close approaches of space vehicles such as the Cassini-Huygens NASA space probe.

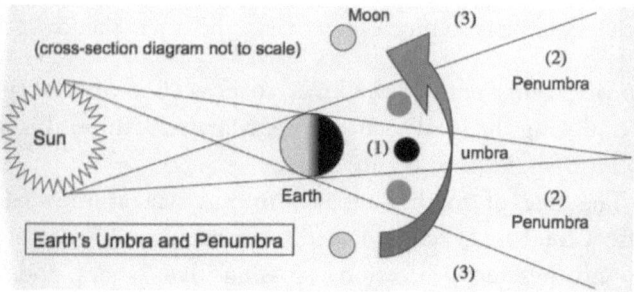

The accompanying diagram displays the Earth's umbra and penumbra, two cones of shadow, one diminishing, the other widening as each extends outward from the planet's dark side. In the diagram, the moon is seen drifting into and through both cones. If we were to imagine standing on the moon during this drift, the sun would initially be seen unobstructed (position 3); partially eclipsed (position 2); and fully eclipsed (position 1). If observed from the Earth, this same drift would show the moon darken as it enters the Earth's penumbra and be darkest within the umbra.

69 From the same diagram, it appears that both a solar and lunar eclipse will occur on every orbit of the moon about the sun. The reason this does not happen is that the moon's plane of orbit is tilted with respect to the Earth's orbit about the sun. For eclipses to occur, two events must occur simultaneously: (1) the moon must be crossing the Earth's plane of orbit; and (2) the crossing must occur when the moon is either in "full" or "new" moon phase. When both events occur simultaneously, an "eclipse season" has opened. During this season, an eclipse must occur. With the moon (new) between the Earth and sun, a solar eclipse will occur. Often, there will be sufficient time for a second eclipse (a lunar eclipse) to occur in the same season, about two weeks later with Earth between the full moon and the sun.

70 Given its distance from us and its apparent size in the sky, our moon can only fully eclipse our sun when conditions during an eclipse are optimal. Optimal conditions include a moon closest to us (larger moon), a sun farthest from us (smaller sun) and a viewing position on our planet that is central to the passing lunar shadow.

71 Optimal conditions are not so essential during a lunar eclipse since the Earth's shadow is so much larger than the lunar shadow.

72 Map displaying path of the lunar shadow (line of totality) over North Africa during the total solar eclipse, March 29, 2006. Data from *NASA 2006 Eclipse Bulletin,* Figure 2, 49.

The line of totality crossed into Africa at the coast of Ghana where a total solar eclipse lasted for 3 minutes 27 seconds. It travelled in a northeasterly direction, crossing the Sahara and entering the Mediterranean Sea at the Libyan–Egyptian border. Total transit time through Africa took 90 minutes. The longest eclipse occurred in southern Libya where the entire sun vanished for 4 minutes 7 seconds. On either side of the line of totality, a partial solar eclipse was visible with durations decreasing with increasing distance from the line. All events occurred in accordance with what had been predicted.

[73] John Greenleaf Whittier, "My Soul and I," in *The Poetical Works in Four Volumes* (Boston: Houghton Mifflin, 1892), v.33. Bartleby.com, 2013. https://www.bartleby.com/372/172. html, lines 130–132.

Chapter 5: Rock

[74] Hendrik van Loon, *The Story of Mankind* (New York: H. Liveright Publishing, 1957), 3.

[75] Percé Rock, a much-photographed landform just off the eastern tip of Canada's Gaspé Peninsula, is a massive limestone monolith rising some 90 metres above the surface of the Gulf of St. Lawrence.

[76] To some degree, the patterns visible along adjacent crustal plate boundaries that testify to processes generating them have their counterparts in similar patterns and processes that operate in the formation and destruction of ice cover over cold ocean surfaces. Both crustal and ice cover exist because prevailing temperatures have dropped below those needed for each material to solidify.

Like crustal cover, ice cover is neither static nor unbroken. In response to various stresses from winds and currents, sea ice moves. When subjected to compression, it buckles and forms ridges. When subjected to tension, it cracks. In many instances, cracks open to form linear channels called leads. Leads are a common phenomenon in ice-covered oceans, breaking apart and displacing various topographic features present in the sea ice surface. Within a single area, different leads usually present themselves at various stages of development and decay. Some may be youthful in appearance, with narrow openings and with sharp margins displaying mirror images of each other. By contrast, older ice may display openings that are frozen over, or margins that have been so modified by considerable lateral movement and erosion that similarities in shape along their margins, and topographic appearances on their surfaces may be minimal or unrecognizable. Sea ice openings easily facilitate new ice formation since heat from the ocean, unimpeded by the insulative cover of ice, can be readily transferred to the atmosphere. Moreover, sea ice openings provide natural spots for marine mammals such as whales and seals to occupy both air and water environments..

Reference to sea ice formation and drift as analogous to the processes found within crustal plates is certainly appropriate. However, major differences are obvious. First of all, the forces that operate to move ice are from above (wind) and below (current). Those that operate on crustal plates are largely from below. Moreover, though both ice and rock are solid materials, rock is far more resistant to ablation than is ice. Since rock maintains its patterns, even after millions of years, a far more complete history is possible, not only of processes along plate boundaries, but also of those topographic features that, through faulting and drifting, nature created long ago. Thus, the rough mirror images of South America and Africa's Atlantic margins are still easily recognized. Moreover, in terms of rock type, age, structure, fossil and mineral content, mountains in Scotland and Scandinavia are still strikingly similar to, and appear continuous with the Appalachian Highlands found through the eastern US and the Canadian Atlantic provinces.

77 The bottom surface of the ocean (hydrosphere) follows the undulating contours of the sea floor. But its top surface, in the absence of wind-forced wave activity, follows the average curvature of the Earth. The top and bottom surfaces of the atmosphere behave in a similar fashion. But while the crust of the Earth can penetrate the entire thickness of the hydrosphere (producing islands and continents when it does), it cannot cut through the atmosphere's entire thickness. Nevertheless, at the crust's highest altitudes, air densities, though not zero, are close to that value.

78 Canada's northern islands need the assistance of both high latitude and altitude to maintain permanent snow and ice conditions. Mountainous areas, as in portions of Ellesmere Island, readily support perennial snow and ice because atmospheric temperatures drop with increasing altitude. In the western Arctic, however, where there is less annual snowfall, and where most surfaces are low in altitude, more rapid summer ablation of thinner snow cover is able to largely destroy what the winter season has managed to deliver. Therefore, no ice fields exist in the western Arctic.

79 The April 2010 eruption of Iceland's Eyjafjallajokull volcano, though relatively small in magnitude, was spectacular in its visual display and significant in its major disruption of air travel. The problem lay not only in the volume of ash that the volcano produced, but also in the altitude

to which the ash was lifted (over 9 000 metres). Prevailing wind currents drove the ash cloud eastward toward western Europe. As a result, about 20 countries in the region closed their air space. These closures affected approximately 100 000 air travellers.

[80] Certain elements within the mantle of the Earth generate heat through radioactive decay. The uneven distribution of these elements means that the mantle's heat energy is unevenly distributed. When this occurs in any fluid, convection currents are generated. Currents work to redistribute heat energy equally. Current movements affect overlying crustal surfaces, buckling crust where they converge, and fracturing crust where they separate.

[81] A trail of volcanic deposition originating from below the Earth's crust is readily apparent along the Pacific seabed, extending from Hawaii in the southeast to the Aleutian Trench in the northwest. The trail is due to the slow migration of the Pacific plate toward the northwest. A prominent change in direction of this drifting plate (occurring some 39 million years ago) is visible halfway along the chain. At the northern extremity of the Emperor Seamount, all further historical data are obliterated as crustal plate materials, along with their geological records, plunge back into the Earth's interior to be destroyed forever. This process is known as subduction. For additional detail regarding Pacific seamount evolution, see the various works of vulcanologist Kenneth Hon, Professor of Geology, University of Hawaii, at Hilo.

[82] Seamounts rising above the surface of the Pacific to form volcanic islands are at present most common in the region of Hawaii, with the largest and youngest island being Big Island. Here, one is able to observe active volcanism at the summits of Mauna Loa and Kilauea.

[83] The furnace from which magma extrudes to form active surface volcanic cones is presently under Hawaii's Big Island. A short distance to the northwest are islands whose volcanoes have become dormant. Further to the northwest, volcanoes have become extinct. The decreasing volcanic activity toward the northwest of Big Island contrasts with its increase toward the southeast. Here, the embryonic active volcanic seamount of Loihi is rising from the seafloor. Presently, its summit is only a kilometre below the ocean surface.

84 The Earth's geographic poles are the two points where the planet's rotational axis intercepts the surface of the planet. Since all planets, and also our sun, rotate, each has a geographic north and south pole. These are not to be confused with the two magnetic poles. Geographic poles represent the most distant points from the spinning object's equator.

Each of the Earth's geographic poles undergoes drift along its surface such that if a stick were to be placed at any instant at either pole, a field of sticks would be formed that would reveal the magnitude of drift of each geographic pole over time. Each field of sticks forms an area the approximate size of a football field within which the geographic poles wander. The poles found on maps represent the average location of each of the Earth's geographic poles, identified as latitudes 90° N and 90° S. When Roald Amundsen reached what his instruments told him was latitude 90° S, he was probably standing very near, but perhaps not precisely at the South Pole's precise position at its time of discovery.

85 The Earth's magnetic field surrounds the entire planet, intercepting its surface at places called magnetic poles. Magnetized needles allowed to swing horizontally align themselves along magnetic lines of force. At each pole, the magnetic lines fall vertically into the Earth. Here, needles, free to pivot vertically, dip 90 degrees to the horizontal. All places where the dip angle is zero degrees lie on the magnetic equator (distinct from the geographic equator). Between this line and each magnetic pole, dip angles lie somewhere between these minimum and maximum values.

86 It is only in recent years that the magnetic secrets of the ocean bed have been revealed. In the Atlantic Ocean, symmetry on either side of the Mid-Atlantic Ridge displays mirror images of the Earth's periodic magnetic polarity reversals. Dating rock strips on either side of the ridge reveals similar ages at similar distances from the ridge. This dating also reveals that age of seabed increases outward on either side of the ridge. All this information about the seabed is possible because new rock becomes magnetized at the time of its formation in accordance with the polarity of the Earth existing at the time the deposited rock solidified. This polarity in the rock is maintained until the rock melts once again.

87 In August 2007, the powerful magnitude 8.0 earthquake that struck the region of Pisco, Peru took its toll in both human life and property.

The quake killed 500 people, destroyed 55 000 buildings, and damaged an additional 21 000 more. It represented a massive snapping along the fault line boundary separating the Nazca and South American plates, part of the Pacific Ring of Fire.

[88] The cross-section diagram through the Bible Lands displays the ruggedness of the terrain and the changes occurring in its topography over relatively short distances. Central to the region is the Jordan Valley, the northern extension of the Great Rift Valley of Africa.

[89] C. S. Lewis, "The Weight of Glory," sermon in *Transpositions and Other Addresses*, (London: Butler and Tanner, 1949), 21–34. [Preached originally in the Church of St. Mary the Virgin, Oxford on 8 June 1941.] Available in the Canadian Public Domain as a Distributors Proofreaders Canada eBook downloadable from:

https://www.fadedpage.com/showbook.php?pid=20141033

Chapter 6: Wilderness

[90] Joseph Barbato, Lisa Weinerman Horak, Lisa Weinerman, eds., *Off the Beaten Path: Stories of Place* (New York: North Point Press, 1998), preface.

[91] Ellesmere, northernmost island in Canada's Arctic archipelago, is a magnificent barren wilderness with only one small settlement (Aujuittuq) and two isolated weather stations (Eureka and Alert). Ellesmere's permanent Inuit residents presently number in the hundreds. Here, mountainous terrain supports the greatest percentage of Canada's glacial ice, while below its surface is continuous permafrost.

[92] Sir Ernest Shackleton, *South* (Cork, Ireland: The Collins Press, 2002), 53. [Shackleton's ship, *Endurance*, locked in and drifting in the pack ice of the Weddell Sea for 10 months in 1915, was crushed and later sank. This began one of the most incredible stories of success amid failure in the cold wilderness of the Antarctic.]

[93] Captain George Tyson, *Arctic Experiences* (New York: Cooper Square Press, 2002), 252, 257, 260.

94   Tyson, *Arctic Experiences*, 261.

95   Cross-section of the Jordan Valley showing the descent of the Jordan River toward the Dead Sea. Except for its headwaters, virtually all river surface is below sea level.

Chapter 7: Water

96   The photo captures the beauty and size of one of nature's most violent storms, the hurricane. Bands of cloud form a spiral about a central eye. Cloud pattern displays the rotation of the system caused by the spin of the Earth below it. Clearly visible below the spiral is the open tropical ocean, the birthplace of hurricanes. High surface temperatures enhance evaporation rates, consuming and storing vast amounts of thermal energy as latent heat within water vapour. In the condensation process, this heat is released along with the precipitation. Heat released from vapours now in the atmosphere further destabilizes the system, illustrating an important characteristic of a positive feedback mechanism in which what happens makes it easier to keep happening.

97   Philip Ball, *Life's Matrix: A Biography of Water* (Berkeley, CA: University of California Press, 2001), 25.

98   The normal behaviour of substances is to contract while cooling or solidifying. Water contracts while cooling, however, only until it reaches the temperature of 4 °C. At this temperature, a given quantity of water is at its smallest volume, and hence its maximum density. Further cooling actually causes water to expand and become less dense. When water freezes, the crystal structure formed within ice significantly increases its volume, meaning that ice becomes less dense than the water surrounding it. Therefore, it floats. Since the density change is small, the amount of ice seen above the waterline is small as well. For this reason iceberg mass is mostly underwater.

99   Sir Ernest Shackleton, *South* (Cork, Ireland: The Collins Press, 2002), 12.

100 Aubrey Podlich, *Barrier Reef Reflections* (Adelaide: Lutheran Publishing, 1990), 75.

[101] Podlich, *Barrier Reef*, 71.

[102] Frederick Buechner, *Sacred Journey* (San Francisco: HarperCollins Publishers, 1982), 19.

[103] Dave Barry [American writer and humorist], from *Dave Barry's Only Travel Guide You'll Ever Need* (New York: Ballantine Books, 1999).

[104] Surprisingly, winter snowfalls are greater in Ontario than in colder regions of Canada. Very cold air can dissolve very little water vapour. Thus, a snowstorm occurring at -40 °C produces little snowfall relative to amounts possible near 0 °C.

Nevertheless, Arctic blizzards can *appear* as great snow events, not because much snow falls, but rather because, during a blizzard, much snow is lifted and redistributed. Moreover, in places where very cold temperatures persist for a long period of time, winter melting of a snowpack is minimal, thus adding to the erroneous conclusion that more northerly regions produce greater amounts of snow.

[105] The Canagagigue Creek, a tributary of southern Ontario's Grand River, travels through the rural communities of Elmira and Floradale. A few decades ago, a dam was constructed on the creek to create the Woolwich Reservoir, part of a series of artificial lakes that now regulate the seasonal flow of the Grand River, reducing the threat of flooding during heavy rains or rapid snow melt. An attractive 12-kilometre hiking and cycling trail encircles the reservoir, traversing stands of pine and spruce alongside fields of corn.

[106] Worldwide, the highest incidence of tornadoes is in the United States, specifically in the mid-western states from Texas and Oklahoma northward toward Missouri and Ohio. Maximum numbers normally occur during afternoon hours in the spring and summer seasons. In May 2013, one of the most powerful tornadoes ever recorded struck the community of Moore, Oklahoma. Assigned the highest score possible on the tornado intensity scale, it developed in a matter of minutes from first sighting to first touchdown, with wind gusts reaching an incredible 300 kilometres per hour. Destruction of property along a twokilometre-wide swath of the city was virtually total. Though injuries were numerous, deaths from this monstrous twister were surprisingly few. Unfortunately

for Moore, it was the third severe tornado to strike the area in a 15 year period.

107 Near the equator, hurricanes track westward. As they leave the lower latitudes, they bend progressively northward, then drift toward the northeast, following the general circulation of the atmosphere. Eventually they link up with mid-latitude depressions, decline further in strength, and gradually disappear.

108 The flooding that accompanied the arrival of Katrina into southern Louisiana was rendered far more serious because of the anatomy of the Mississippi River near its mouth, as well as the entry path of Katrina into the state. When Katrina's rainfall delivered an unusually high volume of water to the region over a short period of time, the river topped its levees and flowed *downhill* onto the surrounding flood plain. Moreover, because of its track and counter-clockwise circulation, Katrina's eastern flank delivered strong onshore winds to the region of New Orleans, triggering a storm surge that inundated ground already overwhelmed by an overflowing river.

109 The dead-end drainage conditions exemplified by the Volga River and Caspian Sea are duplicated elsewhere. For example, the Great Salt Lake in northwestern Utah receives inflow from three major rivers. However, high evaporation rates, combined with high withdrawals for human use have prevented any lake outflow to the sea. A more extreme example is found in California's Death Valley, where very high evaporation rates caused the complete disappearance of Lake Manly, an ancient lake that once contributed water to the Colorado River system. At present, the floor of what was Lake Manly sits at the lowest elevation in North America some 86 metres below sea level. It also boasts of average high daily air temperatures that exceed human body temperature a full five months of the year!

110 The water level of the Dead Sea, presently 434 metres below sea level (as of June 1, 2019, according to the Israeli Water Authority), is the lowest surface elevation in the world. Plans to stop, or even reverse the declining water levels in the Dead Sea include pipeline linkages and inflow from the Red Sea or Mediterranean Sea. Dead Sea level data since 1976 can be

found at: http://www.water.gov.il/Hebrew/Water-Environment/Dead-Sea/Documents/deadsea- from1976.pdf

[111] The spherical shape of a raindrop is significant. Light entering raindrops can be refracted and reflected in equal amounts in every direction. Therefore, what emerges from a water droplet is not a single ray of light but rather a cone of light dispersing in all directions. Moreover, since light's actual point of entry into droplets can vary, a single droplet generates a multitude of dispersing cones of light. Of course, what happens in a single droplet is simultaneously occurring in billions of other droplets at the same time.

One can now imagine an orderly mass production of colour spectra in the sky whenever sunlight intercepts a field of water droplets. However, from the point of view of a single observer, only a sampling of spectra is visible. Given the manner in which the droplets play with incident sunlight, and the position of the observer relative to the various rays of refracted light, one can only see those spectra that fall on an arc of a circle some 42 degrees in diameter. The resulting rainbow is in fact a composition of countless adjacent spectral bands appearing side by side and forming a continuous arc, with the least refracted colour (red) on the outside of the arc.

It is important to realize that the rainbow any one person sees is unique to their point of observation. No person standing elsewhere can see the exact same rainbow since the package of spectral bands within this second field of vision cannot include the exact same set of refracting water droplets.

[112] Sir Walter Scott, "The Battle," canto VI, stanza 5, in *Marmion*.

Chapter 8: Flood

[113] The Missouri Drainage Basin, contributing water to the Mississippi River, moves water toward the east and south through a number of American states. Recently, it has been subject to severe flooding, due primarily to basin surfaces that are relatively flat, and to large volumes of water delivered to the basin over a relatively brief period of time.

114 "The Deadliest Tsunami in History?" in *National Geographic News Online*, December 28, 2004.
https://www.nationalgeographic.com/news/2004/12/deadliest-tsunami-in-history/

115 Under normal conditions the various components of the water cycle are in balance. Globally, the amounts of precipitation are similar to amounts that are evaporated. The amounts transferred back to the oceans via streams match those amounts transferred to land by wind currents. In such circumstances, amounts in residency in oceans, atmosphere, and on land are relatively constant.

However, when abnormal conditions prevail, as with global warming, amounts transferred to and from various residences fall out of equilibrium, resulting in changes to the volumes within each residence. For example, present increases in global temperatures are increasing the rates of melting of ice presently resident on land surfaces. This has increased the net transfer of water to the world's oceans, increasing ocean volumes and raising global sea levels by a few millimetres per year.

116 In terms of world's longest, China's two main rivers rank among the top five, with the Yangtze River almost as long as the Amazon. In terms of total volume, the discharge of the Yangtze, though a mere 15% of the Amazon's, is over 13 times greater than that of the Huang He River. Discharge volumes among the world's rivers are greatly influenced by three principal variables: size of drainage basin; total water delivered to the basin through precipitation; and total water lost from the basin through evaporation and human withdrawals.

117 The energy released by the Indian Ocean earthquake and tsunami of 2004 was estimated to be in the order of 23 000 Hiroshima-type atomic bombs! Along nearby coasts that contained extensive low and flat coastal plains, Indian Ocean water penetrated inland some two kilometres.

118 Tsunamis are most common in the Pacific Ocean. This is not surprising since this massive bowl of water is surrounded by the Ring of Fire, a geologically active zone along which violent plate slippages are common. Tsunami rates of movement are fastest where ocean depths are greatest. As a result, they can traverse the entire Pacific in less than a day.

Little time was required for the tsunami wave to reach the coastal areas like Miyako City in northeastern Japan. Given their experiences with past earthquakes and tsunamis, the people had constructed high sea walls as a defense for coastal towns, believing their height, strong steel construction, and strategic location would afford the people adequate protection. To everyone's horror, as the 2011 tsunami reached shore, it overwhelmed the sea walls and moved inland with seemingly undiminished fury. Surprisingly, the walls, though strong enough, had *not* proven high enough. It was reported that the earthquake that had created the tsunami had also caused subsidence in the ground supporting the sea walls. This had significantly lowered them and largely neutralized them as effective defensive structures to oppose the awesome force of the water.

[119] Hurricanes are violent storms generated over warm ocean water at low latitudes. Most hurricanes originate in the western Pacific and Atlantic oceans and are most common north of the equator. Most impacted land areas are the Philippine and Japanese islands, as well as the southeastern parts of the United States. Maps of hurricane tracks show them to be conspicuously absent along the equator (where forces that produce wind rotation are weak), and at the higher latitudes (where cooler water temperatures provide insufficient energy to fuel hurricanes).

[120] Chart adapted from A. N. Strahler, *Physical Geography*, 2nd edition (New York: John Wiley & Sons: 1960), 289. The chart shows that over 90% of all land surfaces above sea level lies within one kilometre of sea level, whereas over 75% of seabed resides at depths greater than three kilometres below sea level. Thus, continents are mostly lowland and oceans are mostly deep.

[121] David Watson, *Fear No Evil: A Personal Struggle with Cancer* (London: Hodder and Stoughton, 1984), 126. (quoting James Mitchell in *The God I Want*). [What may surprise many are similarly strong expressions of anger directed toward God in the Bible, especially in the Psalms, where we are permitted to eavesdrop on the honest questions and possible doubts of people who struggle to reconcile human travail with the goodness of God. From all this, it appears that God is accepting of the entire spectrum of human emotion, including those that are hardly pleasant.]

Chapter 9: Ice and Snow

122 Gabrielle Walker, *Antarctica* (New York: Houghton Mifflin Harcourt Publishing, 2013), 252. [from comments made by Richard Brandt responding to the author's question, "What do you love about snow?"]

123 Thomas Mann, *The Magic Mountain* (New York: Vintage Books/ Random House, 1996).

124 The Ross Ice Shelf is the largest ice shelf in the world, with approximately 90% of its total mass below the water line. South Pole expeditions during the Golden Age of polar exploration in the early 1900s focused on this shelf as a convenient starting point for a trek to the pole. Early explorers discovered that they could sail closer to the pole in this area than anywhere else on Antarctica's long coastline. However, even utilizing this area as their starting point, they still faced an over-ice round-trip journey of approximately 3600 kilometres, a distance Roald Amundsen covered in 99 days, with approximately 30% of the trek at altitudes greater than 2000 metres above sea level.

125 From the notebook of Sir Joseph Dalton Hooker, assistant surgeon onboard the Erebus, off Ross Island, Antarctica, 1841. http://www.south-pole.com/main.html The two Ross Island volcanic peaks were named after Ross's ships, *Erebus* and *Terror*. These are the same two ships used also by Sir John Franklin, that would disappear in the Northwest Passage four years later.

126 The Beechey Island graves, first discovered in 1851 by searchers for the Franklin Expedition, were the sight of exhumations and post-mortems performed by the forensic anthropologist Dr. Owen Beattie in the mid-1980s on the preserved remains of three Franklin crew members. An interesting account of these investigations is contained in: Owen Beattie and John Geiger, *Frozen in Time: Unlocking the Secrets of the Franklin Expedition* (Saskatoon: Western Producer Prairie Books, 1987).

127 Northern construction of oil and gas pipelines, house foundations, and water and sewage lines must be designed in such a way as to avoid destabilizing surrounding permafrost. For example, the design and construction of the Trans Alaskan Pipeline in the mid-1970s faced

the major challenge of moving heavy crude oil through a region of permafrost. Warmth facilitates flow by reducing oil viscosity. This is something much needed, especially with the heavy type of crude that is extracted from Prudhoe Bay. However, warmth melts permafrost. To avoid the most sensitive permafrost regions, approximately half of the pipeline was constructed above the ground surface.

128   The present holds the keys to the past. This is true because under special circumstances, fragments from the past escape the ravages of time to become recoverable artifacts. Keys that unlock the secrets of the past are frequently found buried. Burial sites include the sediments in seabeds, coral deposits, annular rings of trees, and ice sheets. The longest historical records are contained in the thickest burial sites. Among preferred sites, probably the most outstanding is the Antarctic ice sheet. Among the many *widespread* treasures trapped within its layers are samples of ancient air, imported volcanic dust, and even temperature and snowfall records. Among the more *localized* treasures are wrecks of aircraft, food depots, meteorite fragments, and human remains. Treasures locked in ice are accessed by means of ice core recovery. Sites for ice coring include Antarctica, Greenland, and various alpine sites. Of these, the Antarctic ice sheet contains the longest and least-disturbed historical record. Given recent temperature rises, treasures within alpine ice, especially in the Himalayas and the Andes, are disappearing at a rapid rate.

129   Charles Frances Hall, *Life with the Esquimaux,* Volume 1, Chapter 1 (London: Sampson Low, Son, and Marston, 1864), 23.

130   Munro Ferguson, *EUREKA*. Comic Strip, used by permission.

131   The vast majority of Baffin Bay icebergs come from Greenland's many glaciers that drain its massive ice sheet. Once released into the bay, icebergs are caught up in a current system that first moves them northward, then counterclockwise toward Baffin Island, then southward toward Labrador and the island of Newfoundland. Enemies of icebergs include warm water and wave action. Warmer water facilitates melt while wave action promotes erosion and ice fracture. In general, iceberg numbers and sizes decrease along their track southward. Seldom do they reach much beyond the Grand Banks where they come under the

influence of the warm Gulf Stream. Here, surviving bergs are forced to the northeast.

132 Recently, there has been a sharp decline in both the extent of ice and the amounts of the all-important multi-year ice in the Arctic Basin and Canadian archipelago. This bodes well for future Arctic marine transport. Yet it is a serious concern since open water absorbs more solar energy than does a reflective ice surface, enhancing further warming and ice ablation. World climate specialists speculate that the probability of perennial ice becoming seasonal by mid-century is high, though not certain.

133 Most Arctic and Antarctic exploration has occurred within the last four centuries. Included in the many who ventured into the Earth's highest latitudes are Robert Scott, Roald Amundsen, John Franklin, Robert Peary, Douglas Mawson, Fridjhof Nansen, Otto Sverdrup, and Ernest Shackleton.

134 The map shows two major marine passages through Canada's northern archipelago. The most direct, widest, and deepest is the east-west Parry Channel, which joins Baffin Bay to McClure Strait and the Beaufort Sea. The other follows the eastern half of the Parry Channel, but dips south toward King William Island through Peel Sound, then through Victoria Strait. Traditionally, both routes are plagued by the obstacle of heavy ice concentrations that normally persist year-round, especially in the regions of the McClure and Victoria Straits. Given the level of marine technology available during the nineteenth century, progress through either route was very much dependent upon luck, access to accurate charts, and the particular ice conditions prevailing at the time of attempted transit.

135 Greely's journey northward from Baffin Bay and through Kane Basin took him into more and more restricted waterways and more serious problems with ice that normally flows southward. The relief vessel's failure to resupply his crew was hardly unexpected.

136 Beau Riffenburgh, *Racing with Death* (London: Bloomsbury Publishing, 2008), 71. [Spoken by Belgrave Ninnis.]

137 Lennard Bickel, *This Accursed Land* (London: Macmillan London Limited, 1977), 17. [Bickel offers a vivid description of the severity of the

environment that Mawson and his companions faced at Cape Dennison in 1912 on Commonwealth Bay, Antarctica.]

[138] Beau Riffenburgh, *Racing with Death* (London: Bloomsbury Publishing, 2008), 183. [Attributed to Eric Web, chief magnetician, Australasian Antarctic Expedition, or AAE.]

[139] Lennard Bickel, *This Accursed Land* (London: Macmillan London Limited, 1977), 17. [Commenting on Mawson's response to Antarctica's untrodden alpine grandeur and its timeless solitude, Bickel quotes the explorer's writings on the intangible element of the continent's irresistible attraction.]

[140] Shackleton's ship *Endurance* was lifted and crushed in heavy pack ice in the Weddell Sea and carried in a clockwise circuit to its demise.

[141] Sir Ernest Shackleton, *South* (Cork, Ireland: The Collins Press, 1919), 153.

[142] Shackleton, *South*, 156.

[143] Elspeth Huxley, *Scott of the Antarctic* (New York: Atheneum, 1977).

Chapter 10: Imago Dei

[144] Rebecca Harding Davis, nineteenth century American author and journalist. http:// www.quotegarden.com/thanksgiving.html

[145] As a place of worship, St. Paul's had a humble beginning as a small 1 200-square-foot wooden structure with a tall steeple, opening its doors for services in 1842. Soon afterwards, with the structure unable to accommodate the growing congregation, the original building was moved offsite and a stone church was constructed. From that time on, St. Paul's experienced a series of expansions and renovations to become the largest Anglican church in Toronto. Combining the historic and the modern in a single place of worship, St. Paul's is presently home to a large and diverse congregation.

[146] Galen Gruengerich, a Unitarian pastor, quoted in David Brooks, *The Second Mountain: The Quest for a Moral Life* (New York: Random House, 2019), 128.

147 G. K. Chesterton, "On Lying in Bed," 1909, in *Quotidiana*, ed. Patrick Madden (Nebraska, University of Nebraska Press, 2007).

148 Jerry Seinfeld. http://www.brainyquote.com/quotes/quotes/j/jerryseinf385106.html.

149 Jonathan Edwards, "The Christian Pilgrim," sermon preached September 1733, in *A Bridge Between Two Worlds*, Alister McGrath, featured in *Christianity Today*, June 2012.

150 Thomas Hardy, *Tess of the d'Urbervilles*, Part 2, chapter 15 (Maiden No More), (New York: Harper & Bros, 1891).

151 *What the Bleep Do We Know? It's Time to Get Wise*, directed by William Arntz, Betsy Chasse, Mark Vicente. (Lord of the Wind Films, 2004), film. [Spoken by Fred Alan Wolf.]

152 Johannes Kepler (1571–1630). https://www.goodreads.com/author/quotes/79396.Jo-hannes_Kepler.

153 Fyodor Dostoyevsky (1821–1881). https://www.goodreads.com/author/quotes/3137322.Fyodor_Dostoyevsky.

154 Galileo Galilei (1564–1642). http://www.spacequotations.com/sunquotes.html.

155 David Brooks, *The Second Mountain: The Quest for a Moral Life* (New York: Random House, 2019), 96.

Postscript

156 Frances W. Wile, (1910) "All Beautiful the March of Days," third stanza, Hymn 601, in *The Book of Common Praise* (Anglican Church of Canada, revised 1938).

157 Frederick Buechner, *The Sacred Journey*. (San Francisco, California: HarperCollins Publishers, 1982), 4.

SELECTED BIBLIOGRAPHY

Ball, Philip. *Life's Matrix: A Biography of Water.* Berkeley, CA: University of California Press, 2001.

Bickel, Lennard. *This Accursed Land.* London, UK: Macmillan London Limited, 1977.

Blamires, Harry. *The Christian Mind: How Should a Christian Think?* Ann Arbor, MI: Servant Books, 1963.

Brand, Paul and Philip Yancey. *Fearfully and Wonderfully Made.* Grand Rapids, MI: Zondervan Publishing House, 1980.

Brooks, David. *The Second Mountain: The Quest for a Moral Life.* New York, NY: Random House, 2019.

Brown, Stephen. *The Last Viking: The Life of Roald Amundsen.* Vancouver, BC: Douglas & McIntyre, 2012.

Buechner, Frederick. *The Sacred Journey.* San Francisco, CA: HarperCollins Publishers, 1982.

Capon, Robert F. *The Fingerprints of God: Tracking the Divine Suspect through a History of Images.* Grand Rapids, MI: William B. Eerdmans Publishing Co., 2000.

———. *The Parables of the Kingdom.* Grand Rapids, MI: William B. Eerdmans Publishing, 1985.

———. *The Parables of Grace.* Grand Rapids, MI: William B. Eerdmans Publishing, 1988.

———. *The Parables of Judgment.* Grand Rapids, MI: William B. Eerdmans Publishing Co., 1989.

Frankenberry, Nancy K., ed. *The Faith of Scientists: In Their Own Words.* Princeton NJ: Princeton University Press, 2008.
Giberson, Karl W. *The Wonder of the Universe: Hints of God in Our Fine-Tuned World.* Downers Grove, IL: InterVarsity Press, 2012.
Gould, Paul M. & Daniel Ray, General eds. *The Story of the Cosmos.* Eugene, OR: Harvest House Publishers, 2019.
Holmes, Richard. *The Age of Wonder.* London, UK: HarperCollins, 2008.
Houston, James M. *I Believe in the Creator.* London, UK: Hodder and Stoughton, 1979.
Lansing, Alfred. *Endurance: Shackleton's Incredible Voyage.* New York, NY: Tyndale House Publishers, 1959.
Lewis, C. S. *Miracles.* Revised ed. London & Glasgow, UK: Collins/Fontana, 1960.
_____. *Mere Christianity.* New York, NY: Macmillan, 1968.
Lopez, Barry H. *Arctic Dreams.* New York. NY: Charles Scribner's Sons, 1986.
McGoogan, Ken. *Fatal Passage: The Untold Story of John Rae, the Arctic Adventurer Who Discovered the Fate of Franklin.* Toronto, ON: Harper Collins Publishers Ltd., 2001.
McGrath, Alister. *Glimpsing the Face of God: The Search for Meaning in the Universe.* Grand Rapids, MI: William B. Eerdmans Publishing, 2002.
Potter, Russell A. *The Untold Story of a 165-Year Search.* Montreal, QC: McGillQueens University Press, 2016.
Ryken, L., James C. Wilhoit and Tremper Longman III, General eds. *Dictionary of Biblical Imagery: An Encyclopedic Exploration of the Images, symbols, Motifs, Metaphors, Figures of Speech and Literary Patterns of the Bible.* Downers Grove, IL: InterVarsity Press, 1998.
Salloum, Jerome E. *Iceberg Severity off the Canadian East Coast (An Analysis of the 1991 Iceberg Season).* M.A. thesis, Wilfrid Laurier University, 1993.
Slaymaker, Olav and Richard E.J. Kelly. *The Cryosphere (and Global Environmental Change).* Oxford, UK: Blackwell Publishing, 2007.
Tyson, George E. *Arctic Experiences: Aboard the Doomed Polaris Expedition and Six Months Adrift on an Ice-Floe.* New York, NY: Cooper Square Press, 2002.

Vine's Expository Dictionary of Old and New Testament Words (Reference Library Edition). Grand Rapids, MI: Baker Book House Co., 1981.

Yancey, Philip. *Reaching for the Invisible God*. Grand Rapids, MI: Zondervan Publishing House, 2000.

———. *Rumors of Another World: What on Earth Are We Missing?* Grand Rapids, MI: Zondervan Publishing House, 2003.

ACKNOWLEDGEMENTS

Recently, to a class of young NASA astronauts just beginning their space mission training, an American vice president spoke about the importance of *teamwork*. He began by commenting on their nickname: *The "Turtles."* Alluding to the theme of teamwork, and linking it with an illustration that was both clear and simple, he said, *"If you ever see a turtle sitting on the top of a signpost . . . you know it didn't get there by itself."*

No human endeavour is performed in total isolation. Nor is it the product of a single individual. I am indebted to many people—family, friends, and colleagues, students and parishioners—who came alongside with patience, wisdom, and insight, injecting tidbits of their personal lives and experiences into mine, seldom realizing the gifts they were offering. Among those whose contributions relate specifically to this book, I name the following:

Many friends within the congregation of St. George's Church, and my dear colleague Charlie Masters, with whom I was permitted to work alongside for over a decade, and to dabble in the things of God;

Dave Shantz, my patient, accessible, and computer-literate friend who, without ever alluding to my technological ignorance, tackled and solved many of my frustrations associated with internet and computer software; Terry Brennan for his friendship and wisdom; Jill and David Hicks whose encouragement reflected a critical balance between grace and truth without judgment; Scott Hunt who, without being aware, inspired me to investigate the versatility of the computer as a generator of graphics; Alex Porter who diligently worked with all the elements of maps, photos, and diagrams to render each image printable; and Loria Kulathungam who, with thoroughness and with her phenomenal eye for detail, pored over the manuscript for its final copyedit;

Jane Christmas who, before my pencil touched the paper, shared with me some of her wisdom and experience as an accomplished writer; Marion Baldwin, Jannie Henkelman, and Carole Brennan who were quiet reminders of my place in the grand scheme of things; Alison Mildon whose calm demeanour provided much-appreciated emotional balance to moments of frustration; Mark Henkelman and Dave Diewert, through whose eyes I was enabled to glimpse samplings of Creation's both revealed and hidden wonders; and Gerry Slimmon, my next-door neighbour whose quiet and loving commitment to his wife during her long illness demonstrates what faithfulness and self-sacrifice look like in the face of prolonged adversity;

In addition, a special word of gratitude to the host of companies, organizations and governmental agencies back in the 1980s who provided logistical and financial support for my five forays into Canada's Arctic region: Polar Continental Shelf Project; Canadian Coast Guard; Environment Canada (Atmospheric Environment Service); Energy, Mines and Resources Canada; Esso Resources Canada (Norman Wells & Beaufort Sea Operations); Cominco Mines (Polaris Operations); Bradley Air Services (Resolute NU); The North York Board of Education; The Royal Canadian Geographical Society; and *Ice-Walk 1989* (Student Expedition to Ellesmere Island). These various organizations facilitated access to many remote regions of Canada's north, all of which eventually led to graduate studies in Cold Regions, moving from secondary school to university teaching, then to ordination in the Anglican ministry, and finally into authoring and revision of this book;

With regard to the second edition of *Our World, God's Visible Language*, my thanks to Shaya Snyder, Project Manager at Friesen Press, Victoria, B.C., and its team of specialists for their wise counsel, friendliness, availability, patience and direction, in navigating me through the many steps that convert a rough manuscript into a published book;

I am grateful to the contributors and editors of *The Dictionary of Biblical Imagery* (IVP) for assembling a most valuable resource in *An Encyclopedic Exploration of Biblical imagery: Figures of Speech Employed in Holy Scripture to Communicate Biblical Truths that Reference Elements of God's Natural*

Revelation. In its Introduction, this exhaustive resource is described as "an interdisciplinary enterprise" and "a work of imagination" . . . "bridging the gap between the biblical world and our own world" (see reference in *Selected Bibliography*).

My deepest gratitude is reserved for Nancy, my wife for over five decades, my best friend, and my gracious chief critic, who remained alongside for the entire project, especially in those earliest days when research interests (and just plain fascination with cold regions) took me into Canada's High Arctic when my book writing project had yet to crystallize. When it finally took on a recognizable form and direction, she contributed significantly to the document's readability with her keen eye for proper spelling, expression, sequencing, progression and redundant material, always abounding in honesty mixed with grace. Mercifully, our marriage more than survived the ordeal! She remains my faithful companion, my encourager, and my light.

JES
October 2021.

ABOUT THE AUTHOR

Jerry Salloum is a retired teacher and lecturer in Physical Geography and Earth Science, having taught for over five decades both at the high school and university levels. He is also a recently retired Anglican minister, having served a congregation for ten years. He has had travel experiences, particularly in the High Arctic—an exceptional region of beauty, referred to in scripture as the "treasures of the snow."

At present, he enjoys life with his wife, family, and friends, and has an enduring fondness for English humour, André Rieu concerts, and Baroque music, as well as for maple syrup, raspberries, and cashews. He with his wife Nancy lives in Waterloo, Ontario.

> *"Jerry Salloum, storyteller, university lecturer and muse, paints a canvas of the wonder and magnificence of our world and Cosmos evidencing God's physical language to us. Those who love delightful prose, fascinating scientific observations and questions to ponder will find this book thirst-provoking. I found myself doing many web-searches for the terms introduced and just wanting to learn more. Jerry is neither a ranting preacher, nor a fastidious theologue, rather a seasoned journeyman who commands attention by sharing the relevance of real-life observation and experience."*
>
> *-Jim Klaas, Education Consultant, Online Discipleship*

www.ingramcontent.com/pod-product-compliance
Lightning Source LLC
LaVergne TN
LVHW041742060526
838201LV00046B/878